D1323468

ESSENTIAL GRAPHIC NOVELS

he   Guide

500 ESSENTIAL GRAPHIC NOVELS

The Ultimate Guide • Gene Kannenberg, Jr.

ILEX

500 ESSENTIAL GRAPHIC NOVELS

First published in the UK in 2008 by
I L E X
The Old Candlemakers
West Street
Lewes
East Sussex BN7 2NZ
www.ilex-press.com

Copyright © 2008 The Ilex Press Limited

Publisher: Alastair Campbell
Creative Director: Peter Bridgewater
Rights Director: Roly Allen
Managing Editor: Chris Gatcum
Editor: Tim Seelig
Commissioning Editor: Tim Pilcher
Art Director: Julie Weir
Designer: Ginny Zeal
Design Assistant: Emily Harbison

Any copy of this book issued by the publisher is
sold subject to the condition that it shall not by
way of trade or otherwise be lent, resold, hired
out or otherwise circulated without the publisher's
prior consent in any form of binding or cover other
than that in which it is published and without a
similar condition including these words being
imposed on a subsequent purchaser.

British Library Cataloguing-in-Publication Data
A catalogue record for this book is available from
the British Library.

ISBN 13: 978-1-905814-29-9
ISBN 10: 1-905814-29-1

All rights reserved. No part of this publication
may be reproduced or used in any form, or by
any means – graphic, electronic or mechanical,
including photocopying, recording or information
storage-and-retrieval systems – without the prior
permission of the publisher.

Printed and bound in Thailand

Every effort has been made to credit the artists
and/or copyright holders whose work has been
reproduced in this book. We apologise for any
omissions, which will be corrected in future
editions, but hereby must disclaim any liability.

Glasgow City Council
Cultural & Leisure Services
Libraries Info. & Learning
PK

C 004187692	
Askews	24-Sep-2008
741.509 /PW	£14.99

CONTENTS

INTRODUCTION

GENE KANNENBERG, JR.

When I told people about this book at the start of the project, I'd receive one of two responses. From those folks who didn't know much about comics, I'd get something like this: "Five hundred? Well, I know about *Maus* and *Persepolis*, but... Are there really even more than five hundred graphic novels in total?" And from my more comics-savvy friends, I'd hear: "Five hundred? How are you ever gonna narrow the list down?" While the uninitiated wonder about the possibility of anything "as good" as *Maus*, avid readers have seen an explosion in the medium in recent years, both in the number of titles and their quality.

I hope that this book offers food for thought for both kinds of readers. If you don't know much about graphic novels yet, here's your chance to discover the wide range of titles out there—at least some of which should prove interesting, no matter what your tastes are. Aficionados will find lots of old friends here, but you'll also discover some new ones, since very few people get the chance to see everything that's published.

WHAT IS A GRAPHIC NOVEL, EXACTLY?

To be honest, it's a term that I'm uncomfortable with. Will Eisner popularized it with his seminal *A Contract with God* in 1978; but that book, for all its admirable and groundbreaking qualities, contains three short stories. It's not really a "novel" in a traditional, formal sense. What Eisner was trying to convey with the term was that *A Contract with God* didn't contain the types of stories people generally associated with the term "comic-book." *Contract's* stories focused on the trials and tribulations of normal people, with nary a

superpower, funny animal, or joke-laden picture in sight. It represented a radical departure from popular expectations, especially given its author's perspective as a sixtysomething-year-old man looking back at the circumstances surrounding his formative years.

So in one sense, the term "graphic novel" signals a serious intent: to create a work of lasting value, as opposed to the ephemeral, throwaway nature of the regular monthly comic-book (in America) or the weekly comic (in the UK). It's worth keeping in mind, however, that "lasting value" doesn't necessarily mean "somberly serious"; rather, it's meant to indicate a work that stands the test of time.

FROM EISNER TO THE UNDERGROUND

Will Eisner had been an important artist and publisher of comic books beginning in the 1930s, '40s, and '50s, and was responsible for creating the influential newspaper supplement comic-book, *The Spirit*. Eventually he left the comic-book business altogether and he may never have returned had it not been for his meeting with underground publisher Denis Kitchen at a comics convention. Kitchen introduced Eisner to the world of the underground, from the comics, to the cartoonists, to the business. Although a little startled at these scraggly looking kids "who smelled like funny cigarettes," Eisner saw kindred spirits and, ultimately, inspiration.

The underground comix resembled regular comic-books in form, but their content was decidedly other. These books joyfully, and anarchically, celebrated sex, drugs, and rock'n'roll.

The fact that they looked like "kiddie books" made them all the more subversive. A curious mix of nostalgia and up-to-the-minute counterculture, the comix became extremely popular—so much so that issues were routinely reprinted, something that just didn't happen in mainstream comics. You could go to your local headshop and pick up two or three issues of the same title; underground comix had no sell-by date.

These cartoonists themselves, particularly Robert Crumb, became poster-children for the time, and while some of the cartoonists burnt out, a good number have continued to produce work on a regular basis. Given the tendency to tell continued stories, or stories featuring the same characters, much of this excellent (if occasionally "edgy") work has been collected and published in "real" books.

The work of these cartoonists ranges from humor (Bill Griffith's *Zippy*, Gilbert Shelton's *Fabulous Furry Freak Brothers*) to history (much of Jack Jackson's work as Jaxon), autobiography (Justin Green, Diane Noomin) and more. Trina Robbins, in contrast, has left cartooning itself behind; but fortunately, she has turned her background and knowledge into books about comics, shedding some much-needed light on female cartoonists and female comics readers.

The underground spirit transmogrified into what became known as alternative comics, themselves a breeding ground for future graphic novels. We'll meet them in more detail later in this book, but their name does beg the question: Alternative to what? In a word: Superheroes.

SUPERHEROES AND SUPER-SERIALS
The American comic-book scene has been dominated by superheroes for decades. From the 1960s onward, superhero comic-books began to work like soap operas, so while each issue nominally contained one story, subplots continued from issue to issue, sometimes taking years to play out entirely.

This serial format makes it difficult to collect such comics into anything resembling one coherent story. It's true that some multi-episode mini-epics (like the X-Men's *Dark Phoenix Saga*) form a mostly coherent narrative, but there are still plenty of subplots that might cause a little confusion, whether they seemed to begin before the current storyline or aren't resolved until some later installment.

In the past few years, however, as the general public has begun to embrace comics, mainstream comics publishers have begun to embrace the general public. You can see this change on the shelves of your local bookstore. Most of the newer superhero collections do read more like self-contained stories, rather than just chunks of something larger. Greater public interest leads to bigger sales, but only of the books that are accessible to the general reader. What if you've just seen a Spider-Man movie and would like to read a Spider-Man graphic novel for the first time, and all you could find was something that felt like an incomplete story? You probably wouldn't go back for more.

So publishers have begun thinking in terms of "story arcs," multi-issue stories that are designed in advance to be collected into a single book. Think of this strategy as something comparable to primetime television; shows from *Buffy the Vampire Slayer* to *The Sopranos* have done the same thing. For comics, it's a smart idea: the diehard comics fan can read each monthly issue, and the more casual reader can pick up a goodly sized book at a later date.

1986 AND ALL THAT
It took a coincidental and curious mix of books to bring graphic novels into the media spotlight. Although Eisner continued to produce new work after *A Contract with God*, it took a while for other cartoonists to catch up with him. It wasn't just underground and alternative cartoonists, either; some superhero creators were stretching their own ambitions, too. Things came to a head in 1986, with

the almost simultaneous release of three graphic novels, each of which has stood the test of time.

The Dark Knight Returns, by Frank Miller, featured an older Batman coming out of retirement to restore sanity to a world without balance. Miller's biting social satire, combined with bold and innovative graphics, struck a chord with both fans and older, former fans—and after the 1960s high-camp Batman television series, who couldn't be counted as a sort of former fan?

Writer Alan Moore and artist Dave Gibbons' *Watchmen*, while also in the superhero camp, managed to cross party lines into the larger realm of speculative fiction. Loosely based on action heroes from a defunct publisher, *Watchmen* presented a fully realized, alternate world, one in which American society was suffused with Russian influences, there were action heroes, but only one truly superhero, and the dominant type of comic-book featured pirates. The extra text features at the end of each chapter allowed readers to become familiar with an entirely new society, an experience just as thrilling as (if not more so) than the book's suspenseful plot. Even contemporary television series like *Heroes* and *Lost* owe large debts (acknowledged or not) to *Watchmen's* storytelling. Not content to be just a superior superhero tale, *Watchmen* appealed to a wider range of readers than perhaps anyone involved might have expected.

The third of 1986's Big Three graphic novels was, of course, Art Spiegelman's *Maus*. By this time, Spiegelman had evolved from his underground roots to become a cartoonist and publisher. Starting in 1980, Spiegelman and his wife, Françoise Mouly, founded the influential avant-garde comics anthology *Raw*. Starting in the second issue, Spiegelman began serializing a story about his parents (both Holocaust survivors) as well as his own attempts to make peace with his father. The first six chapters were collected and published by Pantheon Books in 1986, to

widespread acclaim. Spiegelman conveyed his book's serious subject matter with a very straightforward, word-heavy comics style. But most importantly, he tempered the tale with his central visual metaphor: Jews were portrayed as mice, and Nazis as cats. Even more so than *The Dark Knight Returns* or *Watchmen*, *Maus* captured the attention of readers who would never, ever have considered reading "a comic-book." The publication of *Maus II* five years later brought with it even more popular praise, culminating in a special Pulitzer Prize for Spiegelman in 1992.

RECOGNITION AT LAST

The publishing hat trick of 1986 resulted in a glut of media coverage, most of which began with a headline like "Pow! Zap! Wham! Comics Aren't Just for Kids Anymore!" But that attitude is changing—at least in some quarters—like the *New York Times*, which includes comics in its Book Review and runs a comic in its weekly magazine. It's now not uncommon to find reviews, profiles of cartoonists, and industry news scattered throughout newspapers and on "straight" news websites. And it doesn't hurt when bestselling novelists profess their love of comics publicly, like Walter Mosely editing the massive *Maximum Fantastic Four* volume, or Michael Chabon winning a Pulitzer Prize for *The Amazing Adventures of Cavalier and Clay*.

What's caused the change? More than anything else, of course, it's the abundance of quality work that's being published. Some book publishers tried to jump on the graphic-novel bandwagon in the late 1980s and early 1990s, but those experiments rarely panned out (with some notable exceptions, such as *City of Glass*, by David Mazzucchelli and Paul Karasik). The reason is simple: Creating comics takes a long time. For example, it took Art Spiegelman 11 years to complete *Maus*. That's an extreme example, but the point remains that the process of creating comics is complex and time-consuming. Many—if not most—of the graphic novels reviewed in this book were either initially published serially over several years (for example, Seth's *It's a Good Life If You Don't Weaken*) or were subsidized along the way, allowing the cartoonist to survive while engaged in a novel-length project.

Marjane Satrapi's *Persepolis* in particular has garnered international attention. The publication of its first volume in an English translation appeared before its French serialization was even completed. *Persepolis* has reached a height of popularity and praise which, while it doesn't really rival that of Spiegelman's *Maus*, nevertheless eclipsed the popularity and critical attention awarded to much of translated, traditional literary fiction.

RESPECTABILITY IN THE UK

Of course, traditions change from country to country. In the UK, children (and adults) have long been accustomed to at least some long-form, hardcover comics that you're meant to keep. It's a tradition inherited from France and Belgium: the album. To be specific, albums from series such as *Tintin* by Hergé and *Astérix* by René Goscinny and Albert Uderzo.

Originally serialized in children's magazines and newspaper supplements, these were stories that were designed as stories, with beginnings, middles, and ends. This Franco-Belgian school of comics used large pages, with more panels per page than an American comic-book, resulting in a 48-page album that takes a good while to read.

Of course, there were native contributions too. Sometimes overlooked by comics readers is the important body of work produced by Raymond Briggs. While his books are generally classified as children's picture books, one look at them betrays Briggs' debt to—in fact, his excellence at—cartooning. Indeed, his antiwar masterpiece *Where the Wind Blows* managed to escape the "children's literature" label, garnering international praise, awards, and even an animated adaptation. His more traditional children's books are just as innovative.

Apart from titles like these, though, the UK was slow to embrace comics as a more mainstream form. Whereas superheroes came to embody the comic-book in the eyes of the average American, in the UK it was children's comics like *The Beano* and *Bunty*, or more outrageous fare like *Viz* or *Action* or *2000 AD*. But that's changing. One signal breakthrough was the 2001 Guardian First Book Award, which went to Chris Ware (an American, no less!) for his monumental *Jimmy Corrigan, the Smartest Kid on Earth*. Though the award certainly generated a bit of resistance, it also generated lots of praise—and lots more attention to graphic novels as a whole. That's not to say that British cartoonists aren't up to snuff in the awards and recognition department, though. Consider legends such as Posy Simmonds (*Gemma Bovery*), Bryan Talbot (*Alice in Sunderland*), and Raymond Briggs (*Ethel and Ernest*).

MANGA MANIA

1980 saw the publication of some of the first translated manga in America. There was Educomics' 1980 publication of Keiji Nakazawa's *Gen of Hiroshima*, an initial attempt at publishing his *Barefoot Gen*, a four-volume account of a young boy's life before, during, and after the US bombing of Hiroshima in 1945; and an anthology of short science-fiction and fantasy tales titled, simply, *Manga*, from the publisher Metro Scope.

Manga has made an incredible impact on comics publishing—and on publishing in general—in the US and Europe over the past decade. If you take a look at the Graphic Novels section of a large bookstore, at least in the US, chances are that manga will take up significantly more shelf space than all the other types of comics combined. In part it's due to the fact that manga usually appear as multi-volume series; one title can easily take up a whole shelf on its own! But the more important reason, of course, is popularity. For more and more readers, especially younger ones, manga aren't just comics; manga are the only comics.

WHY YOUR FAVORITE BOOK'S NOT HERE

There's no doubt about it: 500 books is a lot. Still, I'm sure that many of you will wonder why title X wasn't included. In many cases, your favorite book was indeed on our list. However, we wanted to make the list as broad as possible, and that made for some extremely difficult choices. For example: With every "must-have, double-bag" superhero title we included, that meant that we'd have room for one fewer title in another category. That's one of the reasons we've included a Further Reading list at the end of each review: In these lists, you can find reference to similar titles that we couldn't include for one reason or another.

Another, and more frustrating issue, was whether or not a given title was in print. What good would it do for us to wax rhapsodic about a book, only to have it unavailable for you when you went out to find it yourself? There are, of course, more and more libraries that stock graphic novels, and it's possible that your local library might have some out-of-print classics. But to make your life a bit easier, we decided to review only those books we knew you could find readily. Again, the Further Reading lists will mention those harder-to-find titles that you'll find worth tracking down if—sorry, when—you develop a deeper interest in graphic novels.

A final frustration came with material first published in a language other than English. Over the past few decades, various companies have published translated editions of some fabulous comics from all over the world. Unfortunately, for many reasons these books haven't always stayed in print for very long, or the publishers themselves have gone out of business. In either case, the end result is that there are some significant cartoonists whose work isn't represented in this book solely because they have no work currently available in an English-language edition. To name but three, the work of Claire Bretécher, Moebius, and Jacques Tardi doesn't appear in this book, yet each has had a profound influence

on comics worldwide, and each has had much of their work translated into English. However, sadly, at the time of this writing, not a single one of any of their English-language books is in print. This is a crime against culture, but nonetheless, we'll meet them again in later chapter introductions.

COMIC-STRIPS COLLECTIONS?

There are a few of these in the book, but only a few because in all honesty, comic strips really deserve a 500 Essential... book of their own—there are certainly enough of them, and most definitely some absolutely outstanding work has been produced by a wide variety of artists.

We thought that a handful, at least, would serve to open up the world of strips to graphic-novel readers, especially as we're now living in a Golden Age of comic-strip reprint projects, with *The Complete Peanuts* leading the charge, as well as deluxe collections of strips like *Calvin and Hobbes* and *The Far Side*.

FINAL THOUGHTS

One thing we're not going to even attempt to do with this book is to answer the question "which was the first graphic novel?" As we've mentioned, Will Eisner popularized the term, but comics fan and critic Richard Kyle coined the term in 1964, although it didn't really circulate beyond a group of hardcore comic-book fans. Even today, some people are willing to search out the very earliest collections of comics they can find, in order to ascribe the "graphic novel" label to them.

Of course, the idea of a graphic novel being, to some degree, a large comic-book, leads to the even thornier question: "Which was the first comic-book?" There are far too many arguments and hypotheses to recite here, and it really doesn't matter.

OK, enough of the generalities. Let's jump to the important stuff: The graphic novels themselves...

HOW TO USE THIS BOOK

As there are a variety of numbers and symbols with each review—and to allow you to navigate this book more simply—this is a brief introduction to help you find your way around a typical entry in this book.

The year given for each graphic novel is the year of its most recent publication—we cross-referenced Amazon, Mars Import, and other online stores to make sure they were available somewhere.

There are a few entries that may be harder to find at the moment, but with companies like Marvel, DC, Image, IDW, NBM, and Fantagraphics constantly repackaging forgotten classics it will only be a short time before they're available once more.

The star ratings given for each entry represent the score out of five for that book—one star representing

a general disappointment, and five stars showing that this is a truly great read.

Every entry also has a recommended readership age, suggesting who the book is suitable for. For ease of reference each age group has a color; "A" (cyan), means "All" ages; 12+ (magenta), over twelve years of age; 15+ (yellow), over fifteen years of age; and 18+ (black), over eighteen years of age.

Each of the chapters (categorized by genre) also has a color assigned to it. A chapter begins with a top ten essential section, and is followed by the "best of the rest" for books that we felt were necessary reading.

We hope you find this book useful and insightful whether you are a newcomer to graphic novels, or an established collector.

CHAPTER 1

ADVENTURE

A ROLLICKING GOOD YARN

A good adventure story has—or should have—everything: heroes and villains, suspense and scares, comedy and tragedy, high drama, and tender emotions. Although it is a dangerous thing to say, the adventure genre has probably produced more great comic strips than any other. Consider classic American newspaper strips such as *Terry and the Pirates, Steve Canyon, and Prince Valiant*; the much-imitated Japanese samurai epics *Lone Wolf and Cub*, or the postmodern *Blade of the Immortal*; and the worldwide adventures of European characters such as Tintin or Corto Maltese, which are part of everyday cultural life in certain areas of Europe.

Like Japan, many European countries have a long tradition of comic books aimed at a general audience, and of collecting stories into albums that are easily affordable. Comics are produced for every age group, but while the Japanese stratify their comics by sex and age, in Europe the most highly regarded strips are those that have a universal appeal and work on many levels. When Georges Remi inverted his initials and created his alter ego Hergé, he set out to produce a strip that would appeal not only to children but to adults, too. Tintin is the perfect adventure hero. He's young enough for children to identify with, but old enough to have some authority. He's honest and plucky, but not stupid, and his job thrusts him into a wildly different, exotic scenario for each adventure, where he encounters beautifully delineated humorous and villainous characters aplenty. Written with a great deal of wit, and drawn in a well-researched, clean, and clear style, Hergé enables everyone to follow the story easily.

Back in 1929, Tintin the boy reporter with his faithful dog Snowy looked a little different, because Hergé was yet to develop the ligne claire or "clear line" style for which he became famous. In ligne claire no sense of depth or movement is given by weighting the lines differently. Instead, panel design and color are used to place the visual emphasis where the artist desires, and movements and emotions are expressed by external lines that indicate speed or shock. Hergé inspired a number of talented ligne claire artists such as Edgar P. Jacobs and Bob de Moor, who had assisted him on the strip, and the style was revived in the 1970s by talented avant-garde artists such as Yves Chaland and Serge Clerc. The greatest of the strips created in the shadow of Tintin is undoubtedly Edgar P. Jacobs's *Blake and Mortimer*, featuring a pair of mature English detectives whose adventures combine the appeal of Agatha Christie murder mysteries with the arch fiends of earlier pulp stories by English novelist Sax Rohmer. Although they appeal to children, the *Blake and Mortimer* stories are complex enough to excite adult readers, the most famous of which is probably *The Yellow "M."*

Subtly sexual and downbeat, yet owing their sense of the exotic to the same tradition, are Vittorio Giardino's *Max Friedman* adventures, represented here by *Orient Gateway*. Max is a man who knows a lot of people. Sometime agent provocateur, sometime spy, he travels through Europe during the turbulent 1930s, slipping past traps as he brushes shoulders with great moments in history—a character the reader can never quite pin down.

Corto Maltese, the other great European adventure hero, is the antithesis of Tintin. He too encounters many famous people and historic events during his many adventures set in the early years of the 20th century. A mysterious sailor with a mystical side, Hugo Pratt's greatest creation started by sharing his adventures with youngsters in *Ballad of the Salt Sea*, but soon became the star of the show. Drawn in an audaciously loose style that became increasingly fluid as the years went by, Corto swashbuckled his way through the Russian Revolution, the Irish uprising,

African wars, and Caribbean piracy, meeting everyone from Rasputin to Jack London along the way.

The European adventure writers seem to be fascinated by both the early 20th century, the period to which the roots of modern global society can be traced, and the medieval period (while their erotic cartoonist contemporaries fill in the gaps with countless works set in the 18th and 19th centuries). Before he became identified with science-fiction epics, Serbian-born Enki Bilal and his writing partner Pierre Christin created historical thrillers such as *The Ranks of the Black Order* and the very highly regarded *The Hunting Party*, in which a group of disgraced Soviet political leaders meet to shoot bear and reminisce, just a few years before the fall of the USSR.

While America can offer Hollywood-style knights in Hal Foster's *sweep*ing, cinematic *Prince Valiant*, in Europe there are a number of long-running medieval adventure series, which are often more cynical and less idealized than their American counterparts. Hermann Huppen's *The Towers of Bois-Maury* is a long-running saga about a dispossessed knight who sees little chivalry in the nobles around him, while André Juillard, who has a soft and delicate drawing style, has produced a number of series notable for their close historical research, including *Les Sept Vies de L'Epervier* and *Bohemond de St Gilles*, which are well worth seeking out if you read French.

Adventure doesn't have to mean historical, of course, and represented in this book are a number of very modern strips. They include *Leave It To Chance*, more Miami Vice than vieilles histoires; *Gunsmith Cats*, a lively manga about female bounty hunters and their day to day misadventures; and the charmingly ordinary *Skidmarks*, ILYA's story of a teenage BMX rider's trials and temptations while coming of age in modern England.

★
★
★
★

Writer: Edgar P. Jacobs
Artist: Edgar P. Jacobs

Publisher: Cinebook Limited, 2007
ISBN: 190546021X

A # THE YELLOW "M"

Plot: In postwar London, a master criminal is destabilizing society with his audacious thefts, including that of the State Crown from the Tower of London. With no idea how to catch the man the populace have dubbed The Yellow "M" and whose symbol appears mysteriously in the streets, Scotland Yard enlists war veteran Captain Blake to help bring him to justice. Blake immediately brings in his old friend, Professor Mortimer, to assist him with the case, but the two are more closely involved than they first realize. The Yellow "M" starts kidnapping members of their club, and engineers the derailment of their train in order to stop them discovering that the victims are all involved in a libel case. But the tenacious detectives don't give up, coming close to capturing The Yellow "M" on several occasions. They eventually discover a complex plot that shakes the foundations of their belief in their fellow man. Blake is finally able to unveil the identity of The Yellow "M," after the mysterious perpetrator interrupts a BBC broadcast to announce he has captured the professor and intends to execute him.

Review: The Yellow "M" is a classic adventure story in the Jack London mold, adding futuristic gizmos and gadgets, and

THE IMPACT IS TERRIFYING! PUSHING EVERYTHING BEFORE IT, IN A MASS OF STEAM AND FLAME, THE EXPRESS LEAPS OVER THE CARRIAGES, WHICH HURTLE INTO EACH OTHER WITH A FEARFUL DIN!

As for this fellow's exploits, I suspect you were—er—embroidering a little.

Really? In that case, how do you explain his invulnerability?

themes such as occultism to the formula established for many years in European serial comics. Having originally run in *Tintin Magazine*, this Blake and Mortimer story is widely regarded as Dutch artist Edgar P. Jacobs's masterpiece. Although its pacing may seem a little slow to modern readers used to more action-packed stories, The Yellow "M" is full of nail-biting moments, and remains an absorbing story that will engross adults and children alike.

Jacobs's ligne claire ("clear line") style was developed while the artist was working extensively with Hergé on Tintin, and as such is gloriously clean and crisp. Every detail is carefully referenced to make sure that no paving stone, car, or even species of tree is out of place, while his London landscapes are particularly beautiful.

FURTHER READING: *Blake & Mortimer: The Mystery of the Great Pyramid; Corto Maltese in Siberia*
SEE ALSO: *Tintin in Tibet*

★
★
★
★

Writer: Carl Barks
Artist: Carl Barks

Publisher: Gemstone Publishing, 2006
ISBN: 1888472367

A # DISNEY'S DUCK TALES STORIES: VOLUME 1

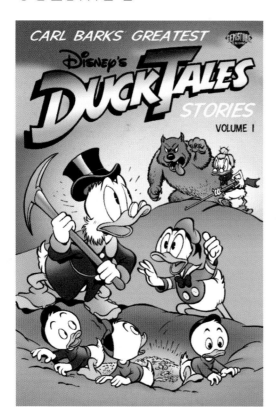

Plot: This collection contains stories from the *Uncle Scrooge* comic series that were later made into animated adventures for the *Disney Duck Tales* series: *Back to the Klondike, Land Beneath the Ground, Micro-Ducks from Outer Space, Lemming with the Locket, Lost Crown of Genghis Khan, and Hound of the Whiskervilles*. In Barks's longer stories, Donald Duck, his Uncle Scrooge, and his three nephews—Huey, Dewey, and Louie—are usually on a treasure hunt of some kind in an exotic location, so these are not all typical stories in that respect. *Back to the Klondike* and *Hound of the Whiskervilles* are tales of Scrooge's past. The first concerns a longstanding rivalry with a possible lost love, Goldie, and is one of the clearest depictions of Scrooge's personality. Meanwhile, *Hound of the Whiskervilles*

takes the ducks back to their ancestral home in Scotland. In *Land Beneath the Ground*, underground beings (the Terries and the Fermies) use earthquakes to threaten Scrooge's fortune. *Micro-Ducks from Outer Space*, unsurprisingly, features aliens, while *Lemming with the Locket* and *Lost Crown of Genghis Khan* are more straightforward tales that allow Barks to take the ducks to Norway and the Himalayas.

Review: Barks worked at Disney before becoming an artist at Western Publishing (and its Dell Comics imprint) on Walt Disney's Comics and Stories and then *Uncle Scrooge*. He gave Donald a personality and created Uncle Scrooge, with his vast wealth and penchant for swimming in the money

he kept in coins in his giant money bin. He populated Duckburg with characters such as the Beagle Brothers, Gyro Gearloose, and the Junior Woodchucks. Though uncredited, the quality of his stories and artwork earned him the nicknames The Duck Man and The Good Duck Artist before he was officially identified. He has since been recognized as one of the greatest comics artists in the world. The inspiration for most current Disney comics, particularly in Scandinavia, Barks has an elegant artistic style, creating simple but richly delineated drawings. Though often dismissed as comics purely for children, Barks's stories can be appreciated by readers of all ages for their fun, slapstick, and sense of adventure. He uses dialog to add layers of context that adults can enjoy and his characterization is not stereotypical—Scrooge succeeds through determination and hard work, in contrast to Donald, whose successes are largely accidental.

FURTHER READING: *Walt Disney's Uncle Scrooge;*
The Life and Times of Scrooge McDuck
SEE ALSO: *Walt Disney Treasures—Disney Comics:*
75 Years of Innovation

★
★
★
★

Writer: Maurice Sendak
Artist: Maurice Sendak

Publisher: Picture Lions, 1991
ISBN: 0006640818

A # IN THE NIGHT KITCHEN

Plot: Woken by a noise in the middle of the night, a young boy, Mickey, falls out of his bed, passes through the floor and, slipping out of his clothes, into the Night Kitchen of the book's title. There, three bakers—each bearing an uncanny resemblance to film star Oliver Hardy—go about their business, baking cake for the morning. They proceed to mix Mickey into the batter, apparently mistaking him for milk, and place the cake mix (and Mickey) into the oven.

Mickey emerges from a half-baked cake dressed in a suit made from the batter and constructs an airplane from the remaining mix, before helping the bakers with their work. As the sun begins to rise in this surreal tale, Mickey—crowing like a cockerel—floats back into his bed.

Review: Many children's books are described as dreamlike, but few manage to capture the essence of a dream as well as Sendak. Things happen randomly and with no logical progression. Mickey floats and flies between panels, his clothes mysteriously vanish and reappear. On entering the Night Kitchen, events swiftly threaten to descend into nightmare. In a sinister turn, the bakers mix Mickey into the batter—either because they don't notice him or don't care—and put him in the oven. Though Mickey subsequently takes control over events, an unsettling tone lingers and doesn't completely vanish until Mickey is safely back in his bed.

In terms of style and content, Sendak has acknowledged his debt to Winsor McCay's *Little Nemo in Slumberland*: Mickey

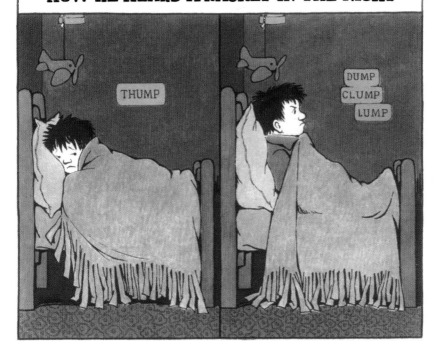

DID YOU EVER HEAR OF MICKEY,
HOW HE HEARD A RACKET IN THE NIGHT

THUMP

DUMP
CLUMP
LUMP

in his bed is a dead ringer for Nemo, and *In The Night Kitchen* clearly draws on themes present in McCay's strip. In the layout, Sendak adopts the panel-based format of the comic strip, occasionally breaking this rule to allow for a number of generous double-page spreads. The most notable of these occurs when Mickey flies his makeshift airplane over a beautifully realized cityscape whose buildings are comprised of kitchen utensils and food packaging.

When released, the book drew criticism from a number of librarians in the US, who objected to the nudity in the book. Others complained of the Freudian symbolism they claimed to have seen in the illustrations, but Sendak has dismissed such interpretations as nonsense.

Though perhaps not as accomplished as Sendak's masterly *Where The Wild Things Are*, *In The Night Kitchen* remains a curiously individual piece of children's fiction, loved by adults and children alike since its original publication in 1971.

FURTHER READING: *Where The Wild Things Are*
SEE ALSO: *Little Nemo in Slumberland*

★
★
★
★
★

Writer: James Robinson
Artist: Paul Smith

Publisher: Image, 2002
ISBN: 1582402531

A # LEAVE IT TO CHANCE VOLUME 1: SHAMAN'S RAIN

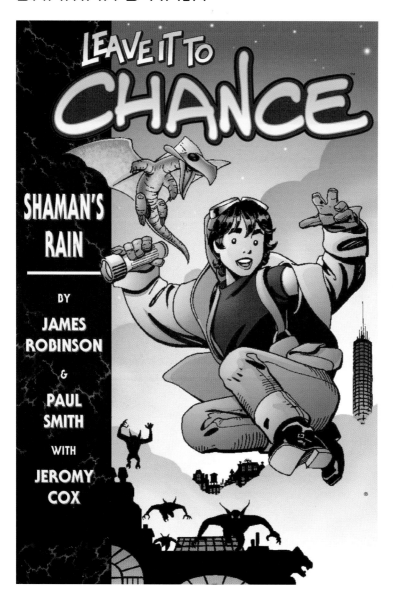

Plot: The *Leave It To Chance* series is set in a fantasy world populated by supernatural beings such as fairies, ghosts, and monsters. In this world, Lucas Falconer is a sorcerer who protects the city of Devil's Echo, the same duty performed by his family for many generations. Lucas has no male heir—only a 14-year-old daughter, Chance, who wants to follow in his footsteps.

However, Lucas feels the role is too dangerous for his daughter and has resisted allowing Chance to start the traditional training regime. He would much rather she married and had children, so he can train her son instead. But Chance isn't going to let her father's fears stop her, and when he leaves the city on a case, she walks into an adventure of her own when she discovers a dead body and a plot to influence the upcoming Mayoral elections.

With her small flying dragon, St George, Chance makes new friends among the city's police force and discovers that the real threat comes from an old foe of her father's.

Review: This series—winner of both the Harvey and Eisner awards—contains elements of *Nancy Drew* and other classic children's fiction alongside darker sources that don't intrude on the overall light tone. James Robinson has succeeded in creating an all-ages comic that seems to be aimed squarely at girls, but has an appeal to boys and adults, too.

Chance is resourceful and tomboyish, without being unfeminine, and is determined to prove to her father that she's fully capable of meeting the challenges of their family's trade. Paul Smith uses a realistic art style that's pretty but energetic, with lush backgrounds and clear storytelling. The stories are fun, fast-paced adventures, charmingly told.

FURTHER READING: *Leave it to Chance Volume 2: Trick or Threat; Leave it to Chance Volume 3: Monster Madness*
SEE ALSO: *Courtney Crumrin; Girl Genius; Buffy the Vampire Slayer*

★
★
★
★

Writer: Kazuo Koike
Artist: Goseki Kojima

Publisher: Dark Horse, 2000
ISBN: 1569715025

15+

LONE WOLF AND CUB VOLUME 1: THE ASSASSIN'S ROAD

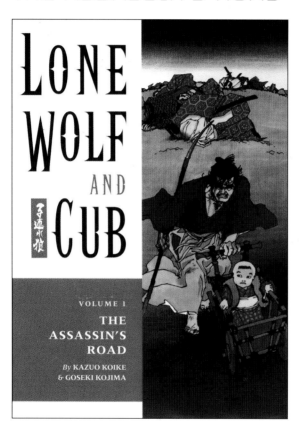

Plot: *Lone Wolf and Cub* is set in 17th century feudal Japan. It is the story of Ogami Itto, the Shogun's executioner, and his infant son, Daigoro—whom Itto pushes in a pram-like cart, bearing a banner to advertise his services: "Son for hire, sword for hire."

Accused of insults against the emperor, Itto is ordered to commit "seppuku" (ritual suicide) and kill both himself and Diagoro. He refuses, and sets out on an epic father-and-son journey, wandering over mountains and through cities, offering his services as an assassin to those in need—and those who can pay.

The *Lone Wolf and Cub* series is extremely popular in Japan, where it began in 1970 and continued for many years, spawning six films and much critical acclaim. *Lone Wolf and Cub* was not published in full in the West until Dark Horse took on the huge and costly task of printing the entire series of 28 volumes in 2000.

Review: *The Assassin's Road* flows at an incredible pace. The stories are jumpy, edgy, and exciting, and each page flashes by—very much like Ogami in his approach to all that stand before him. Goseki Kojima's art is compelling in its simplicity and chiseled accuracy. The small 7 x 4-inch format

does not reduce the tale's impact, but adds to its beauty, as you feel contained by the story and drawn into the Japanese scenery alongside Ogami and his son.

Kojima uses sequential flow like a samurai master uses his sword, drawing the viewer's attention exactly where he wants it, so your eyes glide effortlessly across the page. The storytelling describes a world where you believe in the characters and their actions, and all seems real and natural.

Volume 1 sets the tone beautifully and primes the reader to continue following the series, undaunted by the number of

volumes ahead. The main characters and conflicts are introduced and the stories plot an enjoyable course through Japanese culture, seen through the eyes of a brutal but elegant sword-wielding craftsman and his young son.

FURTHER READING: *Samurai Executioner; Usagi Yojimbo*
SEE ALSO: *Blade of the Immortal; Ronin*

★
★
★

Writer: Vittorio Giardino
Artist: Vittorio Giardino

Publisher: NBM, 1998
ISBN: 1561631841

A **ORIENT GATEWAY**

Plot: No one knows exactly who Max Friedman is working for, but many suspect he was once an officer in the International Brigade. In Europe on the brink of World War II, the appearance in Istanbul of this unremarkable-looking, but extremely resourceful man makes many people nervous, particularly when a would-be Soviet defector is also hiding in the city. Stalinists, the French Intelligence Service, and the network of exiled White Russians all seem to be involving themselves in Max's mission, whatever that really is, and even when he runs into several old friends he's not sure who can be trusted. Although he knows he shouldn't, Max starts a relationship with a Hungarian woman, Magda Witnitz, whose path seems to cross his with startling regularity. She, too, is searching for something, but even Max is surprised when, after cross and double-cross, he discovers her true identity.

Review: Giardino writes literate spy stories that are full of misdirection and betrayal, and orchestrates swift scene changes to keep you up to date with the plots and counterplots among his large cast of characters. At times he makes you work hard to keep up with the story, and his

protagonist slips unnoticed between one party and another, rarely showing the reader his emotions. Often jumpy, and not always heroic, Friedman is a more realistic kind of spy than is usually seen in the movies, although Giardino's evocation of the twisting alleys and sinister shadows of Istanbul owes more than a little to classic spy thrillers.

Having chosen the tense pre-war period as his backdrop, Giardino's desire for verisimilitude can sometimes make his artwork and pacing seem a little stilted, and while his backgrounds are gorgeous—particularly when evoking the

bustle of an exotic city such as Istanbul—they occasionally overwhelm the action. But when the narrative is as subtle and demanding as this, little details can be very important and careful reading ultimately reaps huge rewards.

FURTHER READING: *Hungarian Rhapsody;*
No Pasaran; Adele Blanc-Sec
SEE ALSO: *Blake and Mortimer: The Yellow "M"*

★ **Writer:** Andy Runton   **Publisher:** Top Shelf, 2004
★ **Artist:** Andy Runton   **ISBN:** 1891830627
★
★

A

OWLY: THE WAY HOME & THE BITTERSWEET SUMMER

Plot: Owly is a tiny, gentle owl, who loves gardening and bird-watching. In the first of the two stories in this volume, he rescues a young worm called Wormy, who is separated from his parents by a flood. Owly nurses Wormy back to health and the two become good friends. But Wormy misses his parents, so Owly sets out on a quest to return Wormy to his old home. In the process they learn Thomas Wolfe's truism that "You can never go home again."

In *The Bittersweet Summer*, Owly and Wormy befriend a pair of hummingbirds called Angel and Tiny. When Tiny is captured by a human and locked up in a cage, her three friends mount a daring rescue operation to set her free. Summer soon comes to a close, however, and threatens to bring an end to Owly and Wormy's friendship with the birds, teaching Owly an important lesson about letting go of the ones we love.

Review: Andy Runton's drawing style has a studied simplicity that makes its obvious sophistication seem almost effortless. With just a few well-placed lines, he conjures a whole host of emotions from his seemingly simple characters

and conveys a great sense of their inner and outer worlds. The stories have great rhythm and pace, unfolding so naturally that the reader can't help but feel involved in the stories of Owly and his friends.

Andy has said that *Owly* is a very personal work and that his protagonist is based on himself. Events in the stories mirror Andy's own life and capture his feelings about what happens to him. Taking this into account, we might even consider Owly a unique hybrid of funny animal comics, confessional comics, and all-ages fiction.

What makes *Owly* so special is its ability to deal with weighty themes—the true nature of friendship, what happens when we gain independence from our parents, and the importance of sacrifice in our relationships—dressing these up in simple and engaging stories.

FURTHER READING: *Baby Mouse; Pinky and Stinky*
SEE ALSO: *Gon: Volume 1*

★
★
★
★

Writer: Hal Foster
Artist: Hal Foster

Publisher: Fantagraphics, 1993
ISBN: 1560971231

A

PRINCE VALIANT VOLUME 20: THE PILGRIMAGE

AND AS THEY WATCH, RORY AND HIS MEN RACE TOWARD IT. BUT THE SHIP IS MOORED VIKING FASHION; THE MOORING HOOK IS LIFTED FROM ITS SOCKET IN THE ROCK AND A PULL ON THE ANCHOR ROPE MOVES THE BOAT QUICKLY OUT TO SAFETY.

Plot: *The Pilgrimage* is one of the few *Prince Valiant* newspaper strip collections that—although part of a longer storyline—stands very well on its own terms. The hero of this long-running series is a Viking prince from the kingdom of Thule, who travels to King Arthur's court and becomes a Knight of the Round Table. Many of the stories are based on his knightly quests alongside friends Sir Gawain and Sir Tristan, which take them far afield.

Valiant is very much a remodeling of Mallory's Sir Gawain, who has the strength of ten men because he is pure at heart. Some of the earlier Valiant stories featured magical elements such as dragons and witches, but by this stage the stories

had become much more realistic, with a lightly humorous touch. The focus of *The Pilgrimage* is not Prince Valiant himself, but his true love, Queen Aleta of the Misty Isles, who has returned to her home country after four years to reclaim her throne from her sister, who has been acting as Regent. The sister's husband has other ideas, however, and so do many of the nobles. Aleta struggles with plots and infighting to bring stability to her homeland in a story that centers on intrigue, but includes enough derring-do to keep adventure fans happy.

Review: Hal Foster's stories are set in an indeterminate Arthurian world where Romans and Vikings can happily hang

THEN AT LAST THEIR LUCK RUNS OUT. A WIDE RIVER BARS THEIR WAY.... FROM INLAND COME THEIR PURSUERS, TOWARD THE SEA, THE LAND ENDS IN A ROCKY POINT. TRAPPED!

THIS SEEMS AN UNLIKELY PLACE TO FIND A SHIP, BUT THEY CANNOT TURN BACK NOW. THEIR ENEMIES ARE CLOSE AT THEIR HEELS.

WATER CASKS ARE BEING HOISTED ABOARD A GRACEFUL SHIP. THERE IS NO HURRY, EVEN THOUGH THE PURSUERS ARE NOW ROARING DOWN THE GLEN. EVEN AS THEY CLAMBER ABOARD, RORY STRIDES DOWN THE BEACH.

out together. Although there are some references to real-life events that took place in the 5th century, such as the sacking of Rome, it's very much "Hollywood Medieval," with lots of crusader-style arms and armor, pageboy haircuts, and cloaks. In these clean-cut stories, everyone is exceedingly well scrubbed, and it's all beautifully drawn using a glorious Technicolor style color palette.

Foster's static art technique—with the action described underneath—sits halfway between illustration and cartooning and it's fair to say that it may not be to everyone's taste. But his composition is flawless, and his panoramas and battle scenes are fantastic.

Created as single, dramatic pages, the *Prince Valiant* narrative is limited, but remains a rollicking, if old-fashioned, adventure series for all the family.

FURTHER READING: *Prince Valiant—An American Epic*
SEE ALSO: *The Towers of Bois Maury; Zorro; Thorgal*

★
★
★
★

Writer: Hermann Huppen
Artist: Hermann Huppen

Publisher: Dark Horse, 2002
ISBN: 1569717680

A

THE TOWERS OF BOIS-MAURY VOLUME 1: BABETTE

Plot: A densely plotted, and rather slow-moving morality tale set in 14th century France and packed with period detail. From the pen of Hermann Huppen—better known for his post-apocalyptic teen-survivor story Jeremiah—the complete Bois-Maury series runs to 13 volumes. However, only three volumes have been translated, making it frustrating for those who don't read French.

Sir Aymar de Bois-Maury is a knight who's been dispossessed of his land, but retains his honor. Babette, a local peasant girl, is raped by a member of Aymar's hunting party (who is later found murdered). Babette's would-be lover, Germain, is imprisoned for the deed, but when she tries to help him, Babette's own family beat her to death. Sir Aymar, shocked by the behavior of his fellow knights and the peasants, feels compelled to discover what really happened. Germain is eventually exonerated, but is forced into exile because no one believes he is innocent. By the end of the story he winds up cuckolding a good man just to avoid begging on the streets.

Review: Hermann's stories usually revolve around difficult ethical choices, and the *Bois-Maury* series is no different. There are no heroes, but some characters do have their moments of glory. Aymar is inflexible and judgmental, and acts as a foil for some of the more free-thinking characters as the story slowly unfolds.

Using densely textured panels and his trademark fine, but still sketchy lines, Hermann creates a wonderful sense of place. Few of his characters are beautiful, but each has

unique features and body shape, and he captures their individual expressions superbly. The only downside is the garish color, which tends to fill Hermann's delicate linework in an unsubtle way.

FURTHER READING: *Sur les traces du Dracula; Sarajevo Tango; Les Sept Vies de l'Epervier; Les Passager du Vent; Wind of the Gods*
SEE ALSO: *Remembrance of Things Past*

★
★
★
★
★

Writer: Various
Artist: Alex Toth

Publisher: Image Comics, 2001
ISBN: 1582400903

A

THE COMPLETE CLASSIC ADVENTURES OF ZORRO

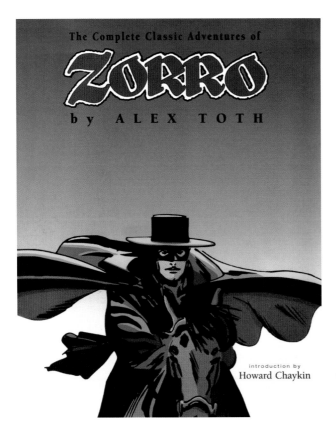

Plot: Diego De La Vega is a Spanish nobleman, returning to Southern California after years in Spain. On his return, he discovers that the villainous Capitan Monastario has become a despot, taxing the poor beyond their means and locking up anyone who dares to disagree or complain. Taking the name El Zorro, and disguising himself behind a domino mask and cape, the sword-wielding nobleman starts to right the wrongs perpetrated by Monastario and his bumbling Sergeant Garcia. At the same time, De La Vega must pretend to be a cowardly, art-loving fool to put those on the trail of Zorro off the scent. But can he put an end to the villainous machinations of Captain Monastario?

Review: Alex Toth is little known outside of the comics industry, but is widely acknowledged to have been one of the masters of pen and ink, right up with Josh Kirby and Steve Ditko; Zorro is one of the reasons why.

Toth's take on Zorro was based on the Walt Disney TV show from the 1950s, and the scripts were largely adapted from the TV scripts. As a result, the writing is hackneyed and full of clichés, but Toth turns it into a tour-de-force of storytelling.

Toth's elegant, sinuous brushwork combines beautifully with his expertise in panel composition, where even the speech

balloons become part of the design. His figure and linework are both fairly minimal, but he uses them to amazing effect, leading the eye across the page with just a few simple lines and a striking use of black and silhouettes. Even his sound effects are integral to the page, as much a part of the flowing composition as the figurework, providing a masterclass in the production of a comic-book page.

Toth rarely drew any of the major characters for DC or Marvel, and never really received the acclaim he deserved until quite recently, shortly before his death. This volume is a great place to start discovering one of the most talented artists to have ever worked in the field of comic-book art, and any up-and-coming artist should look at this book to see exactly how to do everything right.

FURTHER READING: *Toth: Black & White; Toth: One For The Road; Toth: By Design*
SEE ALSO: *Prince Valiant; City Of Glass; Chester Gould's Dick Tracy*

★ **Writer:** J. Torres
★ **Artist:** J. Bone
★

Publisher: Oni Press, 2002
ISBN: 1929998203

A

ALISON DARE, LITTLE MISS ADVENTURES: VOLUME 1

Plot: The child of an archaeologist adventurer and her superhero husband, 12-year-old Alison is sent to live a "normal" life at the St. Joan of Arc Academy for Girls. But it seems like the quiet life just isn't in her blood as she drags her friends, Wendy and Dot, into dangerous encounters with a magical genie, bank robbers, and Baron von Baron—who is intent on world domination. Volume 1 also tells the story of how Alison's parents met; how her father, the Blue Scarab, received his powers; and introduces her uncle, an international super-spy.

Review: J. Torres writes for a young audience, but this is funny and clever enough to entertain older readers. J. Bone's artwork tells the story simply, in a blocky cartoon style that's perfectly suited to the script.

FURTHER READING: *Alison Dare, Little Miss Adventures: Volume 2*
SEE ALSO: *Courtney Crumrin; Girl Genius*

Writer: Alex Simmons
Artist: Various

Publisher: Dark Angel Productions, 2000
ISBN: 0967634105

BLACKJACK: BLOOD AND HONOR

The Graphic Novel

Plot: Arron Day, aka Blackjack, is an African-American soldier of fortune whose adventures are set in the 1930s, against the historical backdrop of the rise of fascism. This story is set in China, where Blackjack is hired as the bodyguard to a Japanese statesman who's opposed to his government's plans. When Japanese agents are sent to kill the statesman, Blackjack finds himself in the firing line, too.

Review: Simmons has created a strong, intelligent character in Blackjack. The artwork isn't as consistent as in the original three-part comic series, but with exotic and well-researched historical settings and strong male and female leads, this is a good, thoughtfully written, action-adventure series.

FURTHER READING: *Sabre by McGregor & Gulacy; Detectives Inc*
SEE ALSO: *Adolf; Golgo 13*

Writer: Jason Shiga
Artist: Jason Shiga

Publisher: Sparkplug Comics, 2007
ISBN: 097427156X

BOOKHUNTER

BOOKHUNTER by Shiga

Plot: It's the year 1973 and books are the most precious commodities in the world. The Library Police are on the trail of a priceless, stolen volume, and they've only got three days to find it, so it's a race against time as the bookhunters use every trick of their trade to hunt down the persons responsible for the theft and bring them to justice.

Review: Jason Shiga uses every cop cliché in the book in this witty parody of '70s cop shows, with every member of the team knowing exactly what to do at the right moment, and the obligatory double-bluff ending. The art is simplistic, but very effective, and as a librarian himself, Shiga draws heavily and effectively on that world. Silly, but very smart at the same time.

FURTHER READING: *Fleep; Double Happiness*
SEE ALSO: *Same Difference & Other Stories*

★
★
★
★
★

Writer: Hiroaki Samura
Artist: Hiroaki Samura

Publisher: Dark Horse, 1997
ISBN: 1569712395

15+ BLADE OF THE IMMORTAL

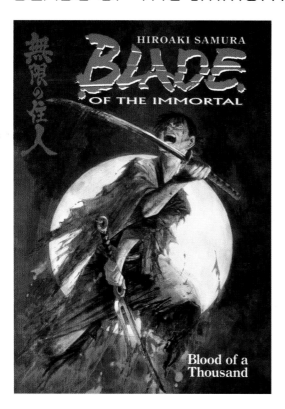

Plot: The ultimate samurai "road movie," set in late 18th century Japan. Manji is a young master swordsman who must kill 1,000 evildoers in order to be free of his immortality. Reluctantly, he teams up with Asano, a girl searching for the men who killed her father. These men, led by a fighter called Anotsu Kagehisa, seek to set up an alternative dojo where all fighting techniques are taught, with the idea that winning at all costs is all that matters.

Review: *Blade of the Immortal* is the most beautiful manga you will ever see. The risks Samura takes with his storytelling will take your breath away, as will the incredible dynamism of his splash pages and fight sequences. Probably the most violent—but simultaneously the most exquisite—work in print, it takes well-worn story concepts and recasts them for the contemporary reader. Always questioning the value of

life against the value of honor, Samura introduces a large cast of characters whose complex emotional entanglements make this much more than just a samurai quest story.

Dana Lewis and Toren Smith's loosely structured, slang-riddled translation plays a large part in the enjoyment of the book. It would be outstanding without such a creative approach to translation, but with it, *Blade of the Immortal* represents the pinnacle of work coming out of Japan. There are currently 17 volumes in this series, with more planned.

FURTHER READING: *Ohikkoshi*
SEE ALSO: *Crying Freeman; Lone Wolf and Cub; Usagi Yojimbo*

★
★
★

Writer: Ian Fleming, adapted by Anthony
Hern and Henry Gammidge
Artist: John McLusky

Publisher: Titan, 2005
ISBN: 1840238437

24+

JAMES BOND: CASINO ROYALE

Plot: British agent James Bond, with the help of Vesper Lynd, is assigned to prevent Soviet agent Le Chiffre winning at the Royale-Les-Eaux casino and funding the militant French trade union that he operates.

Review: Based on the original *James Bond* novels by Ian Fleming, this book includes *Live And Let Die* and *Moonraker* as well as *Casino Royale*. These were the first three James Bond stories adapted into daily strips in the British Daily Express newspaper between 1958 and 1959, predating the *James Bond* films. John McLusky's detailed artwork makes a refreshing change from the now-familiar, movie-style Bond, and the story adaptations by Anthony Hern and Henry Gammidge stick closely to the original books.

FURTHER READING: *James Bond: Dr. No*
SEE ALSO: *Modesty Blaise: Bad Suki*

★
★
★
★

Writer: Masashi Tanaka
Artist: Masashi Tanaka

Publisher: CMX, 2007
ISBN: 1401212735

12+

GON: VOLUME 1

Plot: Gon is a small dinosaur out of time. In each of these four wordless and hilarious adventures, the tiny, T-Rex-like character encounters animals of all sorts. Creatures who treat him well are rewarded with protection against predators, while enemies are subjected to Gon's gigantic wrath...

Review: It's one thing to draw phenomenally well, and another to tell an engaging story without using people or language. Few can combine these two skills like Masashi Tanaka. His near-photorealistic depictions of environments and animals breathe not only authenticity, but life into the story, and although Gon is drawn in a more cartoony style than the other animals, his facial expressions convey his thoughts and emotions precisely.

FURTHER READING: *Gon: Volume 2, Tyrant; Age of Reptiles*
SEE ALSO: *Owly: The Way Home & The Bittersweet Summer*

★
★
★
★

Writer: Kenichi Sonoda
Artist: Kenichi Sonoda

Publisher: Dark Horse, 2007
ISBN: 1593077483

18+

GUNSMITH CATS, REVISED EDITION: VOLUME 1

Plot: Rally Vincent is the owner of a gun store—the Gunsmith Cats of the title—and a bounty hunter. With her business partner, Minnie-May Hopkins, they are two women sharing a love of adventure and mayhem. Rally is an expert shot and driver, while Minnie-May's specialty is explosives. Set in Chicago, recurring characters include their friend, Becky; an ex-criminal, Misty; Goldie, a mob enforcer; Bean, the best getaway driver in the business; and the long-suffering detective, Roy Coleman.

In this volume, Rally pursues and captures Gray, a drug lord and gang leader. In prison, he continues his criminal business until his connections buy his release, leading to a final, fatal confrontation with Rally.

Review: These are fast-paced stories with detailed artwork that shows a keen appreciation of guns, cars, and bombs. Though not exactly politically correct, the action works visually as a comic-book version of Hong Kong cinema. Sonoda has created a well-defined cast of characters, including the villains, who all possess complex motivations.

FURTHER READING: *Gunsmith Cats, Revised Edition: Volumes 2, 3, and 4; Gunsmith Cats: Burst Volume 1*
SEE ALSO: *Oldboy; Crying Freeman; Sin City*

Writer: Kazuo Koike
Artist: Kazuo Kamimura

Publisher: Dark Horse, 2005
ISBN: 1593073852

LADY SNOWBLOOD

Plot: Born for Revenge. Oyuki, the main character, has one thought on her mind. Find and kill those that killed her father and mother. Both deadly and beautiful, she will often use the latter to help disarm her enemies. A gripping tale of sex and fury.

Review: From the same pen as *Samurai Executioner* and *Lone Wolf and Cub*, Koike has written an inspiring tale of vengeance, that has since influenced the making of Quentin Tarantino's two *Kill Bill* movies. The artwork by Kazuo Kamimura is well suited to the story and complements the writing, making this a book well worth reading.

FURTHER READING: *Crying Freeman; Path of the Assassin*
SEE ALSO: *Lone Wolf and Cub*

Writer: David Petersen
Artist: David Petersen

Publisher: Archaia Studio Press, 2007
ISBN: 1932386572

MOUSE GUARD VOLUME 1: FALL 1152

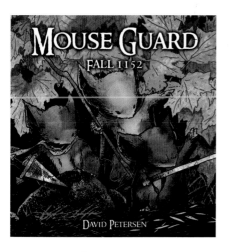

Plot: The Mouse Guard exist to keep the other mice safe, guarding their villages and finding safe passage from one to another. In this volume three members of the Mouse Guard uncover a traitor in their ranks and discover a long-lost hero amid a plot to attack Lockhaven, the home of the Guard.

Review: The initial story in the *Mouse Guard* series isn't particularly strong in terms of either its plot or characterization, but this doesn't take anything away from it. The realistic landscape, and unflinching violence combine with the caped mice and their foes—including crabs and a snake—to create a vivid fantasy setting that's sure to appeal to readers of all ages.

FURTHER READING: *Mouse Guard Volume 2: Winter 1152*
SEE ALSO: *Bone*

★
★
★

Writer: Don Rosa
Artist: Don Rosa

Publisher: Gemstone, 2005
ISBN: 0911903968

A

THE LIFE AND TIMES OF SCROOGE McDUCK

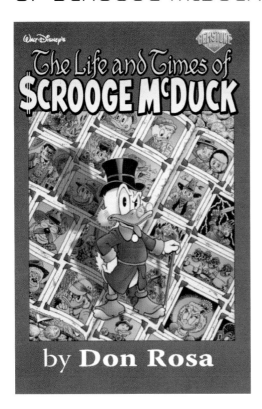

Plot: Originally created for European publisher Egmont in 1991–1993, the 12 stories in this collection were first published in the US by Gladstone in 1994–1995. A Scrooge obsessive, Don Rosa extracts a multitude of facts about the character from Carl Barks's original stories—covering Scrooge's life from 1867–1947, and including activities such as the Alaskan gold rush, meeting Teddy Roosevelt, prospecting in South Africa, and river boating on the Mississippi, weaving them into entertaining twists on the existing tales.

Review: A tour de force by the American heir to Barks, these adventure stories work on a number of levels that allow them to be enjoyed by both children and adults. Rosa has frequently referred to his work as overly detailed, and although self-taught he has evidently studied Will Elder's early art for *MAD*. Rosa is a comics superstar in Europe as a result of these stories, and careful inspection will reward the attentive—or obsessive—reader.

FURTHER READING: *The Life and Times of Scrooge McDuck Companion*
SEE ALSO: *Disney Presents Carl Barks's Greatest Duck Tales Stories Volume 1*

Writer: Masashi Kishimoto
Artist: Masashi Kishimoto

Publisher: VIZ Media, 2003
ISBN: 1569319006

NARUTO: VOLUME ONE

Plot: Naruto wants to become the champion of his village, but what he doesn't know is that a demon was sealed inside him to protect the village when he was born. As a result, the villagers fear him and he's considered a troublemaker, having no friends or family. When Naruto starts ninja school, he meets classmates Sakura and Sasuke and their teacher, Kakashi. As part of their training, the three pupils are given a mission where success will depend entirely on whether they can learn to get along.

Review: Kishimoto has a pleasant, detailed art style. His writing is full of humorous situations and is action-oriented, though there is a dark side to the events. This is an undemanding, but ultimately fun read.

FURTHER READING: *Naruto: Volumes 2-27*
SEE ALSO: *One Piece*

Writer: Dave Stevens
Artist: Dave Stevens

Publisher: Grafton Books, 1991
ISBN: 0586215204

THE ROCKETEER

Plot: In 1938, pilot Cliff Secord discovers a hidden rocket backpack. Using a special helmet to enable him to steer, he becomes The Rocketeer. With his mechanic Peevy and girlfriend Betty, Secord has to outwit Nazi agents who want to steal the secrets of the rocket pack for Germany.

Review: Published sporadically in the 1980s by Pacific Comics, this five-episode story was compiled into a single graphic novel in 1991. Deliberately tongue in cheek, with Secord's girlfriend Betty based on 1950s pinup Bettie Page, and the overall feel of a 1930s movie serial, this fun story rattles along from cliffhanger to cliffhanger. Stevens's artwork is delightful throughout, whether he's drawing Betty's modeling assignments or the equally curvaceous airplanes of the era.

FURTHER READING: *Xenozoic Tales*
SEE ALSO: *Classic Tales*

★
★ **Writer:** ILYA
★ **Artist:** ILYA

Publisher: Active Images, 2004
ISBN: 097405674

12+

SKIDMARKS

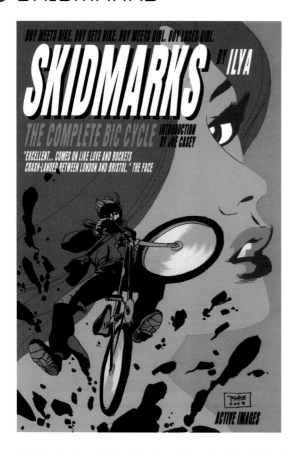

Plot: Bic is a boy cyclist entering the adult world and beginning to realize that girls can be just as interesting as spoke-patterns. When he witnesses a robbery at his local store and sees the thief drop the cash, he picks it up without thinking. Before long it dawns on him that he could buy his dream bike—and impress his dream girl—but there's an annoying little voice telling him he should hand it back...

Review: ILYA plunges the reader into the volatile and emotional teenage world, full of sudden passions and peer pressure. Bic is easy to identify with—weak at times, strong at others, open to temptation, but intensely human—and seen through his eyes, the world is full of possibilities.

By the time he started work on *Skidmarks*, ILYA had self-published many Bic stories, and polished both his storytelling skills and his characters. His experience shows in the pacing of this longer adventure, with his bold, open line style giving the modern morality tale a cool edge, and his assured inking providing a sophisticated finish.

FURTHER READING: *The End of the Century Club; The Eyeball Kid; Alec and In The Days of the Ace Rock'n'Roll Club*
SEE ALSO: *Ghost World*

Writer: Peter David
Artist: LeSean Thomas

Publisher: Dreamwave, 2003
ISBN: 0973278684

TEENAGE MUTANT NINJA TURTLES VOLUME 1

Plot: The graphic-novel adaptation of the 2003 animated television series, the Turtles engage in their usual action-packed heroics, battling the comically sinister Shredder and his Foot Clan, while being mentored by their Sensei, the mutated rat Splinter.

Review: Although this volume draws storylines and events directly from the animated series, its translation into graphic-novel format enhances the stylistic depth. If you're familiar with the *Turtles* series of the early 1990s, this new, slightly more mature effort is far more interesting, with greater attention to the narrative structure. While you may derive some nostalgic pleasure from it, this volume is equally worthy as a fresh work of fiction.

FURTHER READING: *Teenage Mutant Ninja Turtles #1 (Mirage Studios);*
Transformers Generation One
SEE ALSO: *Usagi Yojimbo Volume 1; Ronin*

Writer: Milton Caniff
Artist: Milton Caniff

Publisher: IDW Publishing, 2007
ISBN: 1600101003

THE COMPLETE TERRY AND THE PIRATES VOLUME 1: 1934–1936

a journalist friend, Pat Ryan, in search of a fabled gold mine. "Connie" Confucius, a stereotypical oriental character, becomes their aide and interpreter as the pair take on various villains who seek to interfere with their quest.

Review: Some of the earliest artwork is a little rough around the edges, but Caniff's instinct for gripping plots and captivating characters is there from the outset. In time to celebrate the centenary of Caniff's birth, his dramatically spotted blacks and sinuous linework have been remastered from archived newspapers, and the quality is very good.

Plot: The *Terry and the Pirates* saga begins when Terry Lee, a spirited young American boy, arrives in exotic China with

FURTHER READING: *Meanwhile: A Biography of Milton Caniff*
SEE ALSO: *Ballad of the Salty Sea; Zorro*

★
★
★
★
★

Writer: Hergé
Artist: Hergé

Publisher: Mammoth, 2003
ISBN: 0316357243

A

TINTIN IN TIBET

Plot: On vacation with the Captain and Professor Calculus, Tintin has nightmares of his friend Chang lying half dead in snow. The next day, a letter arrives from Chang, stating that he is flying across Asia to visit London. But a newspaper article brings Tintin's nightmares to reality as it reports that Chang's plane has crashed in the mountains near Katmandu with no survivors. Convinced that Chang is still alive despite all the odds, Tintin and the Captain rush to Tibet to search for their lost friend. But the harsh environment is against them and there are reports of a great monster nearby...

Review: The greatest of Hergé's Tintin stories draws the strongest parallels to the creator's own life. Written and drawn at a time when Hergé was plagued by nightmares, the all-pervading snow represents his sense of being lost. This omnipresent whiteness was so important to Hergé that his initial idea for the *Tintin in Tibet* cover was simply to have Tintin wading through a blank background. As the story progresses, the vibrant color of the earlier adventures is bleached out, blending seamlessly with the ligne claire ("clear line") style the books pioneered.

The character of Chang was based on a friend of the same name who died years before Hergé started the book. His story proved prophetic—after the book's original release the two were reunited, even appearing on Belgian national television together.

The level of accuracy in the drawings of Tibet is staggering for a man who never left Belgium, and outstrips his earlier works. The importance of this book cannot be disputed, and Hergé's respect for Tibet and its people was so great that when a Chinese version was released under the title *Tintin in Chinese Tibet*, his widow demanded the entire run be pulped and reprinted with the original title. *Tintin in Tibet* isn't just an adventure yarn, it's a story about hope, determination, and goodwill against monumental odds.

FURTHER READING: *Tintin: The Calculus Affair; Tintin: Explorers on the Moon; Tintin: The Blue Lotus*
SEE ALSO: *Blake and Mortimer: The Yellow "M"*

Writer: Joe Kubert
Artist: Joe Kubert

Publisher: DC Comics, 2001
ISBN: 1563897814

Ⓐ TOR: VOLUME 1

Plot: The primitive Tor, born to a tribe of mountain people, lives in a fantasy world set a million years ago, where man and dinosaur coexist in a battle for survival. His inquiring mind and great strength set him apart, and he has an apelike companion named Chee-Chee. Defending those less capable than himself, Tor wanders through an untamed landscape encountering savages, monstrous creatures, and natural disasters.

Review: This volume reprints the original 1950s *Tor* stories created by Norman Maurer and Joe Kubert. Kubert wrote and drew the strips, and his flowing, detailed artwork and exciting storytelling are still a joy to behold.

FURTHER READING: *Tor: Volumes 2 and 3; Tarzan; Enemy Ace*
SEE ALSO: *Prince Valiant; Kamandi*

Writer: Stan Sakai
Artist: Stan Sakai

Publisher: Fantagraphics, 1987
ISBN: 0930193350

Ⓐ USAGI YOJIMBO: BOOK 1

Plot: A masterless samurai rabbit named Miyamoto Usagi wanders 17th-century Japan. It is a time of political unrest and he fights injustice while continuing his quest to see the evil Lord Hikiji pay for the death of his former master. Along the way he forms an uneasy alliance with a rhino bounty hunter and befriends a feline bodyguard.

Review: The first book in a series of ten. Some readers may be deterred by Sakai's use of the funny animal style, but he's following a tradition that's been around for decades. Simplicity is the key to the appeal of these stories, and Sakai writes and draws with such charm that it's hard not to fall for his work. The series won a well-deserved Eisner award in 1999.

FURTHER READING: *Usagi Yojimbo: Books 2–10*
SEE ALSO: *Blade of the Immortal*

CHAPTER 2
NON-FICTION

A MAGICAL MYSTERY TOUR

As descriptions go, "non-fiction" is not particularly descriptive. The only thing it promises is some element of fact, and even that may not necessarily be pure. Perhaps a better term is "miscellaneous"—a word full of possibilities. Like a magical mystery tour, you never quite know where you are going to end up.

Nowhere is that more true than in Bryan Talbot's *Alice in Sunderland*. A truly immense and ambitious work, *Alice in Sunderland* explores the history and mythology of an old industrial city in the north of England, linking it first with Alice Liddell, the inspiration for Lewis Carroll's Alice books. From there the story reverberates outward, backward and sideways to link Sunderland to—well, almost everything. Talbot even finds room in his sprawling, meandering epic to explore the roles of the artist and the audience in the telling of tales.

Another book that explores the nature of art is Scott McCloud's *Understanding Comics*. A groundbreaking work, *Understanding Comics* serves as an introduction to, and exploration of, the medium of comics. It's a graphic novel that exemplifies the form of graphic non-fiction. In it, McCloud takes the reader behind the curtain, not just to show how comics work, but how the creative process works as a whole, celebrating the power that lies within every one of us, whether its purpose is to make comics, books, symphonies—or just to blow raspberries.

Everyone has a book in them, as the old saying goes, and that certainly seems to be the case with biography and autobiography, perhaps the two most prevalent forms of graphic non-fiction.

Maus is the work that showed the world the true potential of graphic non-fiction. Often verging on autobiography, *Maus* recounts cartoonist Art Spiegelman's attempt to record his father's experiences in Poland before, during, and immediately after the holocaust. *Maus* explores the dehumanization inherent in nationalist and racist ideologies using the extended metaphor of animals: the Poles are pigs, the Germans are cats, and the Jews are mice. As soon as it was published, *Maus* won international acclaim and an unprecedented Pulitzer Prize. However, Spiegelman was keen to point out that his work was not unique. Back in the early 1970s, cartoonist Justin Green had explored his own take on biographical comics in *Binky Brown Meets the Holy Virgin Mary*. A work of self-discovery, Green used Binky Brown as a tool to explore his religious upbringing and its impact on his obsessive-compulsive disorder, a condition that was poorly understood at the time.

Religious identity is also an important theme of *Blankets*, Craig Thompson's autobiographical, romantic tale of his sexual awakening deep within the religious heartland of the US Midwest. There, amid the long, cold winters, closed minds, and claustrophobic conformity, Thompson weaves a tale of lyrical beauty whose greatest power lies in its silence, when the pages give themselves over entirely to the expressive images.

Examinations of serious medical conditions form another powerful subgenre of graphic autobiography. English artist Al Davison's *The Spiral Cage* explores the artist's experience of living with spina bifida, a theme he would expand on in *The Minotaur's Tale*. By contrast, French cartoonist David Beauchard's *Epileptic* focuses not so much on his own experiences, or even those of his epileptic brother, but on his family as a whole and how they react to his brother's condition. Originally published in France as a six-volume series and now available as a single, 368-page volume in English, *Epileptic* is a sprawling, at times cloying, journey into a family that is both united and divided by a situation that renders them powerless.

The godfather of autobiographical comics is Harvey Pekar. Spurred on by his friend, the legendary cartoonist and fellow jazz fan Robert Crumb, Pekar began to record his reflections on his own experiences in *American Splendor*, focusing primarily on the minutiae of daily life and people's mundane interactions. Unable to draw himself, Pekar attracted a wide variety of artists to illustrate his comics, starting with Crumb.

The last great arena for graphic non-fiction is travel writing. Of the many books that sought to take the reader to purportedly hostile places, two examples stand out. Marjane Satrapi's *Persepolis* is a lively, warm, and engaging tale of a girl growing up in Iran—a country in the throes of revolution and war that is brought to life by the smart, bolshy, vivacious presence of the author. Satrapi swiftly demonstrates what should have been obvious all along—that Iran isn't just populated by religious zealots.

By contrast, *Pyongyang*, based in North Korea, doesn't pretend to offer an insider's view on the country—quite the opposite. Named after the country's capital city, *Pyongyang* is a portrait of alienation, of a culture that is closed off both within and without, to its own people as much as foreigners. Guy Delisle, an animator who visits the city to oversee the outsourcing of French animation to cheaper North Korean labor, acts as a guide to the surreal, impersonal world of the stranger in an hermetically sealed communist state, exploring daily banalities while hinting at the brutality and oppression that remains present, yet unspoken, throughout.

So there, in North Korea, our journey through graphic non-fiction pauses. But the expedition isn't over yet. There are plenty more stops on the magical mystery tour—and, as is so often the case, it is often better to travel than to arrive.

Writer: Bryan Talbot
Artist: Bryan Talbot

Publisher: Jonathan Cape, 2007
ISBN: 0224080768

12+

ALICE IN SUNDERLAND

Plot: Bryan Talbot's *Alice in Sunderland* was four years in the making, combining autobiographical detail from the writer/artist with historical and mythological references, and an eclectic mix of art styles.

The story tells of a performer on the stage of the Sunderland Empire theatre, who relates the area's links to *Alice in Wonderland* to a solitary, and not entirely enthralled, audience member.

The performer projects an outside broadcast onto the rear of the stage, of a pilgrim walking through the modern-day English city of Sunderland and its surrounding area, while talking about the history of the places he visits.

Review: More of a graphic feature-length documentary than a graphic novel, *Alice in Sunderland* sees Bryan Talbot's pilgrim rendered in black and white, while the cityscapes and landscapes of north-east England he describes are in color. The Pilgrim describes the area and its history and talks to some of its people, covering not just historic places such as the venerable Bede's Church of St Peter or the Cathedral at Durham, but also more mundane buildings specific to Charles Dodgson—better known as Lewis Carroll—and Alice Lidell, the inspiration for the fictional Alice of *Alice in Wonderland* and *Through The Looking Glass*.

Both the performer and the pilgrim are obviously the book's writer and artist Bryan Talbot, who is not afraid to intertwine some of his own history into the book, with passing references to his other works—including his best-known character, Luther Arkwright. Even his friends, family, and neighbors make appearances, as does his grandmother's sideboard, which, in the context of the book, is not quite as bizarre as it might sound.

Those who have an interest in history, in Lewis Carroll, or in the geographical area of north-east England may find it more engrossing than those that don't, but with tangential references to people and events outside the main thrust of the narrative, the book rarely gets bogged down by excessive history or geography.

Indeed, the stories within the story—of the *Lambton Worm*, or Lewis Carroll's own nonsense poem *Jabberwocky*, or even the historical background to the phrase "pinning your colors to the mast"—are presented in different art styles, making

them a visual respite, as well as a narrative break from the main thrust of the book.

Talbot's love of his subject and interest in the region shine through as he combines disparate subjects into one continuous train of thought. The greatest achievement of *Alice in Sunderland* is how easy Talbot makes it seem to integrate history and geography into his densely scripted story and his diverse art styles.

FURTHER READING: *The Adventures of Luther Arkwright; Sandman: Fables and Reflections*
SEE ALSO: *The Tale of One Bad Rat; Heart of Empire; The Complete Nemesis the Warlock Vol 1*

★
★
★
★
★

Writer: Harvey Pekar
Artist: Various

Publisher: Ballantine Books, 2003
ISBN: 0345468309,

18+

AMERICAN SPLENDOR: THE LIFE AND TIMES OF HARVEY PEKAR

THE LIFE AND TIMES OF HARVEY PEKAR

Plot: *American Splendor* is a series of autobiographical short stories and snapshots of an everyman's stressful and frustrating life in modern industrial America, working a dead-end job and struggling to make ends meet.

Pekar's tales, by turns amusing and depressing, were first aired in his self-published title in 1976—a time when no one else was making autobiographical and observational comics of that kind. He chronicles the entertaining characters he encounters and the chance conversations he overhears while going about his lacklustre job, glorifying the numbing boredom of working as a filing clerk in an industrial city. As his self-published comic becomes more successful he also offers hilarious looks at the media's attempts to understand the phenomenon.

Review: The 2004 film version of Pekar's life story gave the *American Splendor* "brand" a shot in the arm, and exposed a whole new public to the splendidly neurotic Pekar, second only to Woody Allen for turning self-obsession into an art form without alienating his audience.

His first appearance on the big screen was the 1988 documentary film *Comic Book Confidential*. Pekar's section seems to have had a definite influence on the way the 2004 film was shot.

This extensive collection of the original comic magazine stories gives the reader a wonderful cross-section of his moods, as the author worries about old age and illness, stresses over money and family, shares his enthusiasm for

music, delights at an overheard turn of phrase, or nostalgia for a bygone age.

The key to *American Splendor* is that Pekar is willing to expose everything: all his petty annoyances, his boring hobbyhorses, his peevish grudges; and his obsessions—all the things that real people get up to but often don't want to recognize in themselves or others.

Pekar is big enough to share with us what a little man he can be, and it makes for a compelling read. Pekar has also used an evolving rota of cartoonists to illustrate his scripts, most famously Robert Crumb, who drew some of the funniest sequences. Other underground notables include Spain Rodriguez and Jim Woodring, but the majority of the

stories are delivered by the more workmanlike hands of artists such as Joe Zabel and Gary Dumm. The narrative voice is so strong, however, that it carries you through the less consistent artwork.

FURTHER READING: *American Splendor: Our Movie Year; The New American Splendor Anthology: From the Streets of Cleveland*
SEE ALSO: *Our Cancer Year; Dori Stories; The Playboy; Justin Green's Binky Brown Sampler*

★ **Writer:** Justin Green **Publisher:** Last Gasp, 1995
★ **Artist:** Justin Green **ISBN:** 0867193328
★
★

15+

JUSTIN GREEN'S
BINKY BROWN SAMPLER

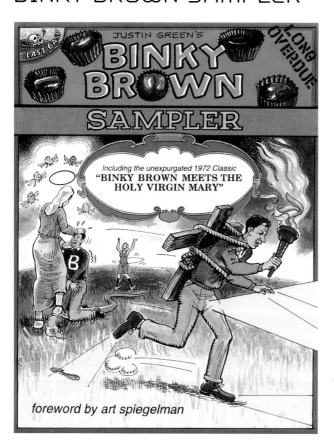

Plot: The centerpiece of this book is the landmark underground comic *Binky Brown Meets the Holy Virgin Mary*, first published by Last Gasp in 1972. This story recounts Binky's (in essence, creator Green's) confused and fearful passage from boyhood to manhood, starting in the crushingly conformist 1950s. Haunted by Catholic dogma, in particular by the image of the Virgin Mary, Binky grows up ashamed of his sexual imagination, and develops a very particular neurosis: he fears affronting the Virgin with his lustful thoughts, which he envisions emanating from him like rays of light. He then devotes his life, obsessively, to either avoiding or atoning for this unavoidable sin (apparently Green has since been diagnosed with obsessive-compulsive disorder). In tune with Binky's mania, the art and story have a hyper-detailed and frequently hallucinatory quality, leavened and yet made more poignant by a constant vein of sly humor. The climax of Binky depicts Green's rejection of Catholicism and first, tentative claims to a life free and unburdened by his compulsions. The rest of the Sampler consists of other essential comix work by Green (from *Show & Tell*, among others)—shorter tales that gain greater significance alongside the central story.

Review: Binky is a classic of confessional comix, and a crucial influence on such creators as R. Crumb, Aline Kominsky Crumb, and Art Spiegelman (who has acknowledged Green as an inspiration for *Maus*). Much of the contemporary passion for autobiographical comix stems from Green's example; in particular, memoirs of disability (such as *The Spiral Cage* and *Epileptic*) owe Binky a great debt. Cartoonists such as Jim Woodring (*The Frank Book*) have hailed Green for his spiritual outlook. More to the point, Binky is a fantastic comic in its own right, brilliant and heart-sore, overflowing with humor, inventive visual metaphors, a constantly and deliberately shifting stylistic palette, and fearsome insight. It's shocking and embarrassing (for author and readers alike) and yet, in the end, entertaining and even oddly uplifting.

FURTHER READING: *Justin Green's Sign Game;*
Music Legends
SEE ALSO: *Furry Freak Brothers; Maus;*
The Frank Book;

★ **Writer:** Craig Thompson **Publisher:** Top Shelf, 2003
★ **Artist:** Craig Thompson **ISBN:** 1891830430
★
★

15+ BLANKETS

an illustrated novel by
CRAIG THOMPSON

Plot: In *Blankets*, writer and artist Craig Thompson presents a semi-autobiographical tale of his experiences of childhood; his first true love, and the conflicts—external and internal—created by being raised in a deeply committed Christian family. He is snubbed for wanting to become an artist, with his creativity viewed as going against his beliefs. As a result, Thompson is castigated for his efforts by both his family and the surrounding community. But when he meets Raina at a religious camp he is introduced to someone both spiritual, and popular, but also someone who puts him on the path to becoming an adult.

Review: This gentle, evenly paced book touches on both the cruelties and joys of life, the burning passion of first love,

and the inevitable heartbreak. Thompson stated that the novel grew out of a simple idea: to describe what it feels like to sleep next to someone for the first time. He also explores themes like separation, for example, that he previously visited in his book *Goodbye Chunky Rice* from 5 years earlier. His artwork is exquisitely simplistic, with minimal lines conveying myriad emotions. Thompson has also won every major US comic industry award—including an Eisner, an Ignatz, and a Harvey. At 600 pages *Blankets* never rushes itself, and like the ever present snow in the story, it settles over you imperceptibly.

FURTHER READING: *Carnet De Voyage*
SEE ALSO: *Goodbye, Chunky Rice; Epileptic*

★ **Writer:** David B.   **Publisher:** Pantheon, 2005
★ **Artist:** David B.   **ISBN:** 0375714685
★
★

15+ # EPILEPTIC

Can we, in fact, get on with our lives? But it's not our choice to make. When the illness took up residence here it didn't seek our permission.

It slumbers inside my brother and, upon awakening, it slithers out and insinuates itself into our lives.

He's back to having three seizures a day.

Like clockwork, imposing a rhythm on our lives.

Plot: The true, and tragic, story of Pierre-Francois (aka David B.), Florence, and their epileptic brother, Jean-Christophe. Whilst growing up in '60s and '70s France, their parents seek help, first from the medical profession, and then—in desperation—turning to the increasingly esoteric practices of alternative therapy in their quest to alleviate Jean-Christophe of his symptoms. David B attempts to make sense of a period of his life dominated by his brother's condition.

Review: This highly emotive and powerful autobiography pulls no punches, and David B. portrays himself with brutal honesty—by turns feeling frustration, anger, sadness, and even savagery toward his burdensome brother. (He dreams of a normal childhood, but the dreams change, to more demonic visions, illustrating his struggle of coming to terms with his feelings for his brother). This is probably the most honest portrayal of a family under pressure ever published in a graphic novel.

FURTHER READING: *Persepolis: The Story of a Childhood*
SEE ALSO: *The Spiral Cage; Jimmy Corrigan; The Minotaur's Tale*

★
★
★
★
★

Writer: Art Spiegelman

Artist: Art Spiegelman

Publisher: Penguin, 2003

ISBN: 0141014083

15+ MAUS: A SURVIVOR'S TALE, VOLUMES 1 AND 2

Plot: A cat-and-mouse story with world-shattering consequences. In order to record and understand his parents' experiences during the Holocaust, underground cartoonist Art Spiegelman re-establishes contact with his father, Vladek. The narrative shifts between Art's present-day life while interviewing Vladek, and Vladek's reminiscences of his earlier life: how he met Anja, his wife and Art's mother; his experiences as a soldier in the early days of World War II; his family's flight from, and eventual capture by, the Nazis; the death of their son; Vladek's and Anja's separate experiences in the camps; and their happy reunion at the end of the war.

Review: Originally serialized in RAW, the highly influential avant-garde comics anthology edited by Spiegelman and his wife, Françoise Mouly, Maus made American readers and critics stand up and take notice of long-form comics. What stands out immediately is the book's visual metaphor: Jews are portrayed as mice, and Nazis as cats. There are also pigs,

who are Poles; dogs, who are Americans; and even frogs, who are French. But instead of falling back on an easy predator/prey comparison, Spiegelman constantly reconsiders that racial metaphor to expose its weaknesses; after all, Hitler's rationale for the Holocaust was that Jews were not truly human.

Contrary to many reports, Maus isn't and doesn't pretend to be a history of the Holocaust; rather, it's a complex, multilayered family saga. The Holocaust does play a large role in the book, but the focus is always on how that incomprehensible event affected Vladek and Anja—and, eventually, their son. Maus deserves all the acclaim it has received, including a special Pulitzer Prize in 1992.

FURTHER READING: *Read Yourself Raw;*
Art Spiegelman: Conversations by Joseph Witek
SEE ALSO: *In the Shadow of No Towers*

SO THE GERMANS SWINGED THEM BY THE LEGS AGAINST A WALL...

AND THEY NEVER ANYMORE SCREAMED.

IN THIS WAY THE GERMANS TREATED THE LITTLE ONES WHAT STILL HAD SURVIVED A LITTLE.

THIS I DIDN'T SEE WITH MY OWN EYES, BUT SOMEBODY THE NEXT DAY TOLD ME. AND I SAID, "THANK GOD WITH PERSIS *OUR* CHILDREN ARE SAFE!"

MAYBE WE SHOULD TRY MY FATHER'S OLD HOUSE. THE JANITOR HAS KNOWN OUR FAMILY FOR YEARS.

LET'S TRY. WE'VE **GOT** TO GET OFF THE STREETS BEFORE DAWN!

I WAS A LITTLE SAFE. I HAD A COAT AND BOOTS, SO LIKE A GESTAPO WORE WHEN HE WAS NOT IN SERVICE. BUT **ANJA** - HER APPEARANCE - YOU COULD SEE MORE *EASY* SHE WAS JEWISH. I WAS AFRAID FOR HER.

NO!

I WON'T GO TO THEIR GAS CHAMBERS!...

AND MY CHILDREN WON'T GO TO THEIR GAS CHAMBERS.

BIBI! LONIA! RICHIEU! COME HERE QUICKLY!

ALWAYS TOSHA CARRIED AROUND HER NECK SOME POISON — SHE KILLED NOT ONLY HERSELF, BUT ALSO THE 3 CHILDREN.

I'M TELLING YOU, IT WAS A TRAGEDY AMONG TRAGEDIES. HE WAS SUCH A HAPPY, BEAUTIFUL BOY!

MY FAMILY SENDS. I WANT THAT YOU ALSO EAT SOMETHING.

MY GOD. SARDINES! BISCUITS! CHOCOLATE!

HE *INSISTED* TO SHARE WITH ME, AND IT SAVED ME MY LIFE.

★
★ **Writer:** Al Davison   **Publisher:** Dark Horse, 2001
★ **Artist:** Al Davison   **ISBN:** 1878574426
★

15+ THE MINOTAUR'S TALE

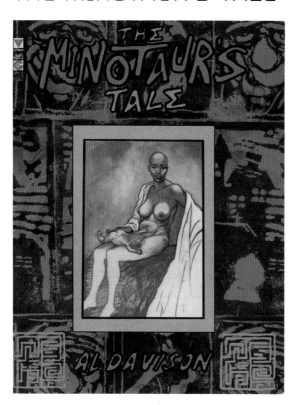

Plot: The ancient Greek myth of *Theseus and the Minotaur* is retold in a child's art project: King Minos is disgusted at his deformed child born of a curse, and shuts the child away in the labyrinth. Years later, as an adult, the half-human, half-bull creature is slain. The action cuts to 1980s inner-city Britain and a destitute man with his own crippling deformity. Beaten senseless by a gang of skinheads, the man, known only as Banshee, is found and winds up in a mental institute. His doctor gives him a book written by one of her former patients, also about the Minotaur. However, this version of the story is very different, and Banshee embarks on a journey of self-discovery.

Review: Al Davison was born with spina bifida. He was never expected to walk, but fought the condition, refusing to comply with its limitations. Perhaps best known for his

autobiographical work *Spiral Cage*, which details some of his experiences of living with a twisted spine, Davison embraces a similar theme in *The Minotaur's Tale*, albeit indirectly. Banshee begins as a pitiful character, wailing in the night and writhing in a filthy, grim world. He is full of self-loathing and almost curses his own birth. His self-hatred and the disgusted looks he receives from passers-by are contrasted sharply with the body ideal depicted in ancient sculpture and legend.

The real strength of Davison's work lies not so much in the book's plot, but in his devastatingly effective artwork. Banshee is seen as a monster, and his life is expressed in Picasso-style abnormality and jarring lines akin to 1920s cinematic Expressionism. The original art project from which Davison takes his title is beautifully rendered in a classical

style, with thick, simple line drawings and straight edges that contrast perfectly with the clunking, uneasy air of Banshee's existence. There's a recurring theme of pregnant women and maternal figures, and as Banshee learns to be comfortable in his own skin, and grows from man-child to man, these figures give way to more sexualized images of women. On his Ulysses-style journey from painful wreck, unable to touch another human being, to romantic lover, the ugly clashes in style dissolve into something more fluid, softer and even beautiful. The implication is that Banshee

and his heavily birthmarked lover find their own place in the world—not by comparing themselves to the Greek ideal, but as something wholly new and different. A triumph of maverick, stream-of-consciousness storytelling, The Minotaur's Tale demands investigation.

FURTHER READING: *Spiral Dreams; 24 Hour Comics*
SEE ALSO: *Spiral Cage; Epileptic*

★
★
★
★
★

Writer: Marjane Satrapi
Artist: Marjane Satrapi

Publisher: Pantheon, 2007
ISBN: 0375714839

PERSEPOLIS:
THE STORY OF A CHILDHOOD

Plot: An Iranian émigré's autobiographical tale of life in Iran—from the 1979 revolution that toppled the pro-Western regime of the Shah, to her experiences of growing up in the Islamic Republic that succeeded it. A thorough knowledge of Iranian history is not necessary to appreciate this tumultuous coming-of-age story.

Review: Can *Persepolis* really be as good as people keep saying it is? Well, bluntly, yes. It is compelling and rewarding, warm and very human. How can you not love a girl who wants to be a prophet and a revolutionary when she grows up? Who convinces religious zealots that her Michael Jackson badge is actually a picture of Malcom X?

Told in a simple style, using inky blacks that are reminiscent of woodcuts, Satrapi conveys the enormity of the revolution and the subsequent Iran-Iraq war in a shockingly matter-of-fact way. This reinforces the horror that tears through Iranian society, the torture and the killings. The creeping realization that the revolution is not going to usher in a better Iran is hammered home via Satrapi's memories of her uncle—a revolutionary who is arrested and eventually killed.

Satrapi herself is a smart woman with a strong voice. More than just a compelling narrator, she is also unflinching and honest in her recollections of her pride and her own petty cruelties, such as the time she betrayed a stranger to the religious authorities to save her own skin. There's a standout passage in which Satrapi recounts her doomed marriage in all its gory detail. But the book is full of standout passages—there's not enough space to do justice to them all here.

Aside from continuing her career as a cartoonist, Satrapi has more recently turned her considerable talents to directing

and overseeing the transformation of *Persepolis* from a comic book into an award-winning animated movie featuring the voice of Catherine Deneuve.

FURTHER READING: *Monsters are Afraid of the Moon*
SEE ALSO: *Chicken with Plums; Embroideries*

★
★
★
★

Writer: Guy Delisle
Artist: Guy Delisle

Publisher: Drawn & Quarterly, 2007
ISBN 0224079905

15+ PYONGYANG

Plot: A travelogue by a French animator whose work takes him to North Korea. At its heart, *Pyongyang* is a tale of globalization and how market forces can open even the most unexpected doors. We discover that no manufactured goods or services, not even animation, are immune from its effect. Globalization brings French-Canadian Delisle to work in the French animation industry, and then to oversee its demise as the bulk of the animation work disappears overseas—first to China (as chronicled in Delisle's other book, *Shenzhen*), and from there to North Korea, where the same work can be done at an even lower price.

Review: Given the notorious secrecy surrounding North Korea, any accounts from behind the DMZ (demilitarized zone) that still divides the Korean Peninsular is bound to be interesting, but Delisle's account is particularly illuminating. With a sparse style that focuses on impressions and anecdotes, and drawing on his experience while creating *Shenzhen*, Delisle conveys the daily monotony of life in North Korea with vividly bland grays and excruciating angles. The conformity is so crushing that the author even looks to the patterns of damp on the ceiling and the grease stains on the tablecloth for some relief.

Told in a series of episodes and vignettes rather than a linear narrative, *Pyongyang* works cumulatively, each incident reinforcing the endless repetitive grind. Not that we get to see much of the ordinary workers—a key feature of the

repressive regime is the power it exercises over its people, and almost all of Delisle's interactions are handled via a series of minders who are afforded greater freedoms than their fellows, but who are also under greater pressure.

In addition to the boredom and conformity, Delisle captures the constant and oppressive atmosphere of terror that permeates the country. There is a wonderful motif of a lineup of ordinary North Koreans. Which one is the villainous traitor? The answer is that any one of them could be found guilty as a traitor, at any time, on an almost arbitrary basis.

But over and above the quotidian struggles, the standout section is undoubtedly Delisle's visit to what could be described as North Korea's main tourist attraction— the International Friendship Museum, a bizarre assortment of objects presented in a bunker that would probably survive a nuclear strike. Its centerpiece is a venerated waxwork of the glorious (and deceased) leader Kim Il-Sung that stands, like North Korea itself, as a testament to one man's brutal cult of personality.

FURTHER READING: *Shenzhen; Berlin*
SEE ALSO: *Persepolis: The Story of a Childhood*

★
★
★
★
★

Writer: Scott McCloud
Artist: Scott McCloud

Publisher: HarperCollins, 1994
ISBN: 006097625

UNDERSTANDING COMICS: THE INVISIBLE ART

Plot: *Understanding Comics* is Scott McCloud's seminal graphic novel about graphic novels. It charts the history of the comic strip, the mechanics of how strips work, and the infinite possibilities that the form offers. McCloud eschews wild speculation about the future in favor of discussing what's on offer for comics creators, potential creators, and creatives of all kinds right now.

Review: As obvious as it might seem now, few people had thought of creating a comprehensive guide to the comics form before *Understanding Comics*—especially one that was a graphic novel itself. Even Will Eisner, arguably the father

of the graphic novel, limited himself to producing an illustrated textbook when crafting his own volume on how comics work, *Comics and Sequential Art*. McCloud shows the courage of his convictions about comics being a medium, not a genre, with its own weaknesses and strengths, by examining the form of the comic strip in the actual form of a comic strip.

Who better to serve as a guide on our grand tour of comics than the author, represented here as an avuncular cartoon version of his physical self. Funny and self-deprecating, the cartoon McCloud is part-teacher, part-raconteur, but never

I'VE ONLY SCRATCHED THE *SURFACE* IN THIS CHAPTER... *TRAJAN'S COLUMN, GREEK PAINTING, JAPANESE SCROLLS...* ALL THESE HAVE BEEN SUGGESTED AND ALL SHOULD BE EXPLORED.

BUT THERE IS *ONE* EVENT WHICH LOOMS AS LARGE IN *COMICS* HISTORY AS IT DOES IN THE HISTORY OF THE *WRITTEN WORD.*

THE INVENTION OF PRINTING.

WORDS AND PICTURES IN COMBINATION MAY NOT BE MY *DEFINITION* OF COMICS, BUT THE COMBINATION HAS HAD *TREMENDOUS INFLUENCE* ON ITS *GROWTH.*

com·ics (kom'iks) n. p... ... form, used with a singular... Juxtaposed pictori... ...er images in deliberat... ...nce, intended to conve... ...n and/or to prod... response in th... 2. Superheroes... costumes, fight... villains who want... ...re world in violent se...

A HUGE RANGE OF HUMAN EXPERIENCES CAN BE *PORTRAYED* IN COMICS THROUGH EITHER WORDS OR PICTURES.

anything less than thoroughly engaging. His linework— simple, smooth, and unfussy—draws you in and propels you through the book. It also belies McCloud's consummate skill as he literally draws us into new directions, altering his natural style to give us lessons in comic styles.

The real meat of the book is its taxonomy of how comics work. It demonstrates the multiplicity of ways in which comics can convey meaning, complete with specially created examples to illustrate each point. Almost every new panel is pregnant with possibilities and bursting with new ideas. Leading by example, McCloud is experimenting for us, and

it's a rare comics creator who wouldn't want to follow these inventive and engaging sample narratives beyond the panels provided.

Importantly, *Understanding Comics* also looks beyond comics to examine approaches to artistic endeavor in general. As a result it is immensely inspirational, not just for comics fans or art lovers, but for everyone.

FURTHER READING: *Reinventing Comics; Zot!*
SEE ALSO: *Making Comics*

★
★ **Writer:** Mark Kalesniko
★ **Artist:** Mark Kalesniko
★

Publisher: Fantagraphics, 2006
ISBN: 1560977450

18+ ALEX

Plot: Cartoonist Alex left his home town to pursue his dream of working for a big animation studio in California, but after failing to make the grade, he's back, and his days are an endless cycle of drinking, watching TV, and listening to his best friend complain about his mother. Forced to face the fact that his life isn't all he expected it to be, he realizes he needs to change things...

Review: *Alex* is a strong story, dealing with one man's struggle with his own failures and the dawning realization that he is destined to become just like his alcoholic art teacher from high school. Although the subject is far from cheerful, Kalesniko makes Alex's story compelling, while elements of black humor bring some much-needed light relief.

FURTHER READING: *Why Did Pete Duel Kill Himself?*
SEE ALSO: *Mail Order Bride; Birthday Riots; Summer Blonde*

★
★ **Writer:** Alejandro Jodorowsky
★ **Artist:** Milo Manara

Publisher: Heavy Metal Comics, 2005
ISBN: 1932413421

18+ BORGIA: BLOOD FOR THE POPE

Plot: Set in 1492, either side of the death of Pope Innocent VIII, the first volume in the *Borgia* series describes the events that led to Rodrigo Borgia becoming Pope Alexander VI. We witness Pope Innocent's desperate attempts to stay alive, Rodrigo's rescue of the mother of his children from the fear inspired by threats of the plague, and Rodrigo's callous machinations to influence the Cardinals to elect him.

Review: Jodorowsky takes the broad facts of history and fleshes them out in an homage of sorts to The Godfather (the Borgias are portrayed as Italy's first Mafia). Manara's gorgeous painted artwork doesn't conceal the blood, violence, sex, and grime of the text.

FURTHER READING: *Borgia: Power and Incest; Piranese: The Prison Planet; Indian Summer*
SEE ALSO: *Casanova's Last Stand; Heart of Empire*

Writer: Osamu Tezuka
Artist: Osamu Tezuka

Publisher: Vertical, 2003
ISBN: 1932234438

Ⓐ BUDDHA VOLUME 1: KAPILAVASTU

Plot: In ancient India, troubled by environmental and social problems, Siddhartha—who is born toward the end of this first, 400-page volume—embarks on a spiritual quest to become the Buddha (the Enlightened One) and bring peace to the land. We meet Naradatta, a monk on a quest to answer a question about life; the slave, Chapra, posing as the son of a general; and the child, Tatta, who is said to have magical abilities.

Review: Tezuka ("the God of Manga") eschews a simple biographical approach, instead providing a context for Buddhist philosophy using a mixture of historical and fictional characters. Maintaining an action-adventure narrative, the story is enlivened by many humorous situations.

FURTHER READING: *Buddha Volumes 2–8*
SEE ALSO: *Adolf; Times of Botchan*

Writer: Marisa Acocella Marchetto
Artist: Marisa Acocella Marchetto

Publisher: Alfred A. Knopf, 2006
ISBN: 0307263576

5+ CANCER VIXEN

PLot: New York "It" girl, shoe obsessive, and cartoonist Marisa discovers she has a cancerous lump in her breast and faces surgery and a lengthy course of chemotherapy and radiation treatment to overcome the disease. Along the way she recounts meeting restaurateur and eventual husband Silvano, her difficult but ultimately loving relationship with her busybody mother, and how family and friends offered support and love.

Review: Marchetto's autobiographical tale about her fight with cancer could easily have been self-indulgent and over-emotional. Instead, it's a smart, funny, entertaining, and moving read, which also manages to include information on cancer treatment without sounding like a government health leaflet. There's genuine warmth and humor to the writing and the brightly colored and instantly accessible cartoon style immediately involves the reader in the story. A wonderful and uplifting piece of work.

FURTHER READING: *Just Who The Hell Is She, Anyway?*
SEE ALSO: *American Splendor: The Life And Times Of Harvey Pekar; Mom's Cancer*

★
★
★
★

Writer: Larry Gonick
Artist: Larry Gonick

Publisher: Bantam Doubleday Dell, 1990
ISBN: 0385265204

 A

A CARTOON HISTORY OF THE UNIVERSE VOLUME 1

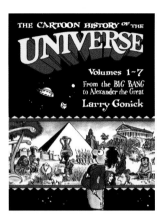

Plot: An irreverent, but informative and alternative way of delivering a history lesson packed with quirky facts. Two more volumes followed this one, and Gonick went on to address modern history and other specific subject areas, having realized that educational cartooning was his niche.

Review: Gonick's great strength—like that of Bill Bryson—is that he knows how to explain complex topics in a simple way, without appearing condescending to the reader. He also manages to be extremely funny about matter and primordial ooze, using his highly expressive figure drawing to underline the points he's making. An amazing achievement—both in terms of cartooning and popularizing history.

FURTHER READING: *A Cartoon Guide to Physics; A Cartoon Guide To Chemistry; A Cartoon History of The Universe Volumes 2 and 3*
SEE ALSO: *Understanding Comics: The Invisible Art*

★
★
★
★

Writer: Hunt Emerson
Artist: Hunt Emerson

Publisher: Knockabout Comics, 1993
ISBN: 0861661095

18+ # CASANOVA'S LAST STAND

Plot: An elderly Casanova, "the world's greatest lover," recounts his past sexploits in order to educate his protégée, Klutz.

Review: Emerson's liberal adaptation of Casanova's memoir is full of bawdy humor and saucy jokes that is entirely befitting of the legendary lothario. Casanova's final seduction is hilariously farcical as he is deluded into believing he is still the great Latin lover, as opposed to the dirty old man he has become. This classic tale is brought vividly to life by underground comic artist Emerson's expert penmanship, which has energy, pizzazz, and eroticism in all the right places.

FURTHER READING: *Lady Chatterley's Lover*
SEE ALSO: *The Rime of the Ancient Mariner*

Writer: Marjane Satrapi
Artist: Marjane Satrapi

Publisher: Pantheon, 2006
ISBN: 0224080458

CHICKEN WITH PLUMS

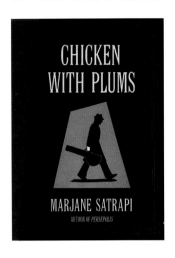

Plot: The story of the author's great-uncle Nasser Ali Khan, a celebrated Iranian musician who gives up on life when his wife breaks his favorite instrument, an irreplaceable tar, and his passion for music can no longer be fulfilled.

Review: Satrapi sticks to the true stories of her family as her subject matter, this time returning to Iran in the mid 1950s. Told in inky blacks, the art style is reminiscent of *Persepolis*, but this tale isn't nearly as uplifting. It's a melancholy story of a lingering week-long suicide, but during that last week we are taken on a journey through Nasser Ali's life and witness what brought him to his fateful, fatal decision. The best stories are often about the telling, and that's certainly true here.

FURTHER READING: *Monsters are Afraid of the Moon*
SEE ALSO: *Persepolis: The Story of a Childhood; Embroideries*

Writer: Dori Seda
Artist: Dori Seda

Publisher: Last Gasp, 1999
ISBN: 0867193751

DORI STORIES:
THE COMPLETE DORI SEDA

Plot: Dori Seda died young, and this volume collects her comics, photo strips, paintings, and ceramics—and a lovely story by Bruce Sterling in which Seda and rock critic Lester Bangs meet and save each other. The confessional stories are terrific, and unlike many autobiographical tales, they are carefully crafted and shaped, with witty dialog and disturbing insights fitting in among the laughs.

Review: Underground comix icon Dori Seda was one of the pioneers of autobiographical comics in the 1970s and '80s, drawing her gap-toothed self in stories that mix humiliation with a delightful joie de vivre. Like Robert Crumb, she is brutally honest, particularly about her sexuality, making this a bundle of laughs, but not for the fainthearted.

FURTHER READING: *Weirdo; Fresca Zizis*
SEE ALSO: *Life's A Bitch: The Bitchy Bitch Chronicles; Stuck Rubber Baby; My Troubles With Women*

★
★
★

Writer: Alexa Kitchen
Artist: Alexa Kitchen

Publisher: DKP, 2006
ISBN: 097100806

A DRAWING COMICS IS EASY (EXCEPT WHEN IT'S HARD)

Plot: Advice and helpful hints on how to draw cartoons. The young author offers a cornucopia of diverse and imaginative depictions of numerous subjects. Meet Denis, Denise, Berto, and a whole host of other characters while learning how to create successful cartoons.

Review: A how-to-cartoon book comprised entirely of the sketches of a seven-year-old girl may not immediately seem like an engaging prospect, but Alexa has an instantly likeable technique. Her style is enormously charming, and comes across as remarkably mature given her tender years, although one suspects she may have had a little help from her Dad—a well-known publisher in the comics industry...

FURTHER READING: *How To Self Publish Comics;*
How To Make Web Comics; Make Your Own Graphic Novel
SEE ALSO: *Fate Of The Artist; Understanding Comics*

★
★
★
★

Writer: Marjane Satrapi
Artist: Marjane Satrapi

Publisher: Pantheon, 2006
ISBN: 0224076086

EMBROIDERIES

Plot: A group of Iranian women gather. The tea flows freely and the gossip—about the lives and loves of those women—soon follows.

Review: Imagine the comics equivalent of *The Vagina Monologues* set in Iran and you have a rough idea of what *Embroideries* is about. Taking its title from the surgical practice of vaginal suture to give the impression of virginity, *Embroideries* is nevertheless a wonderful, warmhearted, and frequently funny collection of other people's secrets. Consequently, it is also compulsive reading. Less polished than Satrapi's *Persepolis*, it possesses great energy and sweeps you up in its own exuberance. Both naughty and nice, *Embroideries* is a life-affirming reminder that people are the same across the globe.

FURTHER READING: *Monsters are Afraid of the Moon*
SEE ALSO: *The Complete Persepolis; Chicken with Plums*

Writer: Raymond Briggs
Artist: Raymond Briggs

Publisher: Pantheon, 2001
ISBN: 0375714472

ETHEL AND ERNEST

Plot: *Ethel and Ernest* charts the life shared by the author's parents, from their first meeting in the late 1920s to their deaths in the early 1970s. It also provides a neatly encapsulated history of the upheavals and social changes faced by Britain—in particular the British working class—during the 20th century. *Ethel and Ernest* is a tribute to Briggs's parents, and a bittersweet recognition of all they lived through together.

Review: *Ethel and Ernest* is a gentler companion piece to Briggs's apocalyptic *When the Wind Blows*. It succeeds in examining a turbulent period of history in microcosm, but ultimately its greatest achievements lie in its carefully assembled personal observations, and its extraordinary tenderness. The artwork, which matches the dialog perfectly, is minutely observed and jewel-like in its grace. The book is a genuinely moving and beautiful distillation of Briggs's career.

FURTHER READING: *The Tin Pot Foreign General; The Man*
SEE ALSO: *Maus; Persepolis; When the Wind Blows*

Writer: Alison Bechdel
Artist: Alison Bechdel

Publisher: Houghton Mifflin, 2006
ISBN: 0618871713

FUN HOME: A FAMILY TRAGICOMIC

Plot: An intelligent and touching autobiographical memoir in which cartoonist Alison Bechdel painstakingly recounts her years growing up in the family home, which doubled up as a funeral parlor. Bechdel concentrates on the tensions that drove the family apart—most importantly, her own coming of age and coming out of the closet, which coincided with the realization that her father was also gay. Balancing pain with Proust, Bechdel attempts to find order and meaning in a past that can never resolve itself.

Review: In *Fun Home*, Bechdel examines her own life as closely as those of her comic-strip characters, and with unflinching honesty. The book's two-tone artwork adds a visual depth and focus that matches the clarity and precision of the narrative, with *Fun Home* receiving a number of awards, including the Stonewall Book Award for non-fiction.

FURTHER READING: *Dykes to Watch Out For*
SEE ALSO: *Stuck Rubber Baby*

★
★
★
★

Artist: Ellen Forney
Writer: Ellen Forney

Publisher: Fantagraphics, 2006
ISBN: 1560977302

15+ I LOVE LED ZEPPELIN

Plot: Eisner-nominated artist/writer Ellen Forney's second book begins with a collection of full-page practical instructions. If you've ever wondered about the best way to discuss drugs with your child, or reattach an amputated digit, the answer lies within these pages. These helpful hints and tips are followed by a series of short comics, in which Forney takes the reader on a whistle-stop tour of all kinds of deviant topics.

Review: Assembling an extensive range of material from around 13 years' worth of work, this is a sharp anthology of sex, drugs, and rock'n'roll. The linework is self-assured and provocative, instantly drawing the eye, and Forney has a natural talent for storytelling, whether her own or someone else's. Enormous fun.

FURTHER READING: *Monkey Food*
SEE ALSO: *Fun Home: A Family Tragicomic; Life's A Bitch*

★
★
★
★

Writer: Hugo Pratt
Artist: Milo Manara

Publisher: NBM, 1994
ISBN: 1561631078

18+ INDIAN SUMMER

Plot: Owing something to Hawthorne's *The Scarlet Letter*, Pratt examines the early, eventually tragic interaction of native Americans and Puritan settlers in 17th century America via the story of a rebellious family, cast out by their more godly neighbors, who try to survive as the uneasy relationship between the two communities breaks down.

Review: Indian Summer offers us two giants of Italian comics at the height of their powers. Pratt provides Manara with a dramatic and moving story that gives Manara the scope to draw something far more complex than sexual satire and reminds us that Manara's artistic skills extend far beyond drawing sexy women. Lushly drawn and splendidly told.

FURTHER READING: *The Model; Piranese: The Prison Planet; Click 2; Borgia: Power and Incest*
SEE ALSO: *Borgia: Blood for the Pope; Click*

Writer: Steven T. Seagle
Artist: Teddy Kristiansen
Publisher: DC Vertigo
ISBN: 1401201091

IT'S A BIRD

"spellbinding and timely..." — GRANT MORRISON

Plot: Steve is a comics writer, but when he's offered the Superman comic, the Holy Grail of comic-book jobs, he initially turns it down. This book follows him through the process of deciding to take the job, while dealing with his father's disappearance, his own impending fatherhood, and the specter of Huntington's disease—an hereditary disease that affects his family.

Review: This is a fascinating book that's a blend of autobiography and meditations on superheroes—*Superman* in particular—all beautifully painted in watercolor by talented Danish artist Kristiansen. Seagle is an engaging voice, and while some of the information about Huntington's is a little preachy, overall he succeeds in conveying his ideas and giving his characters weight. An unusual and extremely worthwhile book.

FURTHER READING: *House of Secrets: Foundation; American Virgin; Grendel Tales: Devil in Our Midst*
SEE ALSO: *Brooklyn Dreams; Our Cancer Year*

Writer: Franz Kafka
Artist/Editor: Peter Kuper
Publisher: NBM, 1995
ISBN: 1561631256

KAFKA: GIVE IT UP AND OTHER SHORT STORIES

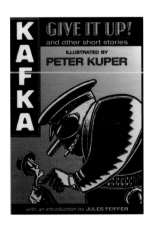

Plot: A collection of nine Kafka tales, presented as brand-new graphic novel adaptations by Peter Kuper, an expert in the field. Included in this collection are the stories *The Bridge*, *The Vulture*, and—a favorite for many Kafka fans—*The Hunger Artist*.

Review: These particularly paranoid works by Kafka were clearly very carefully selected, and the stories have been enhanced by the accompanying graphics. The dark, expressionist illustration style that Kuper uses melds perfectly with the twisted nature of the Kafka source material, creating an anthology that has value not only as an enjoyable work of graphic fiction, but also as an intriguing way to study Kafka's works.

FURTHER READING: *Brownsville; The Adapted Victor Hugo*
SEE ALSO: *Dr Jekyll & Mr Hyde: Graphic Novel*

★
★
★
★

Writer: Ho Che Anderson
Artist: Ho Che Anderson

Publisher: Fantagraphics, 2005
ISBN: 1560976225

15+ KING: A COMICS BIOGRAPHY OF MARTIN LUTHER KING, JR.

Plot: A warts-and-all biography of Martin Luther King Jr. that follows the legendary civil rights campaigner from 1952 up until his death in 1968.

Review: Completed over a period of years, one of the most striking things about *King* is the way in which it conveys the passing of time. Starting with sparse, impressionistic, chiaroscuro sketches, the book adopts a wider variety of styles and colors—skintones, blood reds, and fire yellows—as the narrative increases in scope and the civil rights movement progresses to a crisis point. Anderson takes the established facts of Kings's life and fleshes them out to give his cast new life on the page, with a result that is informative, beautiful, and utterly compelling.

FURTHER READING: *Scream Queen; I Want to be Your Dog*
SEE ALSO: *Palestine; Contract with God Trilogy*

★
★
★
★

Writer: Chester Brown
Artist: Chester Brown

Publisher: Drawn and Quarterly, 2006.
ISBN: 1894937899

15+ LOUIS RIEL: A COMIC-STRIP BIOGRAPHY

Plot: Louis Riel was the Francophone leader of a rebellion by the disenfranchised Métis people of the Canadian Northwest in the 1870s. Brown tells his story in a simply drawn fashion that owes something to Harold Gray's *Little Orphan Annie*. Riel was eventually caught and executed, despite being the founder of Canada's Manitoba province, with Brown's extensive notes leaving the reader to decide whether or not Riel's cause was just.

Review: Let's face it—most non-Canadian readers will have no idea who Louis Riel was, or why they should care. In an attempt to rectify this, Brown tells Riel's story in an easily digestible form that's entertaining as well as informative. Time listed this as one of the best comics of 2003.

FURTHER READING: *I Never Liked You*
SEE ALSO: *The Playboy*

Writer: Nick Abadzis
Artist: Nick Abadzis

Publisher: First Second, 2007
ISBN: 1596431016

LAIKA

Plot: The true story of the puppy that became the Earth's first space traveler. Laika's story is intertwined with that of Soviet space engineer Korolev, and animal lab technician Yelena, who doesn't realize her job's true purpose. Laika's voyage ends too soon, but her story proves irresistible.

Review: *Laika* mixes fact with fiction to create a small masterpiece. Abadzis' expressive, colorful artwork and densely paneled pages lend an engaging complexity to what could otherwise be a simplistic story. It will tug at the heartstrings of young and old alike.

FURTHER READING: *Project: Superior*
SEE ALSO: *The Amazing Mr Pleebus*

★
★ **Writer:** Aline Kominsky Crumb **Publisher:** Fantagraphics, 1990
★ **Artist:** Aline Kominsky Crumb **ISBN:** 1560970170
★

18+ # LOVE THAT BUNCH

Plot: Aline Kominsky Crumb's hilarious memoir about growing up in a nice, middle-class Jewish household on Long Island, where she understands her parents as little as they understand her. Gradually, teenage crushes, the horrors of fat camp, and the longing to be someone different give way to Kominsky Crumb's less than reverent descriptions of dipping her toes in the Greenwich Village scene of the 1960s, then moving to California—where she met her husband, fellow cartoonist Robert Crumb.

Review: Kominsky Crumb's drawing style is naïve and two-dimensional at times, with a great deal of patterning and filling in of space. However, as you become accustomed to it you realize she is a masterful storyteller, revealing all her family's faults and peccadilloes (and her own) with gusto.

FURTHER READING: *The Complete Dirty Laundry Comics; Weirdo by R. Crumb*
SEE ALSO: *Dori Stories, My Trouble With Women*

★
★ **Writer:** Scott McCloud **Publisher:** Harper Collins, 2006
★ **Artist:** Scott McCloud **ISBN:** 0060780940
★
★

MAKING COMICS

Plot: Scott McCloud enthusiastically explores a diverse range of approaches to the subject—and title—of his book: *Making Comics.*

Review: McCloud's third graphic novel about the comics form moves away from the theory to focus on the mechanics of storytelling. Well structured and heavily indexed, each chapter comes with its own set of annotations going into further detail on such areas as the correct types of pens to use for specific tasks. Like McCloud's other books about comics, this is accessible and fun for a general readership, but is a truly indispensable resource of hints, tips, and techniques for anyone thinking of creating their own graphic narratives. Regardless of whether you are a reader or creator, McCloud writes about comics with a passion and infectious enthusiasm that will soon have you appreciating the medium in new ways.

FURTHER READING: *Reinventing Comics; Zot!*
SEE ALSO: *Understanding Comics*

Writer: Andrew J. Helfer
Artist: Randy DuBurke

Publisher: Hill & Wang, 2006
ISBN: 0957789637

5+ MALCOLM X

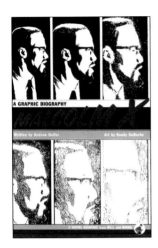

Plot: Linear life of radical Islamic black rights leader Malcolm X shown in the historical context of black experience in America, which explores his journey from petty criminal, to political agitator, to black martyr.

Review: Andy Helfer puts together an honest account of his subject that does not whitewash the more dubious portions of his life, and packs in enough information to make the reader look beyond his iconic status at the factors that led to his popularity and eventual assassination. DuBurke illustrates cleanly and clearly, using sharp black and white and heavy inking to give the history lesson a sense of drama.

FURTHER READING: *Catching The Moon; Che: A Graphic Biography*
SEE ALSO: *King: A Comics Biography Of Martin Luther King Jr*

Writer: Brian Fies
Artist: Brian Fies

Publisher: Abrams Image, 2006
ISBN: 0810958406

5+ MOM'S CANCER

Plot: The true story of the cartoonist's Mom living with incurable lung cancer, from diagnosis onward. This is the print version of the Eisner award-winning web comic that started in 2004. What starts as a visceral response to traumatic and turbulent news soon develops into a series of snapshots of a family responding to a trauma.

Review: As a book, *Mom's Cancer* retains a format similar to a newspaper strip—short and wide. Ostensibly a simple narrative detailing the diagnosis and treatment of one woman's cancer, somewhere in the telling, between the panels, *Mom's Cancer* moves beyond the story of a single individual and reaches out to others in similar situations, becoming a support book for all those who are not dying, but living with cancer.

FURTHER READING: *Dragonslippers*
ALSO SEE: *Our Cancer Year; Cancer Vixen*

★
★ **Writer:** Robert Crumb   **Publisher:** Last Gasp, 2000
★ **Artist:** Robert Crumb   **ISBN:** 0867193743
★

18+ MY TROUBLES WITH WOMEN

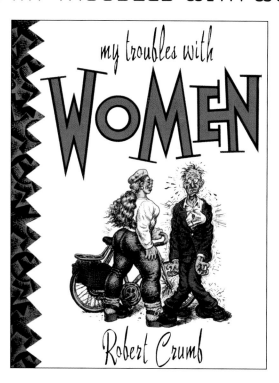

Plot: Underground comix legend Robert Crumb, with great honesty and the input of his wife, Aline Kominsky Crumb, explores his personal relationship with women, detailing what attracts him physically, emotionally, and mentally. In a series of short stories that were originally drawn in the 1980s, Crumb's tales delve back into his family history with *Uncle Bob's Midlife Crisis*, while *Dirty Laundry Comics* brings matters right up to date.

Review: Crumb's autobiographical approach to his stories is so honest that it often frightens people. He's frequently castigated for his misogyny because he says what some regard as unthinkable in an age of political correctness. Pretending such thoughts don't exist isn't going to make them go away, however; it's just that few people have sufficient self-awareness—or enough balls—to put them out there for the world to see.

That aside, even those who accuse him of being a "filthy woman hater" can hardly deny that Crumb is one of the finest living draftsmen we have, able to muster innumerable styles and effects, bringing his stories to life as he tells us about how he wants to hurt women, how he wants to be overpowered by them, and how muscular thighs and odd facial casts turn him on. Crumb explores every crease and wrinkle of his sexual map in public and if you only ever read one Crumb book, this should be it.

FURTHER READING: *Weirdo*
SEE ALSO: *The Playboy; Buddy Does Seattle; Collected Crumb Volume 8*

Writer: Aline Kominsky Crumb
Artist: Various

Publisher: MQPublications, 2007
ISBN-10: 1846011337

3+ NEED MORE LOVE

Plot: A mixed-media autobiography of the artist as a child, lover, 1960s radical, wife, mother, and bon vivant—a woman who is enough of an artist and enough of a woman to hold her own in a marriage with legendary cartoonist Robert Crumb.

Review: Billed as a "graphic memoir," this book is overflowing with photographs, paintings, comic strips, and text—it's not so much a graphic novel, or even a memoir, as much as an annotated guided tour through Kominsky Crumb's scrapbook. A meandering volume filled with beautifully realized grotesqueries of passions, excesses, art, and love, it seems to be made for dipping into at leisure, rather than reading from cover to cover in one sitting. The compelling nature of each brief but startling recollection will keep you coming back for more.

FURTHER READING: *Complete Dirty Laundry*
SEE ALSO: *Love That Bunch; My Troubles with Women*

Writer: Joe Sacco
Artist: Joe Sacco

Publisher: Jonathan Cape, 2003
ISBN: 1560975105

5+ NOTES FROM A DEFEATIST

Plot: Before he became comic books' number one war reporter, Joe Sacco was one of many cartoonists writing and drawing about their own lives. The autobiographical material is entertaining, especially his tales of touring Europe with a rock band as their roadie and cartoonist in residence, but many will be more interested in the short historical pieces about his mother's experience in Greece during World War II, and his even-handed history of the tactical bombing of civilians.

Review: Sacco draws in an open, simple, and appealing style, but this doesn't lend itself to humor, and his writing seems rather pale and unexciting compared to what some other cartoonists were doing at the time in the same genre. However, it's very interesting to see his development, and if you like his later work, this will definitely be of interest.

FURTHER READING: *The Fixer: A Story from Sarajevo; War's End: Profiles from Bosnia 1995–1996*
SEE ALSO: *Palestine; Safe Area Gorazde*

★
★
★
★

Writers: Harvey Pekar, Joyce Brabner
Artist: Frank (Foolbert Sturgeon) Stack

Publisher: Four Walls Eight Windows, 1994
ISBN: 1568580118

15+ # OUR CANCER YEAR

Plot: Filing clerk, underground comic writer, and semi-professional curmudgeon Harvey Pekar discovered he had cancer in 1990, so quite naturally he set out to document his experiences—good and bad—just as he's documented every other aspect of his life. At the same time, his family faced eviction from their home, while Pekar's treatment threatened his ability to support them.

Review: "Uncomfortably honest" is the best description of this unique insight into the horrors and minute irritations of coping with cancer, told from the viewpoint of both Harvey Pekar—a legendary neurotic now with something to really worry about—and his wife, Joyce Brabner. The dual voices sometimes show two sides of the same situation and sometimes pass the narrative from one to the other, which amplifies the sense of stress. The illustrative style may be patchy in places, particularly when dealing with talking heads, but Frank Stack's fluid pen-and-ink drawing ably captures the transience and almost dreamlike quality of many of the events, and suits the fast-moving and often explosive changes in the central characters' emotional states. Pekar has always been brilliant at recording the minutiae of life and making something beautiful out of the most mundane event. Here, he prods his own psyche to examine his emotional responses in a way that is fascinating, but almost terrifying in its openness.

FURTHER READING: *American Splendor: Our Movie Year; American Splendor: From Off The Streets of Cleveland; American Splendor: Unsung Heroes*
SEE ALSO: *American Splendor: The Life And Times of Harvey Pekar; Spiral Cage; My Troubles With Women*

Writer: Judd Winick
Artist: Judd Winick

Publisher: Henry Holt, 2000
ISBN: 0805064036

PEDRO AND ME

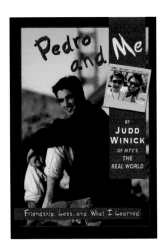

Plot: In 1994, Judd Winick is picked to go on one of the first reality TV shows: MTV's *The Real World*. One of the other members of the cast is a gay man, Pedro Zamora, and the two form an unlikely friendship. Winick depicts their relationship with a humor that can be politically incorrect, but is very funny. Pedro later died of AIDS, but Winick has provided a lasting tribute to his friend in the form of *Pedro and Me*.

Review: A very touching work. The art style is cartoony, but Winick pulls off a trick you may previously have thought impossible—making you actually care about reality TV contestants. Well worth reading.

FURTHER READING: *Road Trip; Frumpy the Clown*
SEE ALSO: *Fun Home*

Writer: Chester Brown
Artist: Chester Brown

Publisher: Drawn & Quarterly, 1992
ISBN: 0969670117

THE PLAYBOY

Plot: The adult Chester Brown goes back in time and commentates (appearing as a kind of little angel) on the actions of his adolescent self during a key moment in his journey to manhood: finding a copy of *Playboy* magazine. The strip examines his adolescent obsession with pornography with great openness.

Review: By creating two autobiographical voices, Brown's examination of his adolescent urges and ideals gains a narrative structure that places *The Playboy* head and shoulders above the many autobiographical comics appearing at the same time, and since. Although it deals with complex issues, the narrative has a humble and honest feel, summoning up a melancholy nostalgia for the simple issues of adolescence without sparing us the self-absorption and gaucheness of growing up.

FURTHER READING: *Yummy Fur; My Mother Was A Schizophrenic*
SEE ALSO: *My Troubles With Women; Dori Stories; Louis Riel*

★ **Writer:** Will Eisner
★ **Artist:** Will Eisner
★
★

Publisher: W.W. Norton, 2006
ISBN: 0393328600

15+ # THE PLOT: THE SECRET STORY OF THE PROTOCOLS OF THE ELDERS OF ZION

Plot: An overview of the history of the *Protocols of the Elders of Zion*, perhaps the most infamous and pernicious anti-Semitic literary fraud ever committed.

Review: *The Plot*, along with his reappraisal of Charles Dickens' character Fagin, provides an opportunity for comics legend Will Eisner to explore Jewish identity (Eisner was born in New York to Jewish immigrant parents). Published shortly before his death, *The Plot* is told in broad strokes over a robust skeleton of detailed research. Its large panels are swathed in inky gray washes, as befits the shadows in which the Protocols were concocted. Each panel breathes out into the page, denying any attempt to cage it. A compelling polemic, there is little doubt that this is an important work by a master of the art.

FURTHER READING: *Fagin the Jew*
SEE ALSO: *Maus*

Writer: Nick Bertozzi
Artist: Nick Bertozzi

Publisher: St. Martin's Press, 2007
ISBN: 0312354851

THE SALON

Plot: Painter Georges Braque seeks his fortune in Paris in 1907—a time when avant-garde painters are being murdered. Thrown in with Gertrude Stein, her brother Leo, her would-be lover Alice B. Toklas, and Pablo Picasso, Braque discovers that some of these artists hide a secret. With the use of a magical blue liquor, they learn how to enter a painting and briefly live in it. Braque discovers that Paul Gauguin is keeping a far bigger secret.

Review: This excellent and highly imaginative story will keep you guessing, while admiring Bertozzi's bold use of color. Perhaps not the kind of comic you'd usually read, but all the more rewarding as a result.

FURTHER READING: *Boswash; The Masochists*
SEE ALSO: *The Extended Dream of Mr D*

Writer: Guy Delisle
Artist: Guy Delisle

Publisher: Jonathan Cape, 2006
ISBN: 0224079913

SHENZHEN

Plot: A graphic travelogue about globalization and life in Shenzhen, one of China's free-trade zones, seen through the eyes of a Westerner.

Review: Although published in English after *Pyongyang*, his book about working in North Korea, Guy Delisle's other graphic travelogue, *Shenzhen*—which covers much of the same subject matter—was actually written first. Both books spring from the author's experiences of overseeing the outsourcing of French animation, but this volume really does read like an early work. Although the art style is the same, the storytelling is less sophisticated, the reminiscences are less organized, and the book is less cohesive. That said, it offers a fascinating insight into the compartmentalized cities and stratified lives in the emerging superpower that is modern China.

FURTHER READING: *Albert And The Others*
SEE ALSO: *Pyongyang*

ESSENTIAL
GRAPHIC NOVELS

500

89

NON-FICTION
Best of the rest

★
★
★

Writer: Al Davison

Artist: Al Davison

Publisher: Active Images, 2003

ISBN: 0974056715

15+ SPIRAL CAGE

Plot: One of the most structurally interesting comic-book autobiographies, Al Davison's *Spiral Cage* documents his extraordinary life. Born with spina bifida, and later suffering from M.E., Davison has much more to say about the human condition than most, as he shows us how his physical state dictated a particular path through life that led to martial arts and Buddhism.

Review: *Spiral Cage* is incredibly intense, and deliberately so. The story is told in a way that compels you to empathize with the narrator as he suffers from bullying and prejudice, even from his own doctors. The narrative structure—linked to the "spiral cage" of DNA, and revolving around repeated visual elements, slight changes between panels, and multiple voices—will either delight or annoy you.

FURTHER READING: *The Alchemist's Easel and Other Spiral Dreams*

SEE ALSO: *The Minotaur's Tale; The Tale Of One Bad Rat*

Writer: Tom Beland
Artist: Tom Beland

Publisher: AiT/ PlanetLar, 2003
ISBN: 1932051090

TRUE STORY, SWEAR TO GOD: CHANCES ARE

Plot: Web designer and cartoonist Tom Beland lands a complimentary trip to Disneyland through the newspaper he works for, and decides to go on his own, little knowing the trip is about to change his life. He meets Puerto Rican journalist Lily Garcia at a bus stop, and the two spend an amazing day together, kindling a romance in the World's Happiest Place. This book follows the initial steps of their burgeoning long-distance relationship as she visits him in Napa and he travels to Puerto Rico, finding it to be far stranger than he imagined—not to mention the fact that Lily is more than a little well known there.

Review: *TSSTG* (as it's known) is a unique entity in today's comics market, in as much as it's an unashamed romance comic, a genre that has few modern-day proponents. Beland's art is very appealing, and suits the style and character of the book well. He's also a fine writer, surprisingly candid about all aspects of his relationship with Garcia—and the sheer wonder that he's found an amazing woman who actually likes him shines through on every page. Beland is a funny guy and his pacing is excellent, letting events play out at their natural rhythm. It's rare to find such an upbeat autobiographical book, and it's a great book to give to a non-comics reader.

FURTHER READING: *True Story Swear To God: This One Goes To Eleven...; Will You Still Love Me If I Wet The Bed?*
SEE ALSO: *Blankets; Locas*

★
★
★
★

Writer: Jim Ottaviani
Artist: Various

Publisher: G.T. Labs
ISBN: 0966010620

TWO FISTED SCIENCE: STORIES ABOUT SCIENTISTS

Plot: A series of 10 stories, ranging from the comic to the serious, including reflections about key figures in modern science, including the fascinating and multi-talented Richard Feynman whose exploits get more than one outing, Nazi sympathizing Heisenberg, and of course Einstein.

Some of the stories blur the lines between reality and fiction, and rely on rumors and attractive, but not necessarily true anecdotes, so you won't learn a great deal of hard science, but you will hopefully gain some insight into how some of the great minds of the century operated. And if it helps enthuse young minds about a subject that's often regarded as nerdy or stuffy, that's certainly a point in its favor.

Review: Writer Jim Ottaviani sets himself a tough goal—to write about science (well, physics mostly) in a way that is visually exciting. To do this he sometimes gets caught up in his own technique. Some of the art is a little rough-and-ready, and the storytelling is not as fluent as it could be at times, but it's a noble effort. Bernie Mireault, Sean Bieri and Colleen Doran all put in solid artistic performances. Although intended for teens, it will provide a lively background to Science 101 for many older readers.

FURTHER READING: *Dignifying Science; Desert Peach*
SEE ALSO: *Laika*

Writer: Natsuo Sekikawa
Artist: Jiro Taniguchi

Publisher: Fanfare/Ponent Mon, 2006
ISBN: 8496427013

THE TIMES OF BOTCHAN

Jiro Taniguchi - Natsuo Sekikawa

The times of Botchan

FIRST VOLUME

FANFARE / PONENT MON

Plot: *The Times of Botchan* is an exploration of the life and works of Natsume Soseki, one of Japan's most famous writers. Soseki was a writer in the Meiji period (1868–1912), a time when Japan opened up to trade with the West and rapidly adapted itself into a state that could compete with the Western powers at the beginning of the 20th century.

Review: In contrast to the sprawling mega-epics so prevalent in some areas of manga, *The Times of Botchan* is a beautiful, lyrical, meandering journey through the themes of Japanese identity in the face of creeping Westernization. A powerful evocation of a fascinating lost age that is still a touchstone in modern Japan.

FURTHER READING: *Berlin*
SEE ALSO: *The Push Man; Yukiko's Spinach*

Writer: Frederic Boilet
Artist: Frederic Boilet

Publisher: Fanfare, 2007
ISBN: 8493309346

YUKIKO'S SPINACH

原作 作画
フレデリック・ボワレ

ゆき子のホウレン草

Yukiko's
Spinach

Frédéric Boilet

Plot: This is the semi-autobiographical tale of a doomed romance between a French cartoonist and a Japanese girl. A manga enthusiast, Boilet draws on a combination of his European comics roots and his passion for Japanese art to create an ebullient fusion of the two.

Review: The "spinach" of the title refers to an apparently common French confusion between the Japanese words for spinach and bellybutton. What could so easily have been a slightly unsavory tale of a Western man with a fetish for Asian women is raised to a whole new level thanks to the art's emphatic urgency. Densely referenced, and with a style verging on photorealism, *Yukiko's Spinach* captures the desperate, syncopated sensations of a new love affair, and the compromises made in the heat of infatuation.

FURTHER READING: *Mariko Parade*
SEE ALSO: *Strangehaven*

CHAPTER 3

CRIME/MYSTERY

LET'S BE CAREFUL OUT THERE...

Before the superhero epidemic took hold, American comics boasted a whole range of genres: westerns, romances, and detective stories of all kinds. Crime scenarios—whether police procedurals, noir, cosy English period pieces, or courtroom battles—have all found their way into the comic book format, some with more success than others. Some of the best, such as *Mr D.A.*, are not well remembered, while others, such as the short run *Cops*, were very much before their time with their intertwined tales of police life on the American streets.

Although popular up to the 1950s, the American market has since seen very few successes in the genre, although *Dick Tracy*, the classic crimefighting strip full of caricatured bad guys and hard-bitten one-liners, is still going strong over 70 years after it was launched in 1931, surviving the death of its creator Chester Gould by 30 years.

The other classic American cartoon crimestopper is *The Spirit*, an altogether more human detective (despite the fact that he began his masked crime-fighting career after erroneously being reported dead), whose strips often feature humor, horror, and heartache, as well as fights with the bad guys. Creator Will Eisner is regarded as one of the giants of the comic book field, introducing a raft of innovative techniques during his dozen years on the original strips.

And then of course there's *Batman*, whose appearances in *Detective Comics* once upon a time reflected the fact that he wasn't superpowered, but a gifted detective whose knowledge of Gotham City's lowlifes and criminal masterminds counted for as much as a powerful upper cut.

With cop- and law-based series constituting the majority of the most-watched shows in the English-speaking TV market, it's not surprising that some comic creators have begun to explore the genre again, although they tend to favor the stylization of classic noir writers or extraordinary investigators over stories of everyday police work. However, lovers of classic police procedurals will enjoy *Kane*, a quirky cop series set in the fictional (and slightly odd) US city of New Eden. By building up a regular cast of characters, creator Paul Grist offers something with as much scope for tragedy, pathos, and humor as popular TV series such as *NYPD Blue*.

Frank Miller's *Sin City* shares Kane's broad, bold, black-and-white approach to cartooning, but is the ultimate macho pulp fiction; a series of brutal stories held together by their common location and their starkly beautiful style of illustration. Successfully filmed by Robert Rodriguez, *Sin City* is one of a surprisingly high number of thrillers that have used comic books as source material. In recent years, Sam Mendes turned long-time crime writer and *Dick Tracy* scripter Max Allen Collins' *Road To Perdition* into a vehicle for Tom Hanks, playing a mob enforcer on the run to prevent his son becoming corrupted. Meanwhile, David Cronenberg adapted *A History of Violence* into a tense drama about a small town coffee-shop owner who may or may not be a former gangster. The criminal mentality is explored in detail in Naoki Urasawa's *Monster*, a recent hit with both Eastern and Western audiences—which has spawned a lengthy animated series— about an idealistic neurosurgeon who saves a child who he later realizes is a psychopath.

Gangster stories feature strongly in work from the Far East. Fumimura and Ikegami's gorgeous *Sanctuary*, with its twisting plot concerning two Cambodian refugees who seek to save Japan from social and economic decline by controlling the government and yakuza, is a fine example of how a political thriller can work in comic-book format—the Japanese parliament is known for breaking into fist-fights, after all, so there's no lack of confrontation and dynamism.

The more traditional detective story remains alive and well in Europe, whether realistic or with more fantastic or horrific elements. The French love Agatha Christie and the first six of what appears to be a complete Christie comic-book adaptation have recently been published in English. Setting up red herrings and clues is something of a challenge with a static visual medium, and it takes superlative storytelling skills to hurry your readers past the real clues and persuade them to swallow the decoys.

Jacques Tardi's novelist heroine, the intrepid but cynical Adele Blanc-Sec, has been delighting audiences with her belle époque investigations into all manner of strange mysteries. Some of Lewis Trondheim's graphic novels offer a similar mix of conspiracy, detection, and the occult but, unusually, his main characters are rather fluid, like character actors who take similar but not identical parts from story to story. Sadly only two of his stories—*Harum Scarum* and *The Hoodoodad*—have been translated into English so far.

If the world of the historical detective isn't engrossing enough, try an-alternate-world version, such as *Rex Mundi*, the Arthurian Grail quest recast as a 1930s murder mystery in a world where the Protestant Reformation never took place. And if you're looking for a really mindbending detective story, look no further than Richard Sala's *The Chuckling Whatsit*, an epic, conspiratorial femme fatale story with a lunatic edge, set in what appears to be an Edwardian college town in a parallel universe. This is one book of which you can truly say, "Nothing is as it seems!"

★
★
★
★

Writer: Brian Azzarello
Artist: Eduardo Risso

Publisher: Vertigo, 2000
ISBN: 1563896451

15+
100 BULLETS VOLUME 1:
FIRST SHOT, LAST CALL

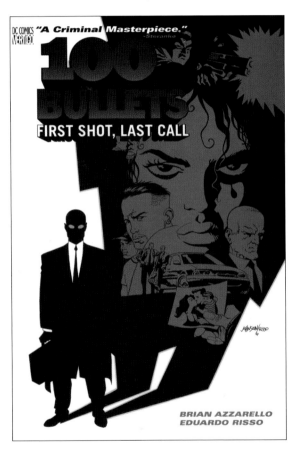

Plot: The mysterious Agent Graves (a cross between Judge Dredd and Charlie from Charlie's Angels) hands his victims—in one way or another—an attaché case containing a gun, 100 bullets, and a promise that if they use the gun against the person they hate, they will have total immunity from prosecution. At first, the killings seem perfectly random, but nothing is what it seems in *100 Bullets*—even words don't mean what you think they mean. As the story develops, we begin to see that Agent Graves may have his own agenda for wanting to see some of the victims dead.

Review: A taut thriller that effectively mixes tense individual "hits" with an overarching storyline involving Graves's past as one of the Minutemen, a now-disbanded group of operatives who worked for a mysterious organization known only as the Trust. The remaining Minutemen seem to want to destroy the Trust, and vice versa. While his literary influences clearly hark back to Hammett and Chandler, Brian Azzarello also looks to modern filmmakers such as Quentin Tarantino and Bryan Singer (*The Usual Suspects*) for inspiration.

Azzarello's stories gnaw at the central tenet of the book—if you have a chance to take revenge, if you know you're in the right, and if the offending person is likely to get away with it if you don't, is it ethically or morally OK to do so?—until it bleeds, and explores the moral ambiguity from every angle. However, no one in *100 Bullets* seems able to have a straight conversation, and the scripts are full of slang, which leads some to wonder whether it's all style over substance. This criticism can't be levelled at Argentinian Eduardo Risso's art, however. Heavily influenced by fellow South Americans Jordi Bernet and José Muñoz, and combining angular, edgy linework with heavy black inking, Risso's drawing on *100 Bullets* is worth the price of admission alone.

FURTHER READING: *Chicanos;*
Simon, Una Aventura Americanos
SEE ALSO: *Sin City; Hard Boiled*

★
★
★
★
★

Writer: Paul Auster
Artist: Paul Karasik/David Mazzucchelli

Publisher: Tandem Library, 2004
ISBN: 0571226337

15+ PAUL AUSTER'S CITY OF GLASS

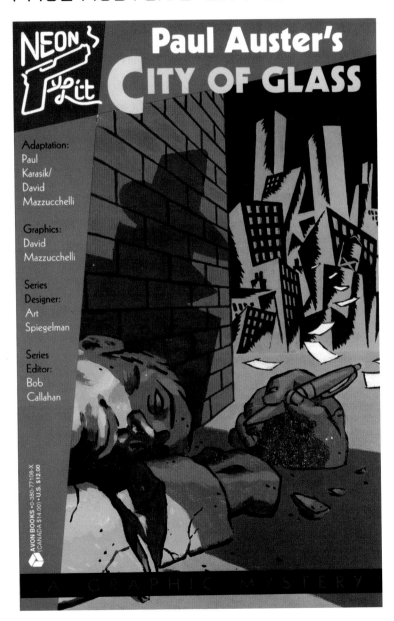

Plot: The comics adaptation of Paul Auster's metafictional detective short story from his popular *New York Trilogy* anthology. *City of Glass*, in its original, plain text form, was a meditation on language and stories. Here, at the expert hands of Karasik and Mazzucchelli, the exploration of language is greatly enhanced by its visual dimension.

Review: On the surface, *City of Glass* is about Daniel Quinn, a writer who loses his mind while impersonating a detective called Paul Auster—not to be confused with the writer of the same name who appears in this story, or the other writer of the same name who actually wrote it. As Auster, Quinn is hired to keep an eye on eccentric academic Peter Stillman—not to be confused with Mr Stillman's abused son, who shares his father's name—a man seeking the divine language of God. There are lots of name games here, but this is only fitting for a story about language. The real author is not a detective, but readers follow the writer of a story like a detective follows a criminal. The story is the crime the author has perpetrated.

Comics are often compared to novels, usually unfavorably, and adapting a short story inevitably invites further unfavorable comparisons, but it is interesting to note that both the plain text and the comic versions tell the same story, using approximately the same number of pages.

Moreover, the comic version actually improves on the original—the illustrations of Peter Stillman Sr.'s meandering route through New York are beyond the power of plain text to depict. But where Mazzucchelli really excels is at the borders of language, when visualizing how words and things used to be interchangeable. This is something comics can do with ease—the drawing of a shadow that forms the word "shadow" literally illustrates the exposition. Then there is the wonderful nine-panel grid that shows a progression of images evoking the treachery of words and pictures, demonstrating how meaning can break down into an inescapable labyrinth.

One could still question the point of adapting a perfectly good short story into a graphic novel; question the meaning of a story that is about language and meaning; question why the reader should tolerate the lies, the nonsense, and the language games perpetrated throughout the narrative. The best answer to such questions is probably supplied by Auster, the writer within the story—it is to give the audience some amusement. This adaptation of *City of Glass* definitely provides plenty of that.

FURTHER READING: *Animal Man :Deus Ex Machina*
SEE ALSO: *Dead Memory; I Shall Destroy All Civilized Planets; Batman: Year One*

★
★
★
★
★

A

Writer: Chester Gould
Artist: Chester Gould

Publisher: IDW Publishing, 2006
ISBN: 1600100368

THE COMPLETE CHESTER GOULD'S DICK TRACY, VOLUME 1: 1931–1933

Plot: This volume covers the first years of the famous comic strip in which Dick Tracy joins the police force after the father of his fiancée, Tess Trueheart, is killed by robbers. After solving the murder, he takes on other murderers and various kidnappers, thieves, and conmen. One of those kidnappings mirrors the famous Lindbergh case, but the story of Little Buddy Waldorf here has a happier ending. Tracy's first unusual villain—the gang leader, Big Boy—is based on Al Capone, and most of the remaining stories in this volume involve Big Boy or members of his gang, who all have names like Broadway Bates, Steve the Tramp, Larceny Lu, and Stooge Viller. Supporting characters include Tess, Chief Brandon, Pat Patton (a fellow detective who's used for comic relief), and Dick Tracy Junior, a homeless boy that Tracy takes under his wing, prompting the boy to name himself after Tracy (later in the series he's officially adopted).

Review: This is the first volume in an ambitious plan to reprint all 46 years' worth of Chester Gould's work on *Dick Tracy*. Originally pitched as *Plainclothes Tracy*, with plots taken from the headlines and remaining firmly in the tradition of James Cagney and Edward G. Robinson gangster movies and the hard-boiled detective fiction of the pulps, *Dick Tracy* took a few years to become the strip that inspired the film, with its bizarre gallery of grotesque villains. Here, the criminals are straightforward police-procedural fare and it's Tracy who is the main protagonist—before his villains started to upstage him. This is a violent comic—Tracy takes few prisoners and the bullets fly graphically though their targets. Though persistent, Tracy is no superman; he's as likely as the next man to crack under torture—and he does. While Tracy is usually the straight man around whom the interesting action takes place, his indefatigable, square-

ESSENTIAL
GRAPHIC NOVELS
500
103
CRIME/MYSTERY
Top 10 crime and mystery graphic novels you must read

jawed pursuit of justice is an important aspect of what makes his character iconic.

At the heart of *Dick Tracy* is Tracy's family—Tess and Junior. The introduction of Junior may have been an acknowledgment of some of the negative aspects of the strip, providing younger readers with someone to relate to. The artwork isn't as polished on the earliest strips as it would later become, but it's interesting to see its early development.

FURTHER READING: *The Complete Chester Gould's Dick Tracy: Volumes 2–4*
SEE ALSO: *Popeye: I Yam What I Yam*

★
★ **Writer:** John Wagner   **Publisher:** DC Vertigo, 1997
★ **Artist:** Vince Locke   **ISBN:** 1563893673
★

18+ A HISTORY OF VIOLENCE

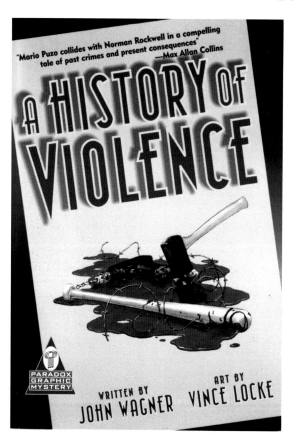

Plot: Tom McKenna is a typical Middle American, unremarkable in every way. He's married, a family man, a member of the local baseball team, and owner of the town diner. In a town where everyone knows your name and nothing much ever happens, Tom has carved himself a cosy existence. But when two traveling killers storm into town with murder and money on their minds, they can think of no better place to stop than the local diner...

Things don't go to plan. Tom violently dispatches them, killing one man and hurling the other through the window. Tom and his family are hurled into the national media as suspicion begins to accumulate among friends and the local

police about Tom's past and identity. Can Tom turn off the media spotlight and deflect the rampant speculation forming against him? But more importantly, with the unwanted attention this brings, can he and his family survive as old foes come to town to claim their revenge?

Review: Criminally overlooked when originally printed by DC's Paradox Press in 1997, but thankfully back into print (in a new format) to coincide with David Cronenberg's film adaptation, *A History Of Violence* is a rare sight in DC's back catalog: a completely ordinary person in an extraordinary situation reacting just like anyone else would—with panic and gut instinct. Wagner and Locke have created a character

so down to earth that he doesn't fight with powers; he fights with his bare hands and firearms. He doesn't fight for truth and justice; he fights for his family's survival.

This everyman sensibility is heightened by Locke's attention to detail in the appearance of Middle America. The realistic look of everyday small towns helps set the story firmly in reality, immersing the reader in the story instantly. As much effort is put into the drawings of diners, baseball fields, malls, and family homes as is shown in scenes of horrific violence and cruelty. And Vince Locke's spattered and scratchy art suits those acts perfectly, with the portrayal of slayings and mutilation going further than even the film adaptation.

John Wagner's script is relentless in its twists and surprises, as a man is thrown into a deadly showdown much against his own will—a theme also seen in his earlier *Button Man* series. Sadistic violence is constant, while revelations about Tom's past lead to the gut-wrenching discovery of what happened to those that Tom left behind.

FURTHER READING: *Button Man; American Freak*
SEE ALSO: *Judge Dredd: The Complete Case Files v1*

★
★
★
★

Writer: Pete Milligan
Artist: Javier Pulido

Publisher: Vertigo, 2003
ISBN: 1563899043

15+ HUMAN TARGET: FINAL CUT

Plot: Pete Milligan's revival of the DC Comics character created by Len Wein and Carmine Infantino. A master of disguise with a twist, the Human Target is a bodyguard-cum-counter assassin. Just as he did with *X-Force* and *Shade the Changing Man*, Milligan's take on this established character is so different from previous versions that he is almost creating something entirely new.

Review: Like many of Milligan's stories, *Human Target* is a meditation on identity—and who better to talk about identity than a man who spends his working life being other people?

Picking up the threads left dangling from Milligan's initial four-issue *Human Target* reboot, the action shifts to Hollywood, where someone with a grudge is killing some of Tinseltown's biggest movers and shakers. Soon,

Christopher Chance, the Human Target, is in character, playing a role—and what better place to be acting than Hollywood? But Chance isn't acting, he's a performing Baudrillardian simulation, a "third order simulacra" in which the copy replaces the original. This is the meat of Milligan's take on the *Human Target*—it's a postmodern romp with critical theory and bullets. Moreover, it's a metafiction—a story about stories—that verges on self-awareness as the characters critique not only each other, but the narrative as a whole.

The artwork is gorgeous. Javier Pulido is a fitting replacement for Edvin BiukoviÐ, the sadly deceased and much-missed artist on Milligan's first stab at reviving *Human Target*. Pulido's lines and inks are further enhanced by the glossy paper and the work of colorist extraordinaire, Dave Stewart. Each page shimmers with Hollywood magic.

At his best, Milligan is a fantastic writer and in *Final Cut* he is on top form. The dialog is trim, but not blunt, and almost every sentence contains a lovely turn of phrase, with a beautifully balanced double meaning that captures the essence of a character. Milligan knows how to play his audience, to raise their expectations in one direction before confounding those expectations and giving the audience something better and more satisfying instead. A taut tale that rewards repeated readings.

FURTHER READING: *X-Force: New Beginnings;*
Human Target: Living in Amerika
SEE ALSO: *City of Glass; Shade the Changing Man:*
The American Scream

★
★
★
★
★

Writer: Paul Grist
Artist: Paul Grist

Publisher: Image Comics, 2004
ISBN: 1582403406

124

KANE BOOK 1:
GREETINGS FROM NEW EDEN

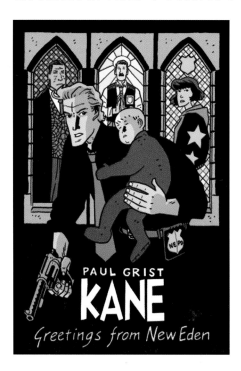

Plot: In the fictional town of New Eden, Detective Kane attempts to keep the streets safe. Returning after an enforced absence of six months for shooting his corrupt partner, Dennis Harvey, Kane finds himself having to deal with vengeful and possibly corrupt colleagues, a recently released old foe in the shape of Edward Fogle, and the city's crime lord Oscar Darke. In addition, he finds himself with a new partner, Kate Felix.

Initially unsure whether he was right to return, Kane shows a cavalier attitude in his approach to his work—not helped by several of his colleagues making it clear that he's a marked man, one even going so far as to tamper with his gun. It takes a quick intervention by Kate during a hostage situation to make sure that Kane isn't killed. Matters are made even worse when the recently released Fogle starts a bombing campaign in New Eden to attract Kane's attention

and seemingly lead him into a trap. We also catch our first glimpse of crime lord Darke as a routine surveillance operation goes disastrously wrong...

Review: Originally published by Grist's own Dancing Elephant Press between 1993 and 2001, *Kane* remains one of the finest examples of the crime genre in comics. Perhaps rivaled only by Frank Miller's *Sin City*, and the works of Brian Michael Bendis and Ed Brubaker, *Kane* is still fondly remembered today. The emergence of Grist's brilliant *Jack Staff* series has contributed to the lack of new *Kane* material in recent years, but it is clear that when the time comes to return to Kane's adventures, and the continuing exploits of the inhabitants of New Eden, there are still plenty of tales to be told.

Grist's artwork is simple and effective throughout, using heavy shadow as favored by Miller on *Sin City* (wonderfully

ESSENTIAL
GRAPHIC NOVELS

500

109

CRIME/MYSTERY

Top 10 crime and mystery graphic novels you must read

parodied in *Kane Volume 5: The Untouchable Rico Costas and Other Short Stories*) and Mike Mignola, to name only two. Despite Grist being British, the town of New Eden, and indeed the New Eden Police Department, owe more to American shows like NYPD Blue, or Batman's Gotham City, than the kind of environments seen on British detective shows, or those later used as Castletown in *Jack Staff*. There are, however, a few nods to Kane's British origins—Kane's car looks like something from British TV series *Inspector Morse*, for instance.

Grist's layouts, though clear and simple, do perhaps suffer initially from sudden flashbacks that are not obviously signposted—which can be a little confusing—but this is all part of *Kane's* charm, and once you get a handle on this storytelling technique it's all part of the joy of the journey. Fun yet gripping.

FURTHER READING: *Kane Volume 2: Rabbit Hunt; Kane Volume 3: Histories*
SEE ALSO: *Jack Staff: Everything Used to Be Black & White; Criminal Volume 1: Coward; Sam & Twitch: The Brian Michael Bendis Collection*

★
★
★

Writer: Max Allan Collins **Publisher:** Paradox Press
Artist: Richard Piers Rayner **ISBN:** 1563894491

15+ ROAD TO PERDITION

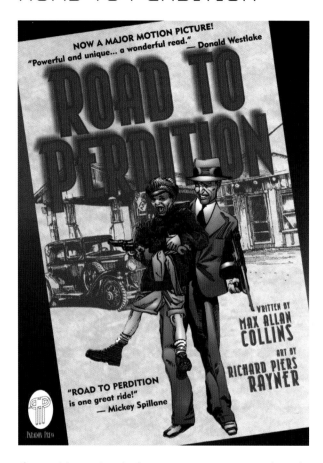

Plot: A twisting, turning tale of vengeance set in 1930s mobland—Rock Island, Illinois. When Michael O'Sullivan (chief enforcer for John Looney, the Irish don) discovers his wife and youngest son murdered by his own employers, he takes his remaining son, Michael Jr., and heads out on the road to perdition, or more accurately, the road to revenge.

Review: There's definitely more of the novel than the graphic in *Road to Perdition*. It possesses an absolutely relentless storyline of revenge, revenge, revenge—and contains so many fedoras, the private detectives' union would blush openly at the sight.

Road to Perdition is an atypical Prohibition-era gangster tale, as it has the added dose of strict family values topped with a penchant for Catholicism.

However, this serves the story well, because without the motives provided by the moral compass, this would be little more than a 302-page killing spree, which would not make it anywhere near as satisfying.

There are some well-rounded characters in *Road to Perdition*, coupled with some mildly interesting panel composition. However, the book is predominantly led by its story. Rayner,

THE CHURCH IS RIGHT. BUT I HAVE A DUTY TO MY FAMILY, AS WELL. THAT MEANS I HAVE TO WORK.

as penciller on the project, displays a clear talent for detail, especially when it comes to character attributes and grizzled gangster faces, but unfortunately, he doesn't appear to have put as much effort into the "noir" feel that typifies the period. As a result, the atmosphere never seems quite as dark or seedy as the narrative suggests.

The narrative has some intriguing twists, and the central characters engage your attention throughout the lengthy tome. *Road to Perdition* has some challenging and thought-provoking aspects, and is, at times, very pacy—but you have to be willing to overlook the occasional flaw.

A movie version of the story was released in 2002, directed by Sam Mendes and starring Tom Hanks, Tyler Hoechlin, and Paul Newman.

FURTHER READING: *Road to Perdition: On the Road; Stolen Away; Dick Tracy: The Collins Casefiles; CSI: Crime Scene Investigation*
SEE ALSO: *Sin City; Lonewolf & Cub*

Writer: Frank Miller
Artist: Frank Miller
Publisher: Dark Horse, 2005
ISBN: 1593072937

★
★
★
★
★

15+ # SIN CITY: THE HARD GOODBYE

Plot: Marv is a brutal man in a brutal town... but his heart is suddenly captured by the mysterious Goldie, a stunning high-class prostitute who makes her move and takes him to bed for the night.

The following morning Marv wakes up with the hangover from hell and finds Goldie dead. Even worse, the corrupt police force are banging on his door determined to arrest the suspect they've been told is the guilty man.

But Marv's not guilty and he sets out to avenge the death of the one woman who's ever offered him love. His bloody quest takes him on a violent rampage through the vice-ridden world of Basin City, as he slowly uncovers a plot led by men who deem themselves untouchable.

Review: *The Hard Goodbye* is, at times, an uncompromising read. In Marv it has an anti-hero who wins your heart despite often committing acts of gut-churning violence. This was Miller's first book in the *Sin City* series and was published in 1991–1992 in 13 parts, in Dark Horse Presents and Dark Horse Presents Fifth Anniversary Special.

Miller started drawing this first story in the series after working as a screenwriter on the film *RoboCop II*, an experience he admits was soul-destroying, as he saw a script he loved go through the Hollywood wringer until it barely resembled the work he'd created. Fortunately, this disillusionment, combined with a two-year lay-off from drawing, saw him return to comics with all guns blazing, determined to create his own properties instead of working

on other people's (i.e. *Batman* or *Daredevil*). Publisher Dark Horse allowed him that freedom, and this brilliant and stylishly violent thriller was the result.

Miller admits he reduced the word count in later *Sin City* sequels as he learned to trust his art to tell the tale, but the stark graphics and the strict use of a black-and-white palette to emphasize the story's gritty noir roots more than makes up for these minor shortcomings. From the opening scenes of intimacy with Goldie, to Marv's trek in the rain, to his brutal murder of those responsible for Goldie's death, Miller's moody pencils and inks never fail. If anything, they become more confident as the tale progresses, and the closing scenes of Marv's defiant end are among the best in the book. The whole project may smack of Tarantino-meets-

Chandler, but that would undersell Miller's achievement in creating a world where justice is hard and fast, and moral codes are enforced with devastating violence. No wonder it proved such visceral source material for the 2005 *Sin City* movie directed by Robert Rodriguez and Miller himself.

FURTHER READING: *Sin City: That Yellow Bastard; Sin City: Family Values; Sin City: The Big Fat Kill; Sin City: A Dame to Kill For*
SEE ALSO: *Road To Perdition; Hard Boiled*

★
★
★
★

Writer: Will Eisner
Artist: Will Eisner

Publisher: DC, 2005
ISBN: 1401207553

A THE BEST OF THE SPIRIT

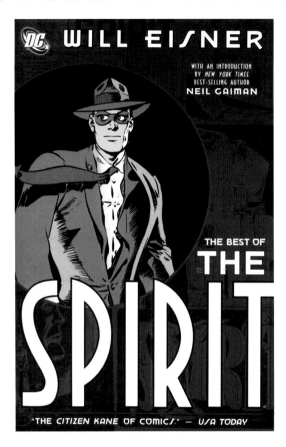

Plot: An excellent starter collection featuring a cross-section of Eisner's classic stories, starting with the 1940 origin story and the debut appearance of Silk Satin, one of Eisner's recurring bombshells, and ending with the strip's demise in 1952. The Spirit is part superhero, part private dick. After investigator Denny Colt is doused with chemicals while battling the villainous Dr. Cobra, he appears to die, but actually enters a state of suspended animation. Crawling from his freshly dug grave, Colt puts on a small mask and proceeds to scare the bejesus out of small-time crooks who believe he's dead. Colt realizes he can use this to his advantage, and is soon handling all sorts of cases, from the patriotic (trailing Nazi war criminals) to the absurd.

Review: Will Eisner is credited with all sorts of innovations—cinematic angles, unusual borders, splash pages, photographic backgrounds, and subjective viewpoints—and *The Best of the Spirit* showcases them all. Eisner loved stories full of intriguing characters, some of whom frequently outwitted his good-natured hero—especially bad girls such as Dulcet Tone, a thief that Colt encounters early in this collection, and who is one of a long list of femmes fatales he would fall for.

Eisner also had a great ear for dialog, and at times his writing is as stark and as sparse as the best hard-boiled detective authors. Modern readers may find his sentimental

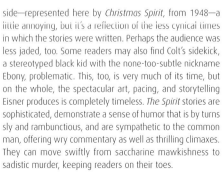

side—represented here by *Christmas Spirit*, from 1948—a little annoying, but it's a reflection of the less cynical times in which the stories were written. Perhaps the audience was less jaded, too. Some readers may also find Colt's sidekick, a stereotyped black kid with the none-too-subtle nickname Ebony, problematic. This, too, is very much of its time, but on the whole, the spectacular art, pacing, and storytelling Eisner produces is completely timeless. *The Spirit* stories are sophisticated, demonstrate a sense of humor that is by turns sly and rambunctious, and are sympathetic to the common man, offering wry commentary as well as thrilling climaxes. They can move swiftly from saccharine mawkishness to sadistic murder, keeping readers on their toes.

At a time when most comics were for children—or only semi-literate adults—Eisner's work on the strip was an outstanding achievement that still looks good today.

FURTHER READING: *The Spirit Archives vol 1-24; Will Eisner's New York; Life in Pictures: Autobiographical stories*
SEE ALSO: *Contract with God Trilogy; Fagin the Jew; The Plot*

★ **Writer:** Greg Rucka   **Publisher:** Oni Press, 1999
★ **Artist:** Steve Lieber   **ISBN:** 0966712714
★
★

15+ WHITEOUT

GREG RUCKA
STEVE LIEBER

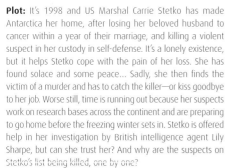

Plot: It's 1998 and US Marshal Carrie Stetko has made Antarctica her home, after losing her beloved husband to cancer within a year of their marriage, and killing a violent suspect in her custody in self-defense. It's a lonely existence, but it helps Stetko cope with the pain of her loss. She has found solace and some peace… Sadly, she then finds the victim of a murder and has to catch the killer—or kiss goodbye to her job. Worse still, time is running out because her suspects work on research bases across the continent and are preparing to go home before the freezing winter sets in. Stetko is offered help in her investigation by British intelligence agent Lily Sharpe, but can she trust her? And why are the suspects on Stetko's list being killed, one by one?

Review: Originally released as a four-part miniseries in 1998, *Whiteout* is an ingenious crime thriller set in one of the most remote places on Earth. The central figure of US Marshal Carrie Stetko is sympathetically written and, although readers don't see too much of her past, there's enough detail included to get a feel of why this intelligent woman opts for a life of isolation in the cold. In fact, the cold, remote location remains a smart metaphor for Stetko's emotional state throughout the book—it's only at the end when, ironically, the weather is about to get even colder,

that she starts to feel emotional warmth for the first time. Sharpe is also a strong character and she comes into her own on a few occasions, but it's Stetko who carries the story, and it's refreshing to have a heroine who's neither pneumatically chested nor stunningly gorgeous. But one of the book's strengths is that all the characters, from the major players to the bit parts, are well worn and look like they have stories to tell.

Steve Lieber's black-and-white artwork conjures up the icy wastes of Antarctica and helps to convey the feel of operating in freezing temperatures in a vast wilderness. A fight scene featuring Stetko, Sharpe, and the killer at the end of Chapter 1 is particularly impressive. Rucka's script is a little too busy in places, and this sometimes conflicts with the need to keep the suspense going, but overall it's clever stuff, elevating a run-of-the-mill detective yarn into something superior. The graphic novel also has cover artwork by Frank Miller and pages by Mike Mignola, Dave Gibbons, and Matt Wagner. A film version is planned for 2008.

FURTHER READING: *Whiteout: Melt; Grendel Tales; Batman: Evolution*
SEE ALSO: *100 Bullets; Brodie's Law; Queen & Country*

★
★
★
★

Writer: Andre Juillard **Publisher:** NBM, 1999
Artist: Andre Juillard **ISBN:** 1561632236

18+ AFTER THE RAIN

Plot: Victor, a photographer who appears in an earlier Juillard work, *The Blue Notebook*, is approached by Abel, a stranger who claims that one of the photos in Victor's exhibition is of his friend Tristan and a beautiful woman they were both courting. Tristan hasn't been in touch for several months and Abel sets about finding him with the help of the photograph.

Review: Andre Juillard is superb at misdirecting the reader and building tension. Best known for his historical epics, his art is detailed and observational. *After The Rain* begins quite casually but picks up the pace toward an explosive and surprising climax that we won't spoil for you. If Hitchcock had drawn comics, they might have turned out like this.

FURTHER READING: *The Blue Notebook; Les Sept Vies de l'Epervier Volumes 1–7*
SEE ALSO: *Streak of Chalk; In Search of Shirley*

★
★
★
★

Writer: Brian Michael Bendis **Publisher:** Marvel Comics, 2003
Artist: Michael Gaydos **ISBN:** 0785108726

18+ ALIAS VOLUME 1

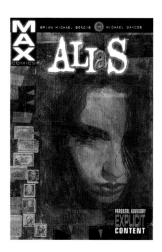

Plot: Former superhero Jessica Jones is no angel in spandex. Now making her living as a private eye specializing in meta-human cases, her life's on a downward spiral. Everything changes when she's duped into almost exposing the identity of a very well-known hero, and a one-night stand turns out to be far more significant than it seems.

Review: From the opening expletive to the decidedly imperfect behavior of Bendis's very flawed hero, it is clear that this isn't a typical superhero book. Jessica is an inspired and convincing character and there are some genuine laugh-out-loud moments that arise as a result of her fiery disposition. Bendis's unconventional storytelling and superb dialog, coupled with Gaydos's realistic and moody artwork, creates a superhero-based narrative that is uniquely grounded in the real world.

FURTHER READING: *Alias Volumes 2–4; The Pulse Volumes 1–3*
SEE ALSO: *Powers: Who Killed Retro Girl?*

Writer: Alan Grant
Artist: David Bircham

Publisher: Markosia, 2007
ISBN: 1905692218

BRODIE'S LAW: PROJECT JAMESON

Plot: Anti-hero Jack Brodie is having a bad day. Sent to steal a scientific file called Project Jameson, he walks into a trap and is forced to go on the run. Subsequently, his wife is killed and his son goes missing. To get his son back and clear his name he has to open up Project Jameson and use the mysterious PM13 formula inside, which allows him to become an entirely different person in body and mind.

Review: A brutal action tale from creators David Bircham and Daley Osiyemi, and writer Alan Grant, this is one of the best UK comics of the last decade. Bircham's art is a fantastic portrayal of the mean streets of South London and extreme close-ups demonstrate his ability to capture amazing detail. Grant's gritty writing style fits the art like a glove.

FURTHER READING: *Brodie's Law: Volume 2*
SEE ALSO: *Kidnapped*

Writer: Richard Sala
Artist: Richard Sala

Publisher: Fantagraphics, 2003
ISBN: 1560972815

THE CHUCKLING WHATSIT

Plot: A hack writer, Broom, finds himself playing detective when a number of astrologists start turning up dead, seemingly murdered by the Gull Street Ghoul, long thought dead himself. Broom is drawn into a complex mystery involving art, the shadowy Mister Ixnay, and a sinister organization called the Ghoul Appreciation Society.

Review: With tongue firmly in cheek, Sala mixes film noir and hard-boiled detective motifs with those from golden-age Hollywood and modern-day slasher horror to create a unique comic experience. Though perhaps undercharacterized, his grand plots are full of twists, misshapen landscapes, grotesque villains, and gruesome deaths.

FURTHER READING: *Mad Night; Peculia; The Grave Robber's Daughter; Delphine*
SEE ALSO: *Meat Cake; Nocturnals*

★ **Writer:** Various
★ **Artist:** Various
★
★

Publisher: Gemstone, 2007
ISBN: 188847274X

THE EC ARCHIVES: CRIME SUSPENSTORIES VOLUME 1

Plot: Obsessed with how the ordinary man or woman can be warped by greed, lust, or despair to commit unthinkable crimes, the stories in *Crime SuspenStories* reinforce the idea that even if the law lets you get away with the crime, karma certainly won't.

Review: Featuring some of the EC stable's more underrated (but extremely reliable) artists, such as Reed Crandall, Jack Kamen and George Evans, occasional bursts of brilliance from Krigstein, and striking—some would say lurid—covers from Jack Davies, *Crime SuspenStories* is a visual feast, even if reading the complete collection may make you feel jaded.

Every story has the familiar EC twist ending, which doesn't always sit well with the preceding narrative, and the scripts tend to be on the wordy side. However, informed by popular radio and TV shows of the 1950s, not to mention the excellent pulps and noir fiction of the time, the language of *Crime SuspenStories* is a cut above the average. As with all the New Direction titles from EC, *Crime SuspenStories* concentrated on the regular person in the street, and created a damp-walled world of skittering shadows where the guilty would always be found out.

FURTHER READING: *Mr District Attorney; Mr A; Cops: The Job*
SEE ALSO: *Two-Fisted Tales; Weird Science; Spirit: The Best of the Spirit*

Writer: Ed Brubaker
Artist: Sean Phillips

Publisher: Marvel, 2007
ISBN: 1845766105

CRIMINAL VOLUME 1: COWARD

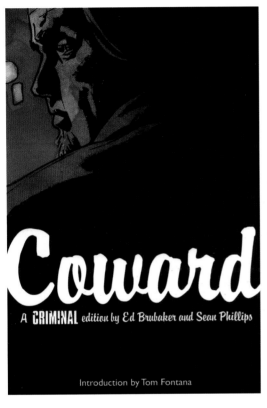

Plot: Leo can plan the perfect heist if you can convince him that it's safe enough. He's a professional, doesn't like guns, and is about to get pulled into a bad job. He's also got to look after the man who taught him all he knows, who is now struggling with senile dementia, and also manage his own heroin addiction. An old friend and a crooked cop come to him with the perfect target, and Leo puts together the ideal crew, despite not entirely trusting his police partners. But on the day of the heist, things do not go well, and when some very unsavory characters pursue the gang, Leo is considered the easiest target. But there's a reason why Leo is so careful, and these guys are about to find out what it is.

Review: The noir crime movies and books of the 1950s and '60s have obviously inspired *Criminal*, where bad things happen to bad people, and nothing's ever black and white. Brubaker's dialog has an authentic ring to it, and the intricate twists and double-crosses are well planned. He makes you care about the central characters, despite their dubious morality, and the violence is both hardhitting and realistic. Phillips' gritty art is well suited to the subject, and the book looks superb.

FURTHER READING: *Sleeper Volumes 1–4; The Complete WildC.A.T.S.*
SEE ALSO: *Scene Of The Crime; History Of Violence; 100 Bullets*

★
★
★
★

Writer: Steve Niles
Artist: Ben Templesmith
Publisher: Dark Horse, 2004
ISBN: 1569719357

15+
CRIMINAL MACABRE:
A CAL MCDONALD MYSTERY

Plot: Cynical supernatural gumshoe Cal McDonald has seen some remarkably strange things, even by LA standards. He works hard, and plays even harder, but no amount of illicit substances can prepare him for his weirdest investigation yet. When asked to look into a relatively straightforward vampire sighting he finds himself in up to his eyeballs, connecting the dots in a case that involves peculiar and unusual monster collaborations, seemingly random murders, and a rash of break-ins, all the while attempting to dissuade the police that he is involved in any way other than being in the wrong place at the wrong time. All this plus shotguns, flea spray, and more blood than you could ask for.

Review: Yes, it's derivative in places, but when the writing is this entertaining, does it really matter? Steve Niles and Ben Templesmith, the creative duo behind *30 Days of Night*, joined forces to create another monster-filled noir escapade.

Each panel evokes a nightmarish atmosphere due in no small part to Templesmith's abrasive artwork. On occasion, this rendering makes it tough to differentiate between human and monster, but this is a slight anomaly, and one that does not detract from the dark and morbid tone that pervades the story. The horror aspect is leavened slightly by the string of genuinely funny oneliners and deadpan comments from the prickly, but likeable, McDonald.

FURTHER READING: *Criminal Macabre: Two Red Eyes*
SEE ALSO: *30 Days of Night*

Writer: Kazuo Koike
Artist: Ryoichi Ikegami

Publisher: Dark Horse, 2006
ISBN: 1593074786

CRYING FREEMAN

Plot: When innocent artist Emu witnesses an assassination, she is struck by the fact that the killer sheds tears throughout; this killer is also an artist, forced to kill impassively while mourning his victims. Emu is sure he'll return to kill her. Instead, he sweeps her off her feet and makes her his wife, to stand beside him at the head of an ancient Chinese secret society.

Review: If you're looking for realism, look elsewhere. Everything about *Crying Freeman* is impossibly romantic and extremely unlikely. Accept it at face value: a story of enduring love punctuated by steamy sex and nailbiting adventures, as Freeman takes on super-soldiers and monsters sent by his enemies. Think *James Bond* meets *Enter The Dragon*. Ryoichi Ikegami's delicate artwork is to die for, subtly shaded with dry brush inking.

FURTHER READING: *Wounded Man; Mai the Psychic Girl; Strain*
SEE ALSO: *Sanctuary; Lady Snowblood; Lone Wolf and Cub*

Writer: Nabiel Kanan
Artist: Nabiel Kanan

Publisher: Image Comics, 2006
ISBN: 1582406170

THE DROWNERS

Plot: James Quinn is a selfmade man, a dot.com millionaire who's built an empire out of nothing. But when his empire starts collapsing around him, dark secrets from his past start to surface, including his involvement in the death of a young girl years before. It soon becomes apparent that nothing and no one are quite what they seem.

Review: As with most of Kanan's work, the artwork is very impressive—beautifully lit and highly expressive. However, the story, while not bad, is a little clichéd, and the characters don't really come across as fully fledged personalities. No one ever really does anything you don't expect. Nothing new, but an enjoyable read and wonderful to look at.

FURTHER READING: *Exit; Lost Girl*
SEE ALSO: *The Birthday Riots; Scene Of The Crime; Billi 99*

★
★
★
★

Writer: Matt Wagner
Artist: Matt Wagner

Publisher: Dark Horse, 2007
ISBN: 159307736X

15+ GRENDEL: DEVIL BY THE DEED

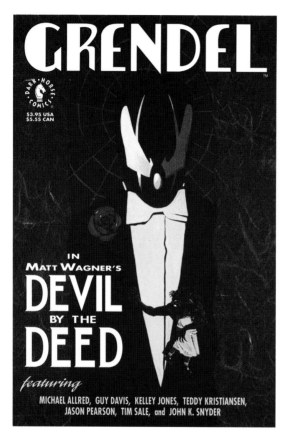

Plot: *Devil By The Deed* iis presented as a novel by the second Grendel, Christine Spar. In it, she recounts the life of Hunter Rose, a wealthy playboy who is also the original Grendel, a crimelord, and a sadistic, masked assassin with near-mystical abilities, whose weapon of choice is a deadly dual-bladed spear. Grendel is obsessed with destroying the werewolf, Argent, who is equally obsessed with bringing Grendel to justice. In the meantime, Rose's adopted daughter and heir, Stacy, has uncovered his secrets, beginning her own descent into madness.

Review: With its pulp overtones and grisly violence, this could have been just another lurid exploitation story, but

Devil By The Deed is beautifully designed and rendered by Wagner, falling somewhere between comic strip and illustrated story. Wagner also looks beyond the surface to examine the nature of violence, its causes and effects. After leaving Hunter Rose, the Grendel power takes on a life of its own, to the point where it becomes a religion, spawning thousands of Grendel warriors in Wagner's later tales.

FURTHER READING: *Grendel: War Child;*
Grendel: Black, White, and Red
SEE ALSO: *Mage; Crying Freeman*

Writer: Rick Veitch
Artist: Rick Veitch

Publisher: Wildstorm, 2003
ISBN: 1563899094

GREYSHIRT: INDIGO SUNSET

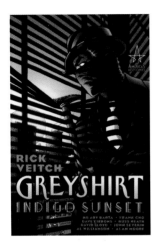

Plot: A masked crimefighter pieces together the clues in an age-old mystery surrounding a number of bizarre deaths and disappearances at Indigo City's abandoned mine.

Review: Originally published by America's Best Comics, this is an obvious homage to Will Eisner's *Spirit. Greyshirt* first appeared in the anthology series *Tomorrow Stories* and wore chainmail under a tailored gray suit, with a scarlet facemask obscuring his features. Veitch's grotesque, thick-edged artwork perfectly suits the old-school crime-comic ambience, and the story is told almost exclusively in flashback, revealing Greyshirt's origins as a lowlife hoodlum. The main narrative is punctuated by short backup strips—featuring artwork from the likes of Frank Cho and David Lloyd—and pages from *The Indigo City Sunset* newspaper offer a wealth of supplementary material.

FURTHER READING: *Tomorrow Stories; Tom Strong*
SEE ALSO: *The Best of The Spirit; Abraxas and the Earthman; Brat Pack; Can't Get No*

Writer: Lewis Trondheim
Artist: Lewis Trondheim

Publisher: Fantagraphics, 1998
ISBN: 1560972882

HARUM SCARUM: THE SPIFFY ADVENTURES OF MCCONEY VOLUME 1

Plot: McConey is asked by a schoolfriend to his father's apartment. On arrival, McConey and his friend Richard discover a monster, but the police don't seem to be interested in their report. Digging deeper, because the police won't, they run up against communist terrorists, and a mad scientist intent on destroying everyone in the city.

Review: Trondheim is a masterful storyteller who uses a minimum of dialog. Using anthropomorphized animals— the sympathetic McConey is a thoughtful rabbit, his friend a sharp alley cat—he creates a completely cohesive and beautifully drawn world that's full of visual tricks and brilliant sight gags but remains scary and full of suspense. His characters are well rounded and his ear for everyday conversation, a joy.

FURTHER READING: *Astronauts of the Future; The Hoodoodad*
SEE ALSO: *Tintin; The Yellow M*

★
★
★
★

Writer: Daniel Clowes
Artist: Daniel Clowes

Publisher: Jonathan Cape, 2005
ISBN: 0224077791

18+ ICE HAVEN

Plot: A deluxe hardback reformatting of Issue 22 of Eightball, Dan Clowes's idiosyncratic, irregular anthology.

Review: Comics maverick Dan Clowes's novella is an intricate series of loose, overlapping vignettes set in the Midwestern town of Ice Haven. At the center of the tale is the disappearance of an unprepossessing child named David Goldberg. The stars of each vignette are all wrapped up in their own, frequently pathetic, little lives, barely aware of Goldberg's plight, yet they are all the more engaging and real as a result. In their blitheness, they are oblivious to Clowes's invocation of the Chicago child killers Leopold and Loeb, but the reader is definitely not. It is touches like this that will drive you on, even through the bleakest of the book's portraits.

FURTHER READING: *David Boring; 20th Century Eightball*
SEE ALSO: *Ghost World*

★
★
★

Writer: David Mack
Artist: David Mack

Publisher: Image Comics, 2001
ISBN: 1887279806

15+ KABUKI: CIRCLE OF BLOOD

Plot: Kabuki is a Japanese assassin who was facially scarred as a little girl and now hides behind a theater mask when she works for a crimefighting organization known as the Noh. When the man who hurt her reappears, she finds herself diverted by thoughts of revenge.

Review: David Mack's work deals with dreamlike states of consciousness and resurfacing memories within the context of a modern Yakuza crime society and a Kill Bill-style revenge plot. Mack's black-and-white art in this volume is a little clumsy compared to his later painted collage approach, and at times there can be a sense of "art for art's sake" in his heavy-handed use of symbolism, but the trippy atmosphere of the story more than makes up for it.

FURTHER READING: *Kabuki: Masks of the Noh; Kabuki: Skin Deep; Elektra Lives Again*
SEE ALSO: *Elektra Assassin; Lady Snowblood*

Writer: Andy Diggle
Artist: Jock

Publisher: Vertigo, 2004
ISBN: 1401201989

THE LOSERS VOLUME 1: ANTE UP

Plot: *The Losers* is a high-octane thriller that follows the actions of a small team of ex-special forces soldiers seeking revenge on those who sold them out and left them to die. While on a covert operation for the CIA—a dirty little black book job—their helicopter was brought down. They were subsequently listed as "killed in action" and their deaths were swept under the carpet. But they're far from dead—and now it's payback time.

Review: Andy Diggle's story is slick and fast. The backdrop to the action is involving enough for the reader to accept, yet it's delivered in a punchy, cinematic, and muscular way that keeps you on the hook all the way through. If Guy Ritchie, David Fincher, Jerry Buckheimer, and Michael Mann all made a comic book together, it would read like this.

Jock's art is sublime. Its craggy, stylized form and confident, cinematic camera angles give the story a gritty reality without becoming stuck in the minutiae of the work. The eye rushes over the page like someone has hit fast forward on a video player. The heavy shadowing and use of slabs of tone is reminiscent of artists such as Frank Miller and Duncan Fregredo, but Jock definitely makes the look his own.

The Losers is a pleasure ride for lovers of the modern thriller; its gutsy delivery doesn't slack off until the final frame.

FURTHER READING: *Losers volumes 2-5; Mega-City Undercover; Hellblazer: Joyride; Faker*
SEE ALSO: *Queen & Country*

★
★
★

Writer: James Robinson
Artist: Paul Johnson

Publisher: Titan Books, 2003
ISBN: 1852861576

15+ LONDON'S DARK

Plot: A ghostly wartime romantic thriller set in the bombed-out streets of London during World War II. One of the few graphic novels published by comics legend Paul Gravett, this was at the vanguard of both creators' professional careers and British graphic novels as a whole.

Review: *London's Dark* is a very raw work, full of experimentation. Johnson's frequently degraded images echo a degraded London, where racketeers are all too eager to put their interests ahead of everything else, even the war effort. While Robinson's script might seem quite straightforward, it is no less engaging for this, and it is enjoyable to see him flexing the writing muscles that he would later use to such great effect on *Starman*.

FURTHER READING: *Starman: Grand Guignol*
SEE ALSO: *Starman: Sins of the Father*

★
★
★
★

Writer: Monkey Punch (Kazuhiko Kato)
Artist: Monkey Punch (Kazuhiko Kato)

Publisher: Tokyopop, 2002
ISBN: 1595320709

18+ LUPIN THE THIRD VOLUME 1 (WORLD'S MOST WANTED)

Plot: Each volume in this series presents a number of short stories featuring the adventures of Arsène Lupin III, the grandson of the gentleman thief of Maurice Leblanc's novels, who travels around the world in search of new things to steal. His chief adversaries are Inspector Zenigata of Interpol and Fujiko Mine—though it's his infatuation with the latter that lands him in danger as much as the fact that she's often seeking the same prize as Lupin himself.

Review: Told with a large helping of madcap humor, both sexual and slapstick, these are engaging, fast-paced, cleverly told thrillers, drawn in a sparse, sketchy style.

FURTHER READING: *Lupin III: World's Most Wanted*
SEE ALSO: *Groo*

Writer: Peter O'Donnell
Artist: Jim Holdaway

Publisher: Titan Books, 2005
ISBN: 184023864

MODESTY BLAISE: BAD SUKI

Plot: Modesty Blaise and Willie Garvin investigate the source of the drugs used by London's hippies. The trail leads them to a small village by the sea and a confrontation with a surprising drug dealer and her henchmen.

Review: Created by author Peter O'Donnell and artist Jim Holdaway for the London Evening Standard newspaper in 1963, Blaise is a reformed gangster working just outside the law with her right-hand man, Garvin. This volume reprints *The Galley Slaves* and *The Red Gryphon* as well as *Bad Suki*, all originally published between 1968 and 1969. O'Donnell's skill as a storyteller and novelist shows through in these plots, with their origins as a daily newspaper strip rarely detracting from the flow of the storyline. Holdaway's gritty art style suits the often frantic pace and violence of the stories.

FURTHER READING: *Modesty Blaise: The Gabriel Set-Up*
SEE ALSO: *James Bond: Casino Royale*

Writer: Naoki Urasawa
Author: Naoki Urasawa

Publisher: Viz Media LLC, 2006
ISBN: 1591166411

NAOKI URASAWA'S MONSTER, VOL. 1

Plot: After choosing to perform an operation on a famous singer instead of an impoverished, dying Turkish man, Dr. Tenma becomes wracked with guilt. Later, faced with a similar situation, the doctor opts to save a young boy instead of the town's mayor, but when the boy vanishes after a series of brutal murders, he realizes that fulfilling his moral obligation to clear his conscience may not have been the wisest course of action.

Review: The first book in this award-winning series is an exhilarating thriller examining the nature of good and evil, and makes the contention that doing the right thing does not always have the best results. The storyline is brisk and zips along at a rapid tempo, while Urasawa displays a real talent for conveying a character's personality with just a few skilful lines.

FURTHER READING: *Parasyte; Benkei In New York*
SEE ALSO: *Old Boy; Why Are You Doing This; Uzimaki; Death Note*

★
★
★
Writer: William Lindsay Gresham
Artist: Spain Rodriguez

Publisher: Fantagraphics, 2003
ISBN: 1560975113

18+ # NIGHTMARE ALLEY

Plot: Stanton Carlisle, a grifter, takes a torrid journey through the underbelly of society, populated by conmen, snake-oil salesmen, sideshow carnival freaks, and femmes fatales. Attempting to mastermind his own scam, Carlisle finds himself on the wrong side of the law.

Review: Adapted from the lurid 1930s pulp novel of the same name, Rodriguez opts for monochrome art, retaining the visual look and feel of his hard-boiled source material. The dialog is heavy and sometimes swamps the artwork, but it also serves to capture the idioms and street talk of the time. Boldly dispensing with any shred of Hollywood-style redemption, no one gains the moral high ground—and escape from the bottom of the barrel is, particularly for Stanton Carlisle, thwarted by personality flaws and unbridled desires

FURTHER READING: *My True Story; Che: A Graphic Biography*
SEE ALSO: *Criminal: Coward; Sin City: The Hard Goodbye*

★
★
★
Writer: Jamie Delano
Artist: Goran Sudzuka

Publisher: Image Comics, 2006
ISBN: 158240707

15+ # OUTLAW NATION

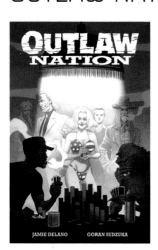

Plot: "Story" Johnson is the black sheep of the Johnson family—a semi-immortal, illuminati-style clan that, in effect, controls America from behind the scenes. After hiding out in Vietnam for 25 years, Johnson returns home to reconcile himself with his past and build a new future, but his eccentric family have other plans for him.

Review: Originally envisaged as a sprawling American road movie serial, commenting on the state of "the Great Satan" (Delano's working title), it was marketed by Vertigo to appeal to fans of the *Preacher* series by Garth Ennis. *Outlaw Nation* draws heavily from the beat writers of the 1950s and the gonzo journalism of Hunter S. Thompson, and mixes it with a dash of social commentary, quasi-science-fiction ideas, and conspiracy theories to create a unique contemporary vision.

FURTHER READING: *Wasteland; Hellblazer: Original Sins*
SEE ALSO: *DMZ; Preacher; Transmetropolitan*

Writer: Garon Tsuchiya
Artist: Nobuaki Minegishi

Publisher: Dark Horse, 2006
ISBN: 1593075685

8+

OLDBOY VOLUME 1

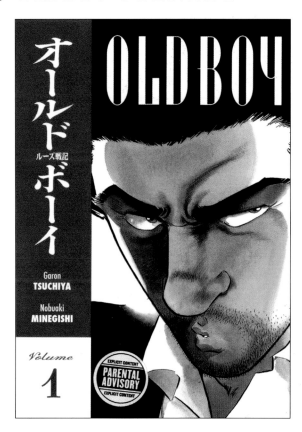

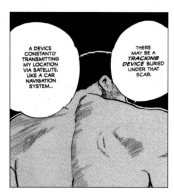

Plot: For ten years he was locked in a tiny room—no reason was given, and by whom he did not know. Ten years he spent doing nothing but keeping his body in peak physical condition and keeping up to date with the outside world by watching television. Then, one day, he is drugged, stuffed in a suitcase, and discarded on the city streets—a free man. *Oldboy* follows the protagonist's attempts to remain sane through his incomprehensible confinement, his first experiences as a free man, and his desire for revenge.

Review: Volume 1 is remarkably fast-paced, without losing any of the emotional or narrative impact. There are some wonderful touches of detail tossed into the plot—one of the best of these comes at the beginning, when we learn that a small private prison was built into a secret floor of the building, between floors 6 and 7. From that moment, a seed is planted that propels our hunger for answers, which in turn adds an additional, subconscious level of empathy with the protagonist, whose own search for answers—and revenge—is the mainstay of the narrative. *Oldboy* was made into a movie in 2003, directed by Chan-wook Park.

FURTHER READING: *Oldboy Volumes 2–8; Takopon*
SEE ALSO: *Naoki Urasawa's Monster; Deathnote; Battle Royale*

★
★
★
★
★

Writer: Greg Rucka
Artists: Steve Rolston, Brian Hurtt,
Leandro Fernandez, Stan Sakai

Publisher: Oni Press, 2008
ISBN: 1932664874

15+

QUEEN & COUNTRY: THE DEFINITIVE EDITION VOLUME 1

Plot: Tara Chase is a secret agent for the Special Section of Britain's Ministry of Intelligence. Designated a "Minder," she is charged with doing the dirty jobs—assassinations, spying, and extracting compromised agents. Tara must travel to Kosovo to kill a General in the Russian Mafia, recover a hidden list of contacts from Afghanistan, and make contact with a defector from an Islamic extremist group in order to find and stop a terrorist attack.

Review: This, the first of four collections, contains the first three storylines (*Operation Broken Ground, Operation Morningstar, and Operation Crystal Ball*) from Greg Rucka's Eisner Award-winning series. Heavily influenced by *The Sandbaggers*—a British TV series shown on the ITV network between 1978 and 1980—*Queen & Country* is (arguably) Rucka's finest work, and one of the best and most important new series of the 21st century.

Topical, relevant, and gritty, not to mention meticulously researched, each artist brings his own distinctive style and interpretation to Rucka's scripts to provide a faultless piece of fiction. *Queen & Country's* only drawback is that it soon becomes dated—*Operation Morningstar's* Taliban-ruled Afghanistan was an anachronism almost before it saw print. But this doesn't detract from the overall quality, and the initial concept has spawned three full-length novels, with a feature film on the way. Currently on hiatus, *Queen & Country* is due to return with a new series in 2009.

FURTHER READING: *Queen & Country: The Definitive Edition Volume 2; Queen & Country: Operation Saddlebags; Queen & Country Declassified*
SEE ALSO: *Whiteout: The Definitive Edition; The Losers*

Writer: Brian Michael Bendis
Artist: Michael Avon Oeming

Publisher: Image Comics, 2006
ISBN: 1582406693

POWERS VOLUME 1:
WHO KILLED RETRO GIRL?

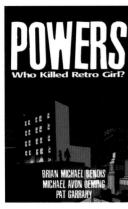

Plot: *Powers* is an exploration of the darker side of the superhero world, seen through the eyes of homicide detectives Christian Walker and Deena Pilgrim. In their first assignment together, Walker and Pilgrim are tasked with solving the grisly murder of beloved superheroine, Retro Girl. In the hunt to uncover the identity of the killer, Detective Walker's troubled past is also revealed.

Review: *Powers* united the superhero and cop-drama genres in a way that had never really been attempted before in mainstream comics. Brian Bendis's snappy, realistic dialog and Michael Avon Oeming's cartoony, but moody artwork worked together to create a convincing world where average-Joe cops rub shoulders with living gods.

FURTHER READING: *Powers Volume 2: Roleplay; Powers Volume 3: Little Deaths; Gotham Central*
SEE ALSO: *Top Ten; Batman: Hush*

Writer: Das Petrou
Artist: John Watkis

Publisher: Image, 2005
ISBN: 1582404259

8+ RING OF ROSES

Plot: Set in an England that's never been free of the political and religious grip of the Catholic Church, scientific progress has been stifled and there have been no world wars. Things might finally be starting to change, however, as hidden forces seem to be promoting a religious war. The Pope arrives in London, but so does the plague, bringing death to thousands. During a search for his missing brother and several prominent clerics, lawyer Samuel Waterhouse uncovers a far-reaching conspiracy. He's never far from becoming a victim himself, though, as he crosses paths with the Secret Brotherhood of the Rosy Cross.

Review: With a sense of claustrophobia evident in both the writing and the artwork, this is a classy mystery.

FURTHER READING: *Deadman: Deadman Walking*
SEE ALSO: *Luthor Arkwright; The Marquis; Rex Mundi*

★ **Writer:** Arvid Nelson   **Publisher:** Dark Horse, 2006
★ **Artist:** Eric J   **ISBN:** 1582403414
★

15+ # REX MUNDI BOOK 1:
THE GUARDIAN OF THE TEMPLE

Plot: It's 1933 in an alternate Paris, where sorcery is commonplace and empires are on the brink of conflict. The inquisitive Doctor Saunière is woken in the dead of night by his friend, a panicky local clergyman. Trusted to guard medieval manuscripts beneath his church, the priest is worried that they've been stolen. As people start dying and the shadowy ruling Inquisition employs heavy scare tactics, the smell of brimstone suggests foul play and occult dealings. What links the Knights Templar, the church, and a mysterious man in white? And will Saunière live to tell the tale?

Review: Rex Mundi is Latin for "The King of The World," a term often used in relation to that age-old preoccupation, the quest for the Holy Grail. Noting the phenomenal success of *The DaVinci Code*, it seems that now is the time for this modern classic to break into the mainstream, with rumors of a film production starring Johnny Depp. Blending Eric J's

moody noir aesthetic with intricate attention to detail—both visually and in the form of written newspaper clippings—fiction is seamlessly mixed with fact.

As the murder-mystery angle on a familiar legend unfolds, author Nelson injects subtle satire and allegory on the modern world into what could otherwise have been just another very good collection. With that extra element, this tale of magic, corruption, and one man's dogged faith in the truth becomes a timeless thriller.

FURTHER READING: *Rex Mundi Book 2: The River Underground; Rex Mundi Book 3: The Lost Kings*
SEE ALSO: *From Hell; Ring of Roses*

Writer: Matt Wagner
Artist: Guy Davis

Publisher: Vertigo, 1995
ISBN: 1563891956

5+

SANDMAN MYSTERY THEATRE: THE TARANTULA

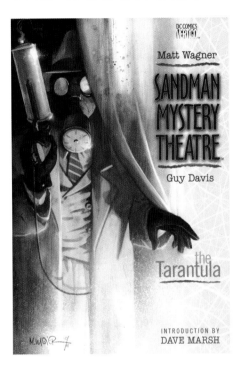

Plot: It's the late 1930s, and America is still partying to celebrate the end of Prohibition, oblivious to the rumblings of war from Europe. Businessman Wesley Dodds, who has recently returned to New York City, is haunted by dreams that lead him to hunt down evil around the city. He conceals his face with a gasmask, and wields a gun that emits a sleep-inducing vapor that also compels its victims to tell the truth. Even with this alter ego, Dodds doesn't seem to be any closer to finding the sadistic kidnapper who's abducting and murdering young socialites. The process is hindered further by Dian Belmont, daughter of the district attorney—a woman destined to make Wesley's life very interesting indeed.

Review: Based on the early years of Justice Society member, The Sandman, this series was launched in the wake of Neil Gaiman's phenomenally successful *Sandman*.

They are linked only by Dodd's dreams, which sometimes feature imagery of the anthropomorphic Sandman character. This is a hard-boiled noir thriller, combined with an acute look at the social mores of pre-war America, with all its glitter and grime—a bundle of contradictions, with casual racism and corruption endemic. Wagner's characters are convincingly flawed, and Davis's art suits its subject perfectly, rendering the fantastic almost mundane.

This is a fascinating examination of a period of American history that's not often approached by comics—and is also a cracking mystery.

FURTHER READING: *Sandman Mystery Theatre: The Face & The Brute; Neil Gaiman's Midnight Days*
SEE ALSO: *Grendel: Devil by the Deed; Scene of the Crime*

★
★
★
★

Writer: Sho Fumimura
Artist: Ryoichi Ikegami

Publisher: Viz Media, 2004
ISBN: 0929279972

15+ # SANCTUARY

Plot: Hojo and Asami, two Japanese refugees from Pol Pot's Cambodia, make a pact to restore Japan to its former glory by becoming heads of the twin forces governing the country's development—Parliament and the Yakuza. Political traditionalists, reformers, the police, and rival gangs stand in their way, but it seems that nothing can withstand their determination to repoliticize the Japanese youth.

Review: *Sanctuary* is an intensely political comic, and has sometimes even been described as fascistic. Nevertheless, it is curiously compelling to watch the two lead characters claw their way to the tops of their careers. Fumimura paints a fascinating picture of the hidden machinations beneath the calm façade: most of the key sequences are talking heads rather than action. Somehow this makes Ikegami's illustrations all the more gripping.

FURTHER READING: *Sanctuary Volumes 2–8;*
Mai the Psychic Girl; Strain
SEE ALSO: *Crying Freeman*

★
★
★
★

Writer: Ed Brubaker
Artists: Michael Lark and Sean Phillips

Publisher: Vertigo, 2000
ISBN: 1563896702

15+ # SCENE OF THE CRIME: A LITTLE PIECE OF GOODNIGHT

Plot: Jack Herriman works as a private investigator, despite only having one eye after being injured by a car bomb as a child. When Jack is hired to investigate a missing-persons case that turns into a murder the next day, the trail soon leads Jack to a new-age hippy commune with more than its fair share of secrets.

Review: An early example of Ed Brubaker's natural flair and talent for the hard-boiled Raymond Chandler-style of crime writing that he has since made his own. Herriman is a tragically flawed everyman character who lacks the almost superhuman skills and determination of most literary P.I.s, making him far more realistic than his peers. Strong characterization is mixed with gritty detail.

FURTHER READING: *Stray Bullets*
SEE ALSO: *Criminal: Coward*

Writer: David Lapham
Artist: David Lapham

Publisher: Vertigo, 2007
ISBN: 1401210481

SILVERFISH

Plot: A tale of love, desire, bad relationships, crimes, and desperate passions set in the heart of suburban America.

Review: For anyone who is familiar with David Lapham's *Stray Bullets*, a sprawling tale of small towns, smaller crimes, and miscellaneous betrayals, *Silverfish* will cover familiar territory: Smalltown America in the 1980s, broken homes, flawed love affairs, and petty secrets that threaten to spill into the open. The art is heavily inked and the panel borders are black, echoing the murky themes of the narrative. But Lapham's real power is his ability to play with our expectations, to raise the tension to a fever pitch and sustain that sense of horror and anticipation for the entire length of the book. Forget Hitchcock— Lapham is the new master of breathless suspense.

FURTHER READING: *Stray Bullets; Murder Me Dead*
SEE ALSO: *A History of Violence*

★ **Writer:** Ken Bulmer
★ **Artist:** Jesus Blasco
★

Publisher: Titan Books, 2005
ISBN: 1845761561

A THE STEEL CLAW: THE VANISHING MAN

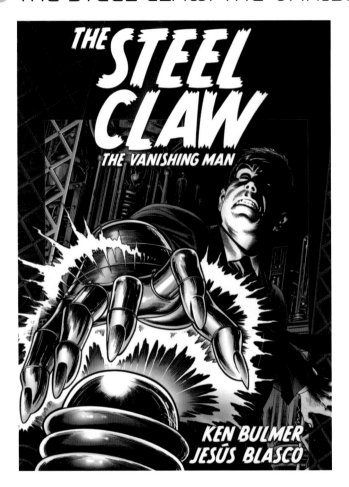

Plot: In 1960s Great Britain, Louis Crandell loses his hand in a laboratory accident and has it replaced with an artificial, but usable, steel one. A second accident—this time electrical—in Professor Barringer's lab turns Louis invisible, except for his steel hand. Taking advantage of the situation, Louis dubs himself The Steel Claw and sets out to make himself rich by extorting money through terrorist acts.

Review: These stories, first published in Valiant comic in 1962, began the long running *Steel Claw* strip that portrayed Louis Crandell as a villain, corrupted by the power forced on him. In this volume, he finally sees the error of his ways and begins to use his invisibility for good. Ken Bulmer's stories have a quick pace and Spanish artist Jesus Blasco's panels are detailed and accurate.

FURTHER READING: *King Of Crooks*
SEE ALSO: *League of Extraordinary Gentlemen*

Writer: Rick Geary
Artist: Rick Geary

Publisher: NBM, 1997
ISBN: 1561631892

A TREASURY OF VICTORIAN MURDER: THE BORDEN TRAGEDY

Plot: "Lizzie Borden took an ax and gave her mother forty whacks"—or so the children's rhyme would have us believe. This, the third in the *Treasury* series, tells the tale of the murders of Abby and Andrew Borden—and their daughter Lizzie, who was accused of perpetrating the whole messy business—in all its graphic glory.

Review: This is probably the most enjoyable and beautiful retelling of this infamous, murderous tale. Geary doesn't take the easy route of exaggerating the facts to make a more gruesome yarn. Instead, he presents the facts in an accurate yet wonderfully executed manner. The artwork is finely detailed, with a little touch of Edward Gorey about it—but Geary has his own unique style that is immediately impressive.

FURTHER READING: *A Treasury of Victorian Murder: The Mystery of Mary Rogers*
SEE ALSO: *From Hell*

Writer: Jason
Artist: Jason

Publisher: Fantagraphics, 2005
ISBN: 1560976551

WHY ARE YOU DOING THIS?

Plot: While watering a friend's plants, Alex spots a stranger in an apartment across the street, and unknowingly sets in motion a chain of events that see him framed for his friend's murder, and on the run—with a hitman on his trail. Hidden by a sympathetic shopkeeper and her daughter, Alex begins to think that things might wind up OK, only to have his hopes dashed.

Review: After several silent stories, Jason introduces dialog for the first time, although very economically and to great effect. His simple artwork is very expressive, and he tells his story beautifully and with surprising depth. As with many of his other books—and indeed, the world in general—bad things happen to good people, and this story will stay with you long after you've finished reading it.

FURTHER READING: *The Living & The Dead; Meow, Baby!; The Left Bank Gang*
SEE ALSO: *Sshhhh!; Silverfish; A History of Violence*

CHAPTER 4

FANTASY

THE LAND OF MAKE BELIEVE

Fantasy is sometimes difficult to categorize because it often crosses over into the realms of science fiction and horror. But what defines fantasy as a distinct genre is a sense of illogical make believe, drawn from elements of childhood imagination—even when those elements become darker and occasionally overtly erotic. Although much of the comic-book subject matter featured in this volume could be construed as "fantastical," in this chapter we are concerned with myth, magic, and, perhaps most importantly, material that rejects science as a restriction when it comes to storytelling. Fantasy, then, spans many different styles—from the highly politically incorrect Conan series to the gentle humor of the *Asterix* books.

The late 1960s and early '70s were the boom years for fantasy—or "sword and sorcery," as the dominant trend was known at the time—when comics really began to embrace the genre with an enthusiasm born of financial self-interest.

Inspired by the popularity of the Lancer paperback reprints of Robert E. Howard's pulp *Conan* tales, Marvel released a monthly licensed comic that, while slow to take off, spawned a whole stable of identikit sword-wielding barbarians in loincloths cleaving demons in half. The look and feel of these traditional fantasy stories in comic-book form perfectly suited the period, with its post-hippy ideals and Roger Dean-style airbrushed LP sleeves.

There were exceptions, however. *Blackmark*, by Gil Kane, was a fantasy/science fiction crossover and is important as one of the very first "proper" graphic novels, paving the way for comic artists' independence from the constraints of major players such as Marvel and DC. Although it failed to achieve great sales at the time, it proved that there was a market for comics in paperback form.

Throughout the '70s, an element of eroticism pervaded many of these sword and sorcery tales, often featuring scantily clad women threatened by slimy-tentacled monsters. The sexual content was even more explicit in Frank Thorne's *Ghita*, serialized as an adult-only, sexually promiscuous version of Marvel's *Red Sonja*.

By the 1980s, interest in the sword and sorcery genre had waned and a more thoughtful approach emerged, steering clear of the worst excesses of the pulps. New writers such as Neil Gaiman turned to the influence of childhood myth and magic in the pages of his *Sandman* series and its spinoff, *Death*. The artist P. Craig Russell perfected a magical, otherworldly art style, adapting Moorcock's *Elric* stories and producing beautiful books based on Mozart's opera *The Magic Flute* and Oscar Wilde's fairytales. Later, Bill Willingham would take the Brothers Grimm approach even further by modernizing the creatures and characters of myth and legend in his award-winning *Fables* series. The DC Vertigo imprint gave many creators the opportunity to blur the distinctions between fantasy, horror, and science fiction, and by the late 1980s fantasy was more about thoughtful character development than simply chopping monsters in half.

Wendy and Richard Pini's *Elfquest* series was a rare example of a more lighthearted fantasy series that has stood the test of time as an independent publication. Initially capturing a cute Californian vision of cartoon elves inhabiting an idyllic world of "free love," it later progressed toward confronting more adult subject matter. The child-friendly art style doesn't always prepare the reader for some of the elf world's liberal sexual customs and practises.

In the UK, Pat Mills' *Slaine* series in 2000 AD drew heavily on ancient Celtic legends. While ostensibly a part of the (no longer fashionable) sword and sorcery subgenre, *Slaine* was used as a vehicle to make subtle references to world politics in the 1980s. Britain also saw the emergence of homegrown talents such as Bryan Talbot, whose Luther Arkwright stories (such as *Heart of Empire*) postulated a curious retro steampunk world, mixing Victorian values, technology, and fashions with those of the 20th century. Arch-fantasist Michael Moorcock was a major influence on Talbot's original vision, but the steampunk genre became popular in its own right, with the American title *Steampunk* taking the idea a stage further with the addition of Japanese manga elements. Although a beautiful book to look at, its heavily cluttered layouts often made it a challenge to follow the story.

Purist manga storytelling became a graphic-novel success story in the West during the 1990s. Fantasy tales were a staple of the genre and often ran over multiple volumes—for example, the *Oh My Goddess* series that pairs the male hero with a beautiful girl claiming to be a goddess. What marked much of Japanese fantasy apart from its European peers was a gentler and more humorous cartoon style, often starring innocent high-school characters, with sparkly bubblegum magic driving the story forward.

The sheer delight of the fantasy genre lies in the multitude of different styles to be found within it. No other genre has such a breadth of talent and ideas. J.M. DeMatteis's graphic novel *Moonshadow*, with its heavily spiritual overtones, is a classic example of the diversity on offer, as is *Abadazad*, which DeMatteis created with the artist Mike Ploog. The latter combines text and full-page illustrations with the more usual sequential art to create a mystical children's tale reminiscent of Frank Baum's *Oz* books and the classic Edwardian storybooks illustrated by master artists such as Arthur Rackham.

★
★
★
★
★

Writer: Jeff Smith
Artist: Jeff Smith

Publisher: Scholastic
ISBN: 0439706408

A # BONE: ONE VOLUME

Plot: Three Bone cousins, Smiley, Phoney, and Fone, become lost after being banished from their village during which time they discover a fantastical valley full of dragons, cow races, and rat creatures. As they are unwittingly caught up in a vast power struggle for control of the valley—between the mysterious Lord of the Locusts and their benefactors, Gran'ma and Rose—the cousins see their newly-adopted home and friends torn asunder, as they struggle bravely on against huge adversities that will change everyone's lives forever.

Review: The best all-ages comic to have been published in the last 15 years. The characters are fully rounded and a genuine empathy is generated for all concerned. The various sideline stories such as the hilarious Great Cow Race and Fone Bone's unrequited love for Rose, simply add more depth and richness, creating a believable world. The supporting cast—from the cheeky possum kids to the enigmatic Red Dragon—are a joy to behold, and seemingly random and inconsequential early meetings reveal greater significance later in the tale.

Much like the *Harry Potter* novels, *Bone* becomes increasingly complex and darker as the story progresses, but never to the point of terrifying or confusing an eight-year-old. The fact that the "stupid, stupid rat creatures" manage to flit from being genuinely scary monsters to light comedic relief, and back again, is testament to Smith's skillful writing and sense of timing. Bone reads as a cross between *Lord of the Rings* and Carl Barks's *Donald Duck* stories, mixed with Walt Kelly—the latter being a huge influence on Smith. Bone's comedy is a mixture of crazy slapstick, sweet embarrassment, and a heavy

dose of modern sensibility infused into a fantasy world, which, surprisingly, blends seamlessly. The whole saga is available as a massive black and white 1,300-page tome or in nine color volumes from Scholastic. Exciting, moving and very, very funny, this is one "all ages" title that both adults and children will be fighting over for years to come. A true classic and an epic in every sense of the word.

FURTHER READING: *Stupid Stupid Rat Tails; Rose*
SEE ALSO: *Elfquest Archives; Castle Waiting*

★ **Writer:** Roy Thomas   **Publisher:** Dark Horse, 2003
★ **Artist:** Barry Windsor-Smith   **ISBN:** 1593070160

THE CHRONICLES OF CONAN VOLUME 1:
TOWER OF THE ELEPHANT
AND OTHER STORIES

Plot: The first of four volumes reprinting Roy Thomas and Barry Windsor-Smith's 24-issue run that first introduced comics fans to Robert E Howard's fatalistic hero back in 1970. Thomas decided when he started the book that each year of publication would reflect a year of Conan's life, so here you find him adapting some of the best early Howard stories (and some of the worst, such as *The Frost Giant's Daughter*). In addition, he fills in gaps with his own ideas, without drawing on the rest of the Howard back catalogue, which was not owned by Marvel at the time.

Tower of the Elephant is fairly subtle for an early Conan story, but it contains all the classic elements. Conan overhears a conversation about a fabulous jewel hidden in the tower of the sorcerer, Yara. After a brawl or two he heads over there, encountering Taurus of Nemidia, known as the Prince of Thieves, and the two join forces to break in and dispatch the lions that roam the grounds. A giant spider kills Taurus, so Conan slays that, too. He presses on and discovers a blind, elephant-headed man, Yag-kosha, kept prisoner by the wizard. Yag-kosha tells him a supernatural tale (inspired by Howard's penpal H.P. Lovecraft) of trans-cosmic beings. Conan agrees to kill him, cuts out his heart (the fabled jewel), and uses it to destroy the sorcerer and his tower.

Review: Florid is the word for these early *Conan* outings. At its worst, Thomas's language becomes a kind of cod-Shakespeare, and Smith's version of the barbarian is a muscular pretty boy fond of jeweled headbands. Although not as ornate as the Pre-Raphaelite-inspired works Smith is best known for, as this collection progresses you can see, almost from page to page, the creeping advance of the decorative finish, especially in the backgrounds.

Initially, Smith's artwork owes a great deal to Jack Kirby, although his anatomy is often dubious and his action quite stiff. Smith uses many of the same tricks as Jim Steranko, such as sequences of cinematic panels in which characters barely move. Both were clearly on a steep learning curve with these early stories, which were considered quite revolutionary in their approach at the time, and by the end of the volume they get into their stride. While lovers of the ornate will enjoy this, *Conan* enthusiasts will probably prefer Thomas's later efforts, when he had his language under control and a better grip on the character—helped by the dependable John Buscema, who understood a great deal more about how to tell a sequential story than Smith ever did.

FURTHER READING: *Savage Sword of Conan; Arak Son of Thunder; Cerebus*
SEE ALSO: *Cerebus: High Society; Tor*

500 ESSENTIAL GRAPHIC NOVELS

Top 10 esssential fantasy graphic novels you must read

★
★
★
★
★

Writer: Bill Willingham
Artist: Lan Medina

Publisher: Vertigo, 2002
ISBN: 1563899426

15+ # FABLES: LEGENDS IN EXILE

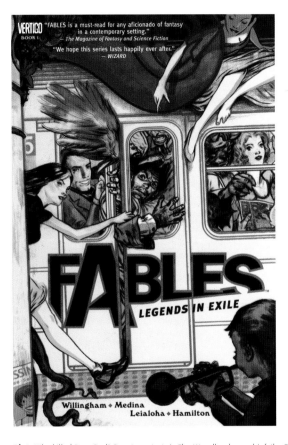

Plot: Who killed Rose Red? Our story starts in The Woodland luxury apartments building in New York, otherwise known as the City Hall for Fables; legends and fairytale characters who have fled their own magical kingdoms, escaping the invading hordes of the Adversary (a dark conqueror from distant lands), and escaped to our world.

Several hundred years later they exist as best they can, led by King Cole, their mayor for life, and the hard-working Deputy Mayor, Snow White—who, after divorcing Prince Charming for sleeping with her sister, works long hours and wears a perpetual frown. When news reaches White of her estranged sister's murder, she insists on helping the security chief, the Big Bad Wolf in human form, with his investigation. But Snow White is also one of the chief suspects.

Review: If you've ever wondered what happens after the words "they all lived happily ever after," this book is a fascinating read. Reinventing classic fable characters and locating them in contemporary New York strips away much of their glamor and naivety, but expands the parameters of the characters, making them more "real." From Beauty and The Beast asking for marriage counseling, to Jack of Jack and the Beanstalk fame running his own dot.com business, it's a peek behind the ever-after. Not every fable character in *Fables* is human however, and those who cannot pass as

such are forced further into exile to a farm upstate, where their otherworldly nature can be concealed more easily. And since many of them are singularly unhappy about that, escape attempts seem to be the norm.

Bigby Wolf adds a touch of noir to the story, as a cynical detective complete with trenchcoat and a chainsmoking habit. He even has an unwelcome house guest in the shape of a talking pig, whose straw house he once blew down.

The intertwining of modern culture and fairy tale ephemera is skillful—flying monkeys provide much of the administrative support in Snow White's office, while Renfield and Boy Blue are drafted in to help recreate blood-splatter patterns in Rose Red's apartment for crime scene analysis. It's a gruesome tale, but the writing style rises above this with some fine humor and a solid plot. An excellent book.

FURTHER READING: *Fables: Wolves; Jack of Fables: The (Nearly) Great Escape*
SEE ALSO: *Fables: 1001 Nights of Snowfall*

★
★
★
★

Writer: Bryan Talbot
Artist: Bryan Talbot

Publisher: Dark Horse, 2001
ISBN: 156971567X

HEART OF EMPIRE:
THE LEGACY OF LUTHER ARKWRIGHT

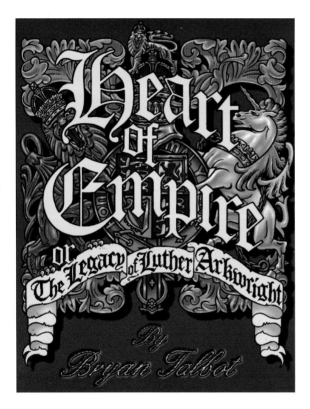

Plot: Talbot's white-haired, psychically attuned Messiah hero, Luther Arkwright, inhabits a complex multiverse where—rather like Michael Moorcock's Jerry Cornelius, on whom he was partially modeled—he fulfils a variety of roles and appears in a number of sometimes contradictory guises. Arkwright hails from Para 00.00 (although he is not a native of that dimension), a version of existence where the highly developed inhabitants are aware of the different, divergent realities and have cast themselves as the multiverse's police force. Luther becomes involved in a royalist coup to overthrow the new Puritan regime in Britain in one parallel existence, and we realize that Luther's (and the multiverse's) fate is intrinsically connected to the rise of the new British Empire.

Returning to the story 20 years later, we find Queen Anne and Luther's daughter, Princess Victoria, suffering strange headaches and visions of her dead brother that may be a precursor to psionic powers inherited from her father, while her mother's empire is threatened by Papist plots and a conspiracy by her own advisors to return to neo-Puritanism. In the wider multiverse, a massive psychic wave is building, the implications of which Victoria doesn't yet understand.

Review: Bryan Talbot has created an exceptionally complex, densely researched alternative England and aligned his cosmic narratives around it, drawing on the history of fascism in Europe, the 17th century Restoration, with a good helping of 1960s New Wave science fiction thrown in to add

ESSENTIAL
GRAPHIC NOVELS
500
151
FANTASY
Top 10 essential fantasy graphic novels you must read

spice. It is a quintessentially English vision that explores many obscure English myths and legendary figures, weaving old and new history together effortlessly. The art is extremely polished, with none of the occasionally awkward figurework of *The Adventures of Luther Arkwright*.

Talbot worked on various Luther Arkwright projects for decades before creating the nine-part graphic novel collected here. Familiarity with his earlier incarnations will help the reader make sense of the complex and multifaceted story, but even those steeped in the Arkwright mythos often struggle to untangle the twisting skeins of Talbot's parallel histories. The only real criticism is that for a Luther Arkwright story, it doesn't have much of Luther in it. When he does

finally appear, he's an emotionally withdrawn figure, watching guardedly from behind the drapery as momentous powers gather. In earlier stories it was Luther who was the sinister and threatening figure, but as more of an onlooker, he leaves the book without a real sense of tension.

FURTHER READING: *The Adventures of Luther Awkwright; The Saga of the Man-Elf; Empire*
SEE ALSO: *The Tale of One Bad Rat; Alice in Sunderland; A Distant Soil*

★
★
★
★
★

Writer: Winsor McCay
Artist: Winsor McCay

Publisher: Checker Publishing Group, 2007
ISBN: 1933160217

A

LITTLE NEMO IN SLUMBERLAND

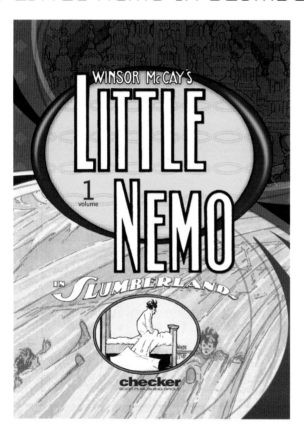

Plot: Nemo, a little boy of five or six years old, is summoned to the palace of King Morpheus as a playmate for the Princess of Slumberland. However, his progress through the kingdom is constantly impeded as his dreams turn to nightmares and result in Nemo waking up, frequently with a bump, as he falls out of bed. Accompanying Nemo through Slumberland are a cast of memorable characters including Flip, a mischievous, cigar-chomping sidekick; Impy, a young cannibal; and Doctor Pill, the physician. Highlights in this volume include the celebrated "walking bed" sequence in which the legs of Nemo's bed grow, before taking Nemo and friends on a moonlit walk over rooftops, and the famous Befuddle Hall episode, in which our heroes are stretched, distorted, and the laws of nature generally turned inside out.

Review: *Little Nemo in Slumberland* has been reprinted a number of times in recent years, but in an unprecedented move, this edition reproduces 110 pages of the celebrated strip in their original dimensions—21 x 16 inches. The sheer scale of the book is impressive, providing a stunning showcase for the magnificent illustrations. The lovingly restored artwork demonstrates Winsor McCay's mastery of color and the stock chosen echoes the off-white newsprint the original strips were printed on.

Those unfamiliar with *Little Nemo* will gain an enviable introduction to one of the greatest comic strips of all time. McCay's Art Nouveau-inspired artwork is simply exquisite. The surreal storylines dazzle with their innovative, experimental

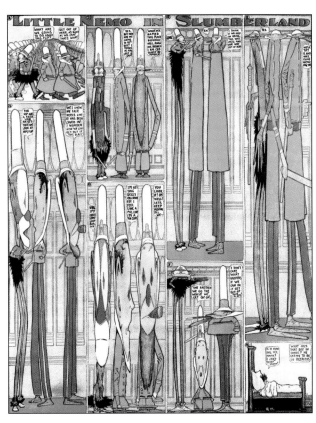

approach. The comic strip itself was barely ten years old when Little Nemo first began and McCay was given free rein with the format. Fluidity of movement from panel to panel is another notable characteristic of the strip, a result of McCay's interest in another burgeoning art form—animation.

The only flaw here is the dialogue, which frequently fails to match the finesse of the artwork. McCay appears to have drawn the speech bubbles first, then packed them with as many words as possible. This leads to sentences being punctuated with meaningless "oh"s, "um"s and "huh!"s in order to fill space. Although this is an unwelcome distraction, it doesn't detract too much from the strip as the artwork is clearly the star, with McCay producing page after page of

consistently brilliant imagery. *Little Nemo in Slumberland* represents a high watermark in comics and serves as a potent reminder of the vast potential of the medium.

FURTHER READING: *Winsor McCay: His Life and Art; Dream of the Rarebit Fiend*
SEE ALSO: *In the Night Kitchen*

★
★
★
★

Writer: Georges Pichard
Artist: Georges Pichard

Publisher: Eurotica, 1995
ISBN: 1561631388

18+

MARIE GABRIELLE

Plot: In a parody of 18th century instructional tales and the Sadeian picaresque format, we are told the history of various salacious, adulterous, or simply feminist women who are being held at a nunnery-come-prison, where an order of sadistic, but starry-eyed Sisters punish them to expurge their sins. Marie-Gabriel and her aged husband visit the nunnery to pick out a servant from among the "saved" women and are told and recount yet more libidinous histories as they tour the facilities. Then, as is obviously going to happen, in an ironic twist of fate Marie-Gabriel finds herself sentenced to be incarcerated in the same place for taking a younger lover and causing the death of her husband. When she has finally accepted that God wants her to be tortured repeatedly

and finds redemption in her suffering she is "rescued" and abused by some rogues, before finally finding happiness with a lusty fellow from the lower orders.

Review: Pichard usually worked with writers or adapted literary works (from erotica such as Apollinaire's *Memoirs of Don Juan* to socialist novels such as Zola's *Germinal*). *Marie-Gabrielle de St Eutrope*, to give it its full title, is one of the few books he wrote himself, a sly parody of early novels that often offered titillating stories on the pretext of denouncing the very subject they were glorifying. Thus Marie-Gabrielle's characters shake their heads in disappointment, or apply the whip with righteousness, when

it is clear they are enjoying every minute of what they pretend to abhor.

In his later works George Pichard developed a unique and beautifully controlled art style, characterized by elaborate (and sometimes hard to follow) decorative page layouts. His extremely vivid figure work often featured comedic men and voluptuous, dark eyed women, which reached its peak in this long-banned volume from the mid 70s. Much of his later erotica looks rushed by comparison.

Pichard taught drawing, so it's hardly surprising that his anatomy and sensitive use of line is amazing. The only problem for most people is that Pichard loved drawing women—especially nuns—being tortured, and if you're not a sadist or masochist then some of the content, even of the edited English language version, is likely to be offputting. This is a great pity as he is a unique stylist with a wry sense of humor, a brilliant draughtsman, and one of the best drawers of women to come out of Europe.

FURTHER READING: *Germinal; The Kama Sutra; Ulysse*
SEE ALSO: *Birdland; Druuna: Morbus Gravis*

★
★
★
★
★

Writer: J.M. DeMatteis　　　**Publisher:** Vertigo, 1998
Artist: Jon J. Muth　　　**ISBN:** 1563893436

15+

THE COMPLEAT MOONSHADOW

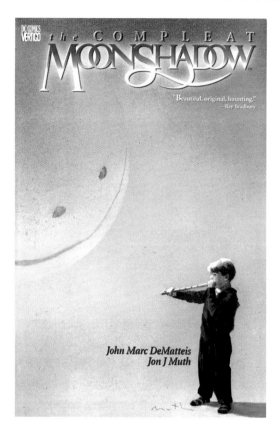

Plot: Born in an alien zoo after his mother was kidnapped by aliens called the G'il Dose, Moonshadow dreams of escaping the race that appears to operate only according to whim. One day he's visited by one of his enigmatic jailers, who may also be his father, and is released into the universe, accompanied by a gruff and disgusting thing called Ira, who looks like a seven-foot-tall teddy bear wearing a bowler hat; his hippy mother, Sunflower; and his cat, Frodo. Things go wrong very quickly, and, reduced to a trio, they find themselves variously committed, locked up, and pressganged into a war that eventually splits Ira and Moonshadow up.

Moonshadow ends up as a nanny to a brood of royal children, a job that ends tragically thanks to scheming cleric Pobidiah Unkshuss, though it does bring him back together with Ira. Unkshuss continues to haunt their lives, until all of the elements of Moonshadow's life come together in a dramatic conclusion—with a revelatory appearance from Moonshadow's father.

The book ends with *Farewell, Moonshadow*—an epilogue that was completed 10 years after the book's initial publication. It tells the story of the rest of Moonshadow's life—and loves—presented as an illustrated novella.

Review: While not as well known as Neil Gaiman's *Sandman*, this is a remarkable work of fantasy, layered and beautifully told, with an incredible amount of depth. Jon

Muth (with the help of fellow masters Kent Williams, George Pratt, and Kevin Nowlan) has produced his magnum opus here, with over 300 pages of beautiful artwork painted in watercolor. His palette is fantastic, and he's able to adapt his style to every mood and situation.

DeMatteis has also outdone himself, with a subtle tone belying the occasional savagery of the tale. Despite the heavy fantasy and science fiction tones, the story never becomes swamped by the themes, and every character is well developed. Moonshadow's emotional development throughout the book is convincingly portrayed, with Ira's "grumpy bastard" character providing the perfect foil to our hero's naivety and belief in people.

As with all the best fantasy, there are parallels with the modern world, with the usual suspects of politics, religion, and war coming in for a battering, but the story is so well written that you can take this on any level and still find it an enormously rewarding experience.

While *Sandman* may be the best-known fantasy comic, *Moonshadow* is arguably the finest.

SEE ALSO: *Blood: A Tale; Brooklyn Dreams*
FURTHER READING: *Greenberg The Vampire; Wolverine & Havok: Meltdown*

★
★
★
★

Writer: Alan Moore
Artist: J.H. Williams III

Publisher: Titan, 2003
ISBN: 1840233702

PROMETHEA

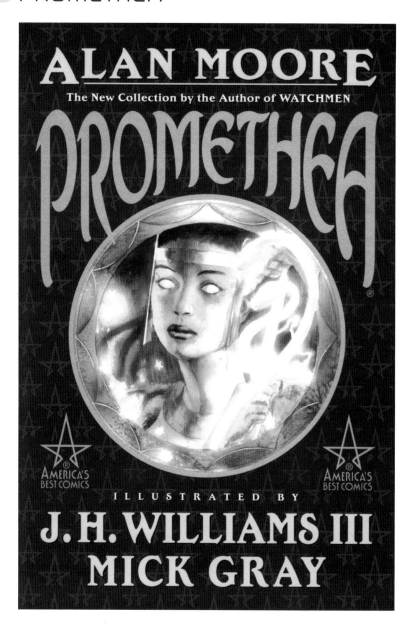

Plot: Sophie Bangs lives in a world that's a little like ours, only with a far higher level of scientific gadgetry and knowledge, and populated by science heroes like the Five Swell Guys and Tom Strong. She's doing a class project on the legend of Promethea, a mythical female warrior who has cropped up in isolated myths and stories going back over two centuries, including a 1920s weekly newspaper strip, pulp magazines, and an ongoing comic series, as well as rumors of real life encounters dating back to the trenches of World War I.

Sophie interviews the widow of the last writer of the Promethea comic, and later that night is attacked by a vicious shadow creature, only surviving when a woman claiming to be Promethea appears and saves her.

Sophie is soon compelled to take on the mantle of Promethea, linking herself to a being who is as much an idea as a real person, and who draws her strength from magic and myth rather than the science that rules the world.

She's soon shocked into action when she's attacked and her best friend is plunged into the Immateria, the world where Promethea's power originates. Sophie is forced into a world that is completely alien to her, where ideas, archetypes, and fables threaten her as much as science villains, magicians, and guns in the real world. She also meets her predecessors, who will help her and get her up to strength before she gets killed.

Review: *Promethea* was one of four titles that Moore launched at the same time, roughly occupying the same universe, and each trying to take its roots from the pulp magazines, instead of the superhero world.

Promethea blends the myriad worlds of *Conan* creator Edgar Rice Burroughs with the mythical roots of *Wonder Woman*, and includes an enormous number of magical references culled from Moore's studies of the subject. It's very smartly written, and if later volumes start to become a little bogged down by the magical element, this one balances it beautifully with the action to present a rip-roaring adventure. J.H. Williams does an astonishing job; he's an impressive figure artist and every page is intricately designed, both in layout and panel placement, with each period and world accompanied by complementary design—Art Deco for the 1920s, and so on.

When Moore balances his own obsessions with the conventions of mainstream superheroes the results are almost always impressive, and this is one of the best examples of recent years.

FURTHER READING: *Promethea Volumes 2–5; Tom Strong; Tomorrow Stories*
SEE ALSO: *Top Ten; Supreme: Story of the Year*

★
★ **Writer:** Neil Gaiman **Publisher:** Vertigo, 1999
★ **Artists:** Kelley Jones, Charles Vess **ISBN:** 1852864419
★

SANDMAN VOLUME 3 – DREAM COUNTRY

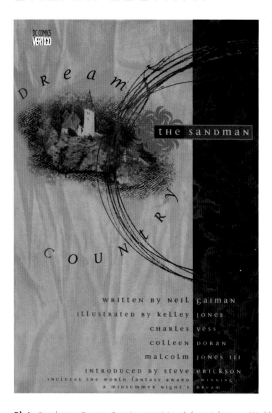

Plot: *Sandman: Dream Country* consists of four tales, continuing the varied and marvellous chronicles of the Sandman (Morpheus). In this anthology we're treated to the story of *Calliope*, the writers' muse and an old flame of the Lord Shaper; *A Dream of a Thousand Cats*, centered around a feline orator with one goal—to return the world to the way it used to be; *A Midsummer Night's Dream*—the first act displaying the Sandman's influence on Shakespeare; and *Façade*, a modern twist on a golden age superheroine.

Review: The third instalment of Neil Gaiman's series has always been a firm favorite among *Sandman* fans. Furthermore, *Dream Country* includes the issue that was—and forever will be—the only comic book to win the

World Fantasy Award (the judging panel declared that comic books would henceforth not qualify for the award).

The opening story, *Calliope*, is the kind of tale that will keep any fiction writer awake at night, and not just because of its subject matter (writer's block). It's a marvelously twisted story that sees the muse of eloquence, Calliope, held hostage so that her captor, a struggling novelist, remains prolific in his ideas.

In *A Dream of a Thousand Cats*, we are permitted a peek at an audience with a cat who has learned the real truth of the relationship between felines and mankind, and is now seeking to change things back to the way they were.

The award-winning *A Midsummer Night's Dream* examines the longstanding relationship between Sandman and Shakespeare, as the play is premièred to an audience of its characters' "true-life" counterparts. This issue is interesting in its development of the Sandman character and his relationship with beings on all planes of existence.

The final tale, *Façade*, is touching and sympathetic, and follows a day in the life of the DC superheroine Element Girl, and her day-to-day struggle against suffocating depression. This story foregoes the character of Morpheus, but the story still centers on the importance of dreams and the difference between fantasy (the superhero lifestyle portrayed in the golden age) and the all-too-uncomfortable reality.

Neil Gaiman has proved his immense worth as a spinner of tales on many, many occasions, and it's a fascinating exercise to peer back into the beginnings of the *Sandman* series and see how well-sculpted these sagas were, even in the character's early life. Kelley Jones's penciling is generally complementary to Gaiman's storytelling, and his art adds personal touches to the tales that enhance them beautifully; certainly in the *Calliope* story, Jones displays his considerable talent for lighting and mood.

FURTHER READING: *Sandman: The Wake; Midnight Days; The Crusades*
SEE ALSO: *Sandman: Preludes & Nocturnes; Death: The High Cost of Living*

★ **Writer:** Pat Mills
★ **Artist:** Clint Langley
★

Publisher: Rebellion, 2006
ISBN: 1904265820

SLÁINE: BOOKS OF INVASIONS VOLUME 1

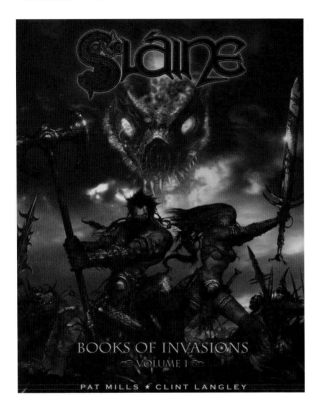

Plot: The adventures of Sláine, a barbarian hero loosely based on Irish folk heros *Sláine mac Dela* and *Cú Chulainn*, are recounted as legend by his dwarf companion, Ukko. Like Cú Chulainn and the Viking berserkers, Sláine is overtaken by an otherworldly frenzy called a "warp spasm" during battle, when the power of the earth surges through his body due to his connection to the earth goddess, Danu.

Having returned to his tribe and become king, one of the major story arcs pits Sláine against the Fomorians, a race of sea demons, before he becomes a living incarnation of Carnun or Cernunnos, the horned god and consort of the earth goddess. In this story, having become High King of Ireland and had many adventures through time, Sláine comes back to his people to find that his old foes, the Fomorians, have returned.

Led by the sadistic Moloch, Sláine struggles with factions who would rather make peace—a peace he believes will not be kept—and, as a result, his wife Naimh is killed. A vast amount of slicing and dicing ensues as a harder, more haggard Sláine seeks his revenge, but discovers that simply killing an enemy leader or three doesn't make for victory.

Review: A definite return to form for Pat Mills's Celtic hero after a period spent time traveling and picking fights with almost every Celtic or ancient British historical figure you can think of. Mills plays with the conventions of his own strip

and develops Sláine's character while returning to one of the strip's central themes: the constraining and wrong-headed nature of a democracy that leads to too much bureaucracy—represented by the tribal council which Sláine, despite being High King of all Ireland, still finds himself disposed to listen to.

Clint Langley's realistic art—which people tend to either love or hate—mixes painting, photography, and digital image-making to produce a rich textural result. Often dark, with details that fill in when subjected to poor printing, it looks much better printed on quality paper than it did in 2000 AD, although some will find Langley's reliance on photographs, particularly for faces, distracting rather than enriching.

While not groundbreaking stuff, *The Books of Invasions* see Pat Mills returning to an old favorite with renewed vigor and paired up with an artist capable of stamping his own visual identity on the character and its world.

FURTHER READING: *Sláine: Warrior's Dawn; Sláine: The Horned God; Sláine The King*
SEE ALSO: *The Book of Ballads; The Chronicles of Conan*

★
★
★
★

Writer: J.M. DeMatteis
Artist: Mike Ploog

Publisher: Hyperion, 2006
ISBN: 0007233388

A

ABADAZAD: THE ROAD TO INCONCEIVABLE

Plot: A young girl, Kate, loses her younger brother, Matt, at a fairground. Five years later, she learns of Abadazad, a fictional storybook world of myth and magic, and is told that her brother has disappeared into this literary setting. Determined to rescue him, she too enters Abadazad with the aid of a glowing blue orb. But what she finds there is far more dangerous than the children's stories suggested.

Review: Reminiscent in places of the fantasy film *Labyrinth* and Clive Barker's *Abarat* series, Abadazad sets out to conjure up the atmosphere and innocence of traditional, old-fashioned children's fairy tales. Unlike most graphic novels, Abadazad experiments with a combination of prose and comic strip to tell its exotic story. (Neil Gaiman's graphic/prose work, *Stardust*, attempted a similar feat in the same genre,

employing a combination of text and full-color paintings). Artist Mike Ploog is a veteran of early 1970s horror comics, and his unique art style—often favorably compared to that of Will Eisner, with his use of wax-like figures—lends this story an enchanting, otherworldly touch. Its strength lies in deploying traditional fantasy elements in a way that is equally appealing to both children and adults.

FURTHER READING: *Abadazad: The Dream Thief*
SEE ALSO: *The Fairy Tales of Oscar Wilde, Volume 1: The Selfish Giant & The Star Child*

Writer: René Goscinny
Artist: Albert Uderzo

Publisher: Orion, 2005
ISBN: 0752866486

(A) # ASTERIX AND THE GREAT CROSSING

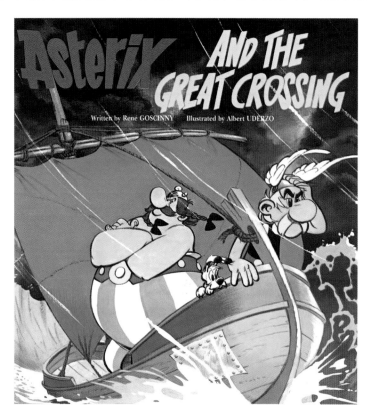

Plot: The year is 50 BC. Asterix the Gaul and his friend Obelix hail from a small village that continues to effortlessly repel its Roman invaders, thanks to a magic potion that gives the drinker superhuman strength. During a fishing trip, the pair are lost at sea after a storm and find themselves—though they don't know it—in North America.

Review: The *Asterix* books are among the best known and most popular of the French bandes dessinées, and have been translated into hundreds of languages. New Asterix adventures have appeared on a regular basis since 1961, and even the death of writer René Goscinny in 1977 has only marginally slowed Albert Uderzo's output. The appeal of the *Asterix* tales lies in their extensive cast of entertaining supporting characters, their punning names (Fulliautomatix

is the village blacksmith), their anachronistic themes and concepts, the running jokes that appear reliably throughout the series, and the fact that the Gauls often resort to—and are hugely fond of—an enormous brawl.

In this volume, much humor is derived from the language barriers Asterix and Obelix encounter, with only Obelix's dog, Dogmatix, able to communicate effectively with a Great Dane belonging to some Hamlet-quoting Vikings. In addition, none of the characters are aware of the magnitude of their respective discoveries: Obelix is convinced that the Native Americans are, in fact, Romans disguised as turkeys.

FURTHER READING: *The Smurfs*
SEE ALSO: *Lucky Luke; Tintin in Tibet*

★
★ **Writer:** Gilbert Hernandez   **Publisher:** Eros Comix, 1992
★ **Artist:** Gilbert Hernandez   **ISBN:** 1560972009

18+ # BIRDLAND

Plot: Fritz, the lisping psychiatrist from Hernandez's *Luba* stories, and her husband Mark form the basis of this highly charged erotic caper. It's less a story than a series of exploits, as both characters have sex with a variety of people, including a pair of strippers who are having problems with rivals stealing their act, and at least one man who seems obsessed with Fritz's lisp. This all leads to a spectacular and epoch-spanning, um, climax.

Review: An unbelievably graphic collection, and certainly not for anyone under the age of 18. Hernandez does squeeze in some plot, but this is essentially a stylistic exercise, and you get the impression he had a lot of fun drawing it. Certainly interesting if you're a *Love & Rockets* fan, but maybe a little repetitive if you're not.

FURTHER READING: *Luba in America; Sloth; Chance in Hell*
SEE ALSO: *Palomar; Locas; Lost Girls*

★
★ **Writer:** Charles Vess & Various   **Publisher:** Tor Books, 2004
★ **Artist:** Charles Vess & Various   **ISBN:** 0765312158

12+ # THE BOOK OF BALLADS

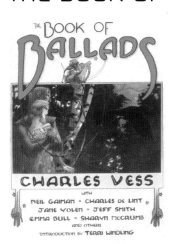

Plot: A collection of works from Charles Vess's self-published miscellany *The Book of Ballads and Sagas*, this volume revisits traditional folk tales and reinvents them for a new audience.

Review: The old ones are often the best, and in this book, Charles Vess, ably assisted by a cast of stellar talents—including Neil Gaiman, Sharyn McCrumb, and Jane Yolen—explores some very old tales indeed.

Folk ballads from all over northern Europe have been told and retold throughout the ages. Here they are adapted for a modern audience, though the book proudly displays the influence of late 19th century illustration. This is obviously a work of love for Vess, whose passions are evident on every page, notably in the intricacy of the linework and the detail of his lettering. It's a beautiful book that should help the ballads live on for another few hundred years.

FURTHER READING: *Stardust; Rose*
SEE ALSO: *Books of Magic; Magic Flute*

Writer: Neil Gaiman
Artists: John Bolton, Charles Vess, Scott Hampton, and Paul Johnson

Publisher: Vertigo, 1993
ISBN: 1852864702

THE BOOKS OF MAGIC

Plot: An assortment of magicians from various DC comics gather to guide and influence Tim Hunter, a young man with the potential to be the most powerful magician of the age, as they introduce him to the prizes and perils of the world of magic.

Review: Ostensibly, this is Neil Gaiman's introduction to the magical fantasy worlds of DC Comics' Vertigo universe, brought to life by his four artistic collaborators whose diverse but sympathetic styles deliver all the magic and majesty of the worlds the writer describes. *The Books of Magic* also offer hints and insights into Gaiman's own *Sandman* series and a variety of other graphic novels from the DC Vertigo stable. Oh, and it manages to fit in the end of the universe, too. An entertaining and rewarding read.

FURTHER READING: *Books of Magic: Summonings; Books of Magic: Girl in a Box; The Names of Magic*
SEE ALSO: *Books of Magic: Bindings; Hellblazer: All His Engines*

Writer: John Ney Rieber
Artist: Gary Amaro; Peter Gross

Publisher: Vertigo, 1995
ISBN: 1563891875

THE BOOKS OF MAGIC: BINDINGS

Plot: Tim Hunter, now informed as to his possible future as the world's greatest magician, seeks to further his understanding by returning to the land of Faerie. However the world of twilight is withering away, threatened by an ancient creature known as the Manticore.

Review: This is the first collection of the 75 issue series that ran after Neil Gaiman's initial 4 part run. By this time Vertigo had established itself away from the DC Universe, and the story furthers Tim's connection with Faerie (something that would continue throughout the series). The art of Peter Gross became the main look for *The Books of Magic*, and John Ney Rieber wrote most of the series, keeping the writing constant, and the series enjoyable.

FURTHER READING: *Books of Faerie; Books of Magic: Death After Death; Books of Magic: Summonings*
SEE ALSO: *Books of Magic; Sandman; Dream Country; Death: The High Cost of Living*

★
★
★

Writer: Linda Medley
Artist: Linda Medley

Publisher: Fantagraphics, 2006
ISBN: 1560977477

15+ CASTLE WAITING

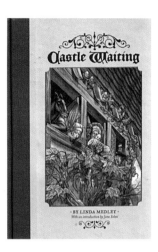

Plot: A series of newly adapted fairy tales, *Castle Waiting* takes *Sleeping Beauty* as its starting point. When Beauty is awakened by her prince, the rest of the kingdom also wakes up, but Beauty abandons her former home for her new life with Prince Charming. The Castle Waiting becomes a legendary refuge for society's misfits, and is sought out by the Lady Jain, a heavily pregnant princess with a secret. Once inside, we're introduced to the castle's inhabitants, and hear their stories of faeries and bearded nuns.

Review: Despite the fairy tale stories and the medieval setting, there's a thoroughly modern sensibility at work in *Castle Waiting*. The characters are endearing and well-rounded, and Medley's art is wonderful throughout, bringing every member of the large cast to life. Not just for readers of traditional fantasy.

FURTHER READING: *Fables: March of the Wooden Soldiers*
SEE ALSO: *Bone; Fables: Legends in Exile*

★
★
★

Writer: Vaughn Bode
Artist: Vaughn Bode

Publisher: Fantagraphics, 1990
ISBN: 1560970421

15+ CHEECH WIZARD

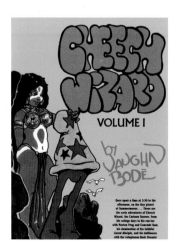

Plot: Plot? What plot? In *Cheech Wizard*, Bode created his own humorous, erotic world full of squishy creatures and rotund humans that has its own internal—and visual—logic. The Cheech Wizard, who speaks a kind of patois, is constantly hidden under an outsize hat from which only his legs protrude. Always looking for a good scam, and frequently drunk or high, he's the antithesis of a guru—but he often offers pearls of wisdom without realizing he'd doing it.

Review: Inexorably linked to the 1960s counterculture, *Cheech Wizard* is a strip you either get or you don't. The confused and poetic language harks back to childhood, while the rounded illustration style and bright colors had a significant influence on 1970s graffiti artists.

FURTHER READING: *Junkwaffel; Deadbone*
SEE ALSO: *The Frank Book; Moomin;*
The Adventures of Tony Millionaire's Sock Monkey

Writer: Wang Du Lu, So Man Sing
Artist: Andy Seto

Publisher: HK Comics Ltd, 2005
ISBN: 9889797275

5+

CROUCHING TIGER, HIDDEN DRAGON VOLUME 1

Plot: Crack swordsman Golden Sword sets out to avenge his father's murder at the hands of another legendary fighter, Grand Yu, while a different kind of warrior, Li Mu Bai, is content to sit on a rock and use his mental powers to divert the flow of the river below him. Golden Sword's men attack Grand Yu and his daughter, Yu Shu Lien, but she is able to fight them off thanks to her extraordinary skills. When Li Mu Bai meets (and fights) her for the first time he is smitten, but discovers that she is already betrothed to another.

Review: Be prepared for the action to move a little slower than in the acclaimed film, based on the fourth of Wang Du Lu's novels. This is an establishing book, where the characters are introduced and the groundwork is laid for the adventures

and tragedies to come. Andy Seto's artwork is very pleasing to the Western eye—highly detailed, much more balanced in composition, and less distorted in form than many Oriental comics. There is no such thing as an ugly character in *Crouching Tiger*, although there is an occasional sense of stiffness and daintiness in the fighting.

FURTHER READING: *Crouching Tiger, Hidden Dragon Volumes 2–12; The Four Constables*
SEE ALSO: *Blade of the Immortal; Crying Freeman*

★ **Writer:** Neil Gaiman
★ **Artists:** Chris Bachalo,
★ Mark Buckingham, Dave McKean

Publisher: Vertigo, 1994
ISBN: 1563891336

15+ DEATH: THE HIGH COST OF LIVING

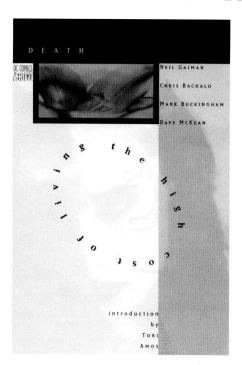

Plot: *Death: the High Cost of Living* centers on a teenage girl named Didi, who at first appears to be an eccentric, orphaned goth, but is acutally the personification of Death. She guides a young boy, Sexton, on a journey of self discovery. In this captivating tale Didi seeks to understand more about the people she visits during their last moments on Earth. In one encounter, Didi and Sexton are confronted by an old woman who has been waiting for Death to help her find her heart—which she had hidden from Death in the first place in an attempt to remain alive.

Review: Written by the award-winning Neil Gaiman, this tale is based on the notion that "One day in every century, Death walks the Earth to better understand those to whom she will be the final visitor." Not unlike Gaiman's *Sandman* series, the story unfolds in a very delicate fashion, offering small nuggets of reality here and there that enable the reader to connect with the story. It will make you smile, and you'll feel a sense of achievement when you finish it.

FURTHER READING: *Death: The Time of Your Life; Death: At Death's Door; Sandman Volumes 1–11*
SEE ALSO: *Sandman: Preludes and Nocturnes; Books of Magic: Bindings*

Writer: Joann Sfar
Artist: Lewis Trondheim

Publisher: NBM Publishing, 2004
ISBN: 1561634018

Ⓐ DUNGEON VOLUME 1: DUCK HEART

Plot: The Dungeon is an immense castle, filled with strange creatures and phantoms. It's a little world in its own right, overseen by the Dungeon Keeper, who can depend on the likes of Herbert the Duck and Marvin the Dragon to help him defend it from the many disgusting things that want its treasures for themselves. Here, they pose as interior decorators in an effort to infiltrate the headquarters of the soul-eating Hooded Ones.

Review: Sfar's zany comedy delights in parodying fantasy adventure stories by pushing everything to the limit and mixing classic scenarios with the absurdly mundane—Conan never called in the interior decorators. Trondheim's visualization of the dungeon creates a cohesive, but very odd, world, and is terrifically entertaining.

FURTHER READING: *Dungeon Volume 2: The Barbarian Princess; Dungeon Parade; Dungeon Twilight; Dungeon: The Early Years; The Professor's Daughter*
SEE ALSO: *Asterix and the Great Crossing*

Writer: Richard & Wendy Pini
Artist: Wendy Pini

Publisher: DC Comics, 2003
ISBN: 1401201288

2+ ELFQUEST ARCHIVES VOLUME 1

Plot: This early independent comics project started as a magazine in the late 1970s and spun off into countless storylines in later comics. *Elfquest* has always attracted a lot of otherwise non-comics-reading fantasy fans. It concerns the adventures of a group of wolf-riding, part-cute, part-sexy elves who are driven out of their home and set out to find a new one away from enemy humans. They encounter numerous other groups of elf-folk along the way, some of whom they previously believed to be legendary.

Review: The earliest and simplest *Elfquest* stories are definitely the best. The Pinis' work is driven by plot and character, and in these early stories the range of characters among the Wolfriders is clearly delineated. Wendy Pini's art is fresh and extremely pretty.

FURTHER READING: *Elfquest Archives Volume 2*
SEE ALSO: *The Book of Ballads; The Chronicles of Conan*

★
★
★

Writer: Bill Willingham
Artists: John Bolton, Charles Vess,
Michael Kaluta, Jill Thompson,

Esao Andrews, Mark Wheatley, Tara
McPherson, Mark Buckingham, James
Jean, Derek Kirk Kim, Brian Bolland.

Publisher: Vertigo, 2006
ISBN: 1401203671

15+ # FABLES: 1001 NIGHTS OF SNOWFALL

Plot: A collection of reinterpreted classic fairy tales wrapped in a framing sequence derived from the story of *Scheherazade* (*The Arabian Nights*). The stories include a whodunnit mystery built around *Snow White and the Seven Dwarves*; a sequel to *Hansel and Gretel*; a morality tale based on *Reynard the Fox*, and the origin of the Big Bad Wolf, among others.

Review: Effectively a prequel to Willingham's ongoing *Fables* title—where characters from myth and folklore are exiled to contemporary America—it's also a showcase for many leading fantasy artists to indulge in flights of fancy. Unfortunately, the individual stories lose much of their impact if you are not already familiar with the characters, or curious about their back stories.

FURTHER READING: *Jack of Fables: The (Nearly) Great Escape*
SEE ALSO: *Fables Volume 1: Legends in Exile; Fairy Tales of Oscar Wilde, Vol. 1*

★
★
★
★

Writer: Oscar Wilde
Artist: P Craig Russell

Publisher: NBM, 2003
ISBN: 156163056X

A # FAIRY TALES OF OSCAR WILDE, VOL. 1: THE SELFISH GIANT & THE STAR CHILD

Plot: Adapting two of Oscar Wilde's classic fairy tales, *The Selfish Giant* tells the story of an ogre-like creature who prevents children from entering his garden, only to discover that doing so brings winter to his land. *The Star Child* features a handsome, but vain and selfish boy who insults a dishevelled beggar, only to find his features become hideous as a result.

Review: Oscar Wilde's turn of the century prose and Russell's art are made for one another. At his finest, Russell's fantasy art resembles a cross between the simple pen and ink style of Aubrey Beardsley and the flamboyant and colourful art nouveau style of Alfons Mucha. The adaptations in this volume are faithful works that preserve the magic of Wilde's original writing.

FURTHER READING: *The Fairy Tales of Oscar Wilde, Vol. 2*
SEE ALSO: *The Magic Flute*

Writer: Jim Woodring
Artist: Jim Woodring

Publisher: Fantagraphics, 2003
ISBN: 1560975342

THE FRANK BOOK

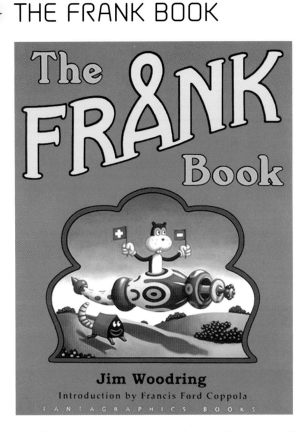

Plot: All two-dozen *Frank* adventures are collected in this beautiful hardback package, introduced by Francis Ford Coppola, no less. Frank is Woodring's "Everyanimal"—mildly curious, furry, of indeterminate species, and wandering through a strange, decorative landscape. Frank is a mostly likeable central character, although he is subject to fits of rage. He looks after other creatures and tries to protect them, and himself, from the base Manhog and the demonic Whim, who seem to represent facets of human nature—even though he often doesn't understand what's going on himself. Wordless, the strips unfold like dreams that often threaten to become nightmares.

Review: Woodring's art, with its rounded figures echoing the style of early Disney characters, extremely controlled linework, and beautiful hatching technique, deserves a showcase like this. An extremely assured storyteller, despite the limitations of his chosen form, Woodring devises an internal visual logic that ties the material together, no matter how strange events seem to become, making this a work that children easily identify with on an intuitive level, yet will still delight adult minds.

FURTHER READING: *Tantalizing Stories; Freaks; The Acme Novelty Library*
SEE ALSO: *Trosper; Jimmy Corrigan; Krazy & Ignatz*

★
★   **Writer:** Yuu Watase
★   **Artist:** Yuu Watase

Publisher: VIZ Media LLC, 2003
ISBN: 156931957X

A FUSHIGI YUGI

Plot: Schoolgirls Miaka and Yui find themselves mysteriously transported into a book called The Universe of the Four Gods that contains a story set in ancient China. Yui manages to return home, but Miaka is told she is a priestess of the phoenix god Suzaku and must find the seven Celestial Warriors, who are her protectors. Then she will find her true love and be able to return home. Later, Yui returns to the world of the book and becomes Miaka's enemy, the priestess of Seiryu.

Review: This begins as a light-hearted romantic adventure, but grows more serious as Miaka's quest continues and the stakes become higher.

FURTHER READING: *Fushigi Yugi: Disciple; Fushigi Yugi: Oracle*
SEE ALSO: *Inu Yasha*

★
★   **Writer:** Rumiko Takahashi
★   **Artist:** Rumiko Takahashi
★

Publisher: VIZ Media LLC, 2003
ISBN: 1569319472

INUYASHA VOLUME 1

Plot: Kagome is a schoolgirl dragged into Japan's past by a demon. She wakes the half-demon InuYasha, and the Shikon jewel he had been searching for, is shattered. Now they must work together to restore the jewel before its power is stolen by numerous other demons who want it for themselves. With help from Myoga the Flea, a servant of InuYasha's, the pair face the malevolent demons who are looking for the jewel shards, all the while (slowly) developing a romantic interest in each other.

Review: Takahashi's romantic comedy (part of an ongoing series) is certainly on a par with her best material. The grotesque demons and dangerous situations make this a more disturbing work than you might expect though.

FURTHER READING: *InuYasha Volumes 2–31*
SEE ALSO: *Ranma ½; Maison Ikkoku*

Writer: Roman Dirge
Artist: Roman Dirge

Publisher: SLG Publishing, 1999
ISBN: 0943151031

LENORE: NOOGIES

Plot: Lenore is a cute little dead girl who doesn't really understand how life (or death) works. Her presence normally results in the death of someone or something—not necessarily due to any malicious intent on her part, simply because she is out of place in the world of the living. The supporting characters are usually dead, too—including Ragamuffin, the eternal vampire scourge, and Mr Gosh, the world's most persistent suitor, who doesn't seem to understand that being repeatedly killed is a sign of rejection.

Review: This is humor at its blackest, but it's often very funny indeed. The twisted Lenore, with her large, round-eyed head on a small, thin body, seems unreal, but is carefully and precisely drawn. Strange, but in a good way.

FURTHER READING: *Lenore: Wedgies; Lenore: Cooties!;*
Something at the Window is Scratching
SEE ALSO: *Hell Baby; Hino Horror*

Writer: Peter Tomasi
Artist: Peter Snejbjerg

Publisher: DC Comics
ISBN: 1401207952

LIGHT BRIGADE

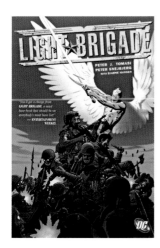

Plot: Stuck in Europe in World War II, a small group of G.I.s, are caught-up in a heavenly battle between angels and demons over the Sword of God, while simultaneously trying to defeat zombie German soldiers!

Review: This excellent tale seems a tad out of step at DC and would have fitted in better at its sister imprint, Vertigo. The story reads like a cross between *Sgt. Rock* and *Preacher*, and Tomasi's skill at pacing, characterization, and dialogue keep the story rattling along. Snejbjerg's art is exquisite—made even better by Bjarne Hanse's stunning coloring—and treads a fine line between the horrific and the humorous. When originally released, the series, unfairly, received very little attention, but this is a gem that's definitely worth hunting out.

FURTHER READING: *Lucifer: A Dalliance with the Damned;*
Damn Nation
SEE ALSO: *Preacher: Gone to Texas; Sgt Rock Archives Vol. 1*

★
★ **Writer:** Vittorio Giardino   **Publisher:** Heavy Metal, 2006
★ **Artist:** Vittorio Giardino   **ISBN:** 1932413626

18+ # LITTLE EGO

Plot: Ego keeps having these strange sexual dreams, and every time she wakes up she wonders what her therapist will make of them. She seems to be consulting an ineffectual shrink, because they return again and again, whenever she goes to bed, and they seem to be getting increasingly odd.

Review: Who would have thought that Vittorio Giardino, best known for his painstakingly twisty spy stories, had so much naughtiness in him? Parodying *Little Nemo in Slumberland*, Giardino creates a series of erotic vignettes for his very sweet and innocent heroine to experience. Although very attractive, the art is a little clinical in its neatness. Some of the early concepts are pretty far out, but the stories soon turn back to more traditional themes like lesbianism and erotic kidnapping.

FURTHER READING: *No Pasaran! Volumes 1 and 2; Butterscotch; Gullivera by Milo Manara*
SEE ALSO: *Click; Omaha the Cat Dancer; Orient Gateway*

★
★ **Writer:** Mike Carey   **Publisher:** Vertigo, 2001
★ **Artist:** Scott Hampton and various   **ISBN:** 1563897334
★

15+ # LUCIFER VOLUME 1:
DEVIL IN THE GATEWAY

Plot: Spinning off from Neil Gaiman's *Sandman*, Lucifer has renounced the throne of Hell, had his wings removed, and is now running a bar with his former consort and protector. When an angel arrives to offer him a job, Lucifer shows that despite his loss of position, he's still more than able to live up to his role as the Prince of Lies, while trying to discover why Heaven is relying on an agent of Hell to do its dirty work.

Review: A worthy spinoff from Gaiman's seminal series. Carey does a great job of capturing the characters, and retains the mix of fantasy and horror that was the hallmark of the *Sandman*.

FURTHER READING: *Lucifer Volumes 2–11; Sandman: Season of Mists; God Save The Queen*
SEE ALSO: *Hellblazer: All His Engines*

Writer: Metaphrog
Artist: Metaphrog

Publisher: Metaphrog, 2001
ISBN: 095349327X

LOUIS: LYING TO CLIVE

Plot: Louis is taken from his home in Hamlet to a bee farm, where he is forced to mine Monetorium from the caves to pay for his wrongdoing. Befriending Clive, one of the bees, Louis makes an enemy of the farm's Chief Executive Officer, Clammy, who hypnotizes Clive into attempting to kill Louis.

Review: Metaphrog's beautifully produced, small-press Louis albums are a visual treat. The colorful artwork is very much in the style of a children's storybook, yet this dark story is set in what is effectively a concentration camp run by Clammy who, feeling humiliated by Louis, is prepared to have him murdered.

This surreal and often disturbing story examines the control of the individual by authority and touches on various aspects of the forced labor camp without entirely fleshing them out. As the second *Louis* book, it does not stand alone easily. While the story may be intriguing, it is ultimately unsatisfying, leaving you wanting to read more about the melancholic Louis and his pet bird.

FURTHER READING: *Louis: Red Letter Day;*
Louis: The Clown's Last Words
SEE ALSO: *Maus*

★
★
★

Writer: Wolfgang Amadeus Mozart; P. Craig Russell
Artist: P. Craig Russell

Publisher: NBM, 2003
ISBN: 1561633518

A THE MAGIC FLUTE

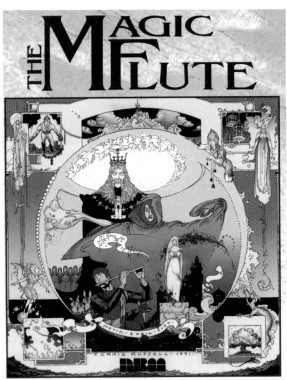

Plot: Sarastro, priest of Iris and Osiris, has captured beautiful Pamina, daughter of the Queen of the Night, and taken her to his temple, where he intends to free her from her mother's influence. Prince Tamino, a traveler lost and alone, is attacked by a serpent. While unconscious he's rescued by three female servants of the Queen of the Night, who kill the serpent, but Papageno, the exotic bird catcher, tricks him into believing it was he who killed the serpent. The Queen offers her daughter's hand to Tamino if he will rescue her, and he sets off with Papageno, carrying with him a magic flute that has the power to change mens' hearts. But on reaching Sarastro's stronghold he realizes the priest is not evil as he'd been told, and agrees to undergo three trials to win Pamina's freedom. Through these he learns about himself and the power of love.

Review: P. Craig Russell's ornate, highly stylized art, influenced by the Aesthetic movement and featuring flowing lines and densely patterned elements, is particularly appropriate to adapting operas—which we are used to seeing with lavish sets and costumes. Russell draws dramatically, with a great sense of broad gesture and exaggerated emotion, and illuminates Mozart's comic tale.

FURTHER READING: *Elric: The Dreaming City;*
Night Music; The Fairy Tales of Oscar Wilde Vol. 2
SEE ALSO: *The Chronicles of Conan; Moonshadow;*
The Book of Ballads; The Books of Magic

Writer: Tove Jansson
Artist: Tove Jansson

Publisher: Drawn and Quarterly, 2006
ISBN: 1894937805

ⒶMOOMIN: THE COMPLETE TOVE JANSSON COMIC STRIP (VOL. 1)

Plot: In an imaginary world, Moomin lives, loves, and longs for peace. Along with his family, his girlfriend Snorkmaiden, his friend Sniff, and an ever-growing cast of characters, Moomin deals with problems such as unwanted guests and shipwrecks with quiet perseverance and a wry sense of humor.

Review: Jansson's *Moomin* novels are better known than her comic strip, which was originally published in England rather than her native Finland. This collection deservedly brings her delightful comic storytelling to a wider audience. Although the Moomintrolls bear a slight resemblance to large hippopotami, Jansson's delicate linework and clean compositions are light and gentle. The strips' subtle use of tiny characters and decorative elements reward repeated reading as much as the sweetly melancholy stories themselves.

FURTHER READING: *Moomin: The Complete Tove Jansson Comic Strip Vol. 2*
SEE ALSO: *Bone: Out From Boneville*

Writer: Kosuke Fujishima
Artist: Kosuke Fujishima

Publisher: Dark Horse, 2005
ISBN: 1845764854

ⒶOH MY GODDESS VOLUME 1

Plot: Impoverished student Keiichi, phoning for a takeout, accidentally calls the Goddess Helpline, and is sent the rather fetching Belldandy to grant him a wish. Without thinking, he wishes she would stay with him forever, but Keiichi soon finds that having a goddess as a roommate isn't easy.

Review: Flirty comedy in the *I Dream of Jeanie* mould that helped establish a manga subgenre. Volume 1 is fairly straightforward as Keiichi tries to hide Belldandy's nature and she tries to use her goddess powers to assist him, often at cross purposes. The art is very pretty, and the pacing extremely swift, which makes up for the fact that the plots are often repetitive and definitely a little absurd.

FURTHER READING: *Oh My Goddess Volumes 2-29*
SEE ALSO: *Maison Ikkoku, Ranma ½*

★
★ **Writer:** Eiichiro Oda **Publisher:** Viz Media LLC, 2003
★ **Artist:** Eiichiro Oda **ISBN:** 1569319014

A # ONE PIECE VOLUME 1: ROMANCE DAWN

Plot: Meet Monkey D. Luffy, the pint-sized would-be pirate who is out to fulfill his dreams and find the fabled One Piece treasure, all with a little help from the rubbery powers he gained from eating the Gum-Gum Devil fruit.

Review: Full of pirates and slapstick silliness, *One Piece* is a prime example of the kind of sprawling adventures that manga does best. From the artwork to the script, the characters' expressions and gestures to the bizarre quests, everything about the strip is exaggerated. The plot may be improbable, the story may go on and on, but it has enough momentum, spirit, and adventure to carry you along with it.

FURTHER READING: *One Piece Vol. 2-17*
SEE ALSO: *Inu Yasha Vol. 1; Fushigi Yugi*

★
★ **Writer:** Farel Dalrymple **Publisher:** Dark Horse, 2003
★ **Artist:** Farel Dalrymple **ISBN:** 1569719349
★

15+ # POP GUN WAR

Plot: An angel crashlands in New York and quickly abandons its wings in a nearby trashcan. Sinclair, a young, emotionally troubled boy, rescues the wings and makes them his own.

Review: A cast of surreal, dreamlike characters populates Dalrymple's narrative in a sublime and understated way. This approach renders scenes such as an airborne Sinclair and a floating fish with glasses more credible and three-dimensional than a horde of caped-crusading, spandex-wearing superheroes. But it's not all whimsy—there is a hard edge to the events that is sometimes uncomfortable, and sometimes implausible. However, all of it is well observed and the story becomes deeply personal for the reader, as well as the writer.

FURTHER READING: *Jenny Finn; Project Superior*
SEE ALSO: *Contract with God Trilogy*

Writer: Jill Thompson
Artist: Jill Thompson

Publisher: Sirius Entertainment, 2000
ISBN: 1579890385

Ⓐ SCARY GODMOTHER: THE BOO FLU

Plot: In this, the fourth book in the *Scary Godmother* series, Halloween is once again fast approaching, but this year, Scary Godmother has caught the dreaded Boo Flu. She's confined to bed, so there's no one to take care of the Halloween preparations. Her friend Hannah Marie volunteers for the task, but swiftly realizes that it's a far bigger job than she'd thought. Will she be able to get it all done in time, even with the help of some fanged friends?

Review: A cross between a comic and a children's book, *Scary Godmother* is little known, but exceptionally good. Jill Thompson's beautiful watercolor art is wonderfully macabre, with all of the horrors set at exactly the right level for kids, without being saccharine. All ages, but with bite!

FURTHER READING: *Scary Godmother: Spooktacular Stories; Scary Godmother: Wild About Harry; Scary Godmother: Ghoul's Out For Summer*
SEE ALSO: *Owly; Bone: Out From Boneville*

Writer: Andi Watson
Artist: Andi Watson

Publisher: SLG Publishing, 1996
ISBN: 0943151120

Ⓐ SKELETON KEY VOLUME 1: BEYOND THE THRESHOLD

Plot: Tamsin Mary Cates lives a life of quiet desperation in a small town where nothing ever seems to happen—until, one Halloween, she finds a very unusual key hidden in a fancy-dress skeleton costume. The Skeleton Key has the ability to unlock a door to anywhere—any dimension, any location—and Tamsin soon meets Kitsune, a Japanese fox spirit addicted to sugary sweets, along with an assortment of weird and wonderful characters who are guaranteed to make sure that life for this teenager will never be the same again.

Review: Strong manga-influenced artwork and kooky, inventive characters make *Skeleton Key* a great read. Andi Watson effortlessly blends Japanese and British cultures and art styles, and his storytelling is superb. This is a delight for any age, but is particularly suited to younger readers.

FURTHER READING: *Love Fights; Glister; Little Star*
SEE ALSO: *Slow News Day; Sandman: Dream Country; Moomin*

★
★
★
★

Writer: Joe Kelly
Artist: Chris Bachalo

Publisher: Wildstorm, 2001
ISBN: 1563897628

15+ # STEAMPUNK: MANIMATRON

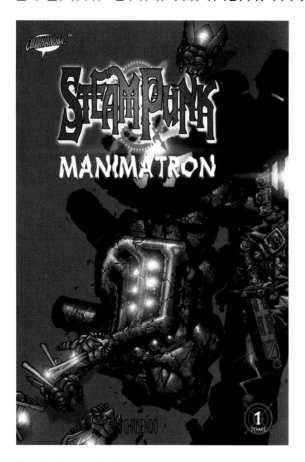

Plot: Cole Blaquesmith wakes up from a coma after more than a century to find that the world has changed radically around him. He's gained a startling new appendage—a mechanical arm—and the drastic changes to Victorian London are all quite alarming. We follow Cole as he leads a resistance effort against the evil Lord Absinthe.

Review: This book is a triumph for the steampunk genre. So many authors and artists have missed the mark so completely that when Bachalo and Kelly entered the fray and released the highly impressive *Steampunk: Manimatron*, it came as a delightful surprise. Bachalo has crafted a tale of revolution within a steampunk world that many will wish had in fact been the reality of Victorian London, while Joe Kelly's artwork has magnificently embraced the spirit of the steampunk style and is peppered with ingenious contraptions.

FURTHER READING: *Steampunk: Drama Obscura*
SEE ALSO: *Girl Genius; The League of Extraordinary Gentlemen; Scarlet Traces*

Writer: Dave Cooper
Artist: Dave Cooper

Publisher: Fantagraphics, 2002
ISBN: 1560973013

SUCKLE: THE STATUS OF BASIL

Plot: Emerging from an egg on a strange, yet familiar world, with psychosexual overtones, Basil travels through bizarre landscapes until he reaches an amazing city and encounters a bewildering array of city dwellers who are out to both help and hinder him in discovering his identity.

Review: Dave Cooper's organic artwork makes what could be a very disturbing book almost cute, with Basil himself an extremely likable naïf, adrift in a world that's far more cynical and screwed up than he is. This is a seriously explicit book, but Cooper's surreal style makes (almost) everything appealing. There are some lovely observations on life and relationships, with a wonderful menagerie of characters, and ultimately this is an extremely rewarding book, with something new to discover on each successive read. Cooper has a very weird imagination, though.

FURTHER READING: *Crumple: The Status of Knuckle; Ripple: A Predilection for Tina*
SEE ALSO: *The Complete Frank; Gregory*

Writer: Jean Van Hamme
Artist: Grzegorz Rosinski

Publisher: Cinebook Ltd, 2007
ISBN: 1905460236

THORGAL: CHILD OF THE STARS

Plot: Although he was raised by Vikings, Thorgal exhibits strange characteristics such as compassion—not exactly a desirable trait for a Viking warrior. His son, Johan, displays supernatural powers, and his daughter, Louve, can talk to animals. Throughout the 29 volumes of this saga, Thorgal and his family struggle to be accepted and to meet the strange challenges he seems destined to encounter. *Child of the Stars (Volume 7)* collects three stories that explore Thorgal's origins.

Review: *Child of the Stars* gives the game away, so you may prefer to start at Volume 1 and read them in order—but all volumes are enjoyable in themselves. Van Hamme is a reliable plotter, and Rosinski an extremely polished artist. Together they've produced a worthy successor to Prince Valiant, with more modern sensibilities.

FURTHER READING: *Code XIII; Largo Winch; The Francis Blake Affair*
SEE ALSO: *Prince Valiant; Slaine: The Books of Invasions*

★ **Writer:** Rich Koslowski **Publisher:** Top Shelf, 2002
★ **Artist:** Rich Koslowski **ISBN:** 1891830317
★
★

15+ # THREE FINGERS

Plot: A dark tale in the form of a documentary that explores the sinister reason why so many classic cartoon characters only have three fingers on each hand...

Review: The first thing you'll notice about *Three Fingers* is its unusual format, wider than it is tall. But the format, with proportions reminiscent of a TV screen, is entirely appropriate for the documentary style of the narrative. In a series of interviews with an assortment of easily recognizable (though non-copyright-infringing) characters based loosely on existing cartoons, we are drawn into a compelling tale of darkness at the heart of the Hollywood dream.

FURTHER READING: *The King*
SEE ALSO: *Cerebus: High Society; Quimby the Mouse*

Writer: Patrick Atangan
Artist: Patrick Atangan

Publisher: NBM, 2002
ISBN: 1561633313

THE YELLOW JAR: TWO TALES FROM JAPANESE TRADITION (VOL. 1)

Plot: This book features two folk tales from Japan. The Yellow Jar is about a fisherman named Nikotuchi, who finds a magical jar that has an enchanted maiden named O Haru San inside. The fisherman wins the maiden's heart and they marry, but when she learns that he lied about the whereabouts of her magical jar, she leaves him. The fisherman realizes he has betrayed his wife's trust and sets off to win her back—but she has been captured by a ferocious demon. The second tale is entitled Two Chrysanthemum Maidens and tells how a renowned gardener named Issa finds two strange weeds that look like women. Issa toys with the idea of destroying them— until they grow into beautiful flowers.

Review: The first in an occasional series from Patrick Atangan, recounting myths from different cultures. These ancient tales offer moral lessons: in the fisherman's case, that true love must be based on real trust, and in the gardener's case, that beauty exists in all things, but it takes an open mind to see it. The stories are charming, but the highlight is Atangan's beautiful artwork. He employs a ukiyo-e style, which translates as "world of floating pictures," and this gives the tales a sense of authenticity. The color palette is so sumptuous that you can luxuriate in the artwork long after the story has been digested.

FURTHER READING: *The Silk Tapestry And Other Chinese Folk Tales*
SEE ALSO: *Buddha: Vol. 1; Usagi Yojimbo*

ESSENTIAL
GRAPHIC NOVELS

500

185

FANTASY
The best of the rest

CHAPTER 5
GENERAL FICTION

THE INFINITE CANVAS

In 1990, comics maestro Scott McCloud set his friend and fellow cartoonist Steve Bissette a challenge: to create a complete 24-page comic, with all art and lettering, in 24 hours. The finished product could be on any subject as long as it was started and finished in a single 24-hour period. Both McCloud and Bissette rose to the challenge and other creators, both professional and non-professional, soon followed, all starting with blank pages—an infinite canvas—and filling them with a made-up story. Many collections of 24-hour comics have been published since.

The genre of graphic fiction is like those 24-hour comics. The comic books in this category may bear little similarity to each other in terms of subject matter, but they are all products of the infinite canvas.

It was the infinite canvas, among other things, that prompted the legendary creator Will Eisner to return to comic-strip fiction in the late 1970s, after years of producing maintenance manuals for the US military. *A Contract With God* was the author's self-conscious attempt to "adhere to a rule of realism that requires that caricature or exaggeration accept the limitations of actuality." The result, the first "graphic novel" to be described as such by its author, was a fiction that attempted to keep itself pure of genre. It wasn't so much a novel as a collection of four tales linked together only by their setting—the New York City slums of the early 20th century that Eisner knew so well, his knowledge demonstrated by small details in the artwork such as the peeling plasterwork and the period costumes. In terms of narrative and structure, *A Contract With God* eloquently expresses Eisner's aspirations for the boundless possibilities of graphic novels, and has provided inspiration for most of the creators that have followed in his footsteps.

Another exceptional piece of graphic fiction that takes full advantage of the infinite canvas is *Cerebus*, by Canadian comics eccentric Dave Sim. Started as a monthly comic in 1977, the year before Eisner's volume, *Cerebus* is nothing if not ambitious. Twenty-six years in the making and running to over 6,000 pages, *Cerebus* follows the life of the eponymous character—a mean, misanthropic, little gray aardvark—from his beginnings as a mercenary in a preindustrial setting, through various political and religious struggles, to his ultimate death in extreme old age in a manner long promised in the narrative. This immense feat of imagination required considerable discipline. Every month, Sim—assisted by the background artist, Gerhard—churned out the pages, crafting storylines that would frequently take years to come to fruition.

The Hernandez brothers, Gilbert and Jaime, shared this commitment to their own idiosyncratic vision. Originally publishing their work together in an anthology entitled *Love and Rockets*, the pair broke new ground in the 1980s by crafting well-developed tales of strong, yet entirely fallible, women. Jaime's stories, collected in *Locas*, usually focus on Maggie, a curvaceous Latina, and her friends living in southern California as they slowly outgrow their younger punk-rock lives. Gilbert's stories, by contrast, focus on the life of Luba, the well-endowed illegitimate child of a beauty queen with mob connections.

The secret of some of the best graphic fiction lies in the details. One great example of this is *Jar of Fools*, Jason Lutes's tale of hope amid the imperfect relationships and urban sprawl of Seattle. Every line, whether written or drawn, is precisely focused on communicating the sense of decay and brokenness that haunts Ernie Weiss, the failed stage magician at the center of the story. The environment mirrors the entropy at the heart of the narrative, and it's evident in every panel—in every tangled telephone wire, garbage-strewn back alley, and dirty overpass.

Building on this highly detailed approach, Lutes has since assumed a greater challenge in the shape of Berlin, a three-volume portrait of the German city during the Weimar period.

As well as being a place of imagination, fiction is an arena where those who are marginalized by mainstream society can explore their identities, ideas, and beliefs. The lesbian, gay, bisexual, and transgender communities, as well as ethnic and religious minorities, have often found fiction to be a powerful mode of expression. With a grass roots approach akin to that employed by the underground comix artists of the 1960s, comics by, for, and about lesbians and gays found their audience on their own terms. Standout examples include Alison Bechdel's *Dykes to Watch Out For*, in which elements of lesbian soap opera are combined with op-ed commentary, and Howard Cruse's *Stuck Rubber Baby*, a coming-of-age tale with a civil-rights message.

Fiction is a place where unpalatable truths can be examined. In *The Tale of One Bad Rat*, Bryan Talbot creates his own stories as well as referring to the works of Beatrix Potter to deal with the subject of child sex abuse in a way that speaks to the reader more eloquently than any official report on the subject ever could—haunting, touching, and ultimately empowering. At the opposite end of the spectrum is Max's *Bardin the Superrealist*, a journey through surreal art and language that exposes the fun, playful side of the infinite canvas.

Of course, the boundaries of fiction are quite arbitrary. Many fiction genres have struck out on their own to claim their own section in libraries, bookshops, and in this very book. What remains is a mixed bag. While they might have little in common in terms of subject matter or form, they all share the desire to make their mark on the infinite canvas.

★ **Writer:** Max
★ **Artist:** Max

Publisher: Fantagraphics, 2006
ISBN: 1560977590
★
★
★

15+ BARDÍN THE SUPERREALIST –

Plot: More a picaresque meditation than a continuous narrative, *Bardín the Superrealist* chronicles a man's search for enlightenment over a series of wildly different, but always surreal, landscapes. From the Andalusian Dog to Saint Ceremonio, Martyr to a bare-bottomed Japanese apparition, Bardín's potential spirit-guides confuse and confound more than instruct. Or do they?

Review: Don't let Max's exquisitely drawn and perfectly colorful art, or the hilarious jokes throughout the book, fool you into thinking this is a comedy. Well, go ahead and chuckle, even though the humor arises from the recognition of—and confusion over—life's possible meaning. After you stop laughing, you'll start thinking; Max's images and ideas will remain long after the laughter.

FURTHER READING: *Bosnian Flat Dog; Maybe Later*
SEE ALSO: *The Extended Dream of Mr. D*

★
★
★
★
★

Writer: Dave Sim   **Publisher:** Aardvaark-Vanheim, 1987, 1988
Artist: Dave Sim and Gerhard   **ISBN:** 0919359094

15+

CEREBUS: CHURCH AND STATE

Plot: Cerebus is an aardvark in a fantasy human world. A fierce, amoral mercenary, he is primarily motivated by the desire for ale and the money to buy it. After acquiring political ambitions in *High Society* (the preceding volume in the *Cerebus* saga), Cerebus returns in *Church and State* to become Prime Minister as an instrument of Adam Weisshaupt, who is trying to organize a union of states against the Cirinists.

When he then causes Cerebus to be appointed Pope of the Eastern Church of Tarim, Weisshaupt's plans start to fall apart as he has reckoned without Cerebus's greed. With no one to stop him, Cerebus uses his absolute power to demand that everyone give him all of their gold or else they'll die horribly. An invasion by the giant, Thrunk, temporarily halts his plans and he is forced to put Astoria, leader of the Kevillists, on trial for the assassination of the Western Pope. During the trial, Cerebus ascends to the moon (as previously predicted), and meets the cosmic Judge, who observes everything and condemns Cerebus for his past actions. The Judge describes the origins of Cerebus's world and predicts that Cerebus will die "alone, unmourned, and unloved." Falling back to earth, Cerebus discovers that, in his absence, the Cirinists have invaded and his empire has collapsed.

Review: Initially a humorous strip parodying Robert E. Howard's *Conan the Barbarian* (as retold by Roy Thomas and Barry Windsor-Smith), Cerebus soon took on a more serious tone. *Church and State* comprises Volumes 3 and 4 of the complete *Cerebus* series and also marks the arrival of Gerhard as a background artist, giving the artwork a greater depth and complexity. The storytelling is more subtle and much darker than earlier volumes, moving away from straightforward adventure plots toward a greater interest in philosophy, religion, and politics. Cerebus's actions have always been callous, but here he really starts to test the audience's understanding, particularly when he throws people off buildings and rapes Astoria. Although Cerebus was always portrayed as something of an antihero, *Church and State* marks a turning point in Sim's depiction of the character. Hereafter no longer a driving force in the plot, Cerebus becomes more and more a forum for Sim's musings on religion and feminism.

FURTHER READING: *First Kingdom; Cerebus: Jaka's Story; Cerebus: Melmoth; Cerebus: Flight*
SEE ALSO: *Cerebus: High Society*

★
★
★
★

Writer: Will Eisner
Artist: Will Eisner

Publisher: W.W. Norton, 2006
ISBN: 0393061051

15+

THE CONTRACT WITH GOD TRILOGY: LIFE ON DROPSIE AVENUE

Plot: This book collects three of Will Eisner's most acclaimed graphic novels, all set on the fictional Bronx street of Dropsie Avenue. The first book, *A Contract With God*, is split into four distinct stories, beginning with Jewish do-gooder Frimme Hersh losing his beloved daughter and rejecting his faith to become an uncaring slum landlord—but rediscovering it moments before his death. The other stories in the first book are *The Street Singer*, about a slum singer with the chance to hit the big time; *The Super*, about a corrupt building supervisor; and *Cookalein*, about a vacation destination where poor city-dwellers escape to the country and penniless social climbers hope to snag rich spouses.

The second book in the trilogy, *A Life Force*, is a single, connected story. It follows the life and times of Dropsie Avenue resident and carpenter Jacob Shtarkah and Wall Street playboy Elton Shaftesbury II, who becomes bankrupt and winds up living on the avenue. The book tells how they, their families, and their friends are affected by events of the early 20th century.

The final book in the trilogy is *Dropsie Avenue*, which chronicles the ups and downs of the street from its origins in 1870 to the 1990s, focusing on key characters such as Jewish lawyer Abie Gold and landlord Izzy Cash.

Review: At just under 500 pages, this trilogy is a daunting read and its subject matter—namely the life and times of a Bronx street and its inhabitants—may not appear to be the most enthralling topic. But it proves to be surprisingly enjoyable; by turns uplifting, disturbing, and sad. *A Contract With God* is the standout story of the first book and, in Frimme Hersh, Eisner creates a character whose good deeds are rewarded with a personal tragedy that prompts him to turn his back on his humanitarian principles. But Hersh's legacy of hope and goodness survives his death, as a street youth is inspired by his original contract. Even though the trilogy is littered with acts of random violence, and with stories of destitute lost causes, the overriding feeling is one of hope and optimism. It's very much this sense of humanity surviving against the odds that permeates the work. The art is highly evocative and Eisner's simple black inks have just enough detail to make sure his characters are fully rounded without ever appearing to be overfussy or showy.

FURTHER READING: *Life in Pictures; Will Eisner's New York; Graphic Storytelling; Invisible People*
SEE ALSO: *The Best Of The Spirit; The Plot: The Secret Story Of The Protocols Of The Elders Of Zion*

★
★
★
★
★

Writer: Dan Clowes   **Publisher:** Fantagraphics, 2001
Artist: Dan Clowes   **ISBN:** 0224060880

15+ # GHOST WORLD

Plot: Enid Coleslaw and her best friend Beck Doppelmeyer are hovering on the cusp of womanhood. By the end of the summer they have to decide the path their futures will take—going away to college, or remaining in the small town they despise. They can't forever inhabit the "ghost world" of no responsibilities and no duties that sits between finishing high school and getting on with the rest of their lives. When Enid is betrayed by her only friend, she's finally spurred into action.

Review: Dan Clowes creates great characters that worm themselves into your consciousness. Everyone starts by wishing they were as ironic, cynical, and smart as Enid, but as the story unfolds we realize how empty her life is. By the end her pranks don't seem so funny and her observations don't seem so clever, as we see how lost she is.

Ghost World develops very slowly, initially functioning as a portrait of the daily life of bored teenagers. Clowes captures

the obsessions and linguistic shorthand as the girls hang out in the local diner fantasizing about unlikely men, or search for iconic kitsch objects at garage sales.

A sense of melancholy hangs over the whole story, which Clowes illustrates in his firm and elegant black-and-white style, using cityscapes to create a sense of isolation and despair. Clowes is excellent at expressing the slightly gawky body movements of his adolescent leads, falling back occasionally on his skill as a caricaturist to give life to some of the supporting cast. The much-debated ending is fascinating and extremely well handled, adding a final layer to a story that is all about going on a journey with Enid, but not seeing where she finally arrives.

FURTHER READING: *Art School Confidential; Like A Velvet Glove Cast In Iron; Pussey!*
SEE ALSO: *Skidmarks; Buddy in Seattle*

★
★
★
★
★

Writer: Jason Lutes
Artist: Jason Lutes

Publisher: Drawn & Quarterly, 2003
ISBN: 1896597726

15+ # JAR OF FOOLS

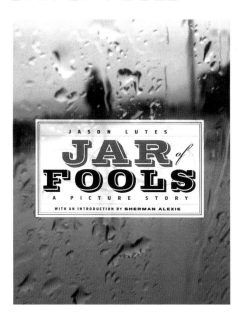

Plot: Unemployed and down on his luck, Ernie Weiss is an alcoholic stage magician troubled by his past. The untimely death of his escape-artist brother and a failed romance with ex-lover Esther O'Dea have resulted in him losing faith in his once-beloved magic. Al Flosso, Eddie's elderly and increasingly senile mentor, acts as confidant for Ernie as he reveals the dreams about his brother that haunt him on a regular basis.

A chance meeting with small-time grifter Nathan Lender leads these disparate characters into a chain of events that will change their lives forever. Nathan is looking for a way to improve life for his 12-year-old daughter Claire, a scheme that involves coercing Ernie into teaching her magic. The trio (accompanied by Flosso, who takes flight from the nursing home he repeatedly breaks out of) take up residence beneath the freeway in Ernie's car, and events spiral out of control, heading toward a heartbreaking conclusion.

Review: *Jar of Fools* is a beautifully written story—the dialog and the characters' relationships are utterly convincing, and it is easy to become attached to them. The comparison of past and present is an overriding theme throughout the story, and the parallels between Ernie's past and his present

are obvious: just as his brother Howard was an escape artist, so Ernie makes a reasonably good stab at escaping the responsibilities of his own life through alcohol and his refusal to let go of the past. Similarly, Flosso spends time reminiscing about his glory days with Ernie.

This is a persuasive tale that tackles its serious subjects of love, bereavement, suicide, memory, and magic in a compelling and lucid fashion. The expressive artwork plays a large part in the power of the story. Lutes fits a lot into the small panels that dominate the book, and the simple graphics often speak volumes. The artwork, and indeed the subject matter, are at times evocative of Daniel Clowes, and although the tone of the book is melancholy at times, and many of the events unfold in dark places—under the freeway, or in heavy rain— this doesn't leave you feeling despondent, but instead quietly contemplative.

FURTHER READING: *Houdini: The Handcuff King*
SEE ALSO: *Ghost World; Berlin: Book 1—City of Stones; Kings In Disguise*

★
★
★
★
★

Writer: Jaime Hernandez

Artist: Jaime Hernandez

Publisher: Fantagraphics, 2004

ISBN: 156097611X

15+

LOCAS: THE MAGGIE AND HOPEY STORIES

Plot: The life story of Maggie Chascarrillo, a Latina woman growing up during the 1980s new-wave explosion in Southern California. The initial stories focus on Maggie's activities as a mechanic, her relationship with her punkette lover Hopey, her misadventures with her crazy friends, and are shot through with the frenetic energy of the region's emergent music scene. Often light and funny, the later stories follow her life through failed relationships and tragedies as she returns to the barrio and tries to settle down.

Review: Summarizing its plot doesn't do Jaime Hernandez's *Locas* series justice. The artist grows up with his characters, and takes them from hedonism to heartbreak in the trip from teenager to adult, adding layer upon layer to our understanding

of a large central cast, often via multiple flashbacks. His story structures and panel design, as well as his use of multiple viewpoints, voices, and shifts back and forth in time, force the reader to make leaps of comprehension. While his first long storyline, *Mechan-X*, is charming, as Maggie takes off with her hunky boss Race Rand to mend a crashed spaceship deep in a jungle inhabited by robots and dinosaurs, it is Hernandez's second major story, *100 Rooms*, that really demonstrates his skill at page composition and pacing.

Although his cast of characters is large, few are as well rounded as Maggie. Although he may take detours to follow other characters, such as millionaire's wife and superheroine-wannabe Penny Century, or the extremely popular Hopey

on the road with her hopeless punk band, he returns, again and again, to the same events in Maggie's life, forcing us to reevaluate not just the reality of what happened, but our previous reactions to those different perspectives.

Hernandez creates a world that is pretty and very cleanly drawn, using an art style that is heavily influenced by *Archie* artists such as Dan DeCarlo, with hints of Kirby and Toth. His stories, by contrast, are a bittersweet examination of the expectations and values of his generation. Maggie grows up, gets fat, and flips burgers to make a living, while people die and love peters out. His punk heroine grows up to be an apartment super, her glamorous friends and adventures long gone, yet these later stories are still gripping and touching.

Hernandez demonstrates enormous control over his material, and over his readers. It's almost impossible not to be thrilled by the audacious way he commands your attention.

FURTHER READING: *Love & Rockets #4 ; Ape Sex*
SEE ALSO: *Palomar: The Heartbreak Soup Stories; Whoa Nellie; Mister X*

★ **Writer:** Neil Gaiman
★ **Artist:** Dave McKean
★
★
★

Publisher: Bloomsbury, 2007
ISBN: 0747588430

15+ # SIGNAL TO NOISE

Why am I writing a film I will never make, writing something no-one will ever see?

The world is always ending, for someone.

It's a good line.

Plot: *Signal to Noise* tells of a dying film director making a film in his head about the end of the world in the year 999 AD. Once again McKean and Gaiman play with the ideas of memory and imagination, posing the question, do film directors always see a much better film in their head than what we get to see on the screen. The director in this film is certain of this. This is the only thing he can be certain about, as his own world slowly comes to an end having been diagnosed with cancer.

This is juxtaposed with the story in his head, reflecting the seemingly inevitable ending coming for the characters in his story. The director doesn't know whether he'll manage to finish the film, because he doesn't know when his life will finish, nor does he want to accept the inevitable.

Finally he stops his treatments, and tries to finish the script with what little time he has left. As he does, he begins to feel better; not because the cancer in his body is in remission, but because the acceptance of his personal Armageddon is a weight off his shoulders.

Review: Gaiman's poignant writing is as sharp as ever, with McKean on top form with his collaged artwork crafted from paintings, pencils, and photographs. The look is reminiscent of his work on *Arkham Asylum*, with new influences such as Barron Storey breaking through towards the end.

More recently the book has been repackaged once again, with a new cover, new introductions, a couple of previously out of print short stories, and a final chapter to *Signal* itself, only previously available as a booklet with the radio version originally produced for BBC Radio 3.

FURTHER READING: *Cages; Neil Gaiman's Midnight Days; Pictures That Tick*
SEE ALSO: *The Tragical Comedy or Comical Tragedy of Mr Punch; Violent Cases*

★
★
★

Writer: Alan Moore
Artist: Oscar Zarate

Publisher: Avatar, 2003
ISBN: 1592910092

A SMALL KILLING

Plot: A fast-living advertising executive, the significantly named Timothy Hole, is desperate for some fresh ideas for his latest campaign, the launch of a new cola in Russia. This could be his career-defining moment, but he's afraid he's going out of his mind. Suffering from strange visions of a demonic child, he returns for the first time in his adult life to his hometown. He hopes to clarify the meaning of the images that haunt him and discover something deep about himself. Or perhaps he simply hopes to make them go away so he can return to his shiny, happy, creative life. Retreating from the media culture where he's comfortable, Timothy begins to question the path his life has taken, and how even his smallest actions impact the lives of others.

Review: *A Small Killing* was a book that could never live up to its publicity. When it was first commissioned by Gollancz, during the height of the UK's "comics are the new rock'n'roll" frenzy of the late 1980s, rumors abounded about how much the publisher had paid for what turned out to be a slight and rather too subtle tale for most readers.

Illustrated by Oscar Zarate in a boldly Expressionistic, painterly style, the book was clearly intended to appeal to a new audience for comics. Zarate already had a considerable reputation as an editorial illustrator, but little track record as a strip artist, and this shows in some of the more awkward narrative passages.

By the time *A Small Killing* was published, Moore already seemed to have moved on to bigger things, although the focus on psychological drama and the inner landscape offered a tantalizing glimpse of some of the non-linear approaches he would take for the sadly unfinished *Big Numbers*. *A Small Killing* is a very interesting stab at reflecting the mores of the 1980s, but ultimately remains a graphic short story, rather than a novel.

FURTHER READING: *It's Dark In London;*
Kling Klang Klatch; Across the Universe
SEE ALSO: *V For Vendetta; Complete Ballad*
of Halo Jones

★
★ **Writer:** Howard Cruse **Publisher:** DC Comics, 2000
★ **Artist:** Howard Cruse **ISBN:** 1563892553
★
★

15+ STUCK RUBBER BABY

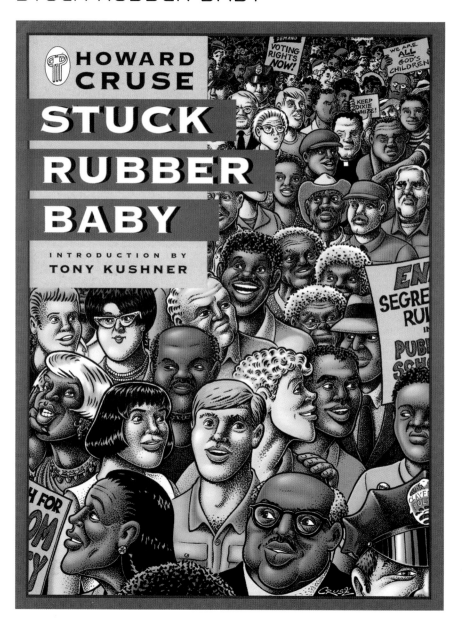

Plot: Small town Southern boy Toland Polk explores his sexuality and political leanings in Kennedy-era America at a time when gay rights were becoming a political issue. His friendship with Sammy Noone, a young sailor, starts expanding his creative horizons too, as he discovers the local TV evangelist's wife was once a steamy cabaret singer, and that her firebrand husband has a gay son.

Pitched into two turbulent worlds Toland becomes involved in the overt black power movement and the more covert world of gay clubs, encountering the gamut of responses to the increasing politicization of the gay lifestyle.

Review: Howard Cruse's experience as a humorous cartoonist stands him in good stead when producing one of the most richly textured, significant, and widely read comics about homosexual relationships ever produced. Which makes it sound a lot stuffier than it is.

Stuck Rubber Baby is a very mature look back at the hesitancy and sexual transience of youth, the fleeting nature of first love, and the uncertainty of our own attractions, which takes you back to a time when homosexuality was

almost universally frowned upon. But it is also packed with warm, entertaining, and funny characters you will grow to care about. Cruse's gentle humor, his gift for human observation, and the wholesome rounded drawing style all served to make the content of this book widely acceptable at the time it was published and expanded the graphic novel's audience. It's an honest and straightforward piece of modern fiction about sex of all sorts and uses the story of one charming but confused boy in the South to represent so many struggles that it moves way beyond being a gay rites of passage story.

It's very easy to read *Stuck Rubber Baby* lightly, and get swept away by the sometimes soap opera style plot, but this ease of reading is underpinned by Cruse's superb control, his mastery of the craft of comic-book storytelling, and his comfortingly cuddly linework—no one can make a character look quite so bright-eyed and naïve as Cruse.

FURTHER READING: *Dancin' Nekkid With The Angels; The Swimmer With A Rope In His Teeth*
SEE ALSO: *Kings In Disguise; Maus*

★
★
★
★

Writer: Bryan Talbot
Artist: Bryan Talbot

Publisher: Dark Horse, 1995
ISBN: 1569710775

THE TALE OF ONE BAD RAT

Plot: Helen is an underage runaway attempting to survive on the streets of London. Her only friend is her pet rat that she talks to. As the story unfolds, we realize she is trying to escape an abusive father, her unconcerned mother, and reality itself. Her love for the work of children's author Beatrix Potter draws her to the Lake District in the north of England, and as she travels, she seems to retreat further into a fantasy world.

When her pet is killed, she creates a giant fantasy rat companion, but when she arrives in the beautiful surroundings previously familiar to her only from books, she finds the will to start trusting people again, and ultimately to confront her father. Having learned to accept what happened to her, she says goodbye to her rat and is able to move forward toward a new life.

Review: *The Tale of One Bad Rat* is a very rare thing indeed in that here we have a quiet, positive story about living through and coming to terms with child abuse that is neither patronizing nor exploitative.

As Talbot slowly builds up a picture of Helen's earlier life, using monotone flashbacks, he doesn't need to spell out what has damaged her—it's there for all to see in the way she holds her body, in the patterning of her speech, and in her reactions to other people. The final pages, where the whole story could so easily have fallen to pieces or become too dramatic, are exquisitely understated.

Talbot is a master craftsman, with numerous techniques at his disposal and the patience to exhaustively research his subject. He uses his skill at pastiche to intermingle elements

of Beatrix Potter's style, and also those of several other early British illustrators, including Alfred Bestall (*Rupert Bear*), into his drawing. Throughout he keeps to a very measured, clean line style, filling in volume with subtle coloring—look carefully and you'll see that different scenes and characters are carefully color-coded.

Color also sets the mood for each scene by indicating the changes in Helen's state of awareness. Figures are kept very simple, and are foregrounded by the use of more lightly delineated and detailed backgrounds.

The Tale of One Bad Rat is a work with truly universal appeal, and is the second most-requested graphic novel in American libraries. Its subtlety and understanding of human nature makes it suitable for the widest possible audience.

FURTHER READING: *Brainstorm Comix; The Adventures of Luther Arkwright; Sandman: Fables and Reflections*
SEE ALSO: *Alice in Sunderland; Heart of Empire*

GENERAL FICTION

209

500

ESSENTIAL
GRAPHIC NOVELS

Top 10 essential general fiction graphic novels

★
★
★
★

Writer: Gene Luen Yang
Artist: Gene Luen Yang; Lark Pien

Publisher: First Second, 2007
ISBN: 1596431520

15+ # AMERICAN BORN CHINESE

Plot: *American Born Chinese* consists of three alternating stories. In the first, Chinese-American Jin Wang's family moves to a new neighborhood, but his ethnicity causes problems in the nearly all-white school. In the second, Danny, who lives in a sitcom world, is embarrassed by his Chinese cousin, the stereotypical Chin-Kee, while in the third tale, the mythical Monkey King wants to become a god. What could these three stories have in common?

Review: The engaging, cartoony, and colorful art immediately grabs you, but the narratives prove equally compelling, with the book's conclusion drawing the three separate stories together in a surprisingly satisfying way. A moving tale of a young person struggling to fit in, the book won the American Library Association's Michael L. Printz Award for Excellence in Young Adult Literature in 2007.

FURTHER READING: *Gordon Yamamoto and the King of the Geeks*
SEE ALSO: *Mail Order Bride; Yellow Jar*

★
★
★
★

Writer: Greg Sadowski and Various
Artist: Bernard Krigstein

Publisher: Fantagraphics, 2004
ISBN: 1560975733

 A # B. KRIGSTEIN: COMICS

Plot: A collection of 34 stories drawn by Krigstein between 1949 and 1956, comprising strips from various publishers—including Atlas, DC, and EC Comics—that cross multiple genres, including romance, crime, horror, war, and western.

Review: Krigstein has long been held to be one of comics most innovative artists, constantly experimenting with techniques to represent the underlying psychology of the script. His use of multiple panels of different sizes is particularly notable. His work for EC Comics is considered the pinnacle of that evolution, with stories such as *Pipe Dream* and *In the Bag*.

FURTHER READING: *B. Krigstein, Volume 1*
SEE ALSO: *Harvey Kurtzman's Mad; EC Archives*

Writer: Hugo Pratt
Artist: Hugo Pratt

Publisher: Harvill, 1996
ISBN: 1860462707

BALLAD OF THE SALT SEA

Plot: *Ballad* is a sweeping story set in the South Pacific just before World War I. Rasputin, a roguish Russian smuggler, rescues two teenagers, Cain and Pandora, and then finds the enigmatic sailor Corto Maltese tied to a raft and left to die.

Review: Pratt's *Corto Maltese* stories are the greatest comic adventures ever created, mixing philosophy and occult mysteries with historical events. From the moment he is introduced, the mercurial Corto—an eternal wanderer who cut his own lifeline into his palm—steals the show. Although the artwork is not as audacious as many of the later instalments, *Ballad* is a beautifully constructed comic, with Pratt demonstrating his intuitive grasp of how much—or how little—it is necessary to draw to achieve the desired effect. If you want to learn about effective storytelling, here's your first lesson.

FURTHER READING: *Corto in Siberia; Corto Maltese: Fable of Venice; Corto Maltese in Africa; Corto Maltese: Mémoires*
SEE ALSO: *Terry & The Pirates Volume 1; Zorro: The Complete Alex Toth*

Writer: Jason Lutes
Artist: Jason Lutes

Publisher: Drawn and Quarterly, 2000
ISBN: 1896597297

BERLIN: CITY OF STONES

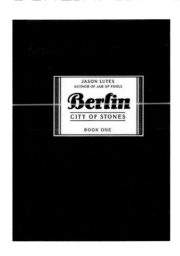

Plot: *City of Stones* follows a cast of characters lead by Kurt Severing and Marthe Muller, a photographer and art student respectively, between September, 1928 and May Day, 1929, in the final years of Germany's Weimar Republic where their everyday lives and dreams are threatened by the rising tide of fascism.

Review: Planned as the first part of a trilogy by the talented, but often overlooked, Jason Lutes, *City of Stones* perfectly captures the mundane and often hard existence of his varied cast of characters. From Jew to Communist sympathizer, their situations are made all the more poignant by what history tells us is coming. Indeed, it is a clash between the political extremes and the police that brings this first volume to its tragic conclusion.

FURTHER READING: *The Fall; Houdini: The Handcuff King*
SEE ALSO: *Jar Of Fools*

★ **Writer:** Nabiel Kanan   **Publisher:** NBM, 2001
★ **Artist:** Nabiel Kanan   **ISBN:** 1561632996
★

15+ THE BIRTHDAY RIOTS

Plot: Max Collins's life should be perfect. Chief adviser to the prospective mayor of London, he's recently moved to a beautiful home in the country with his young family. However, he's having a bit of a midlife crisis—unsure of his political convictions, and tempted by a possible office indiscretion, something he's done once before. At the same time, his daughter is less than happy with her new surroundings, and the recent arrival of a group of travelers is the catalyst that threatens to tear the family apart.

Review: While it's not entirely successful, this is a very worthwhile book. Kanan's art is lovely, and the tale is enjoyable, but other than Max and his daughter, all of the characters are a little one-dimensional. Worth a look if you fancy something a little different.

FURTHER READING: *Exit; Lost Girl*
SEE ALSO: *The Drowners; Slow News Day; Berlin*

★ **Writer:** Kiriko Nananan   **Publisher:** Toptron Ltd T/A Fanfare, 2006
★ **Artist:** Kiriko Nananan   **ISBN:** 8493340979

15+ BLUE

Plot: Two schoolgirls, Kayako Kirishima and Masami Endô, come to terms with the consequences of their friendship as it develops into intense, obsessive love.

Review: This slow-paced, school-based drama is an interesting revelation of Japanese teenage relationships, and the title matches the book's melancholic tone. The fact that Nananan has drawn the two protagonists looking very similar sometimes makes it hard to differentiate between them, and this works both for and against the story, as the two girls become entwined with one another. Sparsely written and lightly drawn, the real tale is inferred between the lines and in the gaps.

FURTHER READING: *Pale Pink; Mail Order Bride*
SEE ALSO: *Yukiko's Spinach*

Writer: Kim Deitch
Artist: Kim Deitch

Publisher: Pantheon, 2002
ISBN: 0375421912

BOULEVARD OF BROKEN DREAMS

Plot: Beginning in 1927 and taking us through to 1993, the story concerns the employees of an animation studio, Fontaine Talking Fables. Ted Mishkin, an alcoholic who may also be insane, is working on a short film featuring Waldo the Cat, the studio "star." Waldo, however, really does exist as Ted's assistant, but has his own malicious agenda. Waldo torments Ted, precipitating his decline through drink, affairs, and visits to a sanatorium. This mirrors the decline of the studio in the face of competition from Disney, corporate politics, and cultural debasement of animation's aesthetic standards.

Review: Deitch's interest in alcoholism and delusional behavior make for unsettling reading (Waldo is a recurring character in his work), but this is a remarkable, twisted history of American animation.

FURTHER READING: *Beyond the Pale; All Waldo Comics; A Shroud for Waldo; The Boulevard of Broken Dreams; Shadowland*
SEE ALSO: *Jimmy Corrigan, the Smartest Kid on Earth; The Chuckling Whatsit*

Writer: Alex Robinson
Artist: Alex Robinson

Publisher: Top Shelf, 2001
ISBN: 1891830198

BOX OFFICE POISON

Plot: This weighty tome (over 600 pages) follows the lives of a group of Generation X friends living in New York, centering on disgruntled bookstore employee Sherman and his best friend Ed, an aspiring comics artist. As the book starts, Sherman meets a new girl, and Ed starts working for golden-age cartoonist Irving Flavor. Both of their lives will change in ways they never expected in the next few years.

Review: Alex Robinson's debut is an amazing piece of work, with the story fully fledged from the first page. Although his drawing is a little stiff to start with, he has an appealing but simple style that gets better page by page. The cast is superb, every character is believable and three-dimensional, and despite its length, you'll wish there was more. A hilarious and essential read.

FURTHER READING: *BOP: More Box Office Poison*
SEE ALSO: *Blankets; Get A Life; Tricked*

★
★
★
★

Writer: J.M. DeMatteis
Artist: Glenn Barr

Publisher: DC Comics, 2003
ISBN: 1401200516

15+ BROOKLYN DREAMS

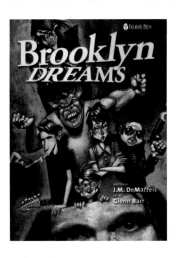

Plot: This is forty-something Carl Santini's memoir of his senior year in high school. It's not necessarily what actually happened, but it's the way he remembers it, and he makes no apologies for that. As he relates the life-changing sequence of events that shaped the year, the narrative bounces around the major events of his life, filling his audience in on the details of his utterly dysfunctional family and how the events have affected his life.

Review: This is a wonderful book, darkly funny and filled with both cynicism and optimism. DeMatteis proves once again that he's a master of the fictional memoir, and Glenn Barr's art goes from painted realism to outrageous surrealism in perfect time with the mood of the story.

FURTHER READING: *Greenberg The Vampire*
SEE ALSO: *Moonshadow; Justice League: A New Beginning; The Playboy*

★
★
★

Writer: Phoebe Gloeckner
Artist: Phoebe Gloeckner

Publisher: Frog Ltd, 2000
ISBN: 1583940286

18+ A CHILD'S LIFE AND OTHER STORIES

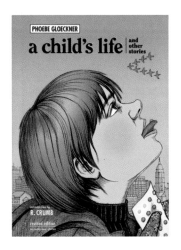

Plot: *A Child's Life* is a collection of stories spanning 20 years, told mainly through the eyes of Minnie, Phoebe Gloeckner's teenage alter ego. Having endured unwanted and unwelcome sexual attention from her stepfather, Minnie takes to the streets of San Francisco, where she encounters an assortment of unsavory and unsuitable men who subject the teenager to a host of drug- and sex-fuelled experiences.

Review: Uneasy reading, as men queue up to take advantage of the youthful protagonist—amplified by the fact that much of the book is semi-autobiographical—Gloeckner creates disturbingly powerful and vivid strips portraying strong feelings of disenchantment, isolation, and revulsion. The artwork is vivid and explicit and the combination of the anatomical and fantastical is mesmerizing, making an uncompromising work, difficult at times, but ultimately very strong.

FURTHER READING: *Diary Of A Teenage Girl*
SEE ALSO: *Life's A Bitch; Summer Of Love*

Writer: Rick Veitch
Artist: Rick Veitch

Publisher: Vertigo, 2006
ISBN: 1401210597

5+ # CAN'T GET NO

"...supremely, magnificently strange, and like nothing else I've read."
— Neil Gaiman

CAN'T GET NO

RICK VEITCH

VERTIGO

Plot: When corporate bigwig Chad Roe wakes from a drunken night out to find himself tattooed from head to toe with one of his own company's super-permanent markers, he quickly falls from grace and undertakes a cathartic journey through the dark heart of America, encountering unlikely allies and making deadly enemies along the way.

Review: The central event of Rick Veitch's intriguing 350-page modern parable is the 2001 terrorist attack on the World Trade Center, in which the protagonist would have been killed were it not for his newfound status as an outcast. His eyewitness experience of the attack inspires a redemptive quest, as well as drawing out the benign and malevolent societal elements that he will encounter on his path to salvation. Veitch's reluctant wanderer suffers as a result of the kneejerk jingoism that followed the September 11 attacks, and is adopted as the figurehead of a mischievous but peaceable countercultural movement.

The story is dialog-free, the script consisting solely of a portentous, stream-of-consciousness "voiceover"—one short caption per image—which complements the main visual narrative and lends the tale an added poetic dimension. Veitch's artwork is monochrome, with no grayscale shading, and the caricatured ugliness of his characters perfectly suits the satirical tone. Unusually for a Vertigo book, Veitch's tale is presented in a half-size format that doesn't fit well on most bookshelves, but which certainly contributes to its overall uniqueness.

FURTHER READING: *Army @ Love Volume 1: The Hot Zone Club*
SEE ALSO: *Abraxas and the Earthman; Brat Pack; Greyshirt: Indigo Sunset; The 9/11 Report: A Graphic Adaptation*

★
★ **Writer:** Dave Sim **Publisher:** Aardvaark-Vanaheim, 1994
★ **Artist:** Dave Sim **ISBN:** 0919359078
★
★

15+ CEREBUS: HIGH SOCIETY

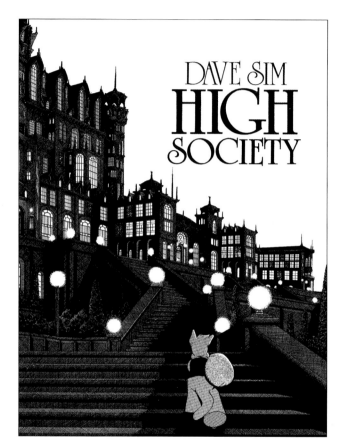

Plot: *High Society* is the second volume of the complete *Cerebus*, the first collection to contain a single (25-issue) storyline. Having arrived in the wealthy city-state of Iest, Cerebus meets Astoria, a femme fatale who encourages him to enter the world of politics and run for Prime Minister. What follows is a joyous satire of the political machine.

Review: Much of the humor in this volume comes from the juxtaposition of the "barbarian" Cerebus and the polite society into which he's thrust. However, with characters such as Lord Julius (based on Groucho Marx), Elrod of Melvinbone (Michael Moorcock's Elric), the Moon Roach (a variable superhero parody, but here, Moonknight), and the Regency Elf (*Elfquest*), there's no shortage of slapstick and witty comedy—the importance of a goat in politics has probably never been so clearly stated. Jaka makes a telling, poignant reappearance, indicating Sim's grander ambitions, and this volume begins to place Cerebus within a more serious social and literary context.

FURTHER READING: *First Kingdom; Cerebus: Jaka's Story; Cerebus: Melmoth; Cerebus: Flight*
SEE ALSO: *Cerebus: Church & State volumes 1 and 2*

Writer: Milo Manara
Artist: Milo Manara

Publisher: NBM, 1993
ISBN: 1561630845

CLICK

Plot: Claudia's husband thinks she's a beautiful but frigid bitch, so he hatches a plan to have her implanted with a device that will arouse her whenever he wishes. Dr Fez, the surgeon carrying out the operation, becomes infatuated with Claudia and steals the remote control. As her husband whisks her off around the world to try and hide her increasingly lewd behavior, Dr Fez and his remote control follow, causing havoc.

Review: Sexual comedy from the Benny Hill school, *Click* is an outrageous soft-porn romp full of gorgeous people enjoying extremely elegant sex. It may be pretty raunchy, but it never loses its sense of fun, and Manara's drawing of the human body is so beautiful, if idealized, that it's hard to think of it offending anyone.

FURTHER READING: *Perchance To Dream; Dies Irae; Indian Summer*
SEE ALSO: *Little Ego; Birdland*

Writer: Seth
Artist: Seth

Publisher: Drawn & Quarterly, 2004
ISBN: 189659784X

CLYDE FANS: BOOK 1

Plot: Two elderly brothers recount their experiences of running a fan factory. Both are introverted by nature, but Abraham, the eldest, has overcome this. In the first half, we see Abraham looking back on 50 years of business life while revisiting the site of his office as he ponders the art of selling, and why the business ultimately failed. The second half concerns his reclusive brother Simon's only attempt to make a sales trip, in 1957, which is completely ineffectual.

Review: Seth's stories progress slowly. Here the focus is on creating two believable voices, drawing the gradual conclusion that while Simon failed abruptly and spectacularly, Abraham has simply dragged the process out over 50 years. The art is heavily influenced by 1950s illustration and matches the sense of wistful longing that permeates the story.

FURTHER READING: *It's A Good Life If You Don't Weaken*
SEE ALSO: *Ghost World*

★
★
★

Writer: Kate Worley
Artist: Reed Waller

Publisher: Amerotica, 2005
ISBN: 1561634514

18+

THE COMPLETE OMAHA THE CAT DANCER VOLUME 1

Plot: Confident and sexy Susie Jensen feels oppressed by the male management in her office so quits to become the stripper Omaha, fully supported by her boyfriend Chuck. Omaha's pro-sex feminist world is soon threatened by all manner of melodrama, from anti-porn protesters trying to shut down her workplace, to gangsters trying to muscle in on the action.

Review: If Waller and Worley thought giving all their characters animal heads and tails would diffuse the outrage their sexual, but very sensitive soap opera might cause, they were wrong. The anthropomorphic nature of the characters doesn't for one second interfere with their horniness. A very positive spin on the sex industry, that's as engrossing as The OC, with the bonus of extremely cutely drawn characters getting it on every few pages.

FURTHER READING: *The Complete Omaha The Cat Dancer Volume 2*
SEE ALSO: *Lost Girls*

★
★
★

Writer: Sarnath Banerjee
Artist: Sarnath Banerjee

Publisher: Penguin, 2005
ISBN: 0143031384

15+ # CORRIDOR

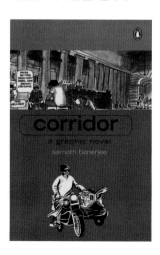

Plot: Jehangir Ragoonwalla, a second hand bookseller in Connaught Place, Delhi, dispenses tea and wisdom to his various customers as they deal with relationships, fear, and the search for happiness.

Review: For a country where the majority of comics are either for children, are adaptations of classic texts like the Maharatba, or increasingly superhero-orientated, *Corridor* is a surprisingly mature and understated work. Banerjee's tableau of life in modern Delhi reads like a graphic novel version of Robert Altman's movie, *Short Cuts*, with the focus shifting from one customer to another as their various tales are recounted. The artwork is basic, but functional, and the fragmented story structure works surprisingly well, giving a fascinating insight into urban Indian life, that is not so different to the West's.

FURTHER READING: *Barn Owl's Fabulous Capers*
SEE ALSO: *Perespolis; Palestine*

Writer: Brian Wood
Artist: Brett Weldele

Publisher: AiT/Planet LAR, 2003
ISBN: 0970936028

COUSCOUS EXPRESS

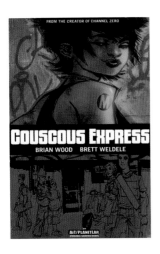

Plot: The tale of three hip young things, street tough and able to give as good as they get, in the middle of a New York vendetta-cum-turf war.

Review: This tale of family and culture set in the classic New York City melting pot sees one girl come to terms with the fact that—shock, horror—she is surrounded by a family who love her, told amid all the shooting and running around of an almost incidental mob story.

But *Couscous Express* is as much about style as substance, and Wedele's rough, degraded images have the freshness, energy, and vitality of an indie film. *Couscous Express* is more than just a tale of the young and the cute—but what's wrong with tales of the young and the cute, anyway?

FURTHER READING: *Channel Zero; The Couriers*
SEE ALSO: *Corridor; Demo*

Writer: Kevin Huizenga
Artist: Kevin Huizenga

Publisher: Drawn & Quarterly, 2006
ISBN: 1894937864

CURSES

Plot: A collection of short, but thoughtful strips, mainly featuring Glenn Ganges, Huizenga's suburban everyman character. Ganges and his wife grapple with the everyday problems that we all face, with subtle and not so subtle diversions from reality. There's a variation on an old folk tale, in which Glenn has to resort to supernatural means to remove an infertility curse from his wife; a meditation on the invasion of starlings across North America; and encounters with ghosts.

Review: Huizenga's beautiful little stories are intensely philosophical—a rarity in American comics, but common in the European comics that have obviously influenced his expressive art style. Philosophical doesn't mean boring, and Huizenga has a wonderfully wry sense of humor that gives these stories real heart.

FURTHER READING: *Ganges; Drawn & Quarterly Showcase Book 1*
SEE ALSO: *Get A Life; Sshhhh!; Paul Has A Summer Job*

★
★
★

Writer: Marc Antoine Mathieu
Artist: Marc Antoine Mathieu

Publisher: Dark Horse, 2003
ISBN: 1569718407

15+ DEAD MEMORY

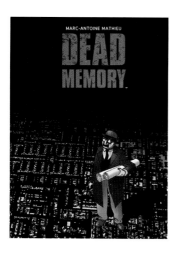

MARC-ANTOINE MATHIEU

Plot: The story of a civil servant called Firmin Huff whose job is to map a city without limits or boundaries. But Huff is soon alarmed to discover that a series of walls is being built within this once-endless metropolis.

Review: The first of Mathieu's works to be translated into English, *Dead Memory* is a claustrophobic, dystopian affair, complete with an unreliable central computer. As the walls continue to go up, the vocabulary available to the local citizens decreases. Like his other works, *Dead Memory* is a rich and playful allegory about the structure of language and meaning. Told in stark black and white, it's a satisfying work that will keep you intrigued until the end.

FURTHER READING: *Museum Vaults; Kafka*
SEE ALSO: *Give It Up & Other Stories; City of Glass; From Hell*

★
★
★
★

Writer: Brian Wood
Artist: Becky Cloonan

Publisher: Vertigo, 2008
ISBN: 1932051422

15+ DEMO

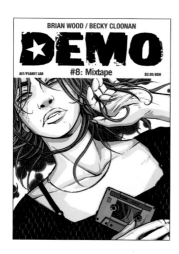

BRIAN WOOD / BECKY CLOONAN

#8: Mixtape

ALT/PLANET LAB $2.99 USD

Plot: Twelve self-contained stories involving young people grappling with emotions and superpowers they are barely able to comprehend, let alone manage efficiently. These stories include the tale of Marie, the telekinetic teenage girl whose powers are suppressed by heavy medication, and a girl who becomes whatever the person who looks at her wants her to be.

Review: Like an indie *X-Men* for the new millennium, *Demo* takes on the conventional subject of superhuman powers and turns it on its head. Wood focuses on the human aspect as we're given a realistic glimpse of what it might be like to be a teenager coping with bizarre powers. Cloonan's artwork is rough and scratchy at times, but that reflects the strong emotions expressed in the stories, and makes them all the more potent.

FURTHER READING: *Channel Zero; American Virgin*
SEE ALSO: *DMZ: On The Ground; Brat Pack; Concrete Volume 1*

Writer: Alison Bechdel
Artist: Alison Bechdel

Publisher: Firebrand Books, 1986
ISBN: 0932379176

DYKES TO WATCH OUT FOR

3+

Review: While successfully tackling and emphasizing society's narrow and oversimplified views of lesbians, Bechdel also deploys her satirical arsenal on the wealth of information she has garnered from lesbians and the politicized sexuality that hampers their loves and lives.

Idiosyncrasies and behavioral traits are lampooned sensitively, but with a certain sympathetic incisiveness. The cartoony style adds rather than detracts from the veracity and authenticity of short but numerous excursions.

Plot: Bechdel presents an appealing series of scenarios depicting the highs and the lows of lesbian relationships. There are some tongue-in-cheek pointers on what to admire and what to avoid in finding the right lesbian partner, maintaining the relationship, and making it work against all the odds.

FURTHER READING: *Dykes and Sundry Other Carbon-based Life Forms to Watch Out For; New, Improved!: Dykes to Watch Out For*
SEE ALSO: *Fun Home*

Writer: Max
Artist: Max

Publisher: Drawn & Quarterly, 2000
ISBN: 1896597262

EXTENDED DREAM OF MR D

5+

Plot: Mr D falls into a deep sleep/coma and embarks on a bizarre journey examining aspects of his life and himself, finding salvation along the way.

Review: Catalonian artist, Max, weaves a mystical tale of philosophical dream-logic, suffused with hidden meanings and surreal moments. D is led through an ever-changing landscape (with Max smoothly altering his art styles appropriately) by three guides—Mr Su, Sarah and Scallywax—whose origins are much closer to home than he could imagine. The book won an Ignatz for Best Foreign Material and was very much a dry run for the artist's later work, *Bardin the Superrealist*.

FURTHER READING: *Bosnian Flat Dog; Maybe Later*
SEE ALSO: *Bardin the Superrealist*

★
★
★
★

Writer: Will Eisner
Artist: Will Eisner

Publisher: Doubleday, 2003
ISBN: 0385510098

15+ FAGIN THE JEW

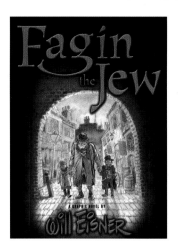

Plot: *Fagin The Jew* centers around the character of Fagin from Charles Dickens' *Oliver Twist*—from his birth and arrival in England, through his childhood, and chronicling his adult misfortunes and misdealings, including the arrival of Bill Sikes and Oliver Twist in his life.

Review: Exploring the tale of Moses Fagin in the Georgian/Victorian era provides an insight into the religious and social history of the time. Arriving from Middle Europe, Fagin's family hopes for a better life, but instead becomes embroiled in the social strife between the Jewish and Christian communities. The young Fagin tries to better himself, but with the word "Jew" having become synonymous with "thief," he finds himself mistrusted wherever he turns. The character of Fagin is a prism through which the hardship many Jewish immigrants had to endure at that time can be examined. Skillfully executed, thought provoking, and enlightening.

FURTHER READING: *Will Eisner's New York; The Dreamer*
SEE ALSO: *The Plot; Jew of New York*

★
★

Writer: Eric Drooker
Artist: Eric Drooker

Publisher: Dark Horse, 2007
ISBN: 1593076762

A FLOOD! A NOVEL IN PICTURES

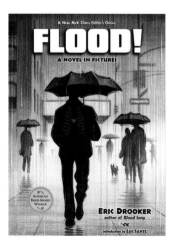

Plot: Drooker's narrative is about the insularity of the modern world, urban pressure, and the process of creation, as his protagonist hurries about his business, ignoring the threatening waters rising around him.

Review: *Flood!* betrays Drooker's background as an illustrator rather than a cartoonist. Using an expressionist woodcut style reminiscent of a ragged Charles Burns, he creates a series of powerful interconnected images, but not a graphic novel. Individually beautiful, they do not, unfortunately, add up to a cohesive whole, and to get a great deal out of the book you need to spend a lot of time studying them and thinking about their nuances, which kills the pace.

FURTHER READING: *Blood Song; Illuminated Poems*
SEE ALSO: *Black Hole*

Writer: Yoshitaka (Henry) Kiyama
Artist: Yoshitaka (Henry) Kiyama
Publisher: Stone Bridge Press, 1999
ISBN: 1880656337

THE FOUR IMMIGRANTS MANGA: A JAPANESE EXPERIENCE IN SAN FRANCISCO, 1904–1924

Plot: Kiyama uses characters based on himself and his acquaintances to describe the experience of Japanese immigrants in San Francisco between 1904 and 1924. The strips cover such events as the earthquake of 1906, the World's Fair of 1915, and World War I.

Review: This 52-chapter story, first published in 1931, was designed to be serialized over a year, like a newspaper strip of the period. Kiyama's style is simple, yet full of background detail, producing a remarkable, fascinating historical document in which humor is used to comment on the social and political conditions of the time.

FURTHER READING: *Will Eisner's New York*
SEE ALSO: *A Contract With God; Persepolis*

Writer: Posy Simmonds
Artist: Posy Simmonds
Publisher: Pantheon, 2005
ISBN: 0224061143

GEMMA BOVERY

Plot: Drawing inspiration from Gustave Flaubert's classic novel *Madame Bovary*, this story tells the tale of the life and death of the eponymous heroine, Gemma, as she emerges, dumpy and unattractive, from the ashes of a ruinous relationship to fall in love with the comfortably middle-class Charles Bovery. As fortune graces her with money, Gemma reinvents herself as a fashionable and desirable lady-about-town—with ultimately disastrous consequences for both her and her loved ones.

Review: A groundbreaking "slice of life" story, originally serialized in the British newspaper *The Guardian*. It's essentially a "fall and rise and fall again" tale, viewed through the eyes of a distanced third-person character. Posy Simmonds's skill as a writer and artist is to document the subtle and absurd behavioral nuances of the prosperous and pretentious middle classes with impressive detail.

FURTHER READING: *Tamara Drewe; Literary Life*
SEE ALSO: *Alex; The Fate of the Artist*

★
★
★
★

Writers: Phillipe Dupuy and Charles Berberian
Artists: Phillipe Dupuy and Charles Berberian

Publisher: Drawn & Quarterly, 2006
ISBN: 1896597793

15+ GET A LIFE

Plot: Dupuy and Berberian have been collaborating on their Mr. Jean character for over 20 years, and this is a collection of all of the early stories, taking Mr. Jean, a young Parisian bachelor, through all the ups and downs life throws at him, including dating, marriage, and fatherhood, all the while juggling the deadlines of his writing career and keeping up with his circle of friends.

Review: The creators collaborate on every part of the art and writing, with incredibly impressive results. Their art is expressive, beautiful, and sympathetically colored, and they demonstrate a striking design sense. They also possess a dry, but charming sense of humor, and this is a constantly witty book, with solid characterization and storytelling throughout.

FURTHER READING: *Maybe Later; Haunted; I Pity You*
SEE ALSO: *Paul Has A Summer Job; Curses; Slow News Day*

★
★
★
★

Writer: James Sturm
Artist: James Sturm

Publisher: Drawn and Quarterly, 2003
ISBN: 1896597718

12+ THE GOLEM'S MIGHTY SWING

Plot: The Jewish Stars of David baseball team are impoverished barnstormers travelling 1920s America and playing exhibition matches in small towns. Led by the book's narrator, coach Noah Strauss, the team allows a schuckster to dress their star player up as a Golem to help improve their finances. The result is disastrous.

Review: Sturm's low-key story is powerful and emotive as he paints a detailed landscape of pre-Depression America, with the black, white, and gray wash artwork transporting the reader back in time. The baseball games, though key, are not the real focus of the story, and the creator ably examines anti-Semitism in the US without becoming preachy.

FURTHER READING: *Lost in the Alps; The Blue Notebook*
SEE ALSO: *Streak of Chalk; Tangents*

Writer: Craig Thompson
Artist: Craig Thompson

Publisher: Pantheon, 2006
ISBN: 1891830090

5+

GOOD-BYE, CHUNKY RICE

Plot: A small turtle by the name of Chunky Rice takes the advice of his best friend, a little mouse, and decides to search for the place where he truly belongs. We follow Chunky on his sea voyage, occasionally heading back to land to catch up with those he left behind.

Review: Heart-wrenchingly beautiful, yet ever so slightly sad, the book consists primarily of three interwoven stories following Chunky's voyage, his little mouse friend's realization of how much she misses him, and his former roommate Solomon's progress with his Chunky replacement—a bird called Merle who just says "Doot." Each story is marvelously crafted, and you'll immediately become attached to the characters and their predicaments: the simplistic Solomon's stories of being forced to drown puppies by his father; Chunky's loneliness during his voyage to an unknown new life; and the little mouse's attempts to express his feelings of loss by tossing hundreds of messages in bottles out to sea—each one containing the solitary line, "I miss you."

This is a tale of friendship, about how important friends can be—though we may not realize it until they are gone—and the loss we feel when they are no longer here. It's also about the memories we share, and the fact that sometimes we all just want to go far, far away. The language is apt, the artwork is simple, and the design is adorable.

FURTHER READING: *Doot Doot Garden*
SEE ALSO: *Blankets*

★
★
★
★

Writer: Dylan Horrocks
Artist: Dylan Horrocks

Publisher: Drawn and Quarterly, 2002
ISBN: 0969887442

15+ HICKSVILLE

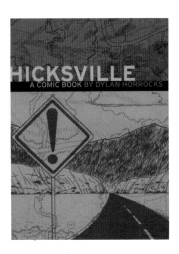

Plot: This is the tale of a journalist in search of a dark secret—a secret that lurks in the past of the world-famous superhero-comic creator, Dick Burger.

Review: A tale of comics history that blends reality with fantasy, the *Hicksville* of the book's title is a town, a wonderful place that many comics fans will have dreamed of: an idyllic village where everyone from the local fisherman to the coffee-shop owner is a passionate comic reader, but most of whom hate the famous Dick Burger. What did he do to deserve such opprobrium? Told in a simple, almost nervous style, *Hicksville* is obviously a work of love—love for comics and their history—but its themes of art and the process of creation are universal.

FURTHER READING: *Ordinary Victories; The Names Of Magic*
SEE ALSO: *Three Fingers; Get A Life; How To Be An Artist*

★
★
★

Writer: Cosey
Artist: Cosey

Publisher: NBM, 1993
ISBN: 1561630683

15+ IN SEARCH OF SHIRLEY

Plot: Two childhood friends, Art and Ian, fought in the Vietnam war together, and both fell in love with Shirley, who questioned their beliefs. Many years later, the two men's lives are at crisis point. Art is facing marital breakdown and drinking too much, while Ian likes to think of himself as a free spirit, but is actually a womanizing dog dentist. Leaving their troubles behind, the two head for Rome to find Shirley again. They discover their femme fatale is now a nun, attempting to rescue a young Vietnamese boy from a refugee camp.

Review: Cosey twists a conventional story (buddies and love rivals on the road, Vietnam war flashbacks, fascinating femme fatale) by removing the raison d'etre—winning Shirley—and turning it into a redemptive quest.

FURTHER READING: *Lost in the Alps; The Blue Notebook*
SEE ALSO: *Streak of Chalk; Tangents*

Writer: Seth
Artist: Seth

Publisher: Drawn & Quarterly, 2003
ISBN: 0224079182

5+

IT'S A GOOD LIFE,
IF YOU DON'T WEAKEN

Plot: Seth is a man infatuated by the past, and not particularly keen on the present. He becomes obsessed with an artist called Kalo, who was published in the New Yorker in the 1940s, and decides to try and track him down. As his quest hits numerous dead ends, he becomes oblivious to the people in his life, and starts withdrawing into his obsession.

Review: This "autobiographical" tale is, in fact, fiction—Seth's tribute to the artfulness and quiet humor of the magazine cartoonist. Kalo himself is also an invention, but that doesn't diminish the power of this tale of quiet desperation. Seth's 1950s-style artwork is exquisite, and a perfect match to the story, creating a funny and moving book.

FURTHER READING: *Wimbledon Green; Vernacular Drawings*
SEE ALSO: *Box Office Poison; Jimmy Corrigan: Smartest Kid In The World; Clyde Fans*

ESSENTIAL GRAPHIC NOVELS
500
227
GENERAL FICTION
Best of the rest

Writer: Ben Katchor
Artist: Ben Katchor

Publisher: Pantheon Books, 1998
ISBN: 0375401040

5+

THE JEW OF NEW YORK

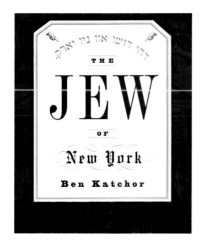

Plot: As one character notes here, "The streets of this city are filled with eccentrics." A disgraced butcher who sleeps in the open air, a businessman with plans to carbonate Lake Eerie, and a fur trapper with an obsession for a one-legged actress, are just some of the memorable characters whose lives are inextricably woven in this tale of New York life in the 1830s.

Review: Katchor's hurried, scratchy line work and quick brush strokes of gray wash give the artwork an immediacy at odds with the measured pace the story demands. Sudden scene shifts from one character to the next halt the flow of narrative, which may irritate readers unfamiliar with the author's particular approach to storytelling. Though not as enjoyable as some of Katchor's earlier work, *The Jew of New York* is an engaging piece with a curious charm quite unlike anything else in comic strip fiction.

FURTHER READING: *Cheap Novelties*
SEE ALSO: *Julius Knipl, Real Estate Photographer*

★
★
★
★

Writer: Gary Panter
Artist: Gary Panter

Publisher: Fantagraphics, 2004
ISBN: 1560975725

15+ JIMBO IN PURGATORY

Plot: Gary Panter's punk everyman, Jimbo, explores a huge infotainment center on Mount Purgatory, where he encounters pop-culture icons such as Frank Zappa and John Lennon, as well as monsters and robots, in a postmodern reworking of Dante's *Purgatorio*.

Review: You either get Gary Panter or you don't. The cartoonist equivalent of a Brutalist building, Panter, hugely influential on other cartoonists, delivers some of his most detailed and ornate artwork. Single-page scenes are resplendent with references to classical illustrators, as he mixes narrative strands from Voltaire, Boccaccio, and Dante to send his hero on an exploration of icons and iconography in the modern media, sprinkled with poetic quotes and obscure allusions.

FURTHER READING: *Jimbo's Inferno; Facetasm*
SEE ALSO: *Big book of Hell; Jimmy Corrigan; Quimby the Mouse*

★
★
★
★

Writer: Ben Katchor
Artist: Ben Katchor

Publisher: Little, Brown and Co., 1996
ISBN: 0316482943

15+ JULIUS KNIPL, REAL ESTATE PHOTOGRAPHER: STORIES

photographing buildings and observing the minutiae of city life. His trawl through the urban landscape leads him to muse on the history of the paper drinking straw, and puzzle over the shape created by a cracked wall.

Review: The short stories in this collection combine to give the reader a palpable sense of the city Knipl inhabits. Ben Katchor's depiction of New York is one of shadowy office blocks, brightly lit neon stores, and discount cafeterias, populated by a collection of memorable eccentrics. It's the little details and their evocation of half-forgotten memories that stay with you long after you've finished reading .

FURTHER READING: *Cheap Novelties:*
The Pleasures of Urban Decay
SEE ALSO: *The Jew Of New York*

Plot: A nostalgic look at New York life seen through the eyes of the title character, Julius Knipl, who wanders the streets

Writer: Chris Ware
Artist: Chris Ware

Publisher: Fantagraphics, 2003
ISBN: 0375404538

JIMMY CORRIGAN, THE SMARTEST KID IN THE WORLD

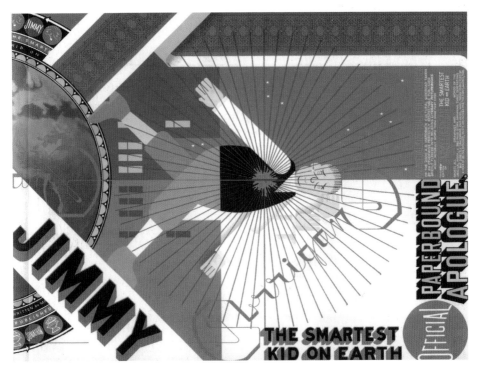

Plot: *Jimmy Corrigan* tells the tale of a lonely office worker who is reconciled with his estranged father one Thanksgiving weekend. The meeting proves to be an awkward experience, as the younger man is unable to engage in any meaningful discussion with his father. Jimmy discovers that he has an adopted sister, Amy, and that his grandfather, also called Jimmy, is still alive. An interesting story about the older Jimmy, told in flashback, acts as an interlude to the principal narrative and deals with the same themes of rejection, isolation, and unhappiness. The book foregoes any real plot to concentrate on the relationship between father and son and their inability to connect after many years apart.

Review: For a story more concerned with character than plot, *Jimmy Corrigan* needs a much more interesting subject at its core to really succeed. Over the course of 380 pages, very little is revealed about Jimmy and the lack of any meaningful insight into his character becomes very frustrating. Chris Ware's visual work, on the other hand, is far more compelling. As an illustrator, designer, and typographer, Ware's skills are unquestionably brilliant. Furthermore, he is clearly a man who understands the unique dynamics of the comic book and is prepared to experiment with the form. Particularly effective are the intricate, diagrammatical layouts that relay the narrative with a wonderful precision and clarity. Not the masterpiece that some critics claim, but on this evidence, Ware can't be far from producing such a work.

FURTHER READING: *Acme Novelty Library;*
Acme Novelty Datebook
SEE ALSO: *Quimby the Mouse; Jimbo in Purgatory*

★ **Writer:** Robert Louis Stevenson
★ **Adapted by:** Alan Grant
★ **Artist:** Cam Kennedy

Publisher: Tundra Books, 2007
ISBN: 1902407385

A KIDNAPPED

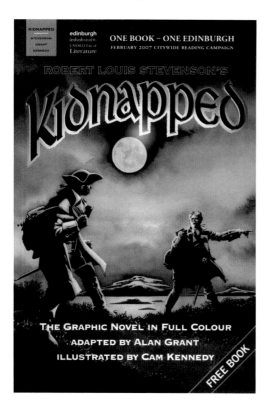

Plot: It is 1751 and recently orphaned Scottish teenager David Balfour sets out for Edinburgh to meet his uncle Ebenezer for the first time. Fearful of his nephew, Ebenezer has him kidnapped and put on a ship sailing for America. When the ship picks up a Scottish rebel, Alan Breck, he befriends David, but both are washed overboard during a storm. Teaming up, they begin to make their way back across the Scottish Highlands to Edinburgh, keeping Alan Breck one step ahead of the English troops, and David Balfour one step nearer to the inheritance his uncle is hiding from him.

Review: Commissioned for the 2007 Edinburgh City of Literature reading campaign, this adaptation of Stevenson's classic novel was promoted as being created by the "Scottish dream team" of Alan Grant and Cam Kennedy. Kennedy spent nine months painting the book and his detailed and atmospheric art complements the action and adventure of the story. A limited number were available free to Edinburgh's citizens, but the title was also released through the normal channels and quickly achieved considerable sales. With Grant remaining true to Stevenson's 1880s language in the initial version, the book was also issued in both modern English and lowland Scots dialect versions, and was eventually translated into Scots Gaelic. Indeed, the success of the different versions led Classical Comics to provide a similar range of alternative text versions for their Shakespearean graphic novels, while Grant and Kennedy were commissioned to adapt *Jekyll and Hyde* for the 2008 reading campaign.

FURTHER READING: *Graphic Shakespeare: Henry V*
SEE ALSO: *King Lear: Graphic Shakespeare; The Strange Case Of Dr Jekyll and Mr Hyde*

Writer: William Shakespeare
Artist: Ian Pollock

Publisher: Black Dog & Leventhal, 2006
ISBN: 190410407X

A KING LEAR: GRAPHIC SHAKESPEARE

Plot: Shakespeare's immortal tale of an aging and vain king who decides to retire and divide his lands between his three daughters. When his daughter Cordelia refuses to flatter him in public, Lear disowns her and sets in place a series of events that will bring ruin to both him and his kingdom.

Review: Usually, graphic adaptations are an abridged retelling of a story in a different medium, but this book retains the entirety of Shakespeare's original text. Unfortunately, as much of the play involves "talking heads" on stage, the comic finds it difficult to illustrate much else. Ian Pollock's art is wonderfully stylized but in no way attempts to be realistic. Faithful students of Shakespeare may find Pollock's images of Lear and the rest of the cast to be a far cry from their own imagination.

FURTHER READING: *Graphic Shakespeare: Macbeth; Manga Shakespeare: Hamlet*
SEE ALSO: *Contract With God Trilogy; Kidnapped*

Writer: James Vance
Artist: Dan Burr

Publisher: W.W. Norton, 2006
ISBN: 0393328481

A KINGS IN DISGUISE: A NOVEL

Plot: When his alcoholic father disappears and his older brother is arrested after trying to steal money, movie-obsessed 12-year-old Freddie sets out on the road for Detroit, where his father was last seen. Befriended by an old, sick wanderer, Sammy, he is introduced to a hobo community who deal with their uncertain futures by pretending they are important people living incognito. The heart of the story is their tragic involvement in labor riots, opening Freddie's eyes to the factors that are really at the heart of the Great Depression.

Review: Vance brings a fresh twist to this coming-of-age story by setting it among the secretive world of American travelers and exploring the dehumanizing horrors of the Depression through the eyes of a boy. Burr's realistic artwork, though sometimes a little stolid, is nonetheless effective in making its point without seeming dogmatic.

FURTHER READING: *Mendel's Daughter*
SEE ALSO: *Skidmarks; Safe Area Gorazde*

★ **Writer:** Jessica Abel
★ **Artist:** Jessica Abel

Publisher: Pantheon, 2006
ISBN: 0375423656

15+ LA PERDIDA

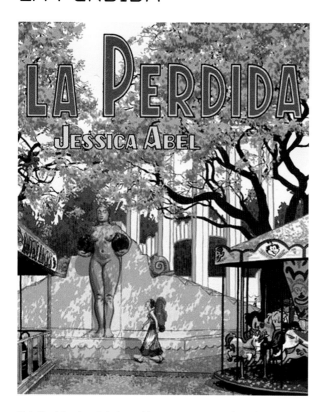

Plot: The folly of a relatively wealthy, naive American girl who wants to live an "authentic" Mexican life. *La Perdida* translates as "the lost girl" but it isn't just a story about loss; at its heart, it is a story of innocence and ignorance—one lost and the other retained.

Review: Carla, the heroine, is on a quest to lose herself in Mexico, and on the surface *La Perdida* is a tale of a cultural battle between Mexico and the United States. It is a conflict that Mexico, ripe with defectors all keen to taste the opportunities and freedoms north of the border, seems doomed to lose.

Jessica Abel's art, reminiscent of David Mazzucchelli and Dylan Horrocks, is fantastically evocative, conveying a real sense of place and the movement of bodies. Unfortunately,

the petty, solipsistic character of Carla undercuts the visual impact that *La Perdida* offers. It isn't that Carla is so resolutely self-centered and lacking in self-awareness, more that interesting questions about her identity remain unexplored. We are told that she's half-Mexican, yet despite returning to the country, she never looks for her father, elaborates on his disappearance, or seeks to uncover additional links to her Mexican roots. For this reason La Perdida remains a frustrating, if occasionally compelling, read.

FURTHER READING: *Soundtrack: Short Stories 1989-1996; Life Sucks*
SEE ALSO: *Mirror, Window; Gemma Bovery; Palomar*

Writer: Alan Moore
Artist: Melinda Gebbie

Publisher: Top Shelf, 2006
ISBN: 1891830740

LOST GIRLS

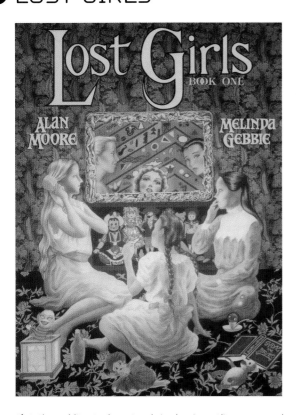

Plot: Three of literature's most enduring heroines—Alice (from the *Adventures in Wonderland*), Dorothy (from *The Wizard of Oz*), and Peter Pan's favorite, Wendy—find themselves, as adults, together in a French hotel in 1913, where they share a selection of their favorite erotic tales and fantasies. These stories take us through the course of their lives, from their first sexual experiences to full-blown orgies, chronicling both their past and their present—and their sexual exploits with the guests of the hotel, and indeed, each other, as history takes shape around them.

Review: Erotic fiction was once a highly respected genre, falling out of favor in the last hundred years. Pornography also has a bad name—in mainstream circles, at least. *Lost Girls* brings them both together and brings the walls of preconception crashing down. The book is very graphic in its approach and doesn't shy away from anything, no matter how explicit—and exercising that artistic freedom is both its purpose and its charm. The beautiful artwork illustrating these very personal and sensual stories contributes silently but effectively to the storytelling, which also covers historical events that are taking place away from the hotel, such as the assassination of Archduke Franz Ferdinand and war clouding the horizon. It took Alan Moore and Melinda Gebbie 16 years to create this stunning, challenging, and thought-provoking work of art, and it was time well spent.

FURTHER READING: *The League of Extraordinary Gentlemen Volume 2; Dark Hunger*
SEE ALSO: *Birdland; Click; Indian Summer*

★
★
★
★

Writer: Mark Kalesniko
Artist: Mark Kalesniko

Publisher: Fantagraphics Books, 2001
ISBN: 1560974109

18+ # MAIL ORDER BRIDE

Plot: Monty, the Canadian owner of a comics store, gets more than he bargains for when he brings Kyung Seo from Korea to start a new life with him in his smalltown home. As his mail order bride displays more interest in Western culture than in being a dutiful Korean wife, it becomes apparent that neither Monty nor Kyung is living up to the imagined expectations of the other, leading to a destructive conclusion.

Review: Kalesniko brings very real emotion to every panel of this inspiring, poignant, and intriguing story. Issues such as racial stereotyping, morality, and identity are tackled and dealt with in a sensitive and forthright manner, with every emotional nuance captured in skillful brushstrokes. The artwork is cartoony, but wonderfully expressive, making *Mail Order Bride* an excellent adult read, in the best sense of the word.

FURTHER READING: *Why Did Pete Duel Kill Himself?*
SEE ALSO: *Alex*

★
★
★

Writer: Lise Myhre
Artist: Lise Myhre

Publisher: Titan Books, 2008
ISBN: 1845765869

15+ # NEMI

Plot: Nemi, a feisty, cynical, romantic, strong-willed goth girl takes the world by storm (Norway in particular), with her rock-chick adventures.

Review: The work of Norwegian cartoonist Lise Myhre, Nemi's adventures have been translated across the globe and have finally been collected into an English edition. *Nemi* is less a linear narrative and more of a series of snapshots of Nemi's rock'n'roll life. A strong character with forthright opinions and desires—whether they're men, work, or chocolate—Nemi is seldom at a loss for words. She is the sexy rock chick you either wanted to date or you wanted to be, and her life is anything but dull. Myhre's smooth lines really bring Nemi's idiosyncrasies off the page.

FURTHER READING: *Nemi Volume 2; Squee*
SEE ALSO: *Lenore: Noogies; Courtney Crumrin & The Night Things*

Writer: Jessica Abel
Artist: Jessica Abel

Publisher: Fantagraphics Books, 2000
ISBN: 1560973846

5+

MIRROR, WINDOW: AN ARTBABE COLLECTION

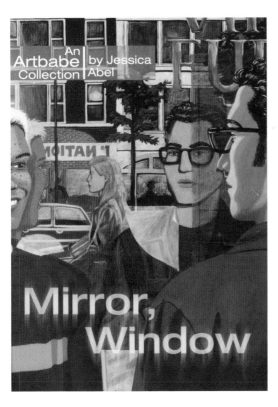

Plot: This a collection of short stories, mainly based around 20-somethings, fresh out of college or just on the cusp of making a life-changing decision. In the first story we see the early stumbling attempts to start a relationship, as seen from both sides of the couple involved. The second deals with a 22-year old ballerina, who fears she's over the hill, and her party-girl best friend as they try to figure out where their life is going to lead them next. The third is about a writer on the verge of moving to New York, abandoning all of his friends, and more importantly his girlfriend, whilst the fourth story deals with a pair of friends—one with an unrequited crush on the other—as their relationship deteriorates. There are also several short strips, mainly short character studies, on similar subjects to the main tales.

Review: This is an uneven collection that's great when it's good, but not entirely successful. Abel's got an excellent ear for dialog, and her characters certainly come across as real individuals, but the flip-side is that many of her characters are deeply unlikable, making it difficult to care in some cases. She paces her stories well, but fails to engage the reader as well as some of her peers. Her art style is great, each of the characters is instantly recognizable, and the world these people live in is beautifully illustrated.

SEE ALSO: *Summer Blonde; Ghost World; Buddy Does Seattle*
FURTHER READING: *La Perdida; Soundtrack: Short Stories; Radio: An Illustrated Guide*

★
★
★
★
★

Writer: Neil Gaiman
Artist: Dave McKean

Publisher: Bloomsbury, 2006
ISBN: 0747588449

18+

THE COMICAL TRAGEDY OR TRAGICAL COMEDY OF MR PUNCH

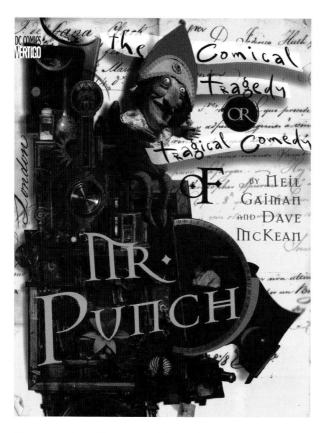

Plot: A young boy, while staying with his grandparents, encounters an ageing Punch and Judy man with a dark and mysterious past. As their lives begin to intertwine, the boy is forced to confront family secrets.

Review: Like *Violent Cases*, this is a story about memory, violence, but also of family secrets and strange puppets. Gaiman wrote the story having recently moved to America, and felt isolated by his new surroundings. To keep himself company, he wrote about old surroundings, with the tale based on bits of his own family life. This is probably McKean's best work, with his style falling halfway between the montages of *Signal to Noise*, and the pen and ink style he would adapt to for his own biographical musings in *Cages*. Gaiman also sees this as his favourite book out of anything that either he or McKean has done. Ironically this was going to be turned into a CD-ROM project, and although that didn't happen, it did sow the seeds for McKean's film career, with some of the crew for that project going on to work on *Mirrormask* in 2005.

FURTHER READING: *Cages; Black Orchid*
SEE ALSO: *Violent Cases; Signal to Noise; Stray Toasters; Arkham Asylum*

Writer: Frank Stack
Artist: Frank Stack

Publisher: Fantagraphics, 2006
ISBN: 1560977809

THE NEW ADVENTURES OF JESUS: THE SECOND COMING

Plot: After performing a much-needed Second Coming, Jesus rapidly realizes, through his encounters with the people he made a sacrifice for some time ago, that he shouldn't have delayed his comeback tour for such a long time. A series of adventures in which Jesus becomes a college lecturer and an army recruit, among other things, convinces him that he faces an uphill struggle to persuade a sceptical world of the merits of his mission of peace and harmony.

Review: Being hailed as an underground-comics landmark and championed by the underground's leading luminaries, Robert Crumb and Gilbert Shelton, does wonders for a comic book's credibility. Stack's portrayal of Jesus as a semi-innocent abroad works effectively enough, and Stack paces his humor throughout, instead of delivering it in one unwieldy, overstuffed gag. This approach also means that we don't just get the same old jokes over and over in new settings. There's much more to Jesus than that, notably the central character's bewilderment and unease at trying to fathom out exactly where his children are at in their spiritual development. Stack doesn't have to fall into lecture mode, either; the answer to the Messiah's question flies off of every page. Social commentary imaginatively concealed in wit and absurdity.

FURTHER READING: *Dorman's Doggie; Naked Glory: the Erotic Art of Frank Stack*
SEE ALSO: *Our Cancer Year*

★
★
★
★
★

Writer: Gilbert Hernandez
Artist: Gilbert Hernandez

Publisher: Fantagraphics, 2003
ISBN: 1560975393

15+ PALOMAR: THE HEARTBREAK SOUP STORIES

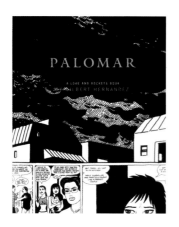

Plot: Palomar, a small Central American town, is agog at the appearance of Luba. She is larger than life in every way (including her breasts), has many children by different fathers, and runs a traveling bathhouse. Although she seems like a free spirit, it becomes apparent that Luba's past harbors dark secrets that could threaten her home.

Review: It's only when you see Hernandez's *Palomar* stories gathered together in one place that you appreciate the scale of his achievement—and the overall shape of the story. Taking a soap-opera structure with a large cast of characters, he weaves elements of magical realism into the often downbeat tales, drawn with the instantly recognizable brushwork that's so adept at expressing subtle reactions as well as outrageous slapstick responses.

FURTHER READING: *Black Hole; La Perdida; Whoa! Nellie*
SEE ALSO: *Locas; Birdland*

★
★
★

Writer: Michel Rabagliati
Artist: Michel Rabagliati

Publisher: Drawn & Quarterly, 2002
ISBN: 1896597548

15+ PAUL HAS A SUMMER JOB

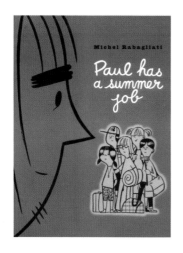

Plot: After leaving school in Montreal during the 1970s, Paul gets a call from an old schoolfriend asking him to come and work at a summer camp for kids. He duly leaves for the countryside, to live among the dirt, outdoor toilets, animals, and insects that invade his space, working with an assortment of hippies while helping disadvantaged kids have an enjoyable vacation. Over the course of the summer his whole outlook on life will change, as he meets two girls who affect him in two very different ways.

Review: This is a very sweet and moving book, not hugely original, but executed with a deft lightness of touch. There's obviously a large helping of autobiography at work here, which adds to the depth of the story, and Rabagliati's gorgeous 1950s-influenced artwork accompanies it admirably.

FURTHER READING: *Paul Moves Out; Paul Goes Fishing*
SEE ALSO: *Get A Life; Alex; My New York Diary*

Writer: Marcel Proust
Adapted by: Stéphane Heuet
Artist: Stéphane Heuet

Publisher: NBM, 2003
ISBN: 1561633488

REMEMBRANCE OF THINGS PAST: WITHIN A BUDDING GROVE

Plot: Young Proust remembers childhood visits to the family house in Combray, recalling his longing for his mother, his precipitation of a family feud with an uncle, the peculiarities of his old aunts, and the people who visited them. Tastes and sounds in the present day trigger memories of specific incidents from the past.

Review: Considering the density of the source material, Heuet does a commendable job of retaining the Proustian voice, but the comic-book rendition is text-heavy and not terribly subtle. Sadly lacking is how the process of remembering affects both past and future, but what remains is a charming series of tableaux, in which Heuet's slightly stiff but well-characterized art allows her to explore her narrator's more whimsical notions visually.

FURTHER READING: *Remembrance of Things Past: Combray; Remembrance of Things Past: Love of Swann*
SEE ALSO: *Streak of Chalk; Violent Cases*

Writer: Samuel Taylor Coleridge
Artist: Hunt Emerson

Publisher: Knockabout Comics, 2007
ISBN: 086166065X

THE RIME OF THE ANCIENT MARINER

Plot: A sailor accosts a guest on the way to a wedding and tells him what happened on a strange sea journey. The Mariner recounts the curious events that occurred after he shot an albatross that appeared to be leading the ship back into charted waters. The sailors encounter Death aboard a ghost ship, and they all die—with the exception of the Mariner, who is condemned to gawp at their corpses for the duration of the voyage. But after seven days, the Mariner is redeemed when he sees slimy sea creatures and perceives their true beauty.

Review: Hunt Emerson's delightful cartooning makes it easy to engage with Coleridge's fascinating symbolic poem. The reactions of the unhappily delayed wedding guest are particularly entertaining. Emerson keeps Coleridge's text intact while adding numerous visual puns and sight gags. Irreverent but very funny.

FURTHER READING: *Casanova's Last Stand; Lady Chatterley's Lover: The Comic Book*
SEE ALSO: *Buddy Does Seattle*

★ **Writer:** Sara Varon   **Publisher:** First Second, 2007
★ **Artist:** Sara Varon   **ISBN:** 1596431083
★
★

A ROBOT DREAMS

Plot: When Dog becomes lonely he builds himself a friend by means of a mail-order robot kit. The two companions share some special moments together, such as taking trips to the library and watching movies. Then, one fateful day, they visit the beach. As Dog swims in the sea, Robot decides to join his friend—and grinds to a halt. Dog panics and abandons his rusty robot chum, leaving the abandoned droid to dream about what could have been, while scavengers pick him clean.

Review: Words are an unnecessary addition to this simple tale of friendship, with its clear and effective drawing style. When Dog attempts to fill the void created by the loss of his companion with a series of unfulfilling friendships with some ducks and a snowman, it becomes clear that the author is examining the complexities of friendship and human relationships.

FURTHER READING: *Chicken And Cat; Sweater Weather*
SEE ALSO: *Monkey vs Robot; Goodbye Chunky Rice*

★ **Writer:** Derek Kirk Kim   **Publisher:** Top Shelf, 2004
★ **Artist:** Derek Kirk Kim   **ISBN:** 1891830570
★

15+ SAME DIFFERENCE & OTHER STORIES

Plot: In *Same Difference*, the first story in this small volume, Simon and his friend Nancy return to Simon's hometown in search of the author of a series of loveletters that were written to a former occupant of Nancy's apartment. Simon is forced to confront some faces from his past, and their quest comes to an unexpected resolution. Also included are an assortment of other stories, some autobiographical, and a few one-page strips featuring Derek Kirk Kim's Oliver Pikk character.

Review: *Same Difference* is the pick of this collected bunch, with Kim's art at its most effective, accompanying a very sweet and funny story. The others vary, with the real-life stuff working better than the strips that show the influence of Adrian Tomine. This is a confident debut, extremely well drawn and showing a lot of promise.

FURTHER READING: *Sleepwalk and Other Stories; Good As Lily*
SEE ALSO: *Chinese Born American; Ghost World; Box Office Poison*

Writer: Al Feldstein
Artist: Various

Publisher: Gemstone, 2006
ISBN: 188847257X

2+

THE EC ARCHIVES: SHOCK SUSPENSTORIES VOLUME 1

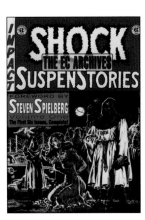

Plot: Another of the EC archives to have been yanked out of the censors' hands to shock, delight, and entertain a new audience. The *Shock SuspenStories* anthologies began as a sampler for the publisher, showcasing tales from various genres, but eventually settled into shock and crime.

Review: Like *Tales From The Crypt*, *Shock SuspenStories* has made a return to our comic-book stores in anthology form. Here, the first six issues from the short lived single issue series are collected in a single volume. Unlike *Tales from the Crypt*, however, *Shock SuspenStories* is quite hardcore in its themes, tackling ultra violence with a dash of Ku Klux Klan, extreme hazing, and murder most foul. Although the penciling seems a little dated, it doesn't detract from the stories.

FURTHER READING: *The Haunt of Fear; The Vault of Horror*
SEE ALSO: *Tales From The Crypt; Weird Science; Two-Fisted Tales*

Writer: Andi Watson
Artist: Andi Watson

Publisher: SLG Publishing, 2007
ISBN: 0943151597

SLOW NEWS DAY

Plot: Katherine Washington is an aspiring American writer, fresh out of college. Her mother learned her trade on a provincial English newspaper, the Wheatstone Mercury, which is suffering from declining sales. Katherine is encouraged to help out by following in her mother's footsteps. However, the locals, including co-worker Owen, are not keen, so Katherine must juggle her own agenda with the needs of a newspaper that covers subjects such as lost pets and parish councils that are far from her own experience. To add to her problems, she has an ambitious boyfriend back home, who is unhappy to be separated from her.

Review: A delightful romantic comedy drawn in a simple, blocky style. Watson perfectly presents the contrast between small everyday routines and big emotional struggles.

FURTHER READING: *Paris; Breakfast After Noon; Geisha*
SEE ALSO: *Paul Has A Summer Job*

ESSENTIAL GRAPHIC NOVELS

500

241

GENERAL FICTION
Best of the rest

★
★
★
★

Writer: Alex De Campi
Artist: Igor Kordey

Publisher: IDW Publishing, 2005
ISBN: 193323928X

18+ SMOKE

Plot: Set in a near future England—that's almost a now future England—a financially and morally bankrupt government spins the wheels of the political machine. Ground up in its cogs are Rupert Cain—an Albino ex-solider turned assassin, his ex- Lucy De Havilland, reporter Katie Shah, and the Machiavellian Lord Lauderdale.

Review: Behind Banksy-inspired covers, lurks a very British tale of Black Ops and political intrigue. US ex-pat writer De Campi taps right into the heart of English sensibilities with great characters like the plastic surgery demanding "Right to Beauty Brigade." The art is Kordey's best, and is beautifully enhanced by Len O'Grady's coloring, which gives the book a very European flavour. Intelligent, funny, and beautiful to look at.

FURTHER READING: *Smoke Volume 2*
SEE ALSO: *DMZ: On the Ground; Queen And Country*

★
★
★
★

Writer: Jason
Artist: Jason

Publisher: Fantagraphics, 2002
ISBN: 1560974974

15+ SSHHHH!

Plot: The second book by Danish cartoonist Jason brings us back to his strange, anthropomorphic world, this time with a series of short, wordless stories that follow a central crow character as he meets a girl, and, despite heroic efforts, loses her. He is then haunted by a strange skeletal figure, meets another girl and has a son, loses his second girl and fantasizes about ways to get her back, and finally becomes invisible, forcing him to commit a terrible deed so people notice him again.

Review: Deceptively simple drawing disguises an incredibly sharp and affecting set of stories, as Jason uses his silent milieu to convey an enormous range of clever observations about life. A quietly powerful book from an exceptional talent, *Sshhhh!* leaves a deep impression.

FURTHER READING: *Hey, Wait...; You Can't Get There From Here; I Killed Adolf Hitler*
SEE ALSO: *Why Are You Doing This?; Skin Deep; Tantrum*

Writer: Terry Moore
Artist: Terry Moore

Publisher: Abstract Studio, 2004
ISBN: 1892597268

5+

STRANGERS IN PARADISE: POCKET BOOK 1

Plot: Katchoo and Francine are best friends, slightly complicated by the fact that bisexual Katchoo is hopelessly in love with the oblivious and very straight Francine. Then Katchoo meets David, a quiet but tenacious young man who's determined to win her heart. Francine also has to contend with her unfaithful ex-fiancé, Freddie, who's proving difficult to shake off. Everything starts going wrong when Katchoo's former employer comes looking for the money she stole, and as her life unravels, she realizes that not everyone in her life is who she thinks they are.

Review: *Strangers in Paradise* is an unusual series in comics, with a narrative based in the real world that combines crime, romance, and humor—not a typical mix. It also features two of the most acclaimed female voices in comics, but is written by a man. It started as a three-issue miniseries, and was followed by a 13-issue second volume, all of which are collected here. The art starts well, but gets better and better until Moore's style becomes pretty much perfect by the final third of this volume—the story, dialog, and characterization are brilliant. Although this is the first of six books, it's self-contained and can be enjoyed on its own. It's particularly recommended as a gateway read for non-comics readers, particularly teens and young adults.

FURTHER READING: *Strangers in Paradise Pocketbooks 2–6; Paradise Too; Wahoo Morris*
SEE ALSO: *Locas; Ghost World*

★ **Writer:** Bill Sienkiewicz **Publisher:** Image Comics, 2007
★ **Artist:** Bill Sienkiewicz **ISBN:** 1582408238
★
★

18+ # STRAY TOASTERS

Plot: Egon Rustemagik is not a well man. He's just been released from a mental institution where he was sent for a crime he didn't commit, so he can catch a monster who is responsible for the deaths of a series of women and children. Before he was locked up, he was a very good cop, and now he's going to need to utilize all his resources to catch the killer—who may, or may not, be human.

Review: The narrative is difficult to follow, because Sienkiewicz makes nothing obvious. Nevertheless, this is an essential read, mainly due to the amazing painted artwork, which is wildly experimental, but was enormously influential on a generation of comics artists. A remarkable and thought-provoking work that can be interpreted on a variety of levels.

FURTHER READING: *Daredevil: Love and War; 30 Days of Night: Beyond Barrow; Voodoo Child: The Illustrated Legend of Jimi Hendrix*
SEE ALSO: *Criminal Macabre; Elektra: Assassin*

★ **Writer:** Miguelanxo Prado **Publisher:** NBM, 1994
★ **Artist:** Miguelanxo Prado **ISBN:** 1561631086
★
★

15+ # STREAK OF CHALK

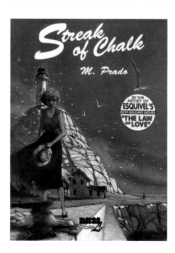

Plot: Raul arrives on a mysterious island. He finds Ana—a woman who seems to be waiting for someone—and Sara and her disturbed son, who run a hotel. Raul tries to court Ana, then attempts to rescue her from two drunken sailors, but he's too fixated on his ineffectuality to realize they raped Sara instead, so turns to her to assuage his guilt. When Ana finally decides to thank Raul for his attempted intervention, she discovers him and Sara together. Shocked by the depth of her feelings, she leaves the island abruptly.

Review: *Streak of Chalk* is a mysterious and compelling story that refuses to allow any easy conclusions. Prado's art, characterized by his use of light pastels on dark backgrounds to create moody and inexplicably threatening landscapes, perfectly matches the uneasy atmosphere of the story.

FURTHER READING: *Peter and the Wolf*
SEE ALSO: *Ghost World; Tangents; In Search of Shirley*

Writer: Adrian Tomine
Artist: Adrian Tomine

Publisher: Drawn & Quarterly, 2003
ISBN: 1896597572

5+ SUMMER BLONDE

Plot: A collection of four stories from Tomine's *Optic Nerve* comic. Each of the tales deals with lonely people and their interactions with the world around them. A writer, stuck on his second book, ends up dating the school-age sister of his high-school crush; a young man starts messing with the girl he's fond of when she begins dating his neighbor; a Korean girl starts prank-calling strangers from the payphone across the street from her window; and a lonely high-school pupil and the class drunk end up forming a bond.

Review: Tomine's central characters are all very similar—the mawkish outsider—but he's so good at writing them that it really doesn't matter. The dialogue and situations are all very authentic, and the artwork is equally strong and effective.

FURTHER READING: *Sleepwalk and Other Stories; 32 Stories: The Complete Optic Nerve Mini-Comics; Shortcomings*
SEE ALSO: *Ghost World; Same Difference & Other Stories; Locas*

Writer: Debbie Drechsler
Artist: Debbie Drechsler

Publisher: Drawn & Quarterly, 2003
ISBN: 1896597653

5+ THE SUMMER OF LOVE

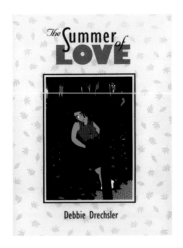

Plot: A rite-of-passage story set in 1967, focusing on the attempts of a teenage girl, Lily, to make new friends and fit in when her family moves to a new home in a nondescript middle American town. After finding everyone and everything boring, she finally meets Steve, a seemingly mature, intelligent young man—but, when their relationship inexplicably cools, she winds up with Keith, who's insensitive and pushy. Meanwhile Lily worries about her younger sister's lesbian explorations.

Review: Drechsler's rounded forms and soft lines, matched by the cool colors, capture the languid and sometimes gawky nature of adolescence, while her writing sensitively explores the confused emotional landscape of puberty. As the new girl in town and at school, Lily's inchoate feelings of angst and anxiety—which most people can readily identify with—are amplified by her unfamiliar situation.

FURTHER READING: *Daddy's Girl*
SEE ALSO: *Ghost World*

★
★
★

Writer: Miguelanxo Prado
Artist: Miguelanxo Prado

Publisher: NBM, 1996
ISBN: 1561631485

15+ TANGENTS

Plot: *Tangents* is a series of interlinked vignettes on the subjects of power and sex, and the effects of time. Each story is a bedroom encounter between two successful people. Though we're rarely shown anything beyond their coupling and brief conversations, we are still led to broad conclusions about their lives and philosophies.

Review: In *Tangents*, Prado meditates on the ineffectual nature of love when compared with power and money. Several of the stories feature former lovers who rejected each other in their youth because of lack of money, or the desire to focus on their careers, who find that they cannot rekindle their old feelings. Each tale is morose and melancholic, but beautifully drawn. Prado has an exquisite eye for the movement of human bodies, and his soft pastel lines create a languid and sensual feel.

FURTHER READING: *Venus in Furs by Guido Crepax;*
The Blue Notebook by Andre Juillard
SEE ALSO: *Streak of Chalk*

★
★
★
★

Writer: Paul Hornschemeier
Artist: Paul Hornschemeier

Publisher: Fantagraphics, 2006
ISBN: 1560976535

15+ THE THREE PARADOXES

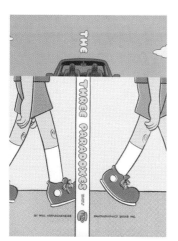

Plot: Paul returns home to Ohio for a short visit with his parents, and prepares for his first meeting with a girl who is a fan of his work and has been writing to him for some time. Paul is also trying to create a new comic strip, and takes some photographs of his childhood haunts to show to his potential new lover. We follow his thought processes as they reveal themselves in comic form.

Review: Hornschemeier deconstructs the idea of autobiographical comics, concentrating on the line at which fact and fiction blur, as the various narratives blend and the voices become interchangeable. The art is gorgeous, changing styles from panel to panel to suit each thread of the story. On the surface it works as a simple narrative, but there's a lot more to it if you look a little deeper.

FURTHER READING: *Mother Come Home; The Complete Sequential;*
Let Us Be Perfectly Clear
SEE ALSO: *Alex; The Playboy; Curses*

Writer: Alex Robinson
Artist: Alex Robinson

Publisher: Top Shelf, 2005
ISBN: 1891830732

5+

TRICKED

Plot: *Tricked* is a glimpse into the seemingly disparate lives of six people, including a fading rock star and a waitress, who go about their lives blissfully unaware of the tragic chain of events that is about to connect them, leading to a violent climax.

Review: Robinson marries the separate lives of this ensemble cast in a skillful and, more importantly, believable manner. His art is very appealing, and his excellent plotting and thought-provoking characterization draw you in page by page, as you head towards the explosive ending. Top marks, too, for the musical references (and nods to the movie *Spinal Tap*) that are sprinkled throughout the book. A smart and memorable book that reads like a Robert Altman film on paper.

FURTHER READING: *BOP! More Box Office Poison*
SEE ALSO: *Box Office Poison; Demo*

★
★
★

Writer: Masakazu Katsura
Artist: Masakazu Katsura

Publisher: VIZ Media LLC, 2004
ISBN: 159116074X

2+

VIDEO GIRL AI
VOLUME 1: PREPRODUCTION

Plot: Yota is a shy and indecisive high-school student whose nickname is "Dateless." He's in love with classmate Moemi, but she only has eyes for his best friend. On a broken machine, Yota plays a video of the cute Ai Amano. To his surprise, she emerges physically from the screen and promises to improve Yota's love life, naturally becoming a focus for his affections herself.

Review: Masakazu Katsura's attractively drawn strip has a darker and more serious tone than other similarly themed romances, but there are plenty of the usual unfortunate coincidences to keep him unsure of his own and others' true feelings. However, the threats to Ai, and the challenges both she and Yota face, help to keep the book consistently interesting.

FURTHER READING: *Video Girl Ai Volumes 2–15*
SEE ALSO: *Maison Ikkoku; Oh My Goddess!*

★
★ **Writer:** Neil Gaiman
★ **Artist:** Dave McKean
★

Publisher: Dark Horse
ISBN: 1569716064

15+ VIOLENT CASES

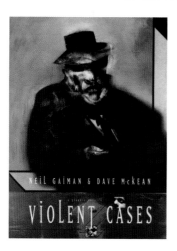

Plot: A narrator begins to explain one of his first memories, when he sustained a dislocated arm while being dragged up to bed by his father. The accident leads to him meeting an ageing osteopath who, during their appointments, begins to recall the time he spent as Al Capone's physician.

Review: This tale meanders between memories and imagination, contrasting childhood events against how we recount memories when we're older, particularly violence. The narrator attempts to piece together the events of his childhood, while at the same time taking stock of the relationship with his own family. Gradually juxtaposing Chicago in the 1920s, and Portsmouth, England, in the 1960s, Gaiman's writing encapsulates the nostalgia perfectly. *Violent Cases* is illustrated in McKean's pre-digital mixed media style, and has a passing similarity to some of Bill Sienkiewicz's work of the time.

FURTHER READING: *Cages; Pictures That Tick*
SEE ALSO: *Signal to Noise; The Tragical Comedy or Comical Tragedy of Mr Punch; Stray Toasters*

★
★ **Writer:** Ross Campbell
★ **Artist:** Ross Campbell
★

Publisher: Oni Press, 2004
ISBN: 1932664076

15+ WET MOON VOLUME 1: FEEBLE WANDERINGS

Plot: Cleo's a goth teenager in the Deep South, just moved out of home and into a dorm at the local art college. Her mysterious new roommate is a bit on the strange side, and there's also a handsome goth boy, and an odd handicapped girl who keeps showing up in the strangest places, plus someone's leaving nasty notes about Cleo all over campus. All of this seems to allude to some bigger mystery, but what exactly is happening?

Review: This is the first book in a series, so not much is revealed, but Campbell sets the scene beautifully, with wonderfully moody, shaded artwork. His dialog is excellent, and the characters are fully fleshed-out, although it's obvious that there's more to most of them than meets the eye. An intriguing and authentic read.

FURTHER READING: *Wet Moon Volumes 2 and 3; The Abandoned*
SEE ALSO: *Black Hole; Strange Embrace; Ghost World*

Writer: Patrick Cothias
Artist: Philippe Adamov

Publisher: Heavy Metal
ISBN: 1879450119

WIND OF THE GODS VOLUME 1: BLOOD FROM THE MOON

Plot: Set in Shinkoku-era Japan (around the 13th century), *Wind of the Gods* contrasts elegant violence with political machination, as the powerful Lord Oshikaga dispatches Tchen Qin and a band of warriors to quash a peasant rebellion. They have barely begun when infighting and intrigue start to threaten the mission. Qin is distracted by a one-eyed peasant who seems to know far more than he does about what is going on, and by a challenge from one of his men, which results in the samurai being ambushed.

Review: If you find all the motion lines and weird angles of Japanese samurai comics a bit offputting, this is the book for you—it's very detailed, and very Western. Cothias is a clever plotter who puts in plenty of twists and turns.

FURTHER READING: *Le Vent des Dieux: Le Ventre du Dragon; Le Vent des Dieux: L'Homme Oublié*
SEE ALSO: *Lone Wolf and Cub; Blade of the Immortal*

Writer: Jaime Hernandez
Artist: Jaime Hernandez

Publisher: Fantagraphics, 2000
ISBN: 1560973838

WHOA, NELLIE!

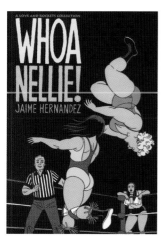

Plot: Xochitl Nava and Gina Bravo are female wrestlers in Texas, friends and tag-team partners. Their friendship is tested when Xo is awarded the Women's Texas Championship, only to lose it in her first fight with upcoming star Katy Hawk. Gina realizes that Xo was only given the belt because the wrestling authorities needed a weaker wrestler for their star to beat. Tensions increase between the two friends, culminating in the two women going up against each other and the strongest female wrestlers in the state in an enormous Battle Royale.

Review: This was Hernandez's first project following the end of the first series of *Love & Rockets*, and combines his two great loves: old-school wrestling and strong women. It's far more lightweight than his Locas work, but is set in the same world, and is beautifully drawn and a lot of fun.

FURTHER READING: *Ghost Of Hoppers; Dicks & Deedees*
SEE ALSO: *Locas: The Maggie & Hopey Stories; Palomar: The Heartbreak Soup Collection*

CHAPTER 5

HORROR

THE RETURN OF THE REPRESSED

The horror comic has been subject to the changing whims of fashion and fortune more than most genres. Constrained by heavy-handed censorship during key periods of its history, horror has struggled at times to maintain the story elements central to its basic premise: the ability to induce fear, terror, and revulsion in the mind of the reader.

If there is such a thing as a year zero for comic-book horror, most would agree that it was 1950—the year that saw the launch of the three EC titles; *Tales From the Crypt*, *The Vault of Horror*, and *The Haunt of Fear*. From the outset, these comics understood that for horror to work it should be unsettling, imaginative, and, at times, gruesome. These early comics pulled few punches with their visceral content and the anthology titles typically consisted of gory stories with surprise endings. The art and writing was generally of a higher standard than most mainstream comics that published at the tail end of the so-called Golden Age, but EC's popularity for delivering such shocking content was to be its own downfall, ushering in an era of heavy censorship that would kill off mainstream horror for a considerable length of time.

A moral crusade against the excesses of crime and horror titles gathered steam in mid-1950s America. The publication of Dr Fredric Wertham's book *Seduction of the Innocent* prompted a Senate subcommittee on juvenile delinquency, that in turn led to the founding of a voluntary Comics Code Authority. In addition to banning violent images, certain horror concepts such as vampires and zombies were also banned, even in child-friendly versions. Although obeying the code was technically voluntary, the moral witch-hunt against publishers who flouted the code meant that no publisher could survive for long if he was seen to be publishing content thought to be a corrupting influence on the young.

A rare exception in the mid-to-late 1960s was the line of black-and-white horror magazines (*Creepy Eerie* and *Vampirella*) published by Warren. These flouted the conventions of the code with a degree of success, mostly because their magazine format meant they weren't sold alongside the color superhero comics of the time. But it wasn't until mainstream publishers challenged the code in the late '60s that some relaxation of the strict rules became a reality. DC launched a series of color horror anthologies in the same format as their superhero titles, but Marvel, in their more experimental period, copied the Warren format and published numerous black-and-white horror magazines such as *Dracula Lives*, *Vampire Tales*, and *Tales of the Zombie*. The new-found horror craze of the early 1970s, boosted by a series of high-profile and suitably disturbing films, gave Marvel the impetus to publish color titles, too, such as the excellent *Tomb of Dracula* series.

By the early 1980s, horror had lost its way in the graphic format, as most of the titles launched in the late '60s and early '70s had folded. But a new wave of horror creators entered the field, led at first by Alan Moore, who revamped an old DC monster character, *Swamp Thing*, with significant critical and financial success. Arguably, Moore's stint on *Swamp Thing* opened the floodgates to a publishing phenomenon. DC decided that the time was right for an imprint for mature readers, centered around fantasy and horror to begin with, and established Vertigo as a home for their more hard-edged titles. Vertigo was responsible for many excellent horror comics, including *Hellblazer* (a spinoff from *Swamp Thing's* tales of working-class magus John Constantine), Neil Gaiman's award winning *Sandman*, Garth Ennis's *Preacher* and the short-lived *House of Secrets*. Having inspired the Vertigo imprint, Alan Moore went on to write another seminal tale of horror, *From Hell*—his own personal take on the Jack the Ripper legend that set a new

literary standard in what has often been regarded as a throwaway pulp genre.

Elsewhere, writer/artist Mike Mignola created *Hellboy*, successfully adopting elements of H.P. Lovecraft's uniquely eldritch horror to create a horror/superhero hybrid in which the eponymous hero fought the forces of darkness, on the side of mankind—despite being a demon himself. The concept was further expanded in a series of related *B.P.R.D.* books.

Independent publishers allowed new writers to experiment with traditional stereotypes. *Thirty Days of Night*, by Steve Niles and Ben Templesmith, stripped away the goth chic that had turned vampires into tragic, misunderstood figures, and returned them to their more frightening, bestial state in an Alaskan town where the sun doesn't shine for a whole month. Robert Kirkman's series *The Walking Dead* was a successful take on the zombie apocalypse scenario popularized by George Romero's ...*Dead* movies, and more recent films such as *28 Days Later*.

Successful franchises were also ripe for adaptation. Clive Barker's *Hellraiser* films were custom-built for the comic-book treatment, and Joss Whedon's well-publicized love of the medium meant that *Buffy the Vampire Slayer* comics were inevitable. In a rare example of a sequel crossing over from one medium to another, Whedon has recently begun Series 8 of Buffy as a monthly comic book, not a TV series.

Perhaps the most unlikely success story of recent years is the *Marvel Zombies* series. Originally a throwaway idea in a *Fantastic Four* title, writer Mark Millar envisaged a parallel Marvel universe where a "rage virus" had infected the super-powered characters. Veering from moments of carefully staged comedy to outright horror, the concept spawned several sequels and shows no signs of stopping.

★
★
★
★

Writer: Garth Ennis
Artist: Will Simpson

Publisher: Vertigo, 1994
ISBN: 1563891506

15+ HELLBLAZER: DANGEROUS HABITS

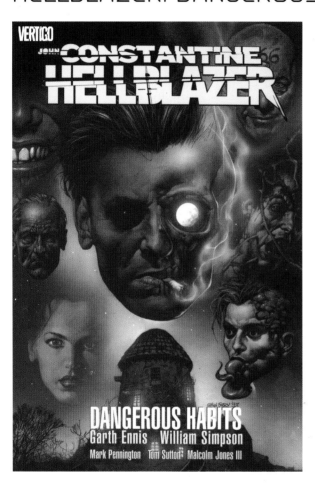

Plot: Everybody's favorite grumpy, chainsmoking, demon-exorcising Liverpudlian, John Constantine, returns to the pages of this graphic novel to receive his death sentence: lung cancer. As if that wasn't bad enough, when the populace of Hell are eagerly awaiting the arrival of Constantine's damned soul, to be delivered personally by the First of the Fallen, well... you could forgive him for being just a little bit more tetchy than usual. This volume comprises issues 41–46 of the series, culminating in a showdown with the three highest denizens of Hell.

Review: This *Hellblazer* story arc should be high up on anybody's list of the best-ever graphic novels. When it was first published it was extremely refreshing, thanks to the new leadership of Garth Ennis, who set out with the very clear intention of pumping some much-needed adrenaline into the series. Ennis succeeded in this goal, ringing in a new era with a story arc riddled with plot twists and some rather marvelous secondary characters that include the deeply and colorfully alcoholic Brendan Finn; Ellie the Succubus; and, of course, The Snob.

There are some very dramatic scenes in which artist Will Simpson has clearly embraced the spirit of the tale, and where the action appears to be more directed than illustrated, affecting the pace and style of the show in a hugely positive way.

This is a challenging and involved storyline that takes you to the very depths of the character of Constantine, and you really have to have an emotional investment in the story before you can start sharing his problems. Constantine isn't the easiest character to get along with at the start of the Hellblazer series, but it's definitely worth putting in the time—the rewards you will gain from the story will far outstrip the effort you put in to it. *Dangerous Habits* is an absolutely essential instalment in the chronicles of Constantine.

FURTHER READING: *Hellblazer: Rake at the Gates of Hell; Hellblazer: Fear And Loathing*
SEE ALSO: *Hellblazer: All His Engines; The Books of Magic; Sandman: Preludes and Nocturnes*

★
★
★
★
★

Writer: Mike Mignola
Artist: Mike Mignola

Publisher: Dark Horse, 2004
ISBN: 1593070918

12+

HELLBOY VOLUME 3: THE CHAINED COFFIN AND OTHER STORIES

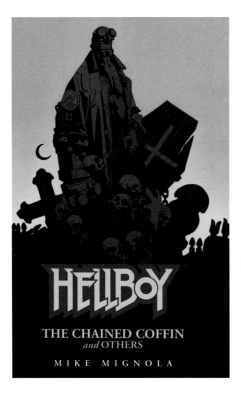

Plot: Accidentally summoned up from Hell as an infant by the Nazis, Hellboy is found by, and chooses to help, Professor Bruttenholm and the B.P.R.D. (Bureau of Paranormal Research and Defense). The stories in this collection include *The Corpse*, in which Hellboy must find a Christian cemetery and bury a corpse before morning, in order to recover a stolen baby; *The Iron Shoes*, in which he must fight a mischievous goblin that lurks in an abandoned tower; and *The Baba Yaga*, a tale of a Russian witch who counts dead men's fingers. *A Christmas Underground* sees Hellboy spending Christmas Eve trying to rescue the long-lost daughter of a dying woman; *The Chained Coffin* sheds light on Hellboy's origins; *The Wolves of Saint Augustus* concerns a cursed village whose population turns into wolves once every seven years; and in *Almost Colossus*, Hellboy must track down a

500-year-old homunculus so that he can save the life of his colleague and friend, Liz Sherman.

Review: This first collection of short stories features some of Mike Mignola's earliest work on his signature character and they just ooze class. Mignola's dark, angular artwork is deceptively simple, providing an incredible amount of atmosphere, and is so wedded to the stories that it's virtually impossible to imagine one without the other.

Influenced heavily by folklore, novelist H.P. Lovecraft, and comics icon Jack Kirby, Hellboy is a wonderful mix of pulp fiction and superhero adventure. The stories in this collection are inevitably a bit of a mixed bag, in terms of content if not quality, due largely to the various sources from which they

ESSENTIAL
GRAPHIC NOVELS
500
257
HORROR
Top 10 horror graphic novels

are culled. The miniseries *Almost Colossus* is the longest story and contributes to the Hellboy mythology as a whole, following up on *Wake The Devil* and introducing the character of Roger the Homunculus. *The Wolves Of Saint Augustus* is notable because it is Mignola's first script for the strip (writer John Byrne took the honors on the debut adventure, *The Seed Of Destruction*).

The remaining adventures are shorter, but are far from being "filler" material. *The Iron Shoes* is admittedly more of a diversion than a story—although it has been animated for the *Hellboy: Blood and Iron* DVD—but in *The Corpse*, we have (arguably) one of Hellboy's finest moments, encapsulating all that is great about the series: it's quirky, silly, funny, spooky, and packed with monsters.

The Chained Coffin and Other Stories is a wonderful assortment of tales, summing up a strip that is one of the finest creator-owned properties of all time, and has since evolved into several animated movies and two live action films, the first released in 2004 and the second in 2008.

FURTHER READING: *Hellboy Volume 1: Seed Of Destruction; Hellboy Volume 2: Wake The Dead; B.P.R.D: Hollow Earth and Other Stories*
SEE ALSO: *B.P.R.D.: Plague of Frogs; Zombieworld: Champion Of The Worms*

★
★
★
★

Writer: Brian Michael Bendis, Steve Niles   **Publisher:** Todd McFarlane Productions, 2006
Artist: Ashley Wood   **ISBN:** 1582405980

15+

HELLSPAWN:
THE ASHLEY WOOD COLLECTION

Plot: Once a solider, Al Simmons makes a deal with a lord of hell to come back to life so he can see his wife one last time. But he's cheated, and gets reincarnated as an agent for the devil: a solider of the damned that facilitates man's downfall in the fight between heaven and hell.

Review: Taking a step back from Todd McFarlane's seminal series, *Hellspawn* focused more on the people around Spawn, and the supernatural aspects of his nature and surroundings. A lot of the time the central character takes a back seat, and the story focuses alternatively on characters

that define who he is and why he's there i.e. a girl on the brink of suicide, a right wing religious zealot who causes far more evil than good, and a journalist trying to uncover the fall in violent crime in the downtown area that Simmons seems to frequent. The overall arc sets Spawn up as an urban legend on a par with characters such as Clive Barker's *Candyman*, and taking him away from his superhero routes definitely does the story a favor.

Ashley Wood's art is certainly the stand out feature of this collection and like all mixed-media illustrators, you either

love it or hate it. With definite influences from Bill Sienkiewicz and Kent Williams, Wood's style is dark and scratchy, while also beautiful and eye catching.

Bendis and Niles give us a decent set of story arcs, and rewrite established characters from the original McFarlane series, such as the angelic host, the Freak, and Cy-Gor, giving them greater depth, as well as giving the covert group led by Jason Wynn a far deeper involvement than previously shown. We also see Simmons go through a metaphysical journey within himself, which establishes the character, at

least for this collection and gives an insight into who he thinks he is. But this occurs quite late in the book, with much of the remaining story dedicated to the Cy-Gor storyline, the climax of which comes quite abruptly, and just stops, making you wish there was a further volume. Unfortunately this is not the case, and you may finish this volume left wanting.

FURTHER READING: *Popbot; Zombies Versus Robots*
SEE ALSO: *Criminal Macabre; 30 Days of Night*

★ **Writer:** Garth Ennis   **Publisher:** Vertigo, 1996
★ **Artist:** Steve Dillon   **ISBN:** 1563892618
★
★

18+ PREACHER: GONE TO TEXAS

ESSENTIAL
GRAPHIC NOVELS

500

261

HORROR
Top 10 horror graphic novels

Plot: Jesse Custer, a preacher in a small Texas town, sees his life change drastically when he is possessed by the child of an angel and a devil, named the Genesis. The possession gives Jesse the power to rival God himself, as well as endowing him with the "Word of God." If Jesse tells someone to do something—anything—they do it.

When this child was born, God surrendered his divine rights. Knowing this, Jesse sets off to find God and return things to normal—if you can call the life they are thrown into normal. He is joined by his former girlfriend Tulip O'Hare and a vampire named Cassidy. They cause commotion wherever they go and soon have the law, as well as supernatural beings sent to stop Jesse, in pursuit.

Review: *Preacher* is a groundbreaking book that allowed Garth Ennis to flex his writing muscles. It takes a good few issues to actually get to the crux of what is going on, and discovering that God has gone AWOL and Jesse is possessed comes as something of a surprise.

Preacher examines a number of interesting religious and philosophical speculations: if God has abandoned his post,

what does that mean for the inhabitants of Heaven and Hell—not to mention Earth—although the appearance of a vampire seems to slightly cloud the issue as a character that doesn't quite fit into this established belief system. That aside, the plot and story are as tight as can be and you soon become immersed in a world of blood, gore, and violence that seems to be part of everyday life. Many of the characters are killed, or shot and seriously injured. One of the main characters is nicknamed Arse Face, for reasons that become obvious when you see him, and throughout the book he speaks a language only his father seems to understand.

There is a charming elegance to this book. Not much really happens in the first story arc, but this never becomes frustrating. Instead, the revealing snippets of the characters' back stories draw you in until you're hooked—a mark of Ennis's considerable storytelling talent.

FURTHER READING: *Dicks; The Boys; Chronicles of Wormwood*
SEE ALSO: *Hellblazer: Dangerous Habits; Lucifer: Devil in the Gateway*

★
★
★
★

Writer: Neil Gaiman
Artists: Dave McKean, Sam Keith,
Mike Dringenberg, and Malcolm Jones III

Publisher: Vertigo, 1996
ISBN: 1563890119

15+

THE SANDMAN VOLUME 1: PRELUDES AND NOCTURNES

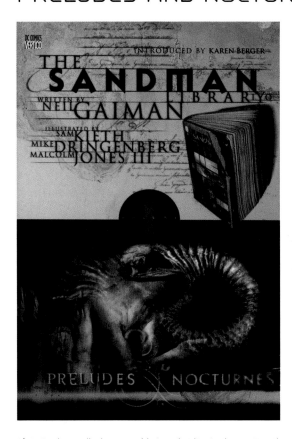

Plot: *Sandman* tells the story of beings that live in the worlds between ours. Dream, one of the Sandman's many names, is one of these Endless. He is imprisoned for decades by an occultist who is seeking immortality. Upon escaping, he must reclaim the objects of power that were stolen from his mortal captors, and rebuild the realm of dreaming that he inhabits, putting right the entire dream world as humans know it. In the process, he confronts a dream junkie, the legions of Hell, and an all-powerful madman.

Review: *Preludes and Nocturnes* co-stars a host of DC characters from the past, including John Constantine, Scott

Free, J'onn J'onzz, Scarecrow, Doctor Destiny, and Cain and Abel from the House of Mystery. It's a mystical tale in which the master of the dreams finds that the objects he uses to manipulate the fabric of dreams are being used for other purposes. His journeys take him into the depths of Hell, where he finds his helmet. Praising the kings of Hell for their honor, he is met with the words, "Tell me why we should let you leave?" The Sandman replies, "What power would Hell have if those here imprisoned were not able to dream of Heaven?" *Preludes and Nocturnes* will leave you pondering such questions yourself, long after you've finished reading.

The artwork is excellent throughout, although it's Dave McKean's stylized yet enigmatic covers that stand out. Lettering was used to depict the main characters, something that has not been done in such flamboyant style since.

Issue 8 does what every comics writer is told not to do, and that is to state clearly what the exposition has been. Death and Dream banter playfully as the Lord of Dreams recounts the adventures that he has endured while retrieving his tools of power. But there are more surprises to come: halfway through the book it is revealed that a mysterious goth girl is the Sandman's sister, who has stopped by to take the soul

of a soccer-playing teenager who keeps interrupting the pair as they speak. A journey with Death, as she collects her day's souls, shows Dream that he now has his power back, and that it is his responsibility to rebuild and maintain the dream world; the place of imagination.

FURTHER READING: *Sandman Volumes 2–11; Sandman: The Dream Hunters; Sandman: Endless Nights*
SEE ALSO: *Death: The High Cost of Living; Sandman Volume 3: Dream Country; Mr. Punch; Violent Cases*

★ **Writer:** Charles Burns   **Publisher:** Fantagraphics, 2001
★ **Artist:** Charles Burns   **ISBN:** 1560973900
★

SKIN DEEP:
TALES OF DOOMED ROMANCE

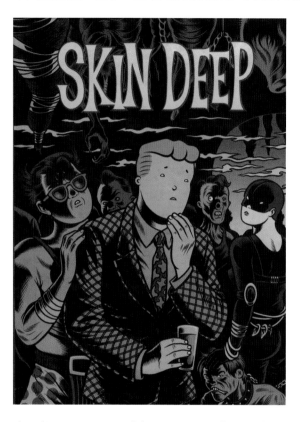

Plot: *Skin Deep* is a series of three stories originally published in comic form between 1988 and 1991. The first, *Dog Days*, tells of a man who needs a heart transplant but can't afford to go to a hospital, so he chooses a backstreet surgeon instead. The surgeon performs the operation but because it was a cut-price deal, transplants the man's heart with the heart of a dog, turning the man into Dog Boy. Dog Boy recounts how this has affected his life in adverse ways, but also how it has helped him win the heart of Rondy, a woman who loves the animal in him.

The second and longest story is *Burn Again*, the tale of a teenage boy who is reluctantly turned into a faith-healing prodigy named Bliss Blister by his crooked father. Aged 16, Bliss flees his father's fake ministry to lead a normal life, but is drawn back into the corrupt business by the woman he loves and by the reappearance of his estranged father, who now has plans to build a faith-healing empire. But the scheme takes a bizarre turn when Bliss is betrayed, then visited by an alien who convinces him to build a massive temple to await the end of the world.

The third and final story, *A Marriage Made In Hell*, begins with a writer looking for inspiration for a new story. The writer tells the tale of newlywed Lydia, who fears her injured war-veteran husband John is having an affair. She follows

him to a motel, confronts him about her fears, and learns the terrible truth.

Review: This offbeat trio of stories is part thriller, part science fiction, and part satire, resembling the spookier episodes of the 1950s TV series *The Twilight Zone* in both tone and style. But among the sometimes dark subject matter there is fun, too. *Dog Boy's* several comedy sequences include one in which he sniffs a woman's bottom in a darkened cinema to make sure she isn't his date. There is parody, too. In *Burn Again*, the commercialization of faith is taken to extreme lengths when Bliss's father and his girlfriend build a theme park to increase their profit potential.

A Marriage Made In Hell is the weakest of the three stories, but it effectively satirizes 1960s romance comics while telling a strange tale of doomed love. The drawing style switches between sympathetic characterization, menacing black inks and shadows, and figures of damaged humanity, drawn in a striking 1960s schlock-horror style. *Skin Deep's* stories may seem anachronistic to a modern audience but they are affectionately written, unnervingly drawn, and always entertaining.

FURTHER READING: *Big Baby*
SEE ALSO: *Tales From The Crypt Volume 1;*
Museum Of Terror Volume 1; Black Hole

★
★
★

Writer: David Hine **Publisher:** Active Image, 2003
Artist: David Hine **ISBN:** 0974056723

15+ STRANGE EMBRACE

Plot: Sukumar is a teenage boy who helps out at his parents' store by delivering groceries, but he's recently been given the job of taking supplies to a spooky antiques store filled with African masks and statues in a derelict part of town.

On one of his trips Sukumar encounters a strange man called Alex, who offers him shelter from a fierce snowstorm, and then tells him the story of the shop and its owner. Alex takes Sukumar to a bizarre café inhabited by ghostly apparitions who all wish to tell their own tales. Sukumar is told how Alex was abused by his parents, and how he discovered his psychic gift. Alex then explains how he discovered the story of the owner of the antiques store, Anthony Corbeau, and

how he painstakingly pieced together details of Corbeau's crazed mother; his father, who ultimately betrayed both Anthony and his mother; how his wife Sarah was driven to suicide; and why Anthony could only find peace with his collection of tribal deities.

Review: English writer and artist David Hine worked as an inker on British Marvel Comics before moving to the *2000 AD* spinoff, *Crisis*. He also worked for a short while on the *Care Bears* comic. But this graphic novel, which collects the four-part black-and-white series originally published by Atomeka Press in 1993, is about as far from that cuddly, fluffy world as it's possible to get.

ESSENTIAL
GRAPHIC NOVELS

500

267

HORROR
Top 10 horror graphic novels

As a writer, Hine weaves the intricate narrative strands of his tale together with consummate skill, so the separate yet connected stories of the three outsiders—Sukumar, Alex, and Anthony—are never confused. If anything, this narrative layering helps to emphasize the key themes of isolation, regret, and repressed sexuality. The plot may be slow to unfold at times, but it never feels boring. The suspense maintained by the three themes that run through the book is like a geographical faultline with the potential to burst forth and cause untold chaos at any moment.

Hine the artist uses a black-and-white palette throughout the book, adding to the brooding, gothic mood. His jagged and spiky inks, when drawing Alex and Anthony in particular, help to confirm their status as outsiders when compared to the more rounded and naturalistic drawing style used for other characters. Part H.P. Lovecraft, part Edgar Allen Poe, *Strange Embrace* is a dark and shadowy story and a gripping read. It was reprinted as an eight-issue series by Active Image in 2007 with the addition of coloring by Rob Steen.

FURTHER READING: *Civil War: X-Men*
SEE ALSO: *From Hell; Hellblazer: All His Engines; Hellblazer: Dangerous Habits*

★
★
★

Writer: Alan Moore
Artist: Steve Bissette and John Totleben

Publisher: Vertigo, 1998
ISBN: 0930289226

12+

SWAMP THING VOLUME 1:
SAGA OF THE SWAMP THING

Plot: A reprint of Alan Moore's first seven issues of *Swamp Thing* (with the exception of his story wrap-up in Issue 20). The book begins with the famous *Anatomy Lesson*, in which a previously rather silly supervillain, the Floronic Man, performs an autopsy on the (supposedly) dead body of Swamp Thing and realizes that he is only superficially human. With a brief detour to explain Swampy's physiology, using nematode worms as an example—Moore would go on to hijack numerous scientific oddities and imagery, such as the Mandlebrot Set, to inform his later work—we discover that Swamp Thing is not scientist Alec Holland at all as

everyone thought (including himself), but an ancient earth elemental of colossal power whose job is to protect an equally ancient concordance called The Parliament of Trees. Awakened by Holland's death in the nearby swamp, he merely thinks he is Holland. In a coma-like state induced by the discovery that he has never been human and therefore cannot ever "regain" his humanity, Swamp Thing retreats deep into The Green, a kind of elemental hive mind. The Floronic Man's attempt to follow him drives him insane, and it's left to Abigail Arcane (the daughter of an old enemy and soon to become Swamp Thing's lover), and The Demon, a

previously little regarded Jack Kirby character, to bring him back and help him say goodbye to Alec Holland forever.

Review: Even though these early stories are full of preparation for later story arcs, they are still perfectly satisfying in their own right—and at times dazzlingly ingenious. Moore takes time to build the characters, while Bissette and Totleben bring an amazing lushness to the art, every bit as detailed as Wrightson's approach, but with the capacity to be beautiful as well as threatening. Totleben's use of stippling and cross-hatching effects gives Bissette's

delicate artwork a depth and texture few comics have replicated since. However, to enjoy Moore's *Swamp Thing* at its best, you should also read *Love And Death*, and *The Curse*, the next couple of volumes, where he really gets into his stride, mixing urban legends, magical tropes, and ecological themes into a heady brew.

FURTHER READING: *Swamp Thing Volume 2: Love and Death; Swamp Thing Volume 3: The Curse; Taboo*
SEE ALSO: *Swamp Thing: Dark Genesis; From Hell; Watchmen; V or Vendetta; Across The Universe*

★
★
★
★

Writer: Al Feldstein
Artist: Graham Ingels and Various

Publisher: Gemstone, 2007
ISBN: 1888472553

THE EC ARCHIVES:
TALES FROM THE CRYPT VOLUME 1

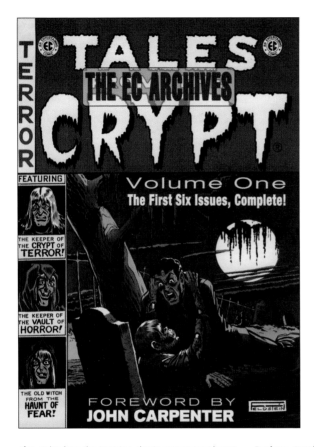

Plot: *Tales from the Crypt* is a classic portmanteau horror anthology from the 1950s single-issue series that's recently been resurrected from the censorship hell it entered during Dr Fredric Wertham's witch-hunt. This collection comprises the first six issues of the Crypt series, including the stories *The Corpse Nobody Knew*, *Madness at Manderville*, and *Zombie!* Each issue is hosted by the infamous Cryptkeeper, with a final fleeting appearance in the last issue from future host, The Old Witch. The majority of the stories are based on the typical B-movie horrors of the time: bodysnatchers, vampires, and ghouls risen from the grave.

Review: Appalling puns, corny plots and abominable dialog... it can only be the return of *Tales from the Crypt*—and about time! Since its demise in 1956 (due in part to the Comics Code Authority's ban on horror and violence), the world has been mourning the loss of these unflappably charming tales of gore, ghouls, and grimness.

It would be very easy to classify this anthology as a republication of "classic" titles, but that wouldn't do justice to their worth in the here and now. The plots and characters may not be particularly challenging, but *Tales from the Crypt*

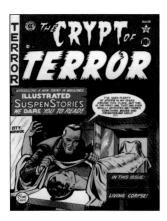
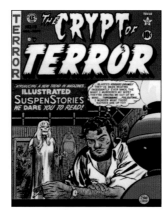

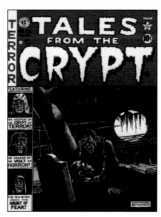

is almost unique in its mastery of anthology horror—packing as many surprisingly engaging tales as possible into a very limited space. Few other comics can rival the sheer quantity of storytelling, while maintaining a standard of quality that bears repeated reading.

There's no denying that the artwork is of the disposable pulp variety that was prevalent at the time (and, some might argue, is equally prevalent today). The horror images are perhaps lacking in the kind of detail we've come to expect now, but the value of this pulp artwork is in its styling; the

panel framing and often bizarre coloring are redolent of the birth of mass production and the 1950s aesthetic, and this disposable appearance is hugely entertaining in itself.

Let's not fool ourselves, *Tales from the Crypt* is no longer likely to keep you up at night, but it's a distinctly enjoyable— and maybe just a little nostalgic—peek at 1950s B-horror.

FURTHER READING: *EC Archives: Vault of Horror*
SEE ALSO: *The EC Archives: Weird Science;*
The EC Archives: Shock SuspenStories

★
★
★
★
★

Writer: Robert Kirkman
Artist: Tony Moore

Publisher: Image Comics, 2006
ISBN: 1582406723

15+

THE WALKING DEAD

Plot: Rick Grimes finds himself in a hospital bed, completely alone, after being shot. Attempting to find out where everyone has gone he finds the hospital's cafeteria packed with the living dead. Barely escaping with his life, he heads for home. Finding it also abandoned, he is hit on the head with a shovel by a young boy named Duane, who believes him to be a zombie. Duane's father, Morgan, explains that while Rick was asleep a plague of the dead swept over the entire world.

Believing that his wife Lori and son Carl went to find shelter in Atlanta, Rick heads off in search of them—but what he finds is a new life, a life that involves living every day with zombies just two feet away.

Review: Robert Kirkman has crafted a world in which zombies not only exist, but seem almost mundane—just another outbreak of disease to contend with. Volume 1 sets the stage for a heartwarming adventure into the complete unknown. Zombie tales are not new, and it's not easy to produce a new take on an almost overexposed genre, but while Kirkman uses the horror of flesh eating monsters to shock and scare, his main aim is to examine the human frailties that are exposed when survival becomes the number one priority.

The artwork by Moore provides the "edge of your seat" horror, though not necessarily in the ways you might expect,

ESSENTIAL
GRAPHIC NOVELS

500

273

HORROR
Top 10 horror graphic novels

and the absence of color gives a sense of balance to the gore on display.

If you have ever wondered what happens in a zombie movie after the end credits have rolled, this story is it. Rick adapts quickly to this new life. Finding his family gives him hope and a sense of leadership, and he takes charge of the situation at hand. A small group of people survive within a makeshift camp, fighting off any unwanted visitors. Rick teaches the group to shoot—including his son Carl—much to his wife Lori's disdain. It is this sense of normality that keeps Kirkman's writing fresh, making you focus on the effects a zombie apocalypse might have on your own daily life. As a

result of this clever storytelling, you almost forget that it is a zombie tale at all, and start to believe that it's perfectly normal to lop the head off the person you have been sharing your food with for the past month when he gets bitten by a random monster from the undergrowth.

FURTHER READING: *The Walking Dead Volumes 2–9;*
Invincible; The Astonishing Wolfman
SEE ALSO: *Zombieworld: Champion of the Worms*

★
★
★
★

Writer: Steve Niles

Artist: Ben Templesmith

Publisher: IDW, 2004

ISBN: 0971977550

15+
30 DAYS OF NIGHT

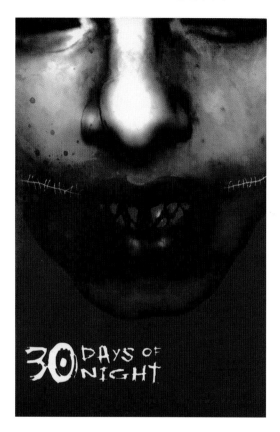

Plot: The northernmost community in the snowy wastes of Alaska is a place called Barrow. It's a tough place to live and every winter the locals are subjected to a full month of darkness. Huddled together in their homes, miles from anywhere, they wait for the dawn to return. But this year the night has eyes—and teeth. Man's undead foes have found a place where their prey is helpless for a full 30 days. They hear the call from far and wide—Barrow is a banquet for all vampires.

Review: With a premise like that it's not hard to see why this graphic novel has been turned into a movie. Steve Niles's story is taut and delightfully grim. It demonstrates all the motivations of the factions involved in the plot against Barrow, and follows the young police chief, Eben, through the events that threaten the town. He's just a guy caught in the middle, and like the rest of the population, he's quickly forced to admit that vampires are very real.

The look is violent, almost deranged, as the feeding frenzy builds, giving the nightmarish events a bloodthirsty fervor. Ben Templesmith's rich graphic touch is crucial in bringing the action to life with a lacerated vitality that makes this dark tale a livid, modern-gothic triumph.

FURTHER READING: *30 Days of Night: Return To Barrow; Dark Days; Beyond Barrow*
SEE ALSO: *Criminal Macabre; Stray Toasters*

Writer: Mike Mignola
Artist: Guy Davis

Publisher: Dark Horse, 2005
ISBN: 1593072880

B.P.R.D. VOLUME 3: PLAGUE OF FROGS

Plot: Mike Mignola's *B.P.R.D.* stories are set in the same world as Hellboy, though Hellboy himself doesn't appear. The adventure concerns a group of unusual agents who work for the Bureau for Paranormal Research and Defense and possess various superpowers and paranormal abilities. The group consists of fish-man Abe Sapien, firestarter Liz Sherman, doctor Kate Corrigan, Roger the Homunculus, and Johann Kraus, a spirit without a body, all searching for an escaped fungus that has gone to ground in a deserted New England town. Shades of H.P. Lovecraft abound as they're attacked by frog monsters, servants of a cult seeking to raise the Old Gods. The unleashing of the frog monsters, linked to an old enemy, Rasputin, sets up the continuing adventures of the B.P.R.D., and explains the origins of Abe Sapien.

Review: Mignola fleshes out the world of Hellboy in an entertaining fashion, with a typically monstrous adventure. As usual, Mignola is more interested in exploring his characters' motivations than writing a neat story, so this is as much about creating an atmosphere and setting the scene for future escapades as it is about solving the mystery of the frogs. Guy Davis's artwork is less stylized than Mignola's, but his fluid lines possess a textural quality reminiscent of Arthur Suydam's fantasies and are entirely in keeping with the dank, dripping, slimy nature of the story.

FURTHER READING: *B.P.R.D.: Garden of Souls;*
B.P.R.D.: The Universal Machine
SEE ALSO: *Hellboy: The Chained Coffin*

★
★
★
★

Writer: Charles Burns
Artist: Charles Burns

Publisher: Pantheon, 2006
ISBN: 037542380X

15+ BLACK HOLE

Plot: The 1970s. Seattle, Washington, USA. High school. Drugs are everywhere, and sex is, too. But even in these pre-AIDS days, sex carries with it fear. And tails. And horns. Being a teenager is bad enough. But what happens when your internal fear becomes visible? What happens when you literally become a monster?

Review: A massive book that was nearly ten years in the making, Burns's first issue of *Black Hole* marked a huge leap in ambition—and excellence. The "teen plague" and social alienation themes of his past works coalesced into a complex and harrowing novel of teenage fear and loathing, not just of society but also of self. Flipping through the book, you can't help but be in awe of Burns's lush, bold, and deeply disturbing images, which are both suggestive and slippery. If you've made it through school, the story will no doubt bring back uncomfortable memories. If you've yet to graduate, well... don't say Burns didn't warn you.

FURTHER READING: *El Borbah; Facetasm; Big Baby*
SEE ALSO: *Skin Deep*

Writer: J.M. DeMatteis

Artist: Kent Williams

Publisher: Vertigo, 2005

ISBN: 1401202632

5+ BLOOD: A TALE

ESSENTIAL
GRAPHIC NOVELS
500
277
HORROR
Best of the rest

Plot: A child is found by two women in a strange, faraway land. As a young boy he is passed over to a teacher, and grows into a man, before escaping his prison in an airship. His life then takes a twist, as he is attacked by vampires and becomes one himself, gaining the name Blood in the process. We follow Blood and his two strange companions as their lives unfold through the centuries and the world changes around them.

Review: This is not a straightforward book. DeMatteis's writing is almost hallucinatory, and very little is ever made explicit, so readers are expected to draw their own conclusions. Williams's artwork is absolutely stunning, and carries you through the confusing narrative, so even when you don't know what's going on, it still looks spectacular.

FURTHER READING: *Spider-Man: Kraven's Last Hunt; Greenberg The Vampire; Batman: Absolution*
SEE ALSO: *Moonshadow; Pop Gun War; Brooklyn Dreams*

★
★
★
★
★

124

Writer: Joss Whedon
Artist: Georges Jeanty

Publisher: Dark Horse, 2007
ISBN: 1593078226

BUFFY THE VAMPIRE SLAYER: THE LONG WAY HOME

Plot: This is the graphic-novel adaptation of the TV show's eighth season, and picks up where Season 7 left off. Buffy has released the potential of slayers the world over, and now finds herself leading a 1,800-strong army of young women. The US government, having investigated the destruction of Sunnydale, brands Buffy a terrorist. Meanwhile, Buffy is coordinating her army from her headquarters in Scotland, where she is accompanied by Xander, Willow, and the increasingly precocious Dawn.

Review: Many have wondered how smooth the transition from screen to page would be for Buffy and the gang, but Joss Whedon knows exactly what he's doing and the characters are given the space to develop independently of each other. Xander no longer trails along behind, but has grown into himself, eye patch and all, while Dawn is getting herself into bigger and bigger trouble. All of the characters behave with a consistency that will keep fans of the series reading to the end, while Georges Jeanty's sweetly evocative artwork captures the very heart of Buffy. The story focuses less on killing monsters, and more on the way that killing the monsters affects those pressed into service. *The Long Way Home* is a very welcome addition to the Buffiverse and a great adjunct to the TV show.

FURTHER READING: *Buffy The Vampire Slayer: Buffy Asylum; Buffy The Vampire Slayer: Slayer Interrupted; Buffy The Vampire Slayer: The Lost Slayer*
SEE ALSO: *Astonishing X-Men; 30 Days Of Night*

★ **Writer:** Clive Barker and Various
★ **Artist:** Alex Ross and various

Publisher: Checker, 2002
ISBN: 0971024928

8+

CLIVE BARKER'S HELLRAISER: COLLECTED BEST, VOLUME 1

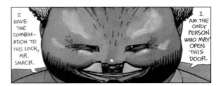

Plot: Clive Barker created the *Hellraiser* mythos over 20 years ago, and it's proved to be his most enduring creation, with new stories and films still appearing. This book collects an assortment of tales from the Marvel (Epic) comics anthology from the 1990s, beginning with an 80-page story written by Barker himself in which a group of strangers are called to a bizarre tourist attraction in the Deep South to open a puzzle that will release a group of the demonic Cenobites—and give them the weapons to destroy it. Neil Gaiman and Dave McKean present the tale of a crossword expert who's also given a peculiar puzzle. This time it contains the secrets of his past and future—and the consequences are predictably gruesome. Mike Mignola, Marc Hempel, Scott Hampton, and many more also contribute tales of the mysterious boxes that open the way to hell.

Review: The first couple of *Hellraiser* movies were creepy, scary, and deservedly popular, but the stories contained here are mostly pale reflections of former glories. Barker's opening story is confusingly written and illustrated, and though it contains some good ideas, the execution is a little dull, as are many of the stories presented here. Most of the artwork is great, and some of the stories—particularly a spooky little tale from Scott and Letitia Hampton—are pretty good, but most of them just aren't very frightening.

FURTHER READING: *Clive Barker's Hellraiser: Collected Best, Volumes 2 & 3; The Great & Secret Show*
SEE ALSO: *Zombieworld: Champion Of The Worms; Sandman: Preludes and Nocturnes*

★
★
★
★
★

A

Writer: Ted Naifeh
Artist: Ted Naifeh

Publisher: Oni Press, 2003
ISBN: 1929998600

COURTNEY CRUMRIN
AND THE NIGHT THINGS

Plot: When Courtney Crumrin's parents are offered the chance to live in a desirable part of town, they inadvisably jump at the chance to move. In the dead of night, however, Courtney discovers the Night Things and finds out that she has a lot more in common with her creepy Great Uncle Crumrin than she could have imagined.

Review: The exploration and development of the relationship between Courtney and Great Uncle Crumrin is a touching adventure in itself, as Courtney's parents are more interested in penetrating the élite social circle of the neighborhood. Ted Naifeh's exquisite style of illustration is accompanied by his equally enchanting storytelling to produce a captivating journey that appeals to the child in us all.

FURTHER READING: *Courtney Crumrin & The Coven of Mystics; Gloom Cookie Volume 1*
SEE ALSO: *Lenore: Noogies*

★
★
★
★

Writer: Tsugumi Ohba
Artist: Takeshi Obata

Publisher: Viz Media, 2005
ISBN: 1421501686

15+ DEATH NOTE, VOLUME 1

Plot: A manga horror tale about a boy who discovers a notebook that once belonged to a bored demon. The notebook contains the power of life and death, but will curse whoever dares to use it.

Review: What makes *Death Note* immediately interesting is its central character, a boy named Light Yagami. He wastes no time in taking the leap to become a Zarathustrian superman, using the demonic book to kill those who have escaped conventional justice. But these killings attract attention and Light is soon engaged in a battle of wits with the mysterious investigator known only as "L," a battle he soon begins to relish. Full of twists, *Death Note* is an intriguing, engaging, and thought-provoking comic with a strong philosophical underpinning. A real page-turner.

FURTHER READING: *Death Note volumes 2-13*
SEE ALSO: *Museum of Terror; Hell Baby*

Writer: Robert Louis Stevenson,
Adapted by: Jerry Kramsky
Artist: Lorenzo Mattotti

Publisher: NBM, 2003
ISBN: 1561633305

DR JEKYLL AND MR HYDE: A GRAPHIC NOVEL

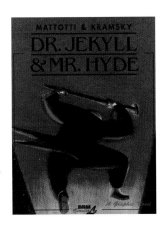

Plot: Robert Louis Stephenson's classic tale of Dr Henry Jekyll's experiments with a serum that releases the personification of the dark side of his soul; Mr Edward Hyde.

Review: There have been countless adaptations of this tale, but few have managed to pull it off with such panache and grace as the dual talents of Mattotti and Kramsky. Between them they have lent an Art Nouveau feel to the narrative that complements the themes and atmosphere in a manner that nobody had even considered before. The warm reds and oranges in the background are eclipsed by the sleek, black shadow of Hyde as he stalks the streets—just one example of the beautiful artistry that has gone into this clearly nurtured and well-loved project.

FURTHER READING: *The Cranky Sun; Murmur*
SEE ALSO: *The League of Extraordinary Gentlemen*

Writer: Eric Powell
Artist: Eric Powell

Publisher: Dark Horse, 2003
ISBN: 1569719985

THE GOON VOLUME 1: NOTHIN' BUT MISERY

Plot: In a town overrun by zombies, The Goon and his pal Franky are the only defense against the forces of the undead and their master, the Zombie Priest. This collection also introduces another recurring character, the mysterious Buzzard.

Review: Eric Powell skillfully mixes brute force with slapstick and cartoon violence, and Buzzard introduces some genuine pathos to the strip, making sure that *The Goon* never becomes two-dimensional. Rounded off with spoof adverts for the foul-mouthed Golden-Age Hero, Atomic Rage, and a vitriolic Afterword by former "publisher" Dwight T. Albatross, *The Goon* is by far the funniest horror book on the shelf.

FURTHER READING: *The Goon—Fancy Pants Edition; Billy The Kid's Old-Timey Oddities; Superman: Escape From Bizarro World*
SEE ALSO: *Marvel Zombies*

★
★ **Writer:** Gerry Finley-Day **Publisher:** Rebellion, 2006
★ **Artist:** Carlos Ezquerra **ISBN:** 1904265642

FIENDS OF THE EASTERN FRONT

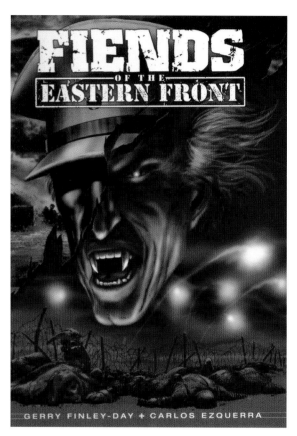

Plot: A diary found by workmen in a Berlin cellar in 1980 tells the story of Hans Schmitt. A German soldier in World War II fighting on the Russian front, Schmitt discovers that his Romanian ally, Captain Constanca, and his mountain troops are vampires. Their unconventional combat methods achieve results against the Russian enemy, but when Romania falls to the Russians, the vampires change sides and Schmitt becomes their target as the Fiends chase the remnants of the German army into the ruins of Berlin.

Review: Ezquerra may be better known for his *Judge Dredd* and *Strontium Dog* artwork in *2000 AD*, but before that he drew war strips for *Battle* comic and this is very much a return to that style. Supernatural characters are unusual in a war story, even by the standards of *2000 AD*, where the strip was originally published in 1980. The mixture of horror and war made little impact at the time, lasting only ten weeks, and would have been forgotten if it weren't for a 2002 return by the *Fiends* in a *Durham Red* story written by Dan Abnett, with art by Ezquerra.

FURTHER READING: *Durham Red; Devlin Waugh: Swimmingin Blood*
SEE ALSO: *Charley's War*

Writer: Hino Hideshi
Artist: Hino Hideshi

Publisher: Blast Books, 1995
ISBN: 0922233128

5+

HELL BABY

Plot: On a dark and stormy night twin girls are born: one completely normal, the other a demon child with a thirst for blood. Thrown in the garbage in a plastic bag, the demon child dies but is resurrected by a bolt of lightning. Seven years later, having survived for this long among the strange denizens of the garbage dump, the demonic child returns to take her revenge.

Review: Hideshi has a unique visual style that never flinches from the visceral—he has directed remakes of notorious "snuff" films and all his work is a dark, oozing distillate of extreme Japanese horror, spiked with the blackest sense of humor imaginable. *Hell Baby* is much loved by goths and those with a taste for bizarre and extreme material.

FURTHER READING: *Panorama of Hell; Dead Little Girl*
SEE ALSO: *Black Hole; Hino Horror 6: Black Cat; Astro Boy*

Writer: Hino Hideshi
Artist: Hino Hideshi

Publisher: DH Publishing, 2004
ISBN: 0974596167

5+

BLACK CAT (HINO HORROR, BOOK 6)

Plot: Three tales of gruesome suspense, all narrated by a wandering black cat. In the first, a circus clown creates a ventriloquist's dummy, and terror ensues—but the twist ending is not what you might expect. Next, a young boy, abandoned by his mother, takes in a pet dog—with murderous consequences. Finally, the wife in an almost comically feuding older couple dies, revealing the husband's real, twisted love for her.

Review: This collection of early Hino tales epitomizes his twin interests: terror and psychology. The cat's outsider perspective enables him to see humans as mere animals, at the mercy of their most base (and literally gut-level) emotions. Disturbing, though not as graphically frightening as Hino's *Hell Baby*.

FURTHER READING: *Hino Horror 5: Living Corpse*
SEE ALSO: *Hell Baby; Museum of Terror*

★
★ **Writer:** Mike Carey   **Publisher:** Vertigo, 2006
★ **Artist:** Leonardo Manco   **ISBN:** 1401203175
★

18+ HELLBLAZER: ALL HIS ENGINES

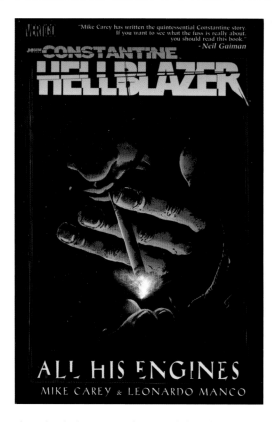

Plot: A bunch of enterprising demons seek deregulation from Hell and begin opening franchised mini-Hells on Earth. Inevitably, there are conflicts of interest as one demon tries to corner the market in freshly tormented souls, and in a decisive marketing move worthy of any fiendish capitalist, an epidemic of comas creates an almost inexhaustible supply of candidates for these fast-food Hells. Enter John Constantine. Constantine has been emotionally blackmailed into the role of supernatural hitman when a close friend's daughter is put in a coma and held hostage in the bowels of the demon, Beroul. To free her, Constantine must put the other demons out of business for good.

Review: This was shrewdly published to coincide with the *Constantine* film starring Keanu Reeves. *All His Engines* is far better, however, with more substance than the over-produced Hollywood style. Mike Carey's narrative is undoubtedly more plausible, and his characterization of Constantine is more courageous, and unflinching in presenting his ambiguous antihero nature. The subtle satire on capitalism leaves a lingering smile—or frown, depending on your persuasion—on your face long after the staple ingredients of occultism and devil worship have been consumed in a haze of sulphur and brimstone.

FURTHER READING: *Hellblazer: Original Sins; Hellblazer: Fear and Loathing*
SEE ALSO: *Hellblazer: Dangerous Habits; Swamp Thing; Sandman; Books Of Magic*

Writer: Pat Mills, Ken Armstrong
Artist: Ramon Sola

Publisher: Spitfire Comics, 2007
ISBN: 9780955473302

COLLECTED HOOK JAW VOLUME 1

2+

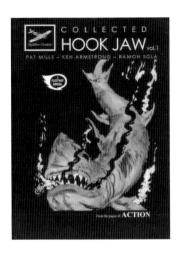

Plot: The crew of a fishing boat in the Caribbean fend off an attack by a Great White shark, leaving it injured with the hook of their gaff in its mouth. Immediately, the shark begins a series of attacks on human swimmers.

Review: From the pages of Action comic in 1976, *Hook Jaw* was a blatant and shameless attempt to cash in on the popularity of the film Jaws. However, unlike the movie, the comic was determined to depict the shark attacks in all their visceral glory, with limbs regularly shown detached from their owners' bodies. Disappointingly, though, while some of the strip's pages were originally published in color, this reprint is in black-and-white. The book collects 31 of the 36 weekly *Hook Jaw* stories that were published before the comic's violent content was toned down.

FURTHER READING: *Judge Dredd: Cursed Earth*
SEE ALSO: *Fiends Of The Eastern Front; Charley's War; Marshall Law*

Writer: Junji Ito
Artist: Junji Ito

Publisher: Dark Horse, 2006
ISBN: 1593075421

MUSEUM OF TERROR VOLUME 1

3+

Plot: A series of stories centering on the disturbing regenerative powers of the beautiful Tomie—a schoolgirl who is murdered by a succession of obsessive admirers. The horror increases for these murderous courtiers as they discover that far from facing the oblivion of death, Tomie is reincarnated over and over again in order to exact her grisly revenge.

Review: The first book in Ito's *Museum of Terror* series is a genuinely unsettling work, brimming with darkness, violence, and revenge. The grotesquely rendered images lurking beneath Tomie's beautiful face work extraordinarily well, and are in stark contrast to the expressions of terror on the faces of the other characters that seem to fill practically every panel. A very unsettling collection, and a wonderful example of manga horror.

FURTHER READING: *Museum Of Horror Volumes 2–4; Gyo; The Ring*
SEE ALSO: *Uzumaki; Hino Horror Volume 6; Hell Baby*

★
★
★
★

Writer: Robert Kirkman
Artist: Sean Phillips

Publisher: Marvel, 2006
ISBN: 0785126082

15+ MARVEL ZOMBIES

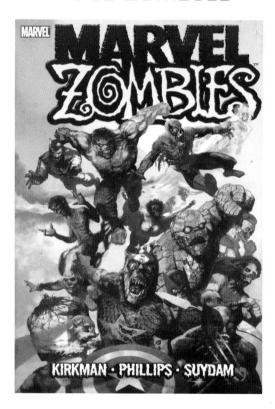

Plot: Marvel's finest superheroes have become zombies—and they are hungry. Starting with Magneto, they begin chomping their way through a menu of Marvel's best-known characters. The Silver Surfer arrives and informs the zombies that Galactus is on his way to devour the planet. Colonel America, Spider-Man, Iron Man, Wolverine, Hulk, and Luke Cage overpower the Surfer and consume him, granting them each a small amount of his Cosmic Power. The newly fed undead crew easily defeats the other heroes, who are angered they weren't also invited to dine on the Surfer. The end is a new beginning, as the zombies gain the power of Galactus and take off to devour their next world.

Review: *Marvel Zombies* is about Marvel's classic characters going head to head in search of food, in an alternate universe where even the superpowered need to feed, as the hunger of being undead clouds their minds and turns them feral. Written by Robert Kirkman, this book helped launch him into the public eye, and Marvel are to be congratulated for taking such a bold step. Seeing Spider-Man as a dribbling zombie, and Captain America (known as Colonel America in this alternate universe) with his brains on show are just two of the many unforgettable moments. Consequently *Marvel Zombies* has become one of the most sought-after books of the last five years.

FURTHER READING: *Marvel Zombies vs. Army of Darkness; Marvel Zombies: Dead Days; Ultimate Fantastic Four; Marvel Zombies Volume 2*
SEE ALSO: *Walking Dead Volume 1; EC Archives: Tales From the Crypt*

Writer: Dan Brereton
Artist: Dan Brereton

Publisher: Olympian, 2007
ISBN: 0978632621

NOCTURNALS VOLUME 1: BLACK PLANET

Plot: Nocturnals is a story of "monsters" who have escaped from the Narn K Corporation's laboratory, where some of them were created. Doc Horror, with his daughter, Eve (Halloween Girl), arrives on Earth after escaping from the Crim—extradimensional conquerors who ravaged his home world and are now working with the Narn K Corporation. He provides a home and family of sorts for these animal-human hybrids and synthetic soldiers—Polychrome, Starfish, Firelion, Komodo, Raccoon, and the undead gunslinger, Gunwitch. Together, from their underground hideout, they protect Pacific City from supernatural menaces.

In *Black Planet*, they are caught between factions fighting for control of the Mob and are hunted by Mister Fane and the Corporation. Eve carries a bucket filled with possessed toys that can grow into monstrous versions of themselves—which makes for an interesting bout of Halloween trick-or-treating in the story Witching Hour. Also included is the new story *Clean Hands*.

Review: Brereton's atmospheric, painted artwork makes this a joy to look at. The characters are intriguing and the plots thrilling. This is a real treat for all lovers of heroes with bizarre powers and pulp-inspired tales of crime and horror.

FURTHER READING: *Giant Killer; The Psycho*
SEE ALSO: *B.P.R.D: Plague of Frogs; Hellboy; The Chuckling Whatsit*

★
★
★
Writer: Osamu Tezuka
Artist: Osamu Tezuka

Publisher: Vertical, 2006
ISBN: 1932234640

18+ # ODE TO KIRIHITO

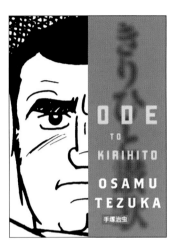

Plot: Dr. Kirihito is studying the sufferers of a fatal disease that makes them look like dogs. When he contracts the disease himself, he realizes that he's been lied to about its origins and that it can be controlled. He finds his life is now at risk and flees, traveling the world looking for a cure and discovering along the way that being different can be very dangerous. All the while, the fate of his fiancée and a colleague are dependent on his own.

Review: This late work by Tezuka (known as "the god of manga") showcases his lifelong interest in medicine, with a mesmerizing, and at times thoroughly weird, examination of the human condition. Experimenting with his own style, yet still distinctly Tezuka, this is a compelling horror/thriller tale.

FURTHER READING: *Adolf; Phoenix; Black Jack*
SEE ALSO: *From Hell; Uzumaki*

★
★
★
Writer: Junko Mizuno
Artist: Junko Mizuno

Publisher: Last Gasp, 2005
ISBN: 0867196300

18+ # PURE TRANCE

Plot: Following a devastating third world war, the earth's surface is noxious and hostile. In order to survive, humankind has gone underground. Many have resorted to popping pills known as Pure Trance, and this brave new world is plagued by another dangerous addiction—hyperorexia (extreme overeating). Keiko Yamazaki is the maniacal director of the Over Eaters Treatment Center 102, and her iron fist dominates the lives of her nurses as she torments and humiliates them.

Review: Bizarre science fiction, dripping with psychedelic illustration and adorable-looking characters, but look a little closer and you'll find these wide-eyed, innocent-looking cuties indulging in bloody violence, demeaning human experimentation, and drug abuse. Don't be dissuaded by the ultraviolence, however—*Pure Trance* is an utterly absorbing and fantastical flight of the imagination.

FURTHER READING: *Junko Mizuno's Hell Babies*
SEE ALSO: *Uzumaki; Museum of Horror; Hell Baby*

Writer: Various
Artist: Various

Publisher: Harper Paperbacks, 2006
ISBN: 0061148725

THE SIMPSONS TREEHOUSE OF HORROR HOODOO VOODOO BROUHAHA

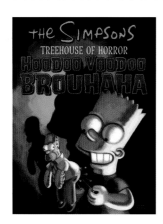

Plot: A collection of Halloween stories, much like the annual episodes of the TV series, covering such classic themes as axe murderers, vampires, and zombies, as well as parodies of books and movies. Homer buys a haunted clown-car in *Krustine*; Mr. Burns becomes a murderer in old London town in *The True Story of Jack the Ripper*; and *The Lord of the Rings* gets a makeover in *Ring Around the Simpsons*.

Review: Told by guest stars of the comics world, the *Treehouse of Horror* titles are always entertaining. This volume includes work by Gail Simone, Scott Shaw, Ty Templeton, Paul Dini, Jill Thompson, and Dan Brereton.

FURTHER READING: *Heebie-Jeebie Hullabaloo; Spine-Tingling Spooktacular; Fun-Filled Frightfest*
SEE ALSO: *Marvel Zombies*

Writer: Killoffer
Artist: Killoffer

Publisher: Typocrat Press, 2005
ISBN: 0954930819

SIX HUNDRED AND SEVENTY-SIX APPARITIONS OF KILLOFFER

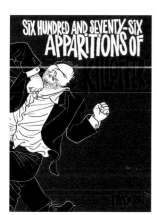

Plot: On a trip to Montreal, Killoffer starts worrying about what might be growing in the sink of dirty dishes he left at home, which soon turns to stress about what might be rotten in his life. Then, after ogling three women in a bar, three other versions of Killoffer turn up—versions who actually went home with each of these women. Each of the decisions he doesn't take sparks another copy of himself, leading to a violent and bloody confrontation between the many apparitions.

Review: A remarkable-looking book, slim but oversized, with each page beautifully designed in a stark, heavy, black-and-white style. Yet the style doesn't overwhelm the substance, and just enough is left unsaid to enable you to draw your own conclusions about what is "real" and what isn't.

FURTHER READING: *Billet SVP; La Clef des Champs*
SEE ALSO: *Pop Gun War; Curses; Can't Get No*

500 ESSENTIAL GRAPHIC NOVELS

HORROR
Best of the rest

★
★ **Writer:** Len Wein   **Publisher:** Vertigo, 2002
★ **Artist:** Berni Wrightson   **ISBN:** 1563890445

12+

SWAMP THING: DARK GENESIS

Plot: Scientist Alec Holland has his laboratory blown up by a villain who wants to steal his secret formula. Splashed with the super serum that he designed to make cornfields out of deserts, Holland flees into a nearby swamp. Here, he transforms into a shambling vegetal being who becomes a spooky, but sympathetic hero.

Review: Gorgeously drawn by noted horror artist Wrightson, this early version of *Swamp Thing* positively drips with decay. The theme of being trapped in a body people find repulsive, unable to reach out to your loved ones, is not new, but Wein wrings out every drop of drama from the premise. This version reprints the Wrightson issue, cutting the ongoing story off cold, but also includes the original *House of Secrets* short story on which the *Swamp Thing* strip was based.

FURTHER READING: *Bernie Wrightson's Frankenstein*
SEE ALSO: *Swamp Thing 1: Saga of the Swamp Thing*

★
★ **Writer:** Marv Wolfman   **Publisher:** Marvel, 2005
★ **Artist:** Gene Colan   **ISBN:** 078510920X

15+ # ESSENTIAL TOMB OF DRACULA: VOLUME 1

Plot: Frank Drake and his friend Clifton Graves journey to the infamous Castle Dracula, intent on reopening it as a spooky tourist attraction. The cynical Graves finds Dracula's corpse and mockingly removes the stake, bringing the Lord of the Undead back to life. Graves falls under Dracula's thrall, but Drake finds new purpose and joins forces with Rachel Van Helsing and the vampire hunter Blade, among others, to hunt and kill the Count.

Review: This book includes the first 25 issues of *Tomb Of Dracula*, plus *Werewolf By Night* #15 and *Giant-size Chillers* #1. Gene Colan's artwork has an eerie sophistication to it, particularly the panels that are thick with ethereal mist. Tremendous fun if you can look beyond the 1970s feel.

FURTHER READING: *Essential Tomb Of Dracula: Volumes 2–4*
SEE ALSO: *30 Days Of Night; Fiends Of The Eastern Front*

Writer: Junji Ito
Artist: Junji Ito

Publisher: Viz Media, 2007
ISBN: 1421513897

3+ UZUMAKI

Plot: Life in the small coastal town of Kurozu-cho rapidly descends into a nightmare as the population are haunted by a mysterious, recurring spiral pattern—in the clouds in the sky, in the smoke drifting from the potter's kiln, and on the corpses that start appearing with alarming regularity. The living are also affected, their bodies becoming twisted and forced into grotesque corkscrews and coils.

Review: Drawing his influences from a wide range of sources, including artist Hideshi Hino and horror writer H.P. Lovecraft, Ito has taken the simple spiral pattern and manipulated it into something truly formidable and disturbing. The spiral design is integrated into the artwork in ever more imaginative and horrific ways, and the theme of obsession is tackled with great intelligence in this authentically creepy story.

FURTHER READING: *Gyo; Museum Of Terror; The Drifting Classroom*
SEE ALSO: *Hino Horror; Hell Baby; Pure Trance*

Writer: Mike Mignola
Artist: Pat McEown

Publisher: Dark Horse, 2005
ISBN: 1593074077

5+ ZOMBIE WORLD: CHAMPION OF THE WORMS

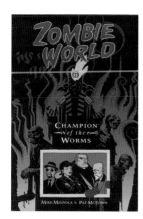

Plot: Called in to investigate a series of strange disturbances at a smalltown museum, Major Damson and his colleagues uncover the living mummy Azzul Gotha and his plot to sacrifice mankind to the Worm Gods.

Review: Displaying the same influences as his Hellboy work, Mike Mignola crafts a story full of his trademark mad ideas and strange monsters. Complimented by Pat McEown's cartoony artwork, which shows flashes of both *Tintin* artist Hergé and comics legend Arthur Adams, *Zombie World* has a lighter air to it than Mignola's other, more famous creation. Sadly, it all ends rather abruptly and has the feel of a pilot episode for a continuing series, rather than a self-contained adventure in its own right. Nonetheless, an interesting side project.

FURTHER READING: *Zombieworld: Winter's Dregs*
SEE ALSO: *Hellboy; Grendel: War Child; 30 Days Of Night*

CHAPTER 7

HUMOR

MAKE 'EM LAUGH

The earliest comic strips, being direct descendents of single-panel editorial cartoons and caricatures, were designed to make people laugh. By the end of the 19th century, Richard Outcault was bending the rules of editorial cartooning in his *Hogan's Alley* series, which featured a popular character that became known as The Yellow Kid. The toothy urchin had ungrammatical messages written in street argot and directed at the reader printed on his long yellow shirt. By 1897, newspaper readers could enjoy the slapstick antics of the rambunctious Katzenjammer Kids, always rebelling against authority, and visual humor of this sort continued to be a mainstay of newspaper humor strips like *Mutt and Jeff* and *Bringing Up Father*. Some of them are sadly dated, although often beautifully drawn.

Early humor strips were often far more surreal than their modern equivalents. Popeye, the spinach-chugging, pipe-puffing sailor man, made his debut in *Thimble Theatre* in the 1920s, a strip that was already populated by strange creatures and quirky characters such as Wimpy. Comics were hugely popular, and newspaper syndicates were willing to pay handsomely for the very best creative teams. One of the strangest yet most engrossingly repetitive strips was *Krazy Kat*, which told the gender-bending tales of a cat of indeterminate sex in love with a mouse (Ignatz) who despises him and constantly seeks to throw a brick at his head. Ignatz's plan is constantly foiled by Officer Pupp, who is obsessed with putting the mouse in jail. Out of this strange slapstick triangle George Herimann creates a work of genius, endlessly embroidering his theme and creating his own little world of empty landscapes and distorted language.

In recent years, cartoonists such as Tony Millionaire and Chris Ware have continued the surrealist line, producing faultlessly drawn short humor strips, often without dénouements, held together with thematic, rather than visual, motifs and informed by a sense of the grotesque. Even more mindbending is Peter Blegvad's *Leviathan*, the hero of which is a faceless baby called Levi. Levi inhabits an incomprehensible world, but is able to raise philosophical points with his stuffed rabbit and pet cat.

Great newspaper strips create their own world of repeated motifs, themes, and archetypal gags. Readers love the comfortable familiarity and look out for the patterns. American newspapers published a host of high-quality material in the 1930s and '40s, including Chick Young's light-hearted *Blondie*; *Little Lulu*, with its gang of appealing, mischievous children; Al Capp's hillbilly adventure *Lil Abner*, and Ernie Bushmiller's simple but stylish *Nancy*. But in 1950, a strip would appear that would surpass them all in popularity: *Peanuts*. Charles M. Schultz's examination of the pains and mysteries of childhood ran for almost 50 years until the death of its creator, and gave us a host of characters that are recognized across the globe. Few recent strips can rival it, but it has at least one natural successor in Bill Waterson's *Calvin and Hobbes*, the adventures of an imaginative but shy little boy, Calvin, who believes his stuffed tiger toy comes alive.

The early strips may have created their own slang, but few drew their humor from puns and wordplay. Comics were, after all, a visual medium and few have focused intently on written humor. An exception is Basil Wolverton, creator of *Powerhouse Pepper*. Despite his reputation for outrageously and creatively ugly cartooning for the seminal *MAD Magazine*, Wolverton produced a clean-cut, generous-spirited hero whose 1940s adventures were indeed peppered with witty dialogue and plays on words. If wordplay is your thing, you may also enjoy Kyle Baker's *Cowboy Wally Show* and *Why I Hate Saturn*—and if you like your cartoons to have an intellectual edge, look to the work of the Langridge brothers, whose *Art D'Ecco* parodies both high- and lowbrow art.

In the 1960s and '70s, underground comics began to appear that parodied the values of modern society, with some achieving great commercial success—including Bill Griffith's *Zippy The Pinhead*. Much of the humor of the time is fairly laidback, such as that in Gilbert Shelton's enduringly popular *Fabulous Furry Freak Brothers*—picaresque tales of three freewheelin' hippies and their sarcastic cat. Shelton's work has endured in part thanks to his beautiful draughtsmanship, but if one person towers head and shoulders over his fellow underground artists it's Robert Crumb, because of his technical craftsmanship and excruciating honesty about his own feelings, particularly toward women. Crumb created a pantheon of counterculture icons, from the fake guru Mr Natural to the oily seducer Fritz The Cat.

The rise of independent comic-book publishing has enabled many cartoonists whose work would be unacceptable in the mainstream to find a voice. Some strips are too violent and contain too much profanity to gain general acceptance. Peter Bagge, whose immensely stylish, but distorted style of drawing is not to everyone's taste, is nevertheless able to address his Generation X audience in his *Buddy Bradley* stories, switching from gross-out comedy and manic action to pondering modern life and back again in an instant.

But for many, the greatest source of humor will always be parody, and the greatest humor comic of them all was EC's *MAD Magazine*, founded by Harvey Kurtzman in 1952. *MAD's* zany take on popular culture, its crazy caricatures, and its fearless attitude to sacred cows made it a title that shaped a whole generation's idea of fun.

★
★
★
★
★

Writer: Peter Bagge   **Publisher:** Fantagraphics, 2005
Artist: Peter Bagge   **ISBN:** 1560976233

15+ # BUDDY DOES SEATTLE

Plot: Snotty loser Buddy Bradley, star of Peter Bagge's *Hate* (from which these stories are collected), finally takes the huge step of moving to Seattle to experience urban slacker culture first hand. On the plus side he doesn't have to deal with his bratty sister and his confused parents any longer, but on the downside he has to endure a series of roommates from hell, neurotic girlfriends, and crappy jobs. For a while things start to go well for Buddy as he begins managing bands, and it looks like he might actually make a living doing something he enjoys, but predictably this happy state of affairs can't last, and by the end of the book he's forced to retreat back home to New Jersey.

Review: Peter Bagge combines scripts full of biting commentary on social interaction and youth culture in the early 1990s, all wrapped up in sharply observed language, with one of the most distinctive drawing styles the comic book has ever seen. Distorted, often deliberately ugly, Bagge's figures explode from the page when angry, twist

and slink when depressed, every line conveying extreme emotion. But they are also beautifully designed, the pages themselves elegantly filled, albeit with goggle-eyed figures attacking each other. Bagge combines freaky, wild cartooning with subtle characterization as Buddy encounters a series of even bigger losers than himself.

The most hilarious interplay is between Buddy and his roomies Stinky, a sexually diseased nonconformist in whose character Bagge can invest all the gross stories you ever heard about young men living alone in squalor; and George Hamilton, a would-be sensitive soul who spends all his time writing mawkish adolescent nonsense in his room while imagining himself a tragic figure. Bagge takes these archetypes and invests them with amazing vivacity and individuality. Compared to them, Buddy starts to look well balanced, until he finds himself on the receiving end from his latest girlfriend, the profoundly masochistic Lisa, whose rants are a thing of beauty.

FURTHER READING: *Buddy Does Jersey;*
Buddy Bites the Bullet; Buddy Has Three Moms
SEE ALSO: *The Complete Crumb; Fun With Milk & Cheese;*

★
★ **Writer:** Bill Watterson   **Publisher:** Andrews McMeel Publishing, 2005
★ **Artist:** Bill Watterson   **ISBN:** 0740748475
★
★

A # THE COMPLETE CALVIN AND HOBBES

Plot: Calvin is a six-year-old boy who lives with his parents on the outskirts of town, giving him easy access to the woods where he spends a great deal of his time. Immensely curious, precocious, and underachieving, his intelligence manifests itself in his arguments with his parents and his elaborate schemes for personal advancement, profit, or simple mischief. His companion in his (mis)adventures is a stuffed tiger called Hobbes. Everyone else sees only the stuffed tiger, but Calvin interacts with a real, slightly more grownup, more cautious version of himself. Hobbes's favorite trick is to pounce on Calvin the moment he comes home from school, so that Calvin's return is at once a great pleasure and a constant source of fear. Hobbes tries to talk Calvin out of his more harebrained schemes, but at best manages to

place himself on the sidelines as Calvin hurtles into space on a sled or drives his mother's car into a ditch.

At school, Calvin is a daydreamer, imagining himself as Spaceman Spiff or as a dinosaur. In winter, he shows off his artistic leanings with snowmen tableaux, often presenting a nightmarish world-view. Neighbor Suzie thinks Calvin is just gross most of the time and Calvin creates a club with no girls allowed, though Hobbes isn't always on Calvin's side where Suzie is concerned.

Situations repeat themselves over time with new twists: his fantasy lives; his friendship and struggles with Hobbes; his desire to be older; Watterson's subtly expressed views on

ESSENTIAL
GRAPHIC NOVELS
500
299
HUMOR
Top 10 humor graphic novels

culture, commercialism, and the human condition, and Calvin's relationships with other people in his life.

Review: Watterson fought several battles to maintain the large size of his strip in newspapers and eschewed merchandising. He gave up *Calvin and Hobbes* after ten years, at the height of the strip's popularity. This is an oversized collection of all the strips in three volumes. It's a great package, if somewhat unwieldy for casual reading. The strip has elements of *Peanuts* (adult-like children), *Krazy Kat* (flights of fantasy), *Barnaby* (companion seen only by the protagonist), and *Pogo* (wordplay and social commentary), but *Calvin and Hobbes* transcends its roots to be simply one of the best comic strips of all time, transporting adults back

to the glorious world of potential that is childhood in a way that can be sentimental but is never mawkish. It's always enjoyable, often works on multiple levels with its frequent visual jokes and metaphors, is beautifully drawn (especially when Watterson stretches out on the Sunday strips), fiercely intelligent, and always fun.

FURTHER READING: *Liberty Meadows Volume 3: Summer of Love*
SEE ALSO: *The Complete Peanuts 1950–1952; Krazy Kat; Book of Leviathan; Liberty Meadows Volume 1*

★ **Writer:** Robert Crumb
★ **Artist:** Robert Crumb
★

Publisher: Fantagraphics, 1992
ISBN: 1560970766

18+

THE COMPLETE CRUMB COMICS: VOLUME 8

Plot: This book is part of a multi-volume series and features Crumb comic strips from 1971 and 1972. Included are stories from regular characters such as sarcastic hippy guru Mr. Natural, the sex-crazed Fritz the Cat, smartass teen Eggs Ackley, and autobiographical strips starring Crumb himself. Also featured is the 22-page strip *Whiteman Meets Bigfoot*, in which Whiteman goes camping and is kidnapped by a tribe of Sasquatches and married to the tribal chief's daughter. Whiteman falls for his new bride but hits problems when he takes his new love back to "civilization." Other stories include *A Gurl*, about a lonely young woman discovering masturbation; *Salty Dog Sam Goes Surfing*, about a black man trying to buy a surfboard; and *Jumpin' Jack Flash*, about a self-styled free-love Messiah.

Review: To his fans, Crumb is the satirical godfather of subversive underground comix who championed freedom of speech and opened up the medium so that other artists could explore explicit or controversial topics. To his detractors, his cartoons are the masturbatory doodlings of a pervert that smack of racism and misogyny.

This book features work to support both arguments. Crumb's drawing of a black man in *Salty Sam* is horribly stereotyped, but he subverts this stereotype by delivering an anti-racism message: When Sam finally gets his surfboard, he discovers that the sea is too polluted for him to use it, and comments that black people only have access to goods after they are no longer of any use to white people. Women are often

large-bottomed, large-breasted objects of sexual ridicule and lust, but Crumb also depicts these women as powerful creatures who are taller than the many feckless and largely unappealing men who populate his universe.

Humor—like sexual and racial politics—has changed a lot since the early '70s, but there is plenty here that is still genuinely funny. Mr. Natural and Jumpin' Jack Flash conning their followers has resonance in a world where the likes of David Koresh still have their moments, and *Whiteman Meets Bigfoot* can be read as a parable of the "natural" versus the "civilized" world. The final strip features the death of Fritz the Cat, one of Crumb's most popular characters who made it onto the big screen in animated form in 1972. Crumb was

apparently not impressed by the movie, so decided to kill off his ever-frisky feline. This strip features strangely touching drawings and dialog as a jaded Fritz realizes he's at the end of the road with this celebrity nonsense. It's not a consistently funny collection but Crumb's best moments still manage to pack a punch.

FURTHER READING: *The R. Crumb Handbook*
SEE ALSO: *The Book Of Mr. Natural; Too Much Coffee Man: Guide For The Perplexed*

★
★
★
★

Writer: Kyle Baker
Artist: Kyle Baker

Publisher: Vertigo, 2003
ISBN: 1401200508

THE COWBOY WALLY SHOW

Plot: The biography of the fictional Cowboy Wally, a man who has taken fat, loud, and obnoxious and turned them into a career. Starting as a kids' TV cowboy, a job he lands thanks to some indiscreet photos of the head of the network, he manages to accrue an incredible resumé of failed TV shows, with no concept too lowbrow or morally ambiguous. Amazingly, bawdy songs, naked ladies, and heavy drinking do not prove to be popular with parents, so he's swiftly moved to primetime, eventually leading to a scandalous Christmas TV appearance that lands him in front of a Congressional hearing. Forced to move behind the scenes, his production company suddenly starts producing hits, as it becomes apparent that Wally himself is the main cause of its failure so far. He decides to move into films, starting with giant monster film *Ed Smith, Lizard of Doom*, and then *Sands of Blood*, a foreign-legion movie that is excerpted in this book. Next up is his version of *Hamlet*, eventually filmed in jail after an incident involving a laundromat, drugs, and a pony. Finally, Wally gets his own late-night chatshow, where his appalling personality finds its natural home.

Review: Kyle Baker's second full-length graphic novel was out of print for many years, and gained a legendary reputation that it doesn't quite deserve (much like Alan

Moore's *Miracleman*); his third book, *You Are Here*, is a far more complete work, but even saying that, *The Cowboy Wally Show* is still a very funny book. Baker has always been a master of comic timing, and his dialogue is superb. His art is far more intricate than in his later work, and although it's a little more stylized and cartoony, this suits the lighter tone of the story and leavens the more grotesque elements of Wally's character.

The film sections are probably the highlights, the prison *Hamlet* particularly, with Shakespeare's words not so subtly brought up to date to hilarious effect. Although the humor is sharp, it's not mean-spirited, which lends a brightness that probably accounts for much of the book's popularity.

A slighter work than some of Baker's later books, but *The Cowboy Wally Show* is still head and shoulders above most of the humor books on the market.

FURTHER READING: *You Are Here; King David; I Die At Midnight*
SEE ALSO: *Why I Hate Saturn; Birth Of A Nation; Sam & Max: Surfin' The Highway*

★ **Writer:** Bob Burden   **Publisher:** Dark Horse, 1998
★ **Artist:** Bob Burden   **ISBN:** 1569712824
★
★
★

15+
FLAMING CARROT VOLUME 3: FLAMING CARROT'S GREATEST HITS

Plot: The Flaming Carrot was an ordinary young man until, brain-damaged by reading 5,000 comics in one sitting, he decided to put on a giant carrot mask and fight crime while uttering the catchphrase, "Ut!". He patrols Iron City, preferably on a pogo stick, protecting it from villains such as The Artless Dodger and Gonzaga. He also saves the city from rather frequent alien invasions. His friends include Uncle Billy, Death, and his mentor, Dr Heller, whose powers of resuscitation are useful when the Carrot has had too much to drink. In this volume, as a member of probably the world's strangest and least effective superhero group, The Mystery Men, Flaming Carrot helps to defeat the Vile Brotherhood, who have let loose clones of Hitler's feet on the city. Members of the Mystery Men include Screwball, The Shoveler, Captain Attack, Jumpin' Jehoshaphat, Red Rover, Mr. Furious, Jackpot, and Bondo-Man— some of whom you may remember from the film version, although the Carrot never appeared.

Review: There is an element of whimsy and wish-fulfilment to Burden's creation, not to mention deliberate political incorrectness—for instance the Carrot has a bunch of groupies called the Bikini Teens who are simply superpowered bimbos. Burden himself describes the Carrot as a "second-string, cut-rate hero of marginal glamor and dubious powers." The Flaming Carrot is only vaguely sane, but his adventures have an old-fashioned appeal and a sense of the absurd that never fails to amuse. Who can resist a comic in which a villain called Don Wiskerando, always accompanied by his flying dead dog, tricks fans of *Dr. Who* and *Star Trek* into helping invading aliens?

FURTHER READING: *Flaming Carrot Volumes 1, 2, & 4*
SEE ALSO: *Frank; Sam And Max: Surfin' The Highway*

★
★
★
★

Writer: Sergio Aragones with Mark Evanier   **Publisher:** Dark Horse, 2001
Artist: Sergio Aragones   **ISBN:** 1569715718

A

GROO: LIBRARY

Plot: He may have the sharpest sword, but he's not the sharpest knife in the drawer. Although the greatest swordsman in the world, Groo tends to slay first and ask questions—such as "Who is on my side?"—later. In this volume, when called upon to protect a village, he manages to reduce it to destitution, while his plot, to steal a valuable sapphire, ends in complete destruction. Why does his faithful dog Rufferto stick with the world's deadliest buffoon? We find out in Rufferto's Reverie, a dog's-eye daydream and one of Aragones's most charming stories.

Review: However it's dressed up, the plot to a *Groo* story is essentially the same—which is why you can pick up any one of the many collections and enjoy it immediately. With *Groo*, Aragones created his own madcap world populated by wonderful recurring characters such as The Sage, who is almost as accident-prone as Groo; Taranto, Groo's former mercenary friend who's now out to kill him; Chakal, a barbarian warrior woman who's the love of Groo's life, but who wants nothing to do with the bandy-legged moron; and the witches Arba and Dakarba.

Greed and stupidity lead people to hire Groo, who proceeds to kill everything in sight, sink fleets, topple towers, and wreak mayhem—on friends and enemies equally.

The glory of the strip lies in the inventive tweaks Aragones introduces in the knowledge that the reader knows exactly what will happen next. Every panel and every page is packed with little visual gags and exaggerated cartooning, so that the pages seem to be bursting with life. Although it began as a sword-and-sorcery parody, Aragones has created a world of his own that goes beyond its initial references. Full of catchphrases and recurring themes, it even has its own linguistic jokes, and with every new story it just gets better and better.

FURTHER READING: *The Death Of Groo; The Groo Chronicles; Groo: The Most Intelligent Man In The World; Louder Than Words; Mad Art*
SEE ALSO: *Little Annie Fanny; The Book of Mr. Natural; Krazy & Ignatz: He Nods In Quiesscent Siesta*

★ **Writer:** Milt Gross   **Publisher:** Fantagraphics, 2005
★ **Artist:** Milt Gross   **ISBN:** 1560976942
★

12+ # HE DONE HER WRONG

Plot: A beautiful female singer arrives at a seedy bar in a remote American town and wows a raucous audience with her sweet voice and innocent manner. But several of the crowd are drunk and follow her to her dressing room—until a simple frontiersman with superhuman strength steps in to defend her honor. The frontiersman overcomes the villains and states his love for the singer. She in turn, impressed by his courage, falls for him. But their happiness is cut short

when a wicked businessman and fur trapper tempts the frontiersman away. While the frontiersman collects a fortune in animal hides, the businessman convinces the singer that her love has died. He then sets about wooing her and, reluctantly, she accompanies him back to the city to begin a new life. The frontiersman eventually returns home and is stunned to find his girl missing. On learning the truth behind her disappearance, he heads off to the city to get her back, but the quest is beset with problems as he adapts to life in the big city, and goes on to take an unexpected twist when the singer and her new fellow become destitute and bankrupt thanks to his gambling addiction.

Review: *He Done Her Wrong* was first published in 1930 and is a cartoon story that presents a feast of slapstick treats from the very beginning. It carries no narrative captions, speech, or thought bubbles throughout its whole novel-length run, and the story's continuing narrative relies entirely on the artist's penmanship to keep the pace moving and the gags coming—and it never disappoints.

Gross learnt his trade as a newspaper cartoonist and this work carries all the tricks of that trade, with an uncomplicated,

no-nonsense drawing style that breathes life and vibrancy into the characters without weighing them down. The sequence where the frontiersman visits a tailor's shop is great fun, and prepares the reader for slapstick fight scenes later in the book that are straight out of the silent movies, an industry where Gross also worked.

There are some quite tender scenes too, which involve the destitute singer alone in the big, bad city and are drawn with slightly more detail and more shade than the rest of the book to highlight her isolation in the dark. This version of the book also features a restored sequence that was previously removed because it was considered racist. In it, the frontiersman finds himself in the dark and mistakes a black man for his arch enemy. This depiction of ethnicity will seem questionable to a modern audience, but this aside, it's a thoroughly entertaining read with the laughs coming thick and fast.

FURTHER READING: *Nize Baby*
SEE ALSO: *Archie Americana Series: Best Of The Fifities; Krazy & Ignatz: He Nods In Quiesscent Siesta*

★
★
★
★

Writer: Frank Cho

Artist: Frank Cho

Publisher: Image Comics, 2002

ISBN: 1582402604

12+

LIBERTY MEADOWS BOOK 1: EDEN

Plot: Frank is the new vet at the Liberty Meadows Animal Sanctuary, whose residents include Leslie, the chronically hypochondriac bullfrog; Ralph, the genius midget bear; Dean, the pig; young Truman, the duck; Oscar, the Weiner dog; Tony, the none-too-smart janitor; and last but not least, Brandy, the animal psychiatrist whom Frank immediately falls head over heels for.

In this volume we meet the cast and join them as they encounter the giant catfish, Khan; Frank meets Brandy's Neanderthal ex-boyfriend, Eric, who really isn't very keen on Frank; Marc DeRail, "manliest man on television," and host of TV show The Great Outdoors, comes to town and gets kidnapped by a deranged Cow; and Frank and Brandy are trapped in an abandoned mineshaft when Frank finally plucks up the nerve to ask Brandy on a date.

Review: *Liberty Meadows* has had a strange history. Starting as a university newspaper strip, it moved to comic-book format, then became a daily strip in several daily newspapers, as Cho had always hoped it would. However, after a year or so, Cho was fed up with the constraints of the cartooning syndicates and their demands to tone down the sometimes racy content, and decided to return to producing a monthly comic book. This means that *Liberty Meadows* has kept a slight edge over the usual bland newspaper fare.

However, let's start with the negative, as there is only one: *Liberty Meadows* is not one of the most original comics out there. It borrows liberally from the likes of *Bloom County* and *Doonesbury* in tone and general style, but that's not really too bad, as Cho takes only the best elements and turns them into something of his own.

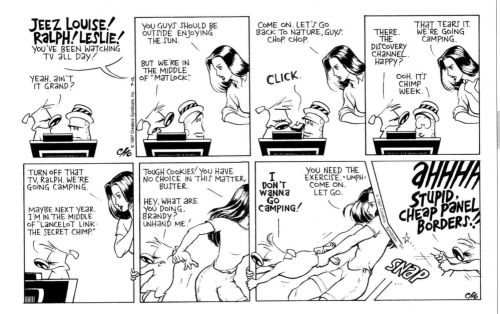

Cho is an excellent artist, and brings an uncommonly fine hand to his panels. He has an incredible mastery of linework, in the tradition of the likes of Beardsley and Howarth, and it's a treat when he breaks the boundaries to draw monkey-men, dinosaurs, or a classical rendering of Brandy to break in a new set of pens.

Cho's a genuinely funny guy. His humor is pretty conventional, but if *Liberty Meadows* doesn't make you giggle at least a few times, you obviously need to relax. This is a cut above the average in every way.

FURTHER READING: *Premillenial Maakies; University*[2]
SEE ALSO: *Liberty Meadows Volumes 2–4; Shanna the She-Devil*

★
★
★
★
★

Writer: Chris Ware
Artist: Chris Ware

Publisher: Jonathan Cape, 2003
ISBN: 1560974559

QUIMBY THE MOUSE

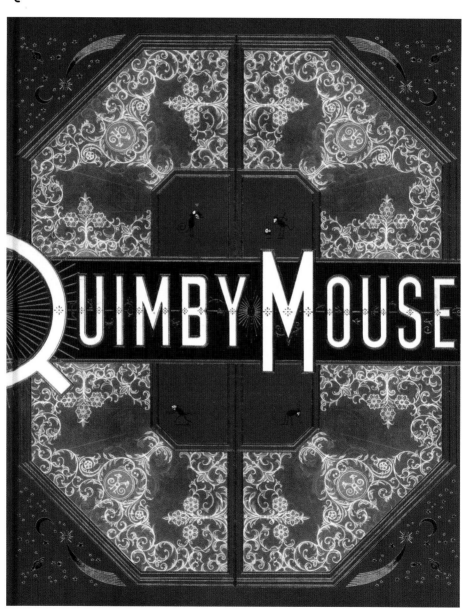

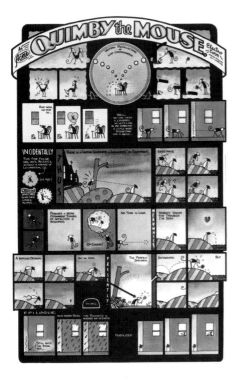

ESSENTIAL
GRAPHIC NOVELS
500
313
HUMOR
Top 10 humor graphic novels

Plot: This book initially appears to be a collection of strips, mainly concerning a cartoon mouse, who sometimes has two heads. However, it swiftly becomes apparent that this mouse is no happy-go-lucky cartoon character, but is beset by insecurities and obsessions that haunt him as he continues on in a dark and cruel world.

The strips soon turn into the author's confessions, as he uses the characters to tell stories of his own youth, and Quimby becomes less important and appears less often. We're also treated to some early stories about Jimmy Corrigan, the star of Ware's award-winning debut book, and several strips in which the autobiographical narrative is squeezed into a completely different style. Ware also includes many small strips and text pieces from early issues of *Acme Novelty Library*, and provides some of his trademark self-deprecating commentary on the material which was largely created while he was at college.

Review: The most immediate thing about this book is that it's an incredibly beautiful package—its intricately designed gold-inlay cover is almost worth the purchase price of the book on its own. It's just as well designed inside, with every page and panel laid out with as many as 60 tiny panels arranged in artful symmetry. Ware may be influenced by the style and typography of the early part of the 20th century, but his writing is razor sharp and contemporary, dark but fueled by a rich, uncomfortable humor. Although the book is only 56 pages long, there's an enormous amount of content, and these are the first steps by a master craftsman, as expert in its ambition as it is in execution.

FURTHER READING: *Acme Novelty Library; Acme Novelty Date Book*
SEE ALSO: *Jimmy Corrigan, Smartest Boy in the World; Maus; Pussey!*

★ **Writer:** Jamie Hewlett and Alan Martin **Publisher:** Titan Books, 2002
★ **Artist:** Jamie Hewlett **ISBN:** 1840234350
★

15+ TANK GIRL: VOLUME 1

Plot: Rebecca Buck was once a tank driver working for the Army in a post-apocalyptic Australia. But after publicly embarrassing the President of Australia by failing to deliver his much-needed supply of colostomy bags, shooting a top-ranking Army officer, and "borrowing" several million dollars from the Army payroll—as well as stealing her tank and turning it into a state-of-the-art killing-machine-cum-all-purpose-home—she went on the run and became the beer-guzzling, gun-toting, shaven-headed, antiheroine outlaw known as Tank Girl.

This book charts her earliest adventures, which include hunting a band of murderous mutant kangaroos, avoiding various assassination attempts, stealing a shipment of beer, making a deal with the Devil in exchange for a holy relic in the form of a bathrobe, and convincing her mutant kangaroo boyfriend Booga to enter the world of professional prizefighting. She also becomes a vengeful Aboriginal spirit and tries to ruin Booga's birthday so she doesn't have to buy him a present. Also introduced are Tank Girl's friends Jet Girl and Sub Girl, her surfer-dude stoner friend Stevie, and her favorite toy, Camp Koala.

Review: Jamie Hewlett and Alan Martin's anarchic outlaw could originally be found in *Deadline* in 1988, a British underground comic founded by *Preacher* artist Steve Dillon,

HUMOR
Top 10 humor graphic novels

315

ESSENTIAL
GRAPHIC NOVELS

500

and Brett Ewings, the *2000 AD* artist behind the strip *Bad Company*. Her creators have described Tank Girl as "*Mad Max* designed by Vivienne Westwood" and this punk-influenced, anti-authoritarian sensibility permeates both the art and the writing. Her adventures are by turns outrageous, violent, and funny. The writing in particular is very lively, particularly when the characters or the narrator address the reader, or even the artist, to complain about the sometimes intentionally crass dialog, the juvenile humor, or just to scrawl messages that have no relevance to the plot. But added to this is a sharp line in parody—note the unflattering portrayal of most of the army characters, or the satire on the film *The Italian Job* when Tank Girl and chums steal a

stash of beer. Hewlett's art is all high energy and it virtually jumps off the page and grabs your attention, but at times it can also be very atmospheric and defy its fanzine roots. *Tank Girl* progressed from a cult comic to an international hit, and made it to the big screen in 1995 in a film adaptation starring Lori Petty, but that's probably best frogtotten. Stick to the books. They're worth keeping.

FURTHER READING: *Tank Girl Volume 2; Tank Girl Volume 3; Tank Girl: The Gifting; The Odyssey*
SEE ALSO: *Judge Dredd: Complete Case Files Volume 1; Preacher Volume 1: Gone To Texas*

★
★
★

Writer: Fred Van Lente
Artist: Ryan Dunlavey

Publisher: Evil Twin, 2006
ISBN: 0977832902

ISBN: 0977832902

12+

ACTION PHILOSOPHERS: VOLUME 1

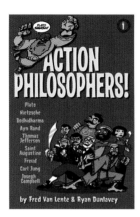

Plot: Plato: wrestling superstar of Ancient Greece! Neitzsche: The Ubermensch! Bodhidharma: Grandmaster of Kung Fu! Freud, Jung, Campbell, Ayn Rand, St. Augustine, and Thomas Jefferson are the other larger-than-life philosophers that are covered here in short, humorous looks at the personalities behind the philosophies.

Review: It's not the most obvious choice for a comic series, but this book actually works surprisingly well. All of the subjects led interesting lives, and the creators have succeeded in conveying the key points of both their lives and philosophies very successfully, while still making it funny and easy to follow. It's a great primer for those interested in the subject, but fascinating reading for anyone.

FURTHER READING: *Action Philosophers Giant-Size Thing Volume 2*
SEE ALSO: *Cartoon History of the Universe*

★
★
★
★

Writer: Nick Abadzis
Artist: Nick Abadzis

Publisher: Orchard Books, 1996
ISBN: 0930289234

ISBN: 0930289234

A

THE AMAZING MR PLEEBUS

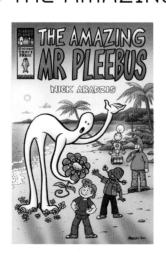

Plot: Joey and Pandora embark on a mysterious quest to other dimensions when the enigmatic Mr Pleebus leaps out of their TV. They band together with a group of bizarre characters in order to defeat the evil Grooblies.

Review: This little-known gem has all the hallmarks of a classic children's story—fantasy, adventure, and danger—without being too scary. Abadzis is a masterful storyteller and keeps the pace rattling along, and his polymorphic Mr Pleebus—who can't speak, except to say his name—is a fantastic character who can wring more emotion out of one word than many can in an entire book. While self-contained, this graphic novel sets up storylines for the next two adventures of Joey, Pandora, and Pleebus.

FURTHER READING: *The Freaky Beastie of Hill Road School*
SEE ALSO: *Laika*

Writer: Tony Millionaire
Artist: Tony Millionaire

Publisher: Dark Horse, 2000
ISBN: 1569714908

2+

THE ADVENTURES OF TONY MILLIONAIRE'S SOCK MONKEY

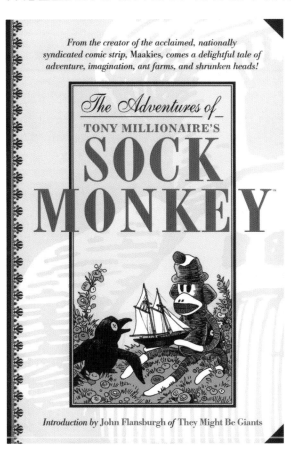

Plot: Take one sock monkey and one button-eyed crow and combine them in a large Victorian mansion filled with bric-a-brac, miscellaneous wild animals, a gas-lit chandelier, the occasional child, alcohol, and a shrunken head from Borneo. Shake well and enjoy; but beware of fire, the treacherous high seas, and "philosophical reorganization!"

Review: Tony Millionaire's artwork is as meticulously beautiful as it is morbidly deranged, and four short stories in this collection perfectly showcase his pen-and-ink

dementia. There's a childlike sense of wonder in these stories—a wonder that invariably leads to chaos at best, conflagration at worst. *Sock Monkey* is not for children, but it is for mature folks who laugh to keep from going mad.

FURTHER READING: *Little and Large; That Darn Yarn*
SEE ALSO: *Premillenial Maakies; Billy Hazelnuts*

★
★
★
★
★

Writer: Edward Gorey
Artist: Edward Gorey

Publisher: Perigee Books, 1980
ISBN: 0399504338

12+

AMPHIGOREY

Plot: The first of the *Amphigorey* anthologies, with 15 works by that most celebrated creator of gothic, illustrated tales, Edward St. John Gorey. Contained within this august tome are *The Unstrung Harp*, *The Listing Attic*, *The Doubtful Guest*, and possibly his most popular work, *The Gashlycrumb Tinies*.

Review: Edward Gorey, in work as well as life, did things a bit differently than everybody else; he wore a fur coat with basketball sneakers, was reclusive, and was prolific in his graphic storytelling, creating over 100 books. *The Doubtful Guest* is a prime example of his work, in which a strange, unnamed creature just appears one day, and proceeds to loiter and cause minor mischief... forever. Gorey's monochromatic, painstakingly cross-hatched illustrations add a new dimension to the writing, and his talent lies in making relatively simple things seem far more sinister.

FURTHER READING: *The Melancholy Death of Oyster Boy;*
The Boy Who Kicked Pigs; Struwwelpeter
SEE ALSO: *Lenore Noogies*

★
★
★

Writer: Paul Castiglia
Artist: Victor Gorelick and Dan DeCarlo

Publisher: Archie Comics, 2002
ISBN: 1879794012

12+

ARCHIE AMERICANA SERIES: BEST OF THE FIFTIES

Plot: A nostalgic look at selected Archie comics from the 1950s. The second in the *Archie Americana* series, tracking Archie's development as the typical American teen.

Review: Considering Archie is a character based on Mickey Rooney, he still commands an extremely loyal fanbase. A good proportion of the groundwork for that loyalty was laid in the 1950s, the era when Archie became the character he is today: instigator of girl-watching contests, school newspaper editor, and all-American teen. This volume demonstrates how the character and the series developed during its most important decade—the same decade that introduced the strip's best-known artist, Dan DeCarlo.

FURTHER READING: *Archie Americana: Best of the Forties;*
Best of the Seventies; Jughead's Diner
SEE ALSO: *Complete Peanuts; Blue Monday: The Kids Are Alright*

Writer: Bob Fingerman
Artist: Bob Fingerman

Publisher: Fantagraphics, 2005
ISBN: 1560976853

BEG THE QUESTION

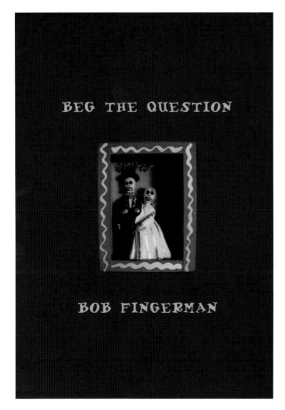

Plot: *Beg the Question* intimately scrutinizes the lives of Rob and Sylvia, a twentysomething couple who live in New York City. Rob is an (ironically) orthodox freelance cartoonist who writes on the side, peddling his wares to a variety of intriguingly titled pornographic magazines. Straight-talking Sylvia, manager of a beauty salon, has her sights set on bigger and better things. Together, the pair encounter a whole host of obstacles and relationship issues, from pregnancy scares to lesbian ex-girlfriends, while hanging out with a supporting cast of friends and oddball acquaintances. Will the relationship last as they try and negotiate their way through the hostile environs of NYC?

Review: Bob Fingerman's 2002 graphic novel is a composite of his signature work, *Minimum Wage*, the beautifully illustrated and candidly erotic account of life in New York City. The strip has been collected and modified into the volume presented here. Supported by a wonderfully eclectic range of characters, we see Rob and Sylvia's relationship evolve in a true-to-life and compassionate manner. It's well written and intelligently conceived, probably due to the fact that much of the book is based on Fingerman's own experiences. The artwork is clean, cartoony, and packed full of detail. An unjustly overlooked work, this is one of the finest slice-of-life narratives of the past 20 years.

FURTHER READING: *Recess Pieces; White Like She; You Deserved It*
SEE ALSO: *Box Office Poison; Buddy Does Seattle*

★
★
★
★

Writer: Matt Groening
Artist: Matt Groening

Publisher: Harper Collins, 2004
ISBN: 0007191650

12+

THE BIG BOOK OF HELL

Plot: The complete collection of Matt Groening's famous *Life In Hell* comic strips, as serialized in US newspapers since 1983. The book explores the gamut of human experience and emotion—from birth to death—while touching on love, work, and school through standalone strips, or as segmented chapters. Every aspect of the theme is covered and advice and solutions are offered for the more trickier situations.

Review: Matt Groening's great talent is for observing the essence of human existence and showing us the funny side. There is no subject that he won't examine with his own brand of caustic, sometimes highly cynical, sense of fun. The drawing style of the characters is relaxed and puts you at ease while your life is dissected and played out by fluffy bunnies. Groening himself even shows up from time to time in the guise of Binky the Rabbit. Alongside the bunny family are the charming characters of Akbar and Jeff, whose disturbing tagline is "brothers or lovers or possibly both." They run a variety of bizarre businesses and are frequently deployed when a generic couple is required. Charming and cheeky, this is a little slice of pre-*Simpsons* Groening that should be treasured by all.

FURTHER READING: *The Huge Book of Hell;*
Binky's Guide to Love
SEE ALSO: *The Simpsons Treehouse of Horror:*
Hoodoo Voodoo Brouhaha

Writer: Various
Artist: Various

Publisher: Puffin, 2006
ISBN: 0142407062

BIG FAT LITTLE LIT

Plot: This is a collection of short stories for children, created by a mix of alternative comic artists and children's book creators. Lemony Snicket and Richard Sala give us a chilly Yeti story; *Maus* creator Art Spiegelman offers a Hassidic fairy tale, *Prince Rooster*; Neil Gaiman and Gahan Wilson present a spooky party; David Mazzucchelli retells the Japanese fable of *The Fisherman and the Sea Princess*; and there are also stories from Maurice Sendak, Otto Seibold, Lorenzo Mattoti, Jules Feiffer, Dan Clowes, amongst many more.

Review: As with most anthologies, this is a mixed bag, but overall the quality is very high, especially on the art side—not surprising considering the caliber of the contributor list. It's especially good for younger kids but there's something in here for almost everyone, regardless of age.

FURTHER READING: *Open Me... I'm A Dog by Art Spiegelman; A Room With A Zoo; Where The Wild Things Are*
SEE ALSO: *Owly; The Amazing Mr Pleebus; Moomin*

Writer: Jay Lynch
Artist: Various

Publisher: Kitchen Sink Press, 1991
ISBN: 0685395081

THE BEST OF BIJOU FUNNIES

Plot: Two books back to back. Bijou Funnies was a seminal underground comic founded by Jay Kinney, Jay Lynch, Robert Crumb, and Skip Williamson, which published most of the notable underground cartoonists, including Justin Green, Gilbert Shelton, Bill Griffith, Bill Stout, Kim Deitch, and Art Spiegelman. Lynch contributed his *Nard'n'Pat* stories, Williamson's *Snappy Sammy Smoot* appeared regularly, and the others produced a range of work from the highly political, to straightforward slapstick humor. The *Apex* half offers profiles of, and a selection of strips by, several of the above.

Review: This collection is jammed with great material and provides a wide-ranging sampler for those who want to see what the original comix underground was producing, while gaining a broader understanding of what those heady days of free love and mind altering drugs were all about.

FURTHER READING: *The Scum Also Rises*
SEE ALSO: *Fabulous Furry Freak Brothers; The Book Of Mr. Natural*

★
★
★
★

Writer: Tony Millionaire
Artist: Tony Millionaire

Publisher: Fantagraphics, 2006
ISBN: 1560977019

A # BILLY HAZELNUTS

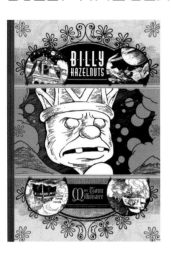

Plot: Beleaguered kitchen mice create the weird and wonderful Billy in an attempt to conquer the "old lady" who prevents them from snacking on their beloved cheese. After several near-fatal encounters, Billy meets budding scientist Becky, and the intrepid duo embark on a breathtaking journey to locate the vanished moon, while clashing with a malevolent steam-driven alligator and his skunk sidekick.

Review: This is a rip-roaring adventure from start to finish, and there are some very funny comedy moments that make the story a joy to read for all ages. Billy is a delightful creation, despite his grimy origins, with the heart of a true adventurer. Millionaire's delicate artwork is a delight, as ever, and this is a loopy and imaginative read that engages the heart and the mind.

FURTHER READING: *Sock Monkey: The Glass Doorknob;*
Der Struwwelmaakies; That Darn Yarn
SEE ALSO: *Amazing Mr Pleebus; Premillenial Maakies;*
Adventures of Tony Millionaire's Sock Monkey

★
★
★
★
★

Writers: Aaron McGruder, Reginald Hudlin
Artist: Kyle Baker

Publisher: Three Rivers Press, 2005
ISBN: 1400083168

15+ # BIRTH OF A NATION: A COMIC NOVEL

Plot: A cynical move on the part of the US Government denies a significant number of black residents from the poor and rundown area of East St. Louis from voting in the presidential elections. In protest, they declare their freedom from the United States and rename East St. Louis "Blackland."

Review: The title is a conscious swipe at the controversial D.W. Griffith film of 1915, which was an historical account of the rise of the Ku Klux Klan after the American Civil War. Due to the pedigree of the collaborators, the issues are couched in wit and shrewdness, addressing the problem of endemic racism and prejudice that still survives and flourishes in some quarters of the American political landscape. It never becomes a didactic rant, but remains both entertaining and informative while adding a significant contribution to the comics landscape.

FURTHER READING: *The Boondocks*
SEE ALSO: *Plastic Man: On the Lam*

★
★
★

Writer: Chynna Clugston-Major
Artist: Chynna Clugston-Major

Publisher: Oni Press, 2003
ISBN: 1929998627

BLUE MONDAY, VOLUME 1:
THE KIDS ARE ALRIGHT

Plot: A rites-of-passage story about life as a teenager, when the clothes you wear, the bands you like, and the people you hang out with mean everything. Bleu L. Finnegan is a retro-obsessed girl who dreams of getting a ticket to an Adam Ant concert and will stop at nothing to do so. Along the way she suffers the slings and arrows of outrageous (mis)fortune as she contends with love, life, and disreputable radio DJs.

Review: A likeable bubblegum take on the high school brat-pack genre, with just a dash of *Cinderella*, by an American creator who's clearly obsessed by Britpop culture. Namedropping of pop groups and counterculture fashion icons is de rigueur throughout the story, which follows a fairly predictable route through the trials and tribulations of late teenage life.

FURTHER READING: *Blue Monday, Volume 2: Absolute Beginners*
SEE ALSO: *Scott Pilgrim: Precious Little Life*

00
00

★
★
★

Writer: Peter Blegvad
Artist: Peter Blegvad

Publisher: Overlook, 2001
ISBN: 1585670987

BOOK OF LEVIATHAN

underworld from which he must lead his phantom parents. In one strip he confronts his nameless dread; in another he goes to Hell and every reader is granted a free indulgence.

Review: *Leviathan* is a surreal experience, driven by its creator's interests in philosophy, art, literature, and language (Blegvad's 1970s progressive rock band, *Slapp Happy*, ploughed a similar furrow with their music). The strips are full of quotes and allusions, but while this means *Leviathan* is occasionally quite dense, it's also wonderfully humorous, weird, dark, and wise.

Plot: Leviathan (Levi) is a faceless infant, son of Aesop and Naomi, whose companions are a cat and a toy rabbit. His adventures are investigations into life's mysteries, whether they're specific to his immediate circumstances or to the wider, adult world. When his parents go out, for instance, he becomes an Orpheus figure, directed by the cat into an

FURTHER READING: *Real Estate Photographer, Julius Knipl*
SEE ALSO: *Calvin and Hobbes; Peanuts*

★
★
★

Writer: Robert Crumb   **Publisher:** Fantagraphics, 1995
Artist: Robert Crumb   **ISBN:** 1560971940

15+ THE BOOK OF MR. NATURAL

Plot: More profane than profound, Robert Crumb's counterculture legend Mr. Natural is a lascivious guru who wanders through life alternately grumbling and looking for women to sleep with. He occasionally dispenses "wisdom," but only when pressed, along with the help of his number-one acolyte, Flakey Foont, who is obsessed with the supernatural charms of Devil Girl. This volume collects all the "freewheeling" underground material that first made Crumb's name.

Review: It's ironic that Crumb, possibly the most unswinging man alive, became famous during the swinging Sixties by parodying the era's susceptibility to cults and swamis, and drawing rather violent sexual material. Mr. Natural's homespun wisdom and lecherous longings survive the test of time, as does Crumb's cartoony, Wolverton-esque early drawing style.

FURTHER READING: *Complete Crumb Volumes 3–7*
SEE ALSO: *Complete Crumb Volume 8: Death of Fritz The Cat; My Troubles With Women*

★
★
★

Writer: Jeffrey Brown   **Publisher:** Top Shelf, 2003
Artist: Jeffrey Brown   **ISBN:** 0971359768

15+ CLUMSY

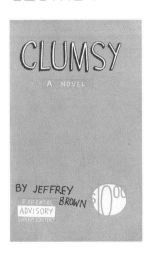

Plot: A bittersweet memoir of a year-long long-distance romance, that was doomed to fail from the start.

Review: Told through short snapshots of everyday life and treasured encounters that are never more than a couple of pages long, Chicagoan Jeffrey Brown's rough, effective, messy art is effectively summed up by the book's title. It is clumsy, but that is the point. *Clumsy* is a book of awkward emotions, compromises, and thwarted desires. It could be described as "Emo comics." To fully appreciate *Clumsy*, you should really read it alongside *Be A Man*, Brown's mini-comic remix of *Clumsy*, in which he satirizes an imagined macho version of his own book.

FURTHER READING: *Be A Man*
SEE ALSO: *Mail Order Bride*

★
★
★
★

Writer: Tom Hart
Artist: Tom Hart

Publisher: Top Shelf, 2000
ISBN: 1891830171

5+

COLLECTED HUTCH OWEN

Plot: Hutch has launched a one-man war against Corporate America and its attempt to co-opt both youth culture and the indigenous cultures of the emerging markets it dominates. His ongoing nemesis is childhood friend Dennis Worner, head of the multinational company Worner Products.

Review: Tom Hart is one of the most politically conscious of the American independent cartoonists who came to fore in the early 1990s. His most popular creation, Hutch Owen, is an itinerant poet who lives in a treehouse or under a bridge and publishes his own writings. Hutch's anger and subversion are tempered by a childlike belief in the basic goodness of his fellow man, and his adventures are notable as much for their humor and poetry as for their biting political insight.

FURTHER READING: *The System; Lowlife; Tricked*
SEE ALSO: *Three Fingers*

ESSENTIAL GRAPHIC NOVELS

500

325

HUMOR
Best of the rest

★
★
★

Writer: Dame Darcy
Artist: Dame Darcy

Publisher: Fantagraphics, 2003
ISBN: 1560975326

5+

DAME DARCY'S MEATCAKE COMPILATION

Plot: Bizarre fairy tales comprise the bulk of the strips in this volume, collected from Darcy's regular comic series. The simplest introduction might be a description of the recurring characters: Strega Pez communicates by means of words on a candy bar that she projects from a wound in her throat. Hindrance and Perfidia are Siamese twins, and Scampi the Selfish Shellfish is kept on a leash by Friend the Girl. The sex pest Wax Wolf is male, but Effluvia is a mermaid and Richard Dirt is actually another female. Got that?

Review: The artwork completely fills the pages, panels have embroidered borders, and words get everywhere. These tell absurd, weird, gothic tales of obsession, love, death, and murder set in a surreal twilight world with sets decorated for a German Expressionist film. Odd, but good.

FURTHER READING: *Frightful Fairytales*
SEE ALSO: *Chuckling Whatsit*

★
★
★
★
★

Writer: Alan Moore
Artist: Alan Davis

Publisher: Rebellion, 2006
ISBN: 1904265480

THE COMPLETE D.R. AND QUINCH

Plot: This fine and, like, utterly mind-blowing tome of coolness, concerns the adventures of two wildly unstable alien high school students, Waldo "D.R." Dobbs and Ernest Errol Quinch. D.R. stands for Diminished Responsibility, while Quinch stands about seven feet tall and has a penchant for neon spats. D.R. is outrageously intelligent, has an IQ of 280, and finds the myriad colors of dangerous weaponry endlessly thrilling. Quinch doesn't speak much, is likely not to be very bright, but he also finds the merciless slaughter of millions of innocents deeply fulfilling.

Plot: Together, D.R. and Quinch are a match made in... Hell? No, wrong plane. The Slime Jungles of Ghoyogi? Whatever. However you put it they are a volatile and potentially lethal combination. They are also very funny. Penned by the bewhiskered wizard of the graphic tale, Mr. Alan Moore, *The Complete D.R. and Quinch* is a must-have for all lovers of egregious acts of callous and totally unjustified violence, and those who appreciate a thinly veiled attack on our own society when they see one. Alan Davis's art is ideally suited to the stories here; stylish and clear with lots of good in-gags, it delivers the story with a nod to newsprint comics, but remains wholly *2000 AD*.

FURTHER READING: *The Complete Ballad of Halo Jones*
SEE ALSO: *Sam and Max: Surfin' the Highway; The Complete Nemesis the Warlock*

Writer: Rick Altergott
Artist: Rick Altergott

Publisher: Fantagraphics, 2002
ISBN: 156097494X

THE DOOFUS OMNIBUS

Plot: Doofus is the ultimate sleazeball. He and his friend, Henry Hotchkiss, an equally creepy loser, live in Flowertown, where they obsess over almost every woman they come into contact with. Populated by a cast of ever-more grotesque dropouts, Altergott's scatological tales plumb the depths of humor as his "hero" sniffs used panties and hides in a dog kennel to watch the dogs have sex.

Review: Very much a cartoonist's cartoonist, Altergott draws heavily on the style of artists such as Wally Wood, producing very tightly drawn and extremely funny ruminations on the world. The clipped and rather aloof narrative voice contrasts with Doofus and his friends' embarrassing attempts to sound like hipsters.

FURTHER READING: *Raisin Pie*
SEE ALSO: *Pussey!; Ghost World; Premillennial Maakies*

Writer: John Kovalic
Artist: John Kovalic

Publisher: Dork Storm Press, 2000
ISBN: 1930964404

THE COLLECTED DORK TOWER VOLUME 1: DORK COVENANT

Plot: *Dork Tower* is a closely observed collection of humorous episodes from the lives of gamers. Matt is the voice of insecurity, Igor is an idiot, Carson is a muskrat (literally), and Ken can be as bloodthirsty as Igor and Carson, but still manages to rise above it all. The humor springs from their reactions to TV, film, comics, and the real and imaginary games they play.

Review: Kovalic has a simple, but effective cartoon style and uses many running jokes. These are often laugh-out-loud funny and as accessible to those who don't know the ins and outs of gaming culture as those who do. Hugely enjoyable.

FURTHER READING: *Dork Shadows; Heart of Dorkness; The Dork Side of the Goon; Livin' La Vida Dorka*
SEE ALSO: *Artesia; Groo*

★ **Writer:** Gilbert Shelton   **Publisher:** Knockabout, 2004
★ **Artist:** Gilbert Shelton   **ISBN:** 086166146X
★
★

15+ # THE COMPLETE FABULOUS FURRY FREAK BROTHERS VOLUME 1

Plot: The three Freak brothers—political activist and experimentally inclined intellectual Phineas T. Phreakears; laidback Freewheelin' Frank, distinguished by his big nose and cowboy attire; and Fat Freddy Freekowtski, a podgy and none-too-bright middle-class kid—are always on the lookout for better sources of drugs, while trying to avoid being caught out by the police and Norbert the Nark, an inept DEA agent who's got it in for them. They also chase chicks, get abducted by aliens, and accidentally form a new religion. Fat Freddy's cat acts as a kind of cynical Greek chorus during their antics.

Review: Like many great humor strips, *Freak Brothers* works by going over the same themes with numerous tweaks and teases. You soon realize that any story that opens with an ordered situation will soon develop into knockabout chaos.

Unlike many underground cartoonists, Shelton's work has stood the test of time and remains as funny today as it was in the late 1960s—particularly if you're a rebellious teenager. This is thanks to his ability to pack so many gags into a page and to the enduring appeal of his archetypal hippies—one dumb but endearing sensualist, one intellectual, and one guy who really doesn't give a damn so long as the world leaves him alone. No matter how bad things seem, somehow the shambolic trio triumph in the end. This volume showcases Shelton's drawing skills at their peak.

FURTHER READING: *The Complete Fabulous Furry Freak Brothers Volume 2*
SEE ALSO: *The Book of Mr. Natural; Justin Green's Binky Brown Sampler; The New Adventures of Jesus*

Writer: Roger Langridge
Artist: Roger Langridge

Publisher: Fantagraphics, 2004
ISBN: 1560976101

FRED THE CLOWN

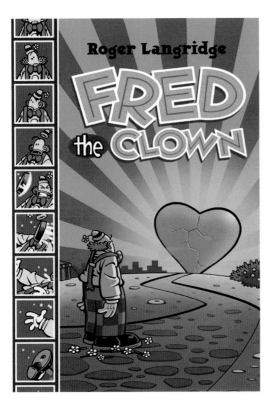

Plot: The definitive collection of the misadventures of Fred, a happy-go-lucky clown whose main joys in life include his relentless search for a female companion. Typically, his tastes run toward the bearded lady, but Fred's not too choosy, and can be very determined when it comes to pursuing his chosen paramour. The book is divided into ten sections, each one a "step to happiness," and so we join Fred on his many adventures, including a trip to the moon and the daring rescue of a spoon millionaire's daughter. Whether or not these steps will lead Fred to the fulfilment he seeks remains to be seen...

Review: Langridge's work combines elements of Python-esque surrealism with that of the Goon Show, Lewis Carroll, and Maurice Sendak, without ever being anything other than truly original. Using a variety of different styles, *Fred the Clown* beautifully satirizes everything from the daily news strips that have appeared in countless papers over the years, to the storytelling stylings of Dr. Seuss, right up to the underground comix of R. Crumb. The artwork is timeless, and the book is full of laugh-out-loud moments. Langridge's writing is effortless and impressive—the back-story that covers the legend of Fred is nothing short of genius—and this is a remarkable and utterly unique book.

FURTHER READING: *Zoot Suite*
SEE ALSO: *Sam & Max: Surfin' The Highway;*
The Cowboy Wally Show; Louche And Insalubrious
Escapades of Art D'Ecco

★
★
★
★

Writer: Evan Dorkin   **Publisher:** SLG, 1997
Artist: Evan Dorkin   **ISBN:** 0943151074

15+ # FUN WITH MILK AND CHEESE

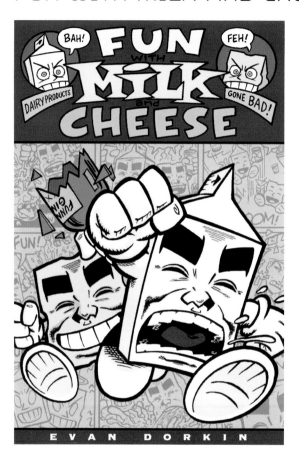

Plot: Evan Dorkin's heroes, "dairy products gone bad," are a brilliant, foul-mouthed pair of characters, prone to violence. In fact they seem to exist solely for the opportunity to beat on brats and idiots of all kinds. Many of the plots, and most of the humor, revolves around them getting drunk and fighting anyone that annoys them. Each story is fundamentally the same, but Dorkin keeps the formula fresh with lots of backchat and clever asides.

target all the blabbermouths, jingoistic jerks, and annoying cretins in one big, cathartic fist-fest—you will find yourself looking forward to the inevitable violence. He brings immense energy (and a very twisted sense of humor) to a series of shorts that target American popular culture, and while some readers may find his rants a bit repetitive, in small doses they are extremely liberating.

Review: Dorkin's smooth artwork, which draws as much on animation as it does cartooning, contrasts nicely with the jarring themes of the strips. His obnoxious protagonists

FURTHER READING: *Dork: Circling the Drain*
SEE ALSO: *The Doofus Omnibus; Too Much Coffee Man's Guide to the Perplexed*

Writer: Lynda Barry
Artist: Lynda Barry

Publisher: Sasquatch Books, 2002
ISBN: 1570612609

THE GREATEST OF MARLYS

Plot: This compendium captures a wide range of Lynda Barry's comic-strip stylings. Her more somber, longer narratives are balanced by nutty and outrageous proclamations by her main character, Marlys. And watch out for what will become your new favorite comedy character—Fred Milton, Beat Poodle.

Review: As Matt Groening (*Life in Hell; The Simpsons*) is fond of saying, "Lynda Barry is Funk Queen of the Universe," and this collection backs up that boast. Her artwork is indeed "funky"—densely packed panels teem with sketchy detail, from freckles to nervous twitches, to antic displays of wild motion. Her captions often fill half the panel, and sometimes leave the images to illustrate unconnected scenes. But Barry's prose is magnificent and her ear for dialog is second to none. She captures melancholy and yearning as easily as she does youthful enthusiasm.

FURTHER READING: *The Freddie Stories; Cruddy*
SEE ALSO: *The Big Book of Hell*

Writer: Marc Hempel
Artist: Marc Hempel

Publisher: Vertigo, 2004
ISBN: 1401202713

A GREGORY TREASURY VOLUME 1

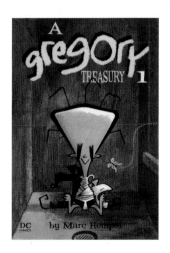

Plot: Gregory is a small boy of indeterminate age who spends his days in a straitjacket, locked up in an asylum, with only a pair of rats for company. In this volume we're introduced to Gregory and his best friend, Herman the Vermin, a loquacious rat with an unfortunate habit for getting himself killed. This book follows them both through a variety of skits, as Gregory meets therapists, cats, and the outside world, while Herman gets to visit the Almighty himself.

Review: A child in the loony bin may not be an obvious comedy scenario, but Hempel's *Gregory* is an inspired creation, bringing a childlike wonder and absurdity to every hysterical situation. Herman provides the voice of sordid reason to proceedings, and the minimal and surreal art perfectly suits the subject. Hilarious and touching.

FURTHER READING: *A Gregory Treasury Volume 2; Sandman: The Kindly Ones; Tug & Buster*
SEE ALSO: *Sandman: Suckle; Sam & Max: Surfin' The Highway*

★
★
★
★

Writer: Graham Annable
Artist: Graham Annable

Publisher: Alternative Comics, 2001
ISBN: 1891867016

15+ # GRICKLE

slight aberration

Plot: *Grickle* is a collection of short strips by storyboard artist Graham Annable, filled with tales of innocence and cruelty. A wannabe-hero confronts a pair of smokers in a nonsmoking restaurant with disastrous results. A group of space explorers argue among themselves and accidentally doom a whole planet. A stalker has an entire relationship with his waitress over a coffee. A quiet, lonely man obsessed with reading on the toilet somehow becomes a popular talkshow host. A tiny man suddenly appears in a stranger's car and haunts his home, doing nothing but drawing strange pictures.

Review: It's difficult to explain just how funny *Grickle* is. Annable's artwork initially seems quite crude, but he produces an astonishing amount of expression from his hapless characters. His stories draw upon the innocence and harsh reality of life, the casual and sudden crushing defeats that sometimes affect us all, told with a sharp and biting sense of humor. He also has an incredibly good sense of comic timing, and his stories can change from hysterical to terrifying, and back, in just a few panels. There are some very sad little tales mixed in with the comedy gold, and they hit the emotional buttons just as effectively as the funny ones. Annable isn't well known, even within the comics field, but he's definitely a talent who deserves acclaim, and if you like your humor dark this is an essential read.

FURTHER READING: *Hickee; Further Grickle*
SEE ALSO: *Mister O; The Big Book of Hell*

Writer: Pete Sickman-Garner
Artist: Pete Sickman-Garner

Publisher: Top Shelf, 2001
ISBN: 1891830066

HEY, MISTER: CELEBRITY ROAST

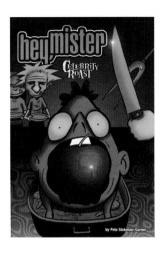

Plot: The misanthropic misadventures of Aunt Mary, Young Tim, Virgil, and Mister himself. Behind these innocuous names lie personalities whose views on life are as hilarious as they are shocking. Punchlines such as "I wish Billy Joel's teen suicide attempt had been successful," and titles like *Young Tim and the Mystery of the Squeezable Playfriend* exemplify the malice, bleakness, and downright inappropriateness of these characters.

Review: The Fates were in literal mood when they gave a cartooning talent like this to a person whose name includes "Sickman." You might hate yourself for finding these one-page jokes and epic-length tragedies funny, but by doing so, you'll just be making Aunt Mary's day.

FURTHER READING: *Hey Mister: After School Special*
SEE ALSO: *Buddy Does Seattle*

Writer: Paige Braddock
Artist: Paige Braddock

Publisher: Girl Twirl Comics, 2003
ISBN: 0974245003

JANE'S WORLD

Plot: As the title implies, this is all about the world of Jane—an ordinary woman with an apartment, a dog, a sort-of girlfriend, and a whole pile of complications that take her into any number of situations that she'd rather stay out of.

Review: In Jane, Paige Braddock has created an entirely believable and highly likeable character, a feat that's much more difficult than you might suppose. Paige's friends say that she steals episodes from their lives and smuggles them into *Jane's World*, and this is perhaps why these characters are so easy to empathize with. The illustration style, as much as the text, draws you in and allows the story to flow beautifully, with great charm and elegance, despite some of Jane's less than glamorous escapades. It's rare to find a strip like this so well realized, and it really is a treat: a comic character who feels like a friend.

FURTHER READING: *Jane's World Volume 2; Stephanie Plum*
SEE ALSO: *Complete Peanuts; Pussey!*

★ **Writer:** Jhonen Vasquez **Publisher:** SLG, 1997
★ **Artist:** Jhonen Vasquez **ISBN:** 0943151163
★
★

15+ # JOHNNY THE HOMICIDAL MANIAC: DIRECTOR'S CUT

Plot: The violent misadventures of a manically depressed psycho who is murderously disappointed in humanity, all laced with plenty of self-loathing.

Review: As a series of brutal and surreal revenge fantasies against the banal annoyances, petty incompetences, and human stupidities of modern life, there is no escaping the fact that *Johnny the Homicidal Manic* is a violent work. But unlike most action movies, it is also far more than that. Johnny is a refreshingly self-aware maniac who is given to self-criticism, but are the surreal monsters that plague him products of his own mind or something else? With its gloriously dark and scratchy expressionist artwork, dark humor, and characters who favor black clothes, Johnny is a comic that will appeal to goths, but is also of interest to a much wider audience.

FURTHER READING: *Squee; I Feel Sick*
SEE ALSO: *Lenore: Noogies*

★ **Writer:** George Herriman **ISBN:** 1560977345
★ **Artist:** George Herriman
★ **Publisher:** Fantagraphics, 2008
★

 A # KRAZY & IGNATZ 1943-1944: HE NODS IN QUIESSCENT SIESTA

Plot: In its 30-year run, the plot of Krazy Kat seldom deviated: Ignatz Mouse hurls bricks at the head of Krazy Kat, who interprets this as a sign of Ignatz's love. Out of a sense of duty, Officer Pup throws Ignatz in jail. Though this basic premise remained unchanged, the strip never lost its freshness and vitality due to Herriman's idiosyncratic drawing style.

Review: This volume features full-color artwork throughout and photographs of unpublished artwork. Considered by many to be the greatest comic strip of all time, this is an excellent place to start.

FURTHER READING: *Krazy & Ignatz (1916 strips);*
Krazy & Ignatz 1925–1926: There Is A Heppy Lend Furfur A-Waay
SEE ALSO: *Quimby the Mouse*

★
★
★
★

Writer: Tim Barela
Artist: Tim Barela

Publisher: Palliard Press, 1993
ISBN: 1884568009

5+ # LEONARD & LARRY:
DOMESTICITY ISN'T PRETTY

Plot: Years before *Will & Grace*, Barela's *Leonard & Larry* was the first gay sitcom, appearing in regular strips in the US. Leonard is an architect, Larry owns a leather goods store on Santa Monica Boulevard, and they've been together for years. They deal with all of the things that most middle-aged couples have to deal with, including Larry's son from a confused marriage years earlier, who is coming out as gay himself.

Review: *Leonard & Larry* is an extremely funny and affecting collection. It doesn't stoop to shock tactics, and it beautifully depicts the ups and downs of any relationship, whether gay or straight. Barela is also a brilliant cartoonist, and you'll end up falling in love with the cast.

FURTHER READING: *Leonard & Larry: Kurt Cobain & Mozart are Dead; How Real Men Do It; Excerpts From The Ring Cycle*
SEE ALSO: *Dykes To Watch Out For; Strangers In Paradise; Fun Home*

★
★
★

Writer: Roberta Gregory
Artist: Roberta Gregory

Publisher: Fantagraphics, 2005
ISBN: 156097656X

3+ # LIFE'S A BITCH:
THE BITCHY BITCH CHRONICLES

Plot: Midge McCracken is Bitchy Bitch, a 40-year-old, politically incorrect harridan who is irritated by the little things in life. In this collection, which sifts through a lifetime of insecurity masquerading as pure bitchery, everything is a target for Bitchy's cynicism: from her co-workers to her relationships with men. The tales span her life, from her appalling childhood, through her teen years, to her current status as a desperate singleton.

Review: Roberta Gregory has created a tour de force in Midge—the slapdash drawing style and exaggerated facial expressions bring a sharp sense of humor into every panel, as does the raging interior monologue that drags you right into the bitchy heart of Midge's surprisingly likeable consciousness. This is painful reading in places, but very funny throughout.

FURTHER READING: *Naughty Bits; Bitchy Butch*
SEE ALSO: *Greatest of Marlys; Jane's World; Fun Home*

★
★
★
★
★

Writer: Thierry Robin
Artist: Louis Trondheim

Publisher: NBM, 2002
ISBN: 1561633356

A # L'IL SANTA

Thierry Robin   Lewis Trondheim

Li'l Santa

Plot: Robin and Trondheim's Santa is an impish little fellow who has to use his wits to overcome the many hurdles he faces while trying to prepare and deliver his annual bounty to children everywhere, in this volume and the follow-up adventure, *Happy Halloween, L'il Santa*. Whether it's numbskull lumberjacks or the big yellow ball of teeth and fur that is the Yeti, there's a problem at every turn.

Review: Told entirely without words, these stories are utterly charming and appeal to tiny tots and senior citizens alike. Trondheim's expressive drawing is an absolute joy.

FURTHER READING: *Happy Halloween, L'il Santa; Mister I*
SEE ALSO: *The Dungeon; Harum Scarum; A.L.I.E.E.E.N.: Archives of Lost Issues and Earthly Editions of Extraterrestrial Novelties*

★
★
★

Writer: Harvey Kurtzman
Artist: Will Elder

Publisher: Dark Horse, 2001
ISBN: 156971519X

18+ # LITTLE ANNIE FANNY: VOLUME 1

Plot: Volume 1 (of 2) reprints the *Annie Fanny* pages that appeared in *Playboy* between 1962 and 1970. Our buxom heroine's adventures (which always involve her losing her clothes) reflect the changing mores of that period—psychedelia, anti-war protests, and swinging. She even has a run-in with The Beatles!

Review: Kurtzman and Elder cook up a mad sexual world full of sight gags, rotund cartooning, and blaring color. The painted detail on the pages is astounding, although no one will believe you if you say you bought it for the backgrounds. Elder was assisted by likes of Frank Frazetta, Russ Heath, and Jack Davis, and the collection also includes sketches and annotations on each segment.

FURTHER READING: *Harvey Kurtzman's Jungle Book; Goodman Beaver; Chicken Fat: Drawings, Sketches, Cartoons and Doodles*
SEE ALSO: *Crime Suspenstories; The Complete Crumb Vol 8*

Writer: Andrew Langridge
Artist: Roger Langridge

Publisher: Fantagraphics, 2006
ISBN: 1560977965

THE LOUCHE AND INSALUBRIOUS ESCAPADES OF ART D'ECCO

Plot: Surreal and unpredictable stories in which Art D'Ecco and his dumb triangular roommate, the Gump—who is oblivious to the cruelty dealt to him by his so called friend—wander through a highly stylized world that frequently references and parodies high art as well as other comics. It's populated by art inspired characters such as the unintelligible Art Nouveau, D'Ecco's negative twin; and the lisping Esch, inspired by the work of Escher.

Review: *Art D'Ecco* is an unapologetically intelligent comic that bombards you with sight gags, puns, and artistic references. The collection contains new material as well as stories from the late 1980s. With parodies of everything from religious zealots to hardline Marxists, it is elegantly drawn and an absolute joy to read.

FURTHER READING: *Bizarro World*
SEE ALSO: *Krazy & Ignatz; Premillennial Maakies; Fred The Clown*

Writer: Rene Goscinny
Artist: Morris (Maurice de Bevere)

Publisher: Cinebook, 2007
ISBN: 1905460112

A LUCKY LUKE ADVENTURE: BILLY THE KID

Plot: Lucky Luke is a cowboy who can shoot faster than his own shadow. With his faithful steed, Jolly Jumper, he travels the Wild West fighting crime and bringing justice to the frontier. Along the way he meets a motley selection of fictional and historical characters such as Calamity Jane; Jesse James; his most persistent foes, the Dalton Family; and in this particular book, Billy the Kid.

Review: Created by Morris, Lucky Luke's adventures are heroic, but humorously told, making the series one of the best-loved comics in Europe, ranking alongside *Asterix* and *Tintin*. Morris's artwork has a fluid look with elements of caricature, but is always rendered realistically.

FURTHER READING: *Spirou et Fantasio; Barbed Wire on the Prarie*
SEE ALSO: *Asterix and the Great Crossing*

★
★
★

Writer: Sam Henderson
Artist: Sam Henderson

Publisher: Alternative Comics, 2004
ISBN: 1891867687

18+ # MAGIC WHISTLE VOLUME 9

Plot: The first annual issue of Sam Henderson's *Magic Whistle* continues in the vein of previous issues, with no joke too disgusting, obvious, or unfunny to escape inclusion. Meet Rex The Exploding Dog; Simperton J. Narcisissy, aspiring artist; Dirty Danny; The Newlyweds, and more hilarious creations, plus loads of single-panel gags and a longer story about a supporting character who's fired from his daily comic strip.

Review: Henderson is a master of the ridiculous, with most of his jokes stripped down to their bare bones. His art is very simple, but suits the slapstick style of the gags very well, and the jokes are often more sophisticated than it may seem at first. Henderson's humor is quite black, and no taboo is safe.

FURTHER READING: *Humor Can Be Funny; The Magic Whistle Blows; Oh That Monroe: The Complete Adventures of Monroe Simmons*
SEE ALSO: *Sam And Max: Surfin' The Highway; Fred The Clown*

★
★
★

Writer: Rumiko Takahashi
Artist: Rumiko Takahashi

Publisher: VIZ Media LLC, 2003
ISBN: 1591160545

A # MAISON IKKOKU: VOLUME 1

Plot: Kyoko is a young widow, the manager of a boarding house called Maison Ikkoku. Her tenants are an odd bunch, including Yusaku, a student dropout. From this unlikely situation a romantic soap opera develops in which the other tenants are comic foils for the nearly on, mostly off, relationship between Yusaku and Kyoko. Constant misunderstandings bedevil their lives and each is pursued by other suitors, prolonging the suspense. Volume 1 sets the scene, introducing Mitaka, tennis coach and rival for Kyoko, and Kozue, a young student who starts to date Yusaku.

Review: The storytelling is fast and full of slapstick, but the incessant teasing does your patience. However, if you enjoy this volume, you'll probably like the whole series.

FURTHER READING: *Maison Ikkoku Volumes 2–14*
SEE ALSO: *Ranma ½; Inu Yashu*

Writer: Louis Trondheim
Artist: Louis Trondheim
Publisher: NBM, 2004
ISBN: 1561633828

MISTER O

Plot: Mister O is a small circular fellow with one problem—how to get to the other side of a chasm in the ground. During the course of 30 strips, he attempts to cross, always ending up plunging into the void no matter what method he tries, while every other character in the book gets across with no problem at all. You'll have to read through to the end to find out whether he ever makes it...

Review: Trondheim is a master of comics minimalism, and can convey an enormous amount with very little in this gut-wrenchingly funny book. The art consists of little more than stick figures, but he does more with this limited palette than most could with any number of complex techniques, creating an amazing little slapstick world.

FURTHER READING: *Mister I; Tiny Tyrant; Harum Scarum Volume 1*
SEE ALSO: *Dungeon Volume 1: Duck Heart; A.L.I.E.E.E.N.; L'il Santa*

Writer: James Kochalka
Artist: James Kochalka
Publisher: Top Shelf, 2000
ISBN: 1891830155

MONKEY VS. ROBOT

Plot: A peaceful tribe of monkeys finds itself drawn into a deadly battle for survival when single-minded, self-duplicating robots encroach on their precious jungle habitat.

Review: At face value, James Kochalka's allegorical tale is a beautifully uncomplicated all-ages adventure, with sparse, essential dialog, and a story that develops mainly through expressive black-and-white illustration. However, Kochalka's simple style is deceptive, and his story touches on the serious themes of conflict, sacrifice, and pyrrhic victory. On an allegorical level, this also explores the conflict between nature and technology, with the organic monkeys attempting to halt the resource-hungry progress of the synthetic robots.

FURTHER READING: *Monkey vs. Robot and the Crystal of Power*
SEE ALSO: *Robot Dreams*

★
★
★

Writer: James Kochalka   **Publisher:** Alternative Comics, 2003
Artist: James Kochalka   **ISBN:** 1891867466

A # PEANUTBUTTER AND JEREMY'S BEST BOOK EVER!

Plot: A story about an unkind crow, and a cat that wears a tie and thinks she works in an office.

Review: James Kochalka is a bit of an indie comics legend—relentlessly creative and prolific, he frequently eschews "craft" such as making his art more representational, in favor of capturing the loose, fluid essence of the moment, the play of a conversation, or a sequence of actions. The result is a joy to read. It isn't really about anything much other than two bickering animals arguing about hats or dollars they can't spend, but it's fun. Fun in the way that childish arguments can be: a stream of oneupmanship, flawed friendships, and silly jokes. It's cute and playful and it will remind you not to swear at Christmas.

FURTHER READING: *Monkey vs. Robot*
SEE ALSO: *American Elf*

★
★
★
★

Writer: Joe Matt   **Publisher:** Drawn & Quarterly, 2003
Artist: Joe Matt   **ISBN:** 1896597270

18+ # PEEPSHOW: THE CARTOON DIARY OF JOE MATT

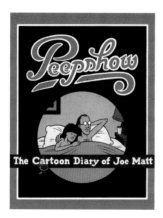

Plot: Collected from his early comic of the same name, Matt's strips center around his fluctuating relationship and the struggle to making a living as an independent cartoonist. He portrays himself as incredibly cheap and obsessed with porn, and is quite shameless about showing himself in a bad light.

Review: You will cringe, you will be shocked, and you will wonder how anyone can bring himself to confess to so much creepy and cowardly behavior (not to mention going into the minutiae of his bowel movements), but in the end Matt seems curiously endearing. He draws pages crammed with tiny panels, displaying his gift for caricature and distortion, and makes everything that ought to be degrading and depressing seem funny.

FURTHER READING: *Spent; Fair Weather*
SEE ALSO: *Pussey!; My Troubles With Women*

Writer: Charles M. Schulz **Publisher:** Fantagraphics, 2004
Artist: Charles M. Schulz **ISBN:** 156097589X

THE COMPLETE PEANUTS 1950-1952

Plot: *Peanuts* is a four-panel newspaper comic strip featuring, among others, eternal loser Charlie Brown, and Snoopy, who never seemed to act like a dog should. This volume contains their first appearances, as well as those of Schroeder, Lucy van Pelt, and Linus, though not yet in their best-known form. There are also several characters who would disappear over the years, including Shermy, Patty, and Violet. Charlie Brown is there from the start, but Shermy is the more frequently used character in gags about how children play together. Of the themes that would become famous, Charlie Brown's persistence in the face of failure and his management of a losing baseball team are both here in the early strips.

Review: *Peanuts* is one of the longest-running, best-loved, and most influential comic strips in the world. Schulz did everything himself, from the script to the finished art and lettering, providing a consistency that few other strips have matched. His artwork was always devoid of ornament, with few backgrounds, as he concentrated on expression and simple movement. Many of these strips have never been reprinted, but despite their lack of polish it's fascinating to watch the strip's development from such simple beginnings to a more sophisticated world-view, as Schultz establishes his characters as exemplars of human rather than just childish behavior.

FURTHER READING: *The Complete Peanuts 1953-1954, 1955-1956, 1957-1958, 1959-1960, 1961-1962, 1963-1964, and 1965-1966*
SEE ALSO: *Calvin and Hobbes; Liberty Meadows*

★
★
★
★

Writer: Walt Kelly
Artist: Walt Kelly

Publisher: Fantagraphics, 2008
ISBN: 1560978694

POGO: THE COMPLETE DAILY & SUNDAY COMIC STRIPS VOLUME 1: INTO THE WILD BLUE WONDER

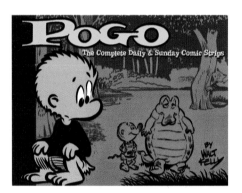

Plot: This first volume of *Pogo*, from the 1940s, introduces a cast of animals living in Okefenokee Swamp, including Pogo; Albert Alligator; the ill-informed know-all Dr Howland Owl; and his love interest, Miss Mam'selle Hepzibah. Also featured is the strip's first politically driven story, where Howland takes an interest in atomic energy.

Review: *Pogo's* elements of political parody may escape younger readers, but the animal versions of US presidents are hilarious. The early strips feature highly polished art and rely a great deal on slapstick humor.

FURTHER READING: *Pogo Revisited; Doonesbury*
SEE ALSO: *The Complete Peanuts 1950-1952*

★
★
★
★
★

Writer: E.C. Segar
Artist: E.C. Segar

Publisher: Fantagraphics, 2006
ISBN: 1560977795

A # POPEYE VOLUME 1: I YAM WHAT I YAM!

Plot: For ten years *Thimble Theatre* had been a popular gag strip with a regular cast of characters before Popeye the Sailor Man was introduced and became a love interest for Olive Oyl. This new reprint publishes all the *Popeye* strips which revolve around Popeye's relationship with Olive, their adopted baby Sweetpea, and saving the day when threatened by crooks and ghosts—not to mention the Sea Hag and her henchthing, Alice the Goon.

Review: An absolute masterpiece. E.C. Segar was always a great craftsman, but the introduction of Popeye to the strip somehow put his comedy skills into overdrive. *Popeye* may take a little getting used to, with its cast of odd but kind bumblers, and perennially thwarted villains, but you'll be hooked soon enough.

FURTHER READING: *Popeye: The 60th Anniversary Collection*
SEE ALSO: *Complete Peanuts; Groo; Krazy & Ignatz*

Writer: Tony Millionaire
Artist: Tony Millionaire

Publisher: Fantagraphics Books, 2006
ISBN: 1560977787

PREMILLENNIAL MAAKIES: THE FIRST FIVE YEARS

Plot: On the high seas, in a ship that changes its appearance from one strip to the next, Uncle Gabby is an Irish monkey prone to drunkenness, and Drinky is a crow. Their employer, the ship's captain, Maak, may have something to do with the title of this comic strip, but then again he might not. Their misadventures are usually concerned with their propensity for drink, violence, and death, but there's no continuity between strips, so death's not as serious as it may seem.

Review: Millionaire's artwork is meticulously detailed, though gloriously at odds with the coarse and irreverent events that he depicts. Very clever, very funny.

FURTHER READING: *When We Were Very Maakies;*
Der Struwwelmaakies;
SEE ALSO: *Tony Millionaire's Sock Monkey*

Writer: Rumiko Takahashi
Artist: Rumiko Takahashi

Publisher: Viz Media, 2003
ISBN: 1569319626

Ⓐ
RANMA ½

Plot: Ranma Saotome has got problems. Not only has his father arranged his marriage, but they have both just suffered unfortunate magical accidents. Ranma knocked his dad into a magic spring and he now takes on the shape of a giant panda whenever he comes into contact with cold water. Even worse, Ranma fell in after him and changed into a girl. Ranma struggles to keep his secret from everyone around him, particularly those at his school.

Review: A charming comedy drama revolving around high-school hijinx, bizarre romantic rivalries, and martial arts battles, *Ranma ½* was one of the earliest and most popular manga series to be translated into English. Takahashi's open and not too stylized art proved a hit with Western audiences, as did her slapstick humor and sensitive portrayal of adolescent concerns.

FURTHER READING: *Ranma ½ Volumes 2–38;*
One Pound Gospel; Mermaid Saga
SEE ALSO: *Inu Yasha; Maison Ikkoku*

★
★ **Writer:** Dan Clowes **Publisher:** Fantagraphics, 2006
★ **Artist:** Dan Clowes **ISBN:** 1560971835
★
★

15+ # PUSSEY!

Plot: Collecting all the exploits of Dan Pussey, Clowes' ultimate comic nerd, *Pussey!* is a bilious but hilarious attack on the fan's vision of how great it would be to be a comic-book creator. Various legends get it in the neck, particularly Stan Lee, as Clowes has his cartoonist protagonist graduate from wannabe to established artist to fan favorite as the creator of the ludicrous superhero Nauseator, all the while obsessed with getting into a woman's underwear. Clowes is not above biting the hand that feeds, either, delivering corruscating comments on his own publishers.

Review: Readers who think Comic Book Guy from *The Simpsons* is funny will certainly get this parade of losers, but to really appreciate *Pussey!* you need to have grown up reading comic books. If you've also retained a sense of humor, it will probably be among the funniest things you'll ever read, with a tiny bit of affection mixed into the bile.

FURTHER READING: *David Boring; Ed the Happy Clown*
SEE ALSO: *Ice Haven; Ghost World*

Writer: Steve Purcell
Artist: Steve Purcell
Publisher: Tell Tale Games, 2008
ISBN: 1569248141

THE COLLECTED SAM & MAX: SURFIN' THE HIGHWAY

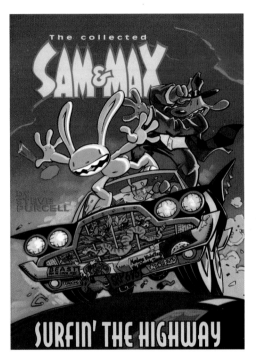

Plot: It's Sam and Max's 20th anniversary this year, and to celebrate, the long out-of-print collection Surfin' The Highway is to be reprinted with a load of new material. Sam and Max are Freelance Police, irreverent and slightly insane, toting guns and determined to bring outrageous ultraviolence and fluffy kittens to the world. They also happen to be a dog and rabbit, respectively. In this collection they deal with terrifying volcano gods, terrorists, baby commandos, alien carnivals, a Spanish galleon pulled by a legion of rats (and the world's largest prairie dog), and demons. They also take a trip to the moon where they meet moonrats and giant cockroaches. All in a day's work for the Freelance Police! Also included are a bunch of full-color two-page strips, and loads more psychotic fun.

Review: One of America's funniest creations; if there was any justice in the world, Sam and Max would be as big as The Simpsons. Far more imaginative and downright smart than America's favorite family, Steve Purcell brings a hefty dose of ultraviolence and strangeness to the proceedings, but still manages to make it incredibly cute, by virtue of his fine artwork and brilliantly surreal dialogue. There's some unbelievably disturbing stuff here on the face of it, but it all works beautifully in context, and is unlike anything else. This first collection remains an essential read for those who like the absurd.

FURTHER READING: *Grickle; Deep Fried*
SEE ALSO: *Gregory Treasury Volume 1; Liberty Meadows Volume 1; Sugar Buzz: Your Ticket To Happiness*

★
★
★
★
★

Writer: Bryan Lee O'Malley
Artist: Scott Pilgrim

Publisher: Oni Press, 2004
ISBN: 1932664084

18+

SCOTT PILGRIM'S PRECIOUS LITTLE LIFE: VOLUME 1

Plot: This is a comic about a guy who's in his early 20s, he's in a band, and they don't suck. He lives with his gay friend in a tiny flat that doesn't have enough furniture. He's dating a high-schooler, even though he's in his 20s, and his friends tease him about it. Basically, he needs to get his life together. Then, he meets the girl of his dreams. Too bad he has to fight her seven or so evil ex-boyfriends to keep on dating her. Oh yeah, he should probably dump his girlfriend too...

Review: *Scott Pilgrim* features highly stylized art that has a strong manga flavour, but it is one that is blended expertly with a simplicity and sense of detail that is rooted to the creator's native Canada. Set self-consciously in his native Toronto, O'Malley captures the city's locations and vibe,

bringing them vividly to life, from the exactness of the libraries to the style of the pizza franchises. But while the flowing art draws us in, it's O'Malley's compelling storytelling that keeps us there, mixing videogame motifs, witty, naturalistic bickering, music, and the odd nod to self-aware post-modernism. It all comes together into a package that is pure joy to read.

FURTHER READING: *Scott Pilgrim Volumes 2-4*
SEE ALSO: *Blue Monday: The Kids Are Alright; Life's A Bitch; Clumsy*

Writer: Ian Carney
Artist: Woodrow Phoenix

Publisher: SLG, 2005
ISBN: 159362008X

SUGAR BUZZ:
YOUR TICKET TO HAPPINESS

Plot: This book collects three issues of *Sugar Buzz*, the best Saturday morning kids' shows that never were. It includes tales of Precious and Percival, two kids on a tropical island with a magical octopus for company; sneaky squirrels the Tattletails; The Lovely Land of Love, where everything is fluffy and sweet; pop stars Bachelor Speedbump, who come to bring the power of rock to town, and to stick it to the Man; and the *Sugar Buzz* favorite, *Where's It At, Sugar Kat?*, starring Sugar Kat, the most popular girl in the world, and her sister Rebecca, who's not even the most popular person in her own pants.

Review: A brilliant homage to the hyperkinetic style of 1980s children's TV, Carney and Phoenix distill the spirit of fun and add their own distinctive twist to proceedings. The humorists of the 1950s are a big influence on Phoenix, and his angular art fits the stories beautifully. Carney is a very witty writer, and you'll find yourself giggling throughout the book, as strangely disturbing things happen to cute and cuddly characters. There's also a thick skin of innuendo, just blatant enough to be slightly icky. If there's any criticism that could be leveled here, it's that the silly occasionally overwhelms the funny, but overall it's comedy gold.

FURTHER READING: *Sugar Buzz: Live at the Budokan; Where's It At, Sugar Kat?*
SEE ALSO: *Fred The Clown; Magic Whistle; Sam & Max: Surfin' The Highway*

★
★ **Writer:** Antonio Prohias   **Publisher:** Watson-Guptill, 2001
★ **Artist:** Antonio Prohias   **ISBN:** 0823050211
★
★

A SPY VS. SPY: THE COMPLETE CASE BOOK

Plot: Two homicidal but inept secret agents, one dressed totally in black, the other in white, go to extreme lengths to liquidate each other in a series of increasingly desperate and inventive murderous ploys.

Review: Originally published in *MAD* magazine between 1960 and 1987, riding on the wave of the fad for all things espionage, the exploits of the agents are light on actual spying but heavy on deadly mayhem. Its modern counterpart would be *The Simpsons* cartoon-within-a-cartoon, *The Itchy and Scratchy Show*. While Cuban-born Prohias's obvious agenda is to entertain with the constant battles of the spies, covert plans, and ill-conceived counterplans, there's plenty of mileage left in this Cold War satire that's relevant today.

FURTHER READING: *Spy Vs Spy: The Joke And Dagger Files*
SEE ALSO: *Krazy And Ignatz; Grickle*

340
500

★ **Writer:** Glenn Dakin   **Publisher:** Active Images, 2004
★ **Artist:** Glenn Dakin   **ISBN:** 0974056758
★

15+ TEMPTATION

Plot: The eternal battle of wills between a hermit and the devil that wants to buy his soul.

Review: Told in a George Herriman-inspired, no-place desert, *Temptation* is one of those deceptively simple strips that frequently deviates from its basic Faustian setup to explore everything from the great philosophical questions, to cheap gags about real-estate agents. Each page is a new story, packed full of invention, and it's brilliantly funny. Notions such as condemning Mickey Mouse to Hell by signing his name on an infernal contract make you laugh out loud, and you'll turn to the next page immediately for more of the same, repeating the process until you discover that you've read the entire book and missed your stop on the train.

FURTHER READING: *Abe: Wrong For The Right Reasons*
SEE ALSO: *How To Be An Artist*

Writer: Jules Feiffer
Artist: Jules Feiffer

Publisher: Fantagraphics, 1997
ISBN: 1560972823

TANTRUM

5+

Jules Feiffer

Plot: Leo is not happy. His life is boring, his kids are ungrateful, and he's depressed. He's sick to death of being 42 years old, and one night he throws the mother of all

tantrums and suddenly reverts to being a two-year-old baby. With a wife and kids that go into meltdown, a mother that follows suit, and siblings that have problems of their own, Leo decides to seek love elsewhere, eventually coming round to the fact he wasn't too badly off in the first place.

Review: First published almost 30 years ago, *Tantrum* is one of the earliest full-length graphic novels, but it has lost none of its bite. It's an hysterical examination of the male midlife crisis, both absurd and savagely direct in its satire of modern morals. Feiffer has a deceptively messy art style, but he captures the expressions and energy of his characters effortlessly, each full-page panel holding a wealth of information. A very funny book and well worth a read.

FURTHER READING: *Passionella; Sick, Sick, Sick*
SEE ALSO: *Why I Hate Saturn; Box Office Poison; Beg The Question*

Writer: Garth Ennis
Artist: Amanda Conner with inks by Jimmy Palmiotti

Publisher: Image Comics, 2007
ISBN: 1582408505

THE PRO

3+

Plot: The Pro is a prostitute who is given superpowers as part of a wager between The Viewer (a parody of The Watcher) and his assistant. When the League of Honor invite her to join their team, they make it worth her while, but not so much that she gives up her night job. They soon begin to regret the invitation as they become more acquainted with her abrasive manners and excessively violent fighting style.

Review: The drawings are cartoony, but stylish and attractive. The script delivers generous amounts of gratuitous sex and violence—a satirical body-blow to the entire superhero genre. Hilarious.

FURTHER READING: *Preacher; Painkiller*
SEE ALSO: *The Complete D.R. and Quinch; Flaming Carrot Volume 3; Justice League of America: A New Beginning*

★
★ **Writer:** Kaz
★ **Artist:** Kaz

Publisher: Fantagraphics, 2004
ISBN: 1560975679

18+ UNDERWORLD VOLUME 5: MY LITTLE FUNNY

Plot: A compilation of short, self-contained comic strips concerning the escapades of various twisted, lowlife cartoon characters.

Review: Kazimieras G. Prapuolenis, or Kaz, has been producing his surreal and entertainingly cynical Underworld strips since 1991. His distasteful cartoon world boasts a sizeable cast of recurring characters, including the appropriately skewed Creep Rat, his criminal associate Snuff, and drug addict Nuzzle. Each four-panel strip builds to a blackly humorous punchline, and deals with such adult themes as drug abuse, cannibalism, and bestiality. Kaz's thick-lined pen-and-ink illustration style mingles cutesy Disney design with the rough idiosyncrasies of self-produced underground comix.

FURTHER READING: *Red Meat; Three Fingers*
SEE ALSO: *Fun With Milk and Cheese; The Frank Book*

★
★ **Writer:** Shannon Wheeler
★ **Artist:** Shannon Wheeler

Publisher: Dark Horse, 1998
ISBN: 1569712832

15+ TOO MUCH COFFEE MAN: GUIDE FOR THE PERPLEXED

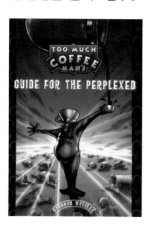

Plot: Too Much Coffee Man is the antithesis of your average superhero. He's often bemused and helpless, and his abilities spring from a combination of caffeine and nicotine rather than mutated genes. As a result he can't sleep and spends hours ruminating on the state of the world at his local coffee shop. He's secretly in love with the abrasive Mystery Woman, but the brief moments of happiness this affords are usually canceled by Too Much Coffee Man's friend, the even lonelier Too Much Espresso Guy.

Review: Begun as a superhero parody in a student paper, Wheeler's mouthpiece is a surreal, pot-bellied figure in sparkly long underwear with a head shaped like a cup of coffee. The humor is gentle and Wheeler's simple pen-and-ink style is very appealing.

FURTHER READING: *Too Much Coffee Man: Parade of Tirade*
SEE ALSO: *Doofus; Flaming Carrot: Flaming Carrot's Greatest Hits*

Writer: Steven Weissman
Artist: Steven Weissman

Publisher: Fantagraphics, 2003
ISBN: 1560975148

WHITE FLOWER DAY

Plot: Weissman's Tykes are a cross between the *Peanuts* gang and the Universal monsters, with L'il Bloody, Pullapart Boy, Kid Medusa, X-Ray Spence, and the rest of the gang causing mayhem all over their hometown. In this collection we meet Pullapart Boy's overachieving cousin, College Boy; Kid Medusa is abused by the gang, and then gets his own back; and L'il Bloody and the Cowboy Twins have bear trouble, leading to fatal results for the lovable vampire.

Review: Weissman's style is unique—a blend of cute strip cartooning and scratchy indie technique, with an imaginative use of its duotone color scheme. The stories are fun and droll, rather than slapstick-hilarious, but they are all sharply written. If you're looking for a bit more bite in your funny books, this is the one to try.

FURTHER READING: *Champs; Mean; Chocolate Cheeks*
SEE ALSO: *Amphigorey; The Greatest of Marlys; Louis: Lying to Clive*

Writer: Kyle Baker
Artist: Kyle Baker

Publisher: Vertigo, 1998
ISBN: 0930289722

WHY I HATE SATURN

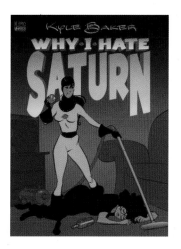

Plot: New Yorker Anne is a smart, pretty, but incredibly lazy writer for an ultra-hip and little-read magazine. She's got a book due in two weeks that she hasn't actually started, and her vegan, ultra-tidy sister Laura—who, incidentally, believes she's the Queen of the Leather Astro-girls of Saturn—has just turned up at her·door with a gunshot wound. Things can only go downhill from here...

Review: Kyle Baker is one of the funniest writers in American comics today, and the fact that he's a damn fine artist as well makes this book essential. The sheer hit-rate of the gags is phenomenal; you'll find yourself laughing out loud nonstop. Anne and her sister are brilliant creations, and we can't recommend this highly enough.

FURTHER READING: *You Are Here; I Die At Midnight; Truth: Red, White and Black*
SEE ALSO: *The Cowboy Wally Show; Plastic Man: On The Lam*

CHAPTER 8

SCIENCE FICTION

WARNINGS FROM THE FUTURE

Comic books have always been a kind of halfway house for science fiction. It's far easier to build a spaceship or blow up a planet on paper than it is on celluloid. And the control of pace, along with the opportunity to provide background information, allows extremely complex stories to be told.

One of the earliest independent comics, *A Distant Soil*, takes advantage of all that the medium has to offer to produce a story of immense scope that strives to portray the alien nature of other races and changes to humanity in the far future. Howard Chaykin's *American Flagg!* bombards the reader with information about a fast-paced, hyper-driven, near-future Earth in a story that revolves around control of information and the media. But while some creators, especially the Japanese and the French, have looked at the complexities of cyberpunk and new-wave science fiction, the visual nature of comic books has always been more appealing to creators of hard-science stories.

In the 1920s, the lurid imagery and imaginative stories of pulp magazines soon spawned newspaper strips like *Flash Gordon*, written and drawn by Alex Raymond, and *Buck Rogers*, adapted for comics by its original pulp creator Philip Francis Nowlan and drawn by Dick Calkins. These strips provided a weekly dose of intergalactic thrills to countless children. Their popularity led to a lot of copycat strips, but these were mostly just adventure strips with fantastical trappings. While literary science fiction developed into all sorts of subgenres, comics were little more than space operas, with muscular action heroes beating up grotesque aliens.

It wasn't until the early 1950s, when EC Comics debuted *Weird Science* and *Weird Fantasy*, that comics began to reflect the radical thinking of the written genre. Although the stories were designed to shock, they were well written and, in common with many EC titles, looked beyond the common Cold War prejudices of the time. But what really made people sit up and take notice was the gorgeous art. Rarely has outer space looked so good.

The other great Western science-fiction creation of the '50s was *Dan Dare*, a strong-jawed space pilot defending Earth against a series of alien menaces. Frank Hampton created the character as the spearhead strip in *The Eagle*, a thoroughly British comic for decent young men. Hampton set the strip in the 1990s, but his vision of the future certainly owed a lot to 1950. Hampton was meticulous in his research and desire for plausibility. He got Arthur C. Clarke on board as a scientific advisor, and hired a studio full of artists and models to assist him in producing two pages a week. Although the strip was still essentially space opera, the *Dan Dare* stories had long, complicated plots, often lasting over a year. This approach gave the pages a slickness that appealed to middle-class parents and children—this was no scrappy pulp nonsense, this was quality!

In the Far East, a very different future was being visualized. In 1951, Osamu Tezuka, known as the God of Manga, created *Astro Boy*, about an android "child" living in a future world where robots and men coexist. Astro Boy's adventures explore the nature of humanity, and raise many ethical issues, which Japanese creators would continue to probe in strips such as *Battle Angel Alita* and *Appleseed*, while creating stranger and more violent giant robot strips. The modern epitome of these is *Neon Genesis Evangelion*, an overblown but hugely enjoyable tale packed with robot-on-robot action. Masamune Shirow's cyberpunk manga *Ghost In The Shell*, about a cybernetically altered police squad fighting technocrime in the far future, continually explores the boundaries between man and machine. The heroine, Motoko Kusanagi, is a human brain in a robot body, deeply conflicted as to her true nature. Modern Japanese science fiction was shaped by the shadow of the atomic bomb. *Akira* contrasts the needs and desires of everyday people struggling to survive in a post-war city with characters that understand the far greater threat to humanity waiting in the wings. The movie version of *Akira* was a breakthrough hit in the West, leading to the strip on which it was based being widely translated.

Science fiction has always used tomorrow to question the morals of today. In *Judge Dredd*, the flagship strip in the British science-fiction weekly *2000 AD*, writer Pat Mills created a character that from one angle is the ultimate fascist policeman, but from another is a darkly humorous satire on British politics. *2000 AD* featured several other notable science-fiction strips, including *ABC Warriors* and *Robohunter*, but its most literate offering was *The Ballad of Halo Jones*, by the then little-known Alan Moore.

If *Judge Dredd* leaves people divided, there can be no such misunderstanding of another of Moore's early strips, *V for Vendetta*. *V* also started as part of an episodic comic, *Warrior*, and is a discursive but profoundly left-wing story of a near-future Britain run by a totalitarian government, told from the point of view of a young orphan who falls in with an unlikely but highly principled costumed freedom fighter. Moore takes great pains to flesh out the motivations of all the characters and to show how easily ordinary people can be led astray, inch by inch.

Currently, science-fiction comics are hobbled by their reliance on movie franchises for sales. Superhero titles such as *Nexus* have often borrowed the futuristic setting, but it's only really in Japan where the genre's many possibilities continue to be exploited to the full.

★
★
★
★

Writer: Katsuhiro Otomo

Artist: Katsuhiro Otomo

Publisher: Dark Horse, 2000

ISBN: 1569714983

15+ AKIRA VOLUME 1

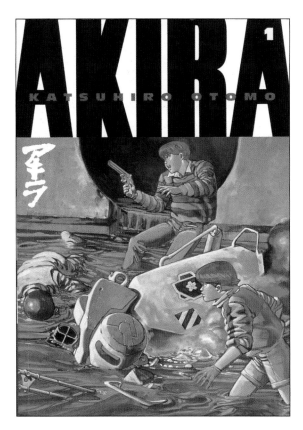

Plot: In 1992, World War III destroyed Tokyo. Thirty-eight years later, a military government is struggling for control of Neo Tokyo against an underground resistance movement. The government is determined never to allow another war that might threaten its fragile stability, and considering the state of most of the city—plagued by criminals and motorcycle gangs looking for violence—you can sympathize. Ryu is one of the underground leaders who believes there is another answer, one that doesn't involve crushing the spirit of the survivors.

The first volume is packed with car and motorcycle chases, as Kaneda, a young biker, rescues a young boy, Tetsuo, and finds himself and his friends trapped in the conflict between the two opposing sides. When Tetsuo starts to manifest strange psychic powers, government forces become desperate to get their hands on him, hoping he will have the power to control a timebomb in their midst which could be more of a threat than any war or atomic bomb. But who or what is Akira?

Review: *Akira* was a groundbreaking comic, and the first manga to be taken seriously in the West following the success of an animated movie that offered a simplified version of the story. Massive, complex, and highly stylized, *Akira* is a great science-fiction tale with spiritual overtones, told in a way that only comics can achieve. Otomo succeeded in creating a beautiful haunted city, full of terrifying grandeur,

with his detailed drawings brought to life by the superb, focused coloring. Against this epic and melancholy backdrop, the central characters are very realistically observed, full of the fire (and bad language) of youth, but often bored and directionless, even bewildered by the conflict they find themselves a part of. Otomo contrasts forces beyond our understanding with the flawed and sometimes pointless actions of his main characters, showing us a gray world in which it's not always easy to tell the good guys from the bad guys.

Toren Smith and Studio Proteus deserve a tip of the hat for their gutsy approach to translation, which allows the liveliness of the original to shine through in English. As well

as a complex plot and extensive character development, Otomo's script examines some fine philosophical points as he examines the deep-seated fear in Japanese society of youth running wild, and the ramifications of the Hiroshima and Nagasaki atom bombs.

FURTHER READING: *Domu; Legend of Mother Sarah*
SEE ALSO: *American Flagg; Ghost in the Shell; Nausicaä of the Valley of the Wind*

★
★
★
★

Writer: Paul Chadwick
Artist: Paul Chadwick

Publisher: Dark Horse, 2005
ISBN: 1593073437

12+

CONCRETE VOLUME 1: DEPTHS

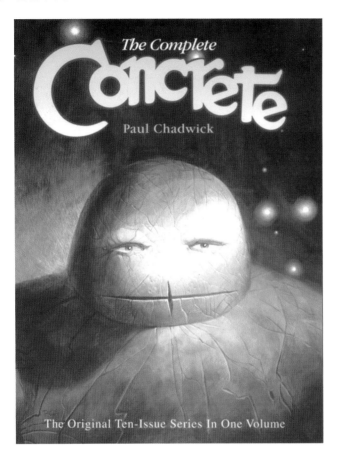

Plot: Ron Lithgow wakes up in a colossally heavy body that is virtually indestructible, not knowing how he got there. He can travel from one continent to another without diving equipment, jump out of an airplane without a parachute, and survive bomb blasts and hostile environments. The downside of these apparently liberating powers is that he can never feel the touch of a loved one's hand, or feel sand between his toes. He soon realizes he can use his powers to do good deeds—rescuing miners when a shaft caves in, for example—but also that to survive he needs to pursue a commercial course, appearing on television, building his "brand" and engaging a team of support workers who can cope with finding an armchair for a seven-ton man at short notice. The early stories mix adventure, quirky character comedy (as in the story when he becomes bodyguard to a neurotic rock star), and quiet rumination, as Concrete tests himself and tries to come to terms with the limitations and opportunities he will face in the future.

Review: Paul Chadwick made a huge splash with *Concrete* in the mid-1980s. This was the kind of independent comic that many regular comics fans could support. It took a very grown-up look at a common fantasy. Not only is Chadwick's art super-smooth and his pages well balanced, but his stories

deal with comfortably familiar superhero tropes in a fresh, exciting, and more intellectually stimulating way.

Many comics fans have asked themselves what they would do if they suddenly obtained superpowers. Chadwick offers some possible answers to that question, as his plots mix heroics with expeditions and media marathons, all the while sharing his character's inner turmoil as the ineluctability of his future dawns on him. He searches for an explanation for his transformation, but the solution he finds seems random and meaningless, a truth that doesn't transform his life at all, and certainly doesn't set him free. People expect Concrete to be as tough and emotionless as his stony exterior, and of course he isn't. There are Lee/Kirby-style romantic subplots and charming supporting characters, but most of all there is the excitement of reading a book in which character development really does come first.

FURTHER READING: *Concrete: Further Dilemma; Concrete: Killer Smile; Concrete: Fragile Creature*
SEE ALSO: *Nexus Archives; Watchmen; God-Land*

★
★   **Writer:** Masamune Shirow   **Publisher:** Dark Horse, 2004
★   **Artist:** Masamune Shirow   **ISBN:** 1593072287
★
★

15+ GHOST IN THE SHELL VOLUME 1

Plot: The Puppeteer—a master cybercriminal—has committed numerous crimes in the city by forcibly entering and controlling the minds of the populace, an act referred to as "ghost hacking." Pursued by the intelligence branch of the National Public Safety Commission, The Puppeteer is revealed to be part of a top-secret artificial intelligence project and is subsequently symbiotically fused with the part-cyborg squad leader of the intelligence branch.

Review: *Ghost in the Shell*, one of the most far-reaching ınd successful manga series, is a magnificent example of the cyberpunk genre. It explores the relationships between human and machine in a similar manner to the *Matrix* franchise. Throughout the book Masamune Shirow challenges

our perceptions of what it means to be human, and examines the difference between violation and enhancement, while wrapping everything in spectacular visuals.

In fact, the book is so beautiful to look at that it's easy to ignore its more philosophical elements. This is a mistake, however, as the driving force of all good cyberpunk literature is that it offers a critique, as well as a celebration of technology, making you question what is—and what should be—acceptable in a technologically advanced society.

As with many manga, there are some extra-narrative touches that serve to involve us more closely with the characters, period, and locations that we are introduced to.

In this case, Shirow includes some extremely detailed footnotes on the technological advances and sociopolitical environment of his story—further demonstrating that this highly talented artist and writer has not just created a graphic novel, but has painstakingly sculpted his vision of society. As a result, *Ghost in the Shell* is an extremely involved work that demands a certain level of commitment if you are to reap its full benefits.

FURTHER READING: *Ghost in the Shell Volume 2; The Sprawl trilogy; The Matrix Comics Volumes 1 & 2; Black Magic; Appleseed Volumes 2-4*
SEE ALSO: *Hard Boiled; Appleseed volume 1*

★
★
★
★

Writer: Frank Miller
Artist: Geoff Darrow

Publisher: Dark Horse, 1992
ISBN: 1878574582

15+ HARD BOILED

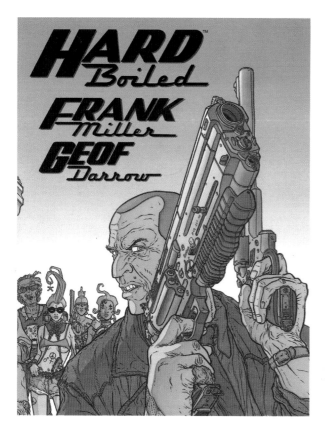

Plot: Carl Seltz thinks he's a loving husband and a devoted father to his two wonderful kids. He also thinks he's a meager insurance investigator stuck in the grind of the daily 9–5 in a futuristic city... But in his dreams, he's an ultraviolent, gun-toting, mayhem-creating tax collector called Nixon, who regularly turns the cityscape into a scene of blood-soaked, bullet-riddled, corpse-laden carnage.

But is Seltz really an insurance investigator—or is he really Nixon, who in turn is actually an android assassin called Unit Four, whose sole purpose is to wipe out the commercial competition for the all-pervasive Willeford Home Appliances Company? And if he ever acknowledges either of his true identities, will he help free all the other imprisoned androids?

Review: Originally published as a three-part miniseries by Dark Horse Comics in 1990, this collaboration between writer Frank Miller and artist Geoff Darrow owes much to the Philip K. Dick novel *Do Androids Dream Of Electrical Sheep*, which also formed the basis for the 1982 Ridley Scott movie *Blade Runner*. But even though this story inhabits similar territory— killer androids on the loose—*Hard Boiled* is scripted tongue firmly in cheek by Miller, so it's a much less somber, and highly entertaining science-fiction pastiche.

The scenes in which Unit Four fights his would-be ally, a female android, and lays waste to a large part of the city while simultaneously conducting a regular conversation, is Miller doing ultra-bleak black humor and is very funny. The

subsequent scenes, with a badly damaged Unit Four attempting to head home in rush hour with only a sarcastic robot dog for company, are also very entertaining.

This book adopts a slightly larger format than most comics, making it possible to luxuriate in the visuals. And this is a good thing; Darrow's artwork is hugely impressive, with lots of stunning and intricately drawn single- and double-page splashes. The detail in some of these is mind-boggling: they're like a *Simpsons* episode where you can go back and notice visual gags you'd previously missed. An earlier segment, where Nixon makes love to his wife while recalling scenes of utter carnage that he is responsible for, demonstrates that Darrow can do intimate as well as violent,

and this page in particular is a welcome break from the action. It's graphic, it's brutal, it's funny, and Darrow's breathtaking artwork steals the show.

FURTHER READING: *The Big Guy And Rusty The Boy Robot; The Matrix Comics Volumes 1 and 2*
SEE ALSO: *The Life And Times Of Martha Washington; Tank Girl*

★
★
★
★
★

Writer: Grant Morrison
Artists: Steve Yeowell and Jill Thompson

Publisher: Vertigo, 1996
ISBN: 1852867213

18+

THE INVISIBLES VOLUME 1: SAY YOU WANT A REVOLUTION

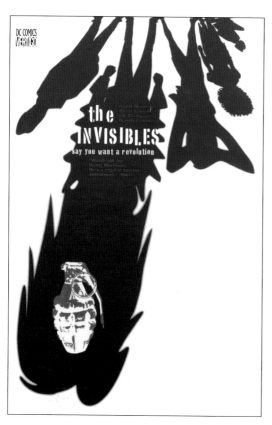

Plot: Beginning as a fin de siècle tale of terrorist heroes fighting to overcome the forces of oppression and control, this gradually evolves into a postmodern epic, encompassing teenage rebellion, time travel, religion, and psychedelia. This first volume is extremely idiosyncratic and underperformed on its initial release to such an extent that it prompted the publisher to reboot the entire series twice.

Review: Grant Morrison's first stab at his own creator-owned, extended series of graphic novels is very much of its time, or at least rooted in a world almost unimaginably different than the one we inhabit today. Somehow terrorist heroes seem a lot more difficult to identify with in these post-9/11 days. Not that Morrison necessarily intended to portray terrorists as paragons of virtue even back in the mid-1990s—or to glorify the behavior of young hooligan Dane McGowan, the book's lead character.

But *Say You Want a Revolution* feels awkward. The art style shifts abruptly halfway through the volume, from the smooth strokes of Steve Yeowell to the finer, scratchier, more complicated lines of Jill Thompson. The narrative also shifts radically, from the initiation of a new recruit into an exploration of grand ideas of liberty and sexuality. Characters

are given free rein to explore their petty passions and we are given the opportunity to watch their excesses in all their awful glory. It's strong stuff, and not entirely successful as either a standalone tale or an opening salvo in an ongoing narrative. *The Invisibles* is about time, changing expectations, and shifting perceptions; it is also a story that loops back on itself. Eventually we are invited to re-evaluate our opinions of the terrorists who are cast as the heroes (almost) unproblematically at the start of the book.

The subsequent volumes may be more compelling and easier to read, but *Say You Want a Revolution* introduces all

the themes that are revived, reviewed, and re-examined later in the series. It's a complicated, messy, slightly off-putting opening, but everything that happens here is relevant and warrants repeated readings—it just isn't the most accessible graphic novel on the shelf.

FURTHER READING: *The Invisibles: Counting to None; The Invisibles: The Invisible Kingdom*
SEE ALSO: *Doom Patrol: Crawling From The Wreckage; Animal Man Volume 1*

★
★ **Writers:** John Wagner and Various **Publisher:** Rebellion, 2005
★ **Artists:** Carlos Ezquerra and Various **ISBN:** 1904265790
★

12+

JUDGE DREDD:
THE COMPLETE CASE FILES 01

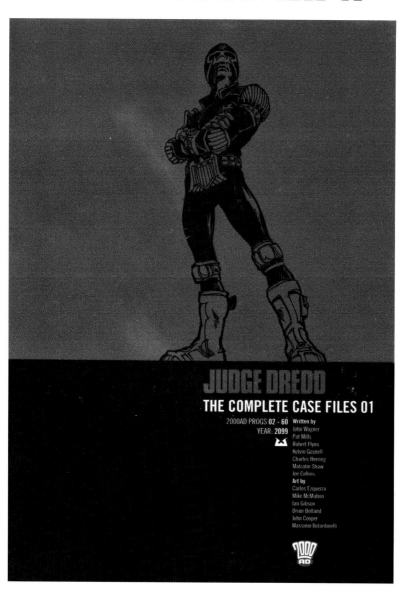

Plot: It is 2099 and 800 million people live on the east coast of North America in the massive conurbation of Mega City One. The only way to keep the massive city under control is the strict rule of law. Permanently wearing his Judge's helmet, Joseph Dredd is the faceless, emotionless, and apparently indestructible law bringer. Riding a powerful motorcycle with impossibly wide wheels, carrying a handgun loaded with a variety of increasingly deadly bullets, and with The Law on his side, he cruises the city streets handing down immediate punishments to anyone, or anything, breaking that law—from muggers to psychotic talking cars.

Review: Many *Judge Dredd* stories have been reprinted over the years, but this is the first in a series of books to start at the beginning and continue chronologically. This book covers the first 59 Dredd stories published in the weekly comic *2000 AD* between 1977 and 1978. *Judge Dredd* would evolve from these unsteady beginnings into the comic's single best-known character, spawning his own title, novels, computer games, and even a movie starring Sylvester Stallone.

Created by writer John Wagner and artist Carlos Ezquerra, a considerable number of different writers and artists were

tried on the strip over the course of that first year. While few of the writers made any lasting impact, the pairing of artists Ian Gibson and Mike McMahon, plus Brian Bolland in the later stories, did much to define the look of the strip. Indeed, for many fans Brian Bolland remains the definitive *Dredd* artist and this book includes his earliest *Dredd* artwork.

Most of the stories are standalone tales, but the book does covers the two earliest story arcs. In the first, the homicidal robot Call Me Kenneth leads almost all the robots of Mega City One in a rebellion against "the fleshy ones" which lasted for nine episodes. In the other, Dredd is made Judge-Marshal of the moon colony Luna-1, allowing the stories to escape the Mega City and explore a Wild West-style environment.

Extras include the very first Dredd story with art by Carlos Ezquerra and nine episodes of *Walter The Wobot*, the tongue-in-cheek tales of Dredd's serving droid.

FURTHER READING: *Judge Dredd: The Complete Case Files 02*
SEE ALSO: *Judge Dredd: Origins; The Complete Nemesis The Warlock; ABC Warriors: Black Hole*

★
★ **Writer:** Alan Moore **Publisher:** Wildstorm, 2002
★ **Artist:** Kevin O'Neill **ISBN:** 1563898586
★
★

15+ THE LEAGUE OF EXTRAORDINARY GENTLEMEN VOLUME 1

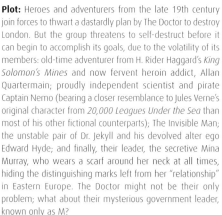

Plot: Heroes and adventurers from the late 19th century join forces to thwart a dastardly plan by The Doctor to destroy London. But the group threatens to self-destruct before it can begin to accomplish its goals, due to the volatility of its members: old-time adventurer from H. Rider Haggard's *King Solomon's Mines* and now fervent heroin addict, Allan Quartermain; proudly independent scientist and pirate Captain Nemo (bearing a closer resemblance to Jules Verne's original character from *20,000 Leagues Under the Sea* than most of his other fictional counterparts); The Invisible Man; the unstable pair of Dr. Jekyll and his devolved alter ego Edward Hyde; and finally, their leader, the secretive Mina Murray, who wears a scarf around her neck at all times, hiding the distinguishing marks left from her "relationship" in Eastern Europe. The Doctor might not be their only problem; what about their mysterious government leader, known only as M?

Review: Forget the loud, brain-dead Sean Connery movie that took this book and made a complete mockery of it—by adding Tom Sawyer, for instance, and making him a gung-ho action hero— Alan Moore's original plot is as intricate as it is engrossing, creating a world that might have been, if fiction were fact. The characters' complex, often monstrous, psychologies make their interactions at least as suspenseful as the action itself. Kevin O'Neill's scratchy pen line gives this Victorian world a rough and highly detailed texture, with images that reward close attention. And the very last page sets up an even bigger story for Volume 2. H.G. Wells would have approved.

FURTHER READING: *Marshall Law; The League of Extraordinary Gentlemen: The Black Dossier*
SEE ALSO: *Watchmen; From Hell; Planetary*

★
★
★
★
★

Writer: Tom Veitch **Publisher:** Dark Horse, 2006
Artist: Cam Kennedy **ISBN:** 0752209876

12+

STAR WARS: DARK EMPIRE I AND II

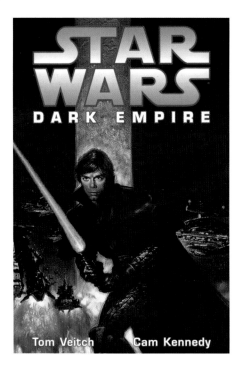

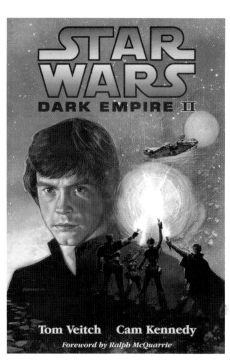

Plot: The first graphic novel is set five years after *Return of the Jedi*—the last of George Lucas's *Star Wars* films. The New Republic that has replaced the Empire is founded on the model of its predecessor, with the major drawback that there are no Jedi Knights to defend it.

Meanwhile the Empire has started to win back sectors that were previously under its control. Using the force, Luke discovers that the Emperor has returned and now poses the biggest threat the New Republic has ever faced. In order to save the Republic and revive the Jedi Knights, Luke agrees to become the Emperor's apprentice, like his father—Darth Vader—before him.

Luke's hidden agenda is to study the Dark Side so he can learn how to conquer it and sabotage the Emperor's military machine from within. Needless to say, this doesn't work out and Luke is overwhelmed by the Dark Side, falling under the Emperor's control. It is left to Leia Organa Solo, now pregnant

with her third child and a Jedi in her own right, along with her husband Han Solo, to rescue Luke from himself and set out to save the galaxy.

The second graphic novel picks up the threads from the first, with Luke discovering that some Jedi Knights survived Darth Vader's attempts to exterminate them. In the company of Kam Solusar, a Jedi who Luke rescued from the Dark Side, Luke sets off on a quest to the planet Ossus, once a center of Jedi teaching, to retrieve important artifacts that will help revive the Jedi.

The Alliance, meanwhile, is planning to undertake a daring attack on Byss, the planetary headquarters of the Imperial forces. It hopes to take advantage of new technology to strike right at the heart of the Empire and defeat it once and for all. What they don't know is that they are playing right into the hands of Emperor Palatine—who once again has managed to evade staying dead.

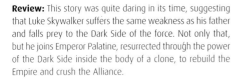

Review: This story was quite daring in its time, suggesting that Luke Skywalker suffers the same weakness as his father and falls prey to the Dark Side of the force. Not only that, but he joins Emperor Palatine, resurrected through the power of the Dark Side inside the body of a clone, to rebuild the Empire and crush the Alliance.

It's hard to imagine now, but before *The Phantom Menace* and its two sequels fed the demand for more *Star Wars* stories, *Dark Empire* was a major event for fans of the saga. Some have even claimed it revitalized the franchise. It certainly kickstarted a slew of spinoff novels and a highly successful comic series from Dark Horse.

FURTHER READING: *Mara Jade: By The Emperor's Hand; Star Wars: Crimson Empire; Heir To The Empire*
SEE ALSO: *Lone Sloane; Dan Dare; Kidnapped*

★
★
★
★
★

Writer: Warren Ellis **Publisher:** Vertigo, 1998
Artists: Darick Robertson **ISBN:** 1563894459

18+

TRANSMETROPOLITAN: BACK ON THE STREET

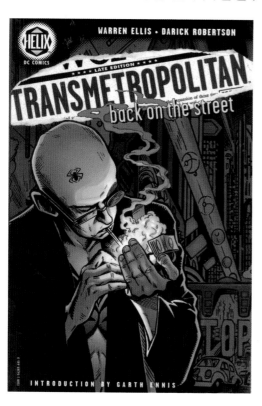

Plot: Spider Jerusalem is The City's top political columnist and gonzo journalist, a media darling and the toast of the press—and he can't stand it. Unable to get to the truth and losing the will to write, Jerusalem flees to the hills with the advance money from various unfulfilled book contracts.

Five years later, Jerusalem broods in his compound, naked, and with his advance all spent. His editor is demanding work, the food and drugs are gone, and mice are stealing his cigarettes. Jerusalem is depressed, leading him back to the one place he hates, but the only place he can write—The City. A place where a new religion is created every six hours, changing species is a fashion craze, and the highest-rating kids' show is called Sex Puppets.

Transmetropolitan is a vision of a world of warped morality, where one journalist rallies against bent cops, corrupt politicians, phony religions, technology cults, and a monster of a presidential candidate.

Review: A mixture of cyberpunk, cultural exploration, and gonzo journalism was always going to be a hard sell. But despite *Transmetropolitan's* originally low sales figures, it was the only strip in DC's Helix line to escape the axe after the imprint's closure, which speaks volumes for its scope and quality.

The lead character is a Hunter S. Thompson for the 21st century, seeking truth and honesty even if it kills him.

Jerusalem's sometimes self-righteous rants read like nothing else in American comics thanks to Warren Ellis's British sensibilities and penchant for some truly inventive swearing. Stalking the streets of The City with a manic smile, pounding a truly heroic amount of stimulants and additives into his system, and looking like a skinhead in 3D glasses, Jerusalem shoots, beats, or bowel-disrupts anyone who gets in his way of the facts.

The comic narrative is unique in breaking from regular panel-by-panel sequences, moving straight into transcripts of Jerusalem's articles with art representing his research photography. This adds to the sense of world-building, with the art bringing all aspects of The City to life.

Darrick Robertson's portrayal of The City is staggering, and never shies away from the high-tech concepts and strange social cults that the scripts portray. The art never feels static and there isn't a single panel that seems rushed or haphazard. Gloriously disgusting, honest, and great.

FURTHER READING: *Transmetropolitan 2–10;*
Lazarus Churchyard; Hellblazer: Setting Sun
SEE ALSO: *Planetary: All Over The World*
And Other Stories; Global Frequency

★
★
★
★
★

Writer: Alan Moore
Artist: David Lloyd

Publisher: Vertigo, 2005
ISBN: 1401207928

15+ # V FOR VENDETTA

Plot: *V for Vendetta* is a complex, densely plotted work concerning the attempts of a mysterious, anarchic figure to wage war against a totalitarian government. Events take place in a post-apocalyptic Britain, which, though emerging physically unscathed from the conflict, has succumbed to a fascist leadership.

V, a masked figure in a Guy Fawkes outfit, attacks the existing regime, destroying symbolic London landmarks, killing high-profile figures associated with the ruling party, and using state television to relay his own messages to the people. His actions prompt the launch of a police investigation into the "terrorist," headed by Eric Finch who endeavors to uncover V's motives and identity. The subplots deal with various characters connected to the government. Later, when cracks start to appear, we see the internal divisions and power struggles within the regime. Evey Hammond, the principal female protagonist, is rescued by V early in the story. Through her that we learn more about V, and come to understand, and question, his motives.

Review: *V for Vendetta* was one of several early works by writer Alan Moore that took an unconventional approach to the costumed superhero comic—something he would later explore in more detail in the groundbreaking *Watchmen*. While retaining some of the conventions of the genre, Moore was keen to introduce adult themes, explore the logistics of

the superhero, and examine the motives of a vigilante. In *V for Vendetta*, Moore and artist David Lloyd reject the traditional comic-book simplicity of "heroes versus villains" in favor of a morally ambiguous storyline that pits an anarchist against a fascist state. Even the act of dressing the hero in costume, a rather archaic device to some, has validity here. Aside from protecting his anonymity, V's flamboyant appearance elicits shock and fear from the people of a country devoid of theatrics.

Stylistically, David Lloyd's shadowy black-and-white imagery is a radical departure from the comic-book artwork of the time and gives the book a more naturalistic feel. When first serialized in *Warrior* magazine, the artwork was printed in black and white, but color was added to the strip when DC Comics opted to republish the series in 1988. The muted color palette added a new depth to the artwork while sympathetically retaining the gloomy atmosphere of David Lloyd's original imagery.

While many regard *Watchmen* as the superior work, *V for Vendetta* remains a powerful piece of storytelling and an essential piece of comic-book fiction.

FURTHER READING: *Miracleman; Brought to Light*
SEE ALSO: *Watchmen; League of Extraordinary Gentlemen; A Small Killing*

★ **Writer:** Jamie Delano
★ **Artists:** Frank Quitely, Warren Pleece,
★ James Romberger, and Steve Pugh
★

Publisher: Speakeasy Comics, 2005
ISBN: 0973703997

15+ # 2020 VISIONS

Plot: Four separate dystopian visions of a fractured America in the year 2020, linked by the blood relationships between the main characters. In *Lust For Life*, a plague is sweeping through New York that triggers uncontrollable sexual urges before killing the host. In *La Tormenta*, a female-to-male cross-dressing detective investigates the case of a missing girl in Miami, that leads her into a seedy world of surgical S&M practices. In *Renegade*, Montana is the setting for a neo-western tale of penal servitude and warring cattle barons. The final story, *Repro-Man*, is a punk road-movie romance that offers closure to this sprawling anthology.

Review: Delano foresees a broken down and morally bankrupt America, where national unity and social brotherhood is low on the agenda. As dystopian visions go, his stories show considerable flair and imagination in what is a heavily mined genre. The practice of rotating artists between each story arc to match their art styles with the subject matter works very well, and the thematic links between characters are obvious enough without being labored. Each story arc explores a different genre of writing (horror, crime, western, and romance), giving the impression of a very broad canvas. Despite the pessimism inherent in the setting, the stories invariably offer some hope for redemption in an otherwise bleak and unforgiving world.

FURTHER READING: *The Territory; Global Frequency*
SEE ALSO: *Transmetropolitan; Outlaw Nation*

Writer: Pat Mills
Artist: Simon Bisley and S.M.S.

Publisher: Rebellion, 2005
ISBN: 1401205860

A.B.C. WARRIORS: THE BLACK HOLE

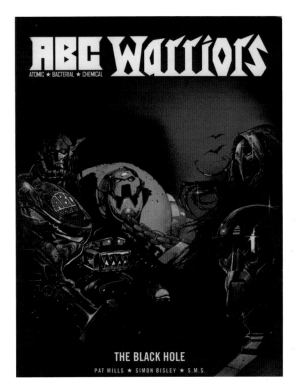

Plot: Dispatched by Nemesis the Warlock into the time wastes of the evil Termight Empire, the A.B.C. Warriors must shut down a black hole created by the Termights' time-travel experiments. Unfortunately the Warriors' arrival is expected by their adversaries. Will the Warriors' own personalities, hidden agendas, and mutual distrust tear the group apart before they complete their mission?

Review: This much-anticipated sequel appeared a full eight years after the Warriors' debut. Disappointed by the use of multiple artists in *The Mek-Nificent Seven* (even though they comprised the cream of British artistic talent), writer and cocreator Pat Mills refused to write any further *A.B.C. Warriors* tales despite their enormous popularity. He was eventually moved to reintroduce the characters in the pages of *Nemesis The Warlock*, and *The Black Hole* finally saw the Warriors back in their own adventures.

Making his debut alongside Mills is comics legend Simon Bisley, his artwork already so distinctive and refined that it came as no surprise when he was given *Sláine* to paint on the strength of his work here. Ably assisted by the mysterious S.M.S., *The Black Hole* has a more artistically coherent feel than the earlier strips of the Warriors, and Mills is on fine form. At its heart, *The Black Hole* is a robot shoot-em-up that reveals a more serious examination of warfare when you delve a little deeper. The distinct personalities of the robot warriors make certain that the warfare doesn't just take place in the Termight wastelands, but also within the robots' own ranks.

FURTHER READING: *A.B.C. Warriors: The Mek-Nificent Seven; A.B.C. Warriors: Khronicles of Khaos*
SEE ALSO: *The Complete Nemesis The Warlock*

★
★ **Writer:** Rick Veitch   **Publisher:** King Hell Press, 2006
★ **Artist:** Rick Veitch   **ISBN:** 0962486485

15+ # ABRAXAS AND THE EARTHMAN

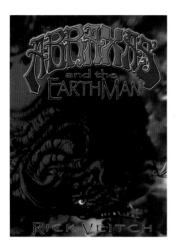

Plot: The mad, bad, and dangerous to know space-whaling alien, Captain Rotwang, kidnaps two humans from a naval research mission. Stripped of their skin and surgically mutated by intelligent alien insects to survive the pressures of space, the humans find themselves trapped on Rotwang's ship as slave labor as the Captain sails through the void, *Moby Dick* style, hunting Abraxas—a red leviathan whale.

Review: A thoughtful, psychedelic, space-faring fantasy that mixes Carlos Castaneda-style spiritualism with ecological messages, visceral horror, and trippy weirdness. Originally serialized in the pages of Marvel's *Epic* magazine, it's a powerful story that at times resembles the closing sequence of *2001* with the addition of LSD. Colors explode and soak through the page, adding to the lysergic acid atmosphere.

FURTHER READING: *Heartburst*
SEE ALSO: *Can't Get No; Bratpack*

★
★ **Writer:** Lewis Trondheim   **Publisher:** First Second, 2006
★ **Artist:** Lewis Trondheim   **ISBN:** 1596430958
★

12+ # A.L.I.E.E.E.N.: ARCHIVES OF LOST ISSUES AND EARTHLY EDITIONS OF EXTRATERRESTRIAL NOVELTIES

Plot: Very cute aliens suffer various horrors while frolicking through bizarre landscapes. In the first story, one alien loses its eyes, so its friend takes it to an eye doctor. The doctor has an assistant clean the wounds with its tongue and then climbs inside the patient to complete its examination.

Review: Trondheim claims to have found the comic while on vacation, its "alien" dialog being a clue to its extraterrestrial origins. In keeping with this concept, the volume is cleverly designed to give it an aged appearance. With great attention to detail, especially in the creatures' expressions, it's always clear what is happening. A fun, enjoyable, read.

FURTHER READING: *Astronauts of the Future*
SEE ALSO: *The Frank Book; Harum Scarum; Dungeon; Li'l Santa*

Writer: Mark Verheiden
Artist: Mark Nelson, Dennis Beauvais, and Sam Keith

Publisher: Dark Horse, 2007
ISBN: 1593077270

5+

ALIENS OMNIBUS VOLUME 1

Plot: Originally released in 1990, the *Aliens* comics continued the stories of space marine Hicks and colony survivor Newt, who made it to the end of the *Aliens* movie. Both characters were later killed off in *Alien³*, so here they become Wilks and Billie, two other survivors of a mission gone wrong.

In the first part, *Outbreak*, Wilks and Billie—back on Earth but still haunted by the memories and friends that they left behind on the doomed colony—are sucked into a mission to visit the Aliens' home world as the Company tries to find even more powerful creatures than the Aliens. Meanwhile, on Earth, a Queen has been hatched by the Company, and is somehow communicating with a cult that believes the Aliens are gods.

In the second, *Nightmare Asylum*, an insane military commander attempts to train an army of Aliens; and in the third, *Female War*, Wilks and Billie are joined by an old friend as they try to capture another Alien Queen, part of a plot to rid Earth of the Alien infestation.

Review: Artistically, these comics are a triumph, with Beauvais's gorgeous painted artwork in the middle a particular standout. They're well written, but changing the characters' names affects things enormously and everything becomes very confusing, particularly when they seemingly screw up and use the original names in a few places. Fun, but only if you've seen the films.

FURTHER READING: *Alien vs. Predator Omnibus Volume 1; Aliens Omnibus Volume 2*
SEE ALSO: *Scarlet Traces; Astronauts In Trouble*

★
★ **Writer:** Howard Chaykin
★ **Artist:** Howard Chaykin
★

Publisher: Titan Books, 2008
ISBN: 1845760778

15+ AMERICAN FLAGG

Plot: The year is 2031. America is run by a corporate government that has decamped to Mars, and Africa and South America are the new superpowers. Former TV star Reuben Flagg is drafted into the Plexus Rangers as a morale-boosting exercise. The disgruntled Flagg is dispatched to Chicago, where he discovers widespread corruption and subliminal messages in the Plex-controlled TV shows, which are causing outbreaks of gang violence. He and his partner, Krieger, interrupt the broadcasts, causing the Plex to send in secret agents in an attempt to neutralize the situation. But the death of his partner only increases Flagg's determination to reveal the truth that is being hidden from the populace.

Review: Very much ahead of its time, Howard Chaykin creates a frenetic visual world full of signs and slogans into which his typically hard-bitten characters are dropped. Reminiscent of Philip K. Dick's paranoid visions, Chaykin's future America is by turns wry, ironic, and vicious, drawn in a crowded style full of sound and lettering effects. Throughout the series Chaykin experiments with page structure and storytelling, leaving the reader to extrapolate the narrative from the many hints provided, and his dense, rough inking style makes everything look worn and tawdry. Flagg is a deliberately flawed hero who is forced to decide between the bad and the very bad. The plot moves quickly, frequently picks up on trends and parodies popular culture, and features lots of Chaykin's trademark hard-boiled dialog (and hard-boiled sex).

FURTHER READING: *Black Kiss; Empire: A Visual Novel; Cody Starbuck*
SEE ALSO: *Sanctuary; Sin City*

Writer: Masamune Shirow
Artist: Masamune Shirow

Publisher: Dark Horse, 1995
ISBN: 1593076916

APPLESEED BOOK 1: THE PROMETHEAN CHALLENGE

Plot: The adventures of a female soldier, Duenan Knute, and her cyborg partner, Briareos, trying to survive in a post-World War III landscape of abandoned cities and military wasteland known as the Badside. Taken to the apparently perfect city of Olympus, one of the last strongholds of civilization, they join the local police force, and quickly discover that things are not as ideal as they seem.

Review: Masamune contrasts the human/machine bond between Duenan and Briareos with the threat to humanity's continued existence in the form of the cyborgs that threaten Olympus. He creates a fantastically detailed future world full of amazing robots, but behind all these science fiction trappings are fundamental questions about what it means to be human.

FURTHER READING: *Appleseed Book 2: Promethean Unbound*
SEE ALSO: *Ghost in the Shell; Neon Genesis Evangelion; Battle Angel Alita*

Writer: Osamu Tezuka
Artist: Osamu Tezuka

Publisher: Dark Horse Comics, 2002
ISBN: 1569716765

ASTRO BOY VOLUME 1

Plot: Astro Boy is a robot created by Doctor Tenma to replace his dead son. Disappointed that Astro Boy isn't really his son, however, Tenma rejects him and Astro Boy finds himself working at a circus. While he's there, he's seen by a colleague of Tenma's, who, believing that Astro Boy has the ability to experience human emotions, becomes his guardian. Astro Boy then becomes a crimefighter, battling against robot-hating humans, robots gone berserk, and alien invaders. This volume contains the stories *The Birth of Astro Boy, The Hot Dog Corps,* and *Plant People.*

Review: These volumes reorganize the original manga episodes (the first-ever manga to be adapted for animation) to present the episodes chronologically. Tezuka uses the characters to explore issues such as personal responsibility and prejudice while wrapping them in an apparently juvenile action-adventure series format. It's all hugely enjoyable.

FURTHER READING: *Astro Boy Volumes 2–23*
SEE ALSO: *Phoenix, Appleseed*

★
★
★
★

Writer: Larry Young
Artists: Matt Smith and Charlie Adlard

Publisher: AIT/planetLar, 1999
ISBN: 0967684714

12+

ASTRONAUTS IN TROUBLE: LIVE FROM THE MOON

Plot: When billionaire industrialist Ishmael Hayes invites the Channel Seven news crew to accompany him on a flight to the moon to establish a permanent outpost, it's news, for sure. It's also the first step on a journey in which anything that can go wrong probably will. Lost rocket? Check. Dropped communications? Check. Rogue nuclear missile, fired at the moon by the mob? Check. Safe return to Earth? Stand by...

Review: While some of the science here might be a little suspect, the suspense is genuine. Apart from typical spaceflight hazards, Young ups the ante with corporate malfeasance, political intrigue, and organized crime. The reporters, who learn too much, naturally get caught in the middle. It's a packed plot executed with finesse, aided by the chiaroscuro suggestiveness of artists Smith and, later, Adlard, who make offices of power look as forbidding as the surface of the moon—and vice versa.

FURTHER READING: *Planet of the Capes; Proof of Concept; Astronauts in Trouble: One Shot, One Beer*
SEE ALSO: *The Walking Dead*

Writer: Alan Moore
Artist: Ian Gibson

Publisher: Titan Books, 2004
ISBN: 1905437188

COMPLETE BALLAD OF HALO JONES

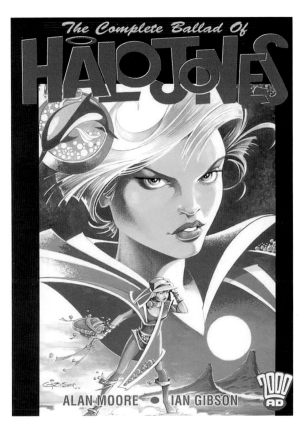

Plot: The three main *Halo Jones* story arcs started life in *2000 AD*. Halo Jones begins as an ordinary young woman on a future Earth, living in a floating housing complex called The Hoop, where society has broken down to such an extent that when she and her friends go shopping, they need a grenade launcher just to reach the mall. They all hope for a better future, and to escape the boredom of their world.

The second story focuses on individual tales set on the space cruiser where Halo has taken a job as a stewardess. In the third story arc, Halo has been forced to join the army, fighting an inexplicable war. When her service is over she hopes to rendezvous with her old friends, but eventually realizes they never set foot out of the Hoop.

Review: *Halo Jones* provides a tantalizing taster of Alan Moore's power as a storyteller. It begins as quirky science fiction, but soon develops into a coming-of-age tale. Ian Gibson's open, dynamic linework and heavy inking ably match Moore's scripts. The art is deliberately inelegant, because it deals with Halo's disturbing, ugly reality as an uneducated worker and army grunt.

FURTHER READING: *Brought To Light*
SEE ALSO: *Martha Washington; V For Vendetta; Skizz*

★
★
★
★

Writer: Yukito Kishiro
Artist: Yukito Kishiro

Publisher: VIZ Media LLC, 2003
ISBN: 1569319456

12+ BATTLE ANGEL ALITA VOLUME 1

Plot: Alita is a cyborg suffering from memory loss. All she remembers is the Panzer Kunst, a very powerful fighting technique. Condemned to the Scrapyard, Alita is found and rebuilt by the scientist, Ido. To uncover the secrets of her past, Alita must find a way to survive fights against other cyborgs in the Motorball arena, until she can reach the floating city of Tiphares, which is forbidden and fiercely protected.

Review: The sharp artwork grabs your attention and the storytelling grows in depth in later volumes, as the underlying theme of what it is to be human comes to the fore.

FURTHER READING: *Battle Angel Alita Volumes 2–9;*
Battle Angel Alita: Last Orders
SEE ALSO: *Ghost in the Shell; Appleseed*

★
★
★

Writer: Koushun Takami
Artist: Masayuki Taguchi

Publisher: VIZ Media LLC, 2003
ISBN: 1591829461

18+ BATTLE ROYALE

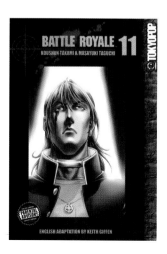

Plot: In the near future, a class of 42 ninth graders from Shiro Iwa Junior High School has been kidnapped, marooned on an island, and forced to compete in an extremely popular reality TV show called *The Program*. If no one dies within 24 hours, the collars around their necks will be detonated. The only way to survive, is to be the last one alive.

Review: *Battle Royale* has gained quite a reputation. You may be familiar with the two movies based on the manga series, or at least heard rumors about its violent content. While there may be some justification for this moral outrage, the violence is appropriate to the narrative and is juxtaposed with the psychological trauma of being thrust into such an extreme situation. The book portrays characters that strive to find alternatives to violence, as well as those who want to actively compete in the sick game.

FURTHER READING: *Old Boy; Death Note*
SEE ALSO: *Ghost in the Shell*

Writer: Sarah Byam
Artist: Tim Sale

Publisher: Dark Horse, 2002
ISBN: 1569718199

BILLI 99

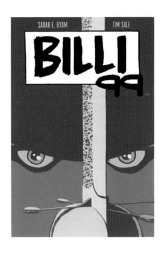

Plot: In a not too distant future, the gulf between the rich and poor has never been wider, but the poor are protected by the Toreador, a shadowy cross between Batman and Robin Hood. But when the man behind the mask is murdered, and the blame is placed squarely on his adopted daughter, Billi, she's forced to vanish into the ghettos, taking on the Toreador role herself and trying to find out who murdered her father.

Review: This is a cracking, politically conscious adventure that pulls you in with an appealing blend of characters and situations, and keeps you guessing until the end. Tim Sale, chief artist on the hit TV show *Heroes*, provides the moody black-and-white artwork, but it's a shame that writer Byam never did much else after this.

FURTHER READING: *Batman: The Long Halloween; Daredevil: Yellow; Superman For All Seasons*
SEE ALSO: *Batman: Year One; DMZ: On The Ground*

Writer: Gil Kane
Artist: Gil Kane

Publisher: Fantagraphics, 2002
ISBN: 1560974567

BLACKMARK

Plot: Centuries after a nuclear holocaust has thrown Earth back into a pre-technological Dark Age populated by mutated monsters and the remnants of mankind, Blackmark is born with the collected knowledge of Earth's ancient science implanted inside his head, so he can preserve it for future generations. But when his parents are murdered, the child Blackmark falls into the hands of slavers and grows up as a gladiator in the arena.

Review: Notable as one of the very first graphic novels, *Blackmark* was an ambitious project for its time, but stalled due to poor distribution. Gil Kane is obviously influenced by the popular Barbarian genre of the late 1960s and early 1970s, but mixes this with the post-holocaust idea of technology as witchcraft. This volume also includes the previously unpublished sequel.

FURTHER READING: *Green Lantern Archives: Vol 1*
SEE ALSO: *Chronicles of Conan Vol 1; Fafhrd and Gray Mouser*

★
★   **Writer:** Colleen Doran   **Publisher:** Image Comics, 2001
★   **Artist:** Colleen Doran   **ISBN:** 1887279512

15+ A DISTANT SOIL VOLUME 1

Plot: A brother and sister, unaware of their psychic powers, grow up in a mental institution, but are separated during an escape attempt. They find themselves caught up in two different and possibly conflicting alien resistance armies in a complex universe where mythological figures are real. The armies are fighting against a race of alien near-immortals who kill any of their own kind that are found to have psychic abilities, and who have enslaved The Avatar, a godlike being who is continually reborn.

Review: No brief plot summary can capture the complexity of this science-fiction epic. *A Distant Soil* was one of the earliest independent comics published in the 1970s. This version is a reworking of the original, which includes extra information on some areas of the plot (child molestation was hinted at back then, but is covered in quite graphic detail now). The original took advantage of its independent status and included graphic sexual scenes, particularly homoerotic ones, but this has been toned down.

The earlier episodes are not perfect by any means, mainly because there's so much plot that the narrative sometimes suffers. Doran lacks the skills to interweave the huge cast of characters and often jumps from one scene to another in a style that's closer to Japanese romantic and science-fiction comics than most Western examples.

FURTHER READING: *Girl to Grrrl Manga: How to Draw The Hottest Shoujo Manga; Dead In The West*
SEE ALSO: *Akira; Heart Of Empire*

Writer: Frank Hampson
Artist: Frank Hampson

Publisher: Titan Books, 2004
ISBN: 1840236442

Ⓐ CLASSIC DAN DARE: VOYAGE TO VENUS PART 1

Plot: By 1996 the Earth's food shortage has hit crisis point. The Interplanet Space Fleet launches a mission to Venus to find out whether the planet could be used for food production, but contact is lost with the ships. Colonel Dan Dare leads a rescue team to discover what has happened to the initial expedition and to save the Earth from starvation.

Review: Dan Dare, one of the most iconic British comic characters, was created by artist Frank Hampson for the *Eagle* comic in 1950, a time when Britain was still under rationing and other comics were mainly in black-and-white. Dare's colorful battles against the evil Venusian, Mekon, proved an instant hit and almost 60 years later the detailed art remains an inspiration to comics professionals and readers alike.

FURTHER READING: *Classic Dan Dare: Voyage To Venus Part 2*
SEE ALSO: *Ministry Of Space*

Writer: Pat Mills, John Wagner, Steve Moore
Artist: Dave Gibbons

Publisher: Panini, 2004
ISBN: 1904159370

Ⓐ DOCTOR WHO: THE IRON LEGION

Plot: The peace of a contemporary English village is shattered by a force of Roman Empire robots fighting a war through an interdimensional portal. The Doctor uses the Tardis to pass through the portal before being captured by Roman soldiers and thrown into the arena at the mercy of the Ectoslime.

Review: Based on the BBC television series and originally published in the first 38 issues of Marvel UK's *Doctor Who* Weekly between 1979 and 1980, all five stories reprinted here feature the Tom Baker incarnation of the timeless Timelord, with his robotic canine companion K-9 appearing in the latter three. *2000 AD* regulars Pat Mills, John Wagner, and Steve Moore take the opportunity to pit the Doctor against aliens that would be impossible on a television budget and are ably assisted by Dave Gibbons's clear artwork.

FURTHER READING: *Doctor Who: Dragon's Claw*
SEE ALSO: *Judge Dredd: The Complete Case Files 01*

★
★ **Writer:** Paulo Eleuteri Serpieri   **Publisher:** Heavy Metal Magazine, 1997
Artist: Paulo Eleuteri Serpieri   **ISBN:** 0878162224

 18+ # MORBUS GRAVIS I: DRUUNA

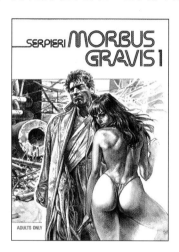

Plot: Most of the population have been turned into zombies by a mysterious plague, and those who remain must take a special serum to survive. Druuna's boyfriend has half mutated, and she will do pretty much anything to obtain the extra serum needed to stop him from turning into a flesh-crazed creature. But when she receives a mysterious telepathic message, she sets off on a quest to save the city from destruction by an unknown force.

Review: Serpieri is a superb draughtsman; only Georges Pichard has a better eye for Rubenesque anatomy. His rosy-cheeked, rotund-buttocked heroine inhabits a world where every background is filled in as lovingly as the swell of Druuna's breasts. As the series progresses, the stories become more sadistic, and in later volumes several sequences have been removed, making them read unevenly.

FURTHER READING: *Survivor*
SEE ALSO: *Click; Lone Sloane; Marie-Gabrielle*

★
★
★
★
★ **Writer:** Howard Chaykin   **Publisher:** Dark Horse, 2007
Artist: Mike Mignola and Al Williamson   **ISBN:** 1593077130

12+ # FAFHRD AND GRAY MOUSER

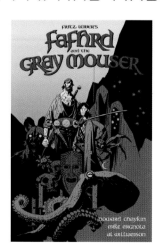

Plot: Former ship's boy to a pirate, Fafhrd, and former wizard's apprentice, Gray Mouser, are reunited in the city of Lankhmar. Reluctantly agreeing to honor a promise Fafhrd made to his true love, Vlana, and enact revenge on her former torturers, the Thieves Guild, the two friends infiltrate their home, initiating a tragic series of events.

Review: Chaykin does an impressive job adapting seven of Fritz Leiber's original tales. A contemporary of H.P. Lovecraft, Lieber's work has influenced writers such as Terry Pratchett and Michael Moorcock. Regarded by Mignola himself as his best pre-*Hellboy* work, his art shows more detail than the style he now employs—but it is still recognizable as his, making this an essential read for Mignola fans.

FURTHER READING: *Rocket Raccoon; Hellboy: Strange Places*
SEE ALSO: *The Chronicles of Conan Volume 1; Hellboy Volume 3*

Writer: Darren Aronofsky
Artist: Kent Williams

Publisher: Vertigo, 2006
ISBN: 1401200583

THE FOUNTAIN

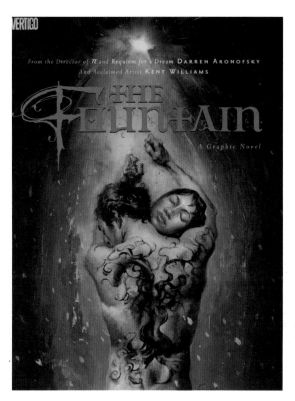

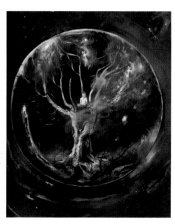

Plot: In South America, in the year 1535, a conquistador embarks on a dangerous journey to a Mayan temple to steal a mythical tree that grants eternal life to those who drink its sap—but the Mayans will not surrender it without a fight. The narrative jumps forward to the year 2463; a space traveler journeys toward a collapsing star once worshipped by the Mayans, hoping that the power it unleashes will breathe life into the dying tree that has granted him eternal life, allowing him to continue his attempts to resurrect his dead lover. The story then jumps to the present day; a research scientist struggles to find a cure for a brain tumor that threatens the life of the woman he loves. An ancient Mayan tree may hold the answer he seeks.

Review: Film director Aronofsky's tale of obsessive love spanning a thousand years is remarkably moving and never resorts to obvious sentimentality. The conquistador, the scientist, and the traveler are all remarkably human and the love that drives them is a believable and almost tangible force. The sparse script allows the artwork to tell the story, and Williams's paintings are incredibly atmospheric, from the blood-red, Francis Bacon-like sections based in the 16th century, to the more sterile world of the research doctor, to the mystical, fantastic world of the star traveler. A film version starring Hugh Jackman and Rachel Weisz was released in 2006.

FURTHER READING: *Havok And Wolverine: Meltdown*
SEE ALSO: *Blood: A Tale; Ronin; Sandman Volume 3: Dream Country*

★
★
★

Writer: Hiromu Arakawa
Artist: Hiromu Arakawa

Publisher: VIZ Media LLC, 2005
ISBN: 1591169208

15+ # FULL METAL ALCHEMIST

Plot: Hugely popular manga about Amestris, a country where machines are steam powered and alchemy works. Edward and Alphonse are brothers who work for the government as alchemists, though not entirely voluntarily. Due to an accident when they tried to revive their dead mother, Edward now has two cybernetic limbs and his brother's spirit is trapped inside a metal body. Together they use their mix of science, magic, and brainpower to thwart a series of bad guys, from corrupt priests to hijackers, but there are hints that much darker forces are gathering as the story progresses.

Review: While its constituent parts may not be wholly original, Arakawa's mix of intriguing situations for the brothers to work out and the unusual setting sets her work apart.

FURTHER READING: *Jushin Enbu; Stray Dog*
SEE ALSO: *Ghost in the Shell*

★
★
★

Writer: Phil and Kaja Foglio
Artist: Phil and Kaja Foglio

Publisher: Studio Foglio, 2002
ISBN: 1890856193

A # GIRL GENIUS VOLUME 1:
AGATHA HETERODYNE
AND THE BEETLEBURG CLANK

Plot: Set in a fantasy world where steam is still a major source of power, Agatha Clay is an assistant at the Transylvania Polygnostic University. Unknown to her she is a "spark"—someone with exceptional scientific skills, and therefore an enemy of the ruthless Baron von Wulfenbach, who knew her biological parents. He has suppressed the "sparks," who he considers a threat to his rule, and now sets his sights on Agatha.

Review: Described as "a gas lamp fantasy with adventure, romance, and mad science," this is an engrossing, humorous tale, and it's well worth seeking out the further volumes.

FURTHER READING: *Girl Genius Volumes 2–6*
SEE ALSO: *Steampunk; The Witching Hour; Full Metal Alchemist*

Writer: Nicolas De Crécy
Artist: Nicolas De Crécy

Publisher: ComicsLit, 2007
ISBN: 1561634832

GLACIAL PERIOD

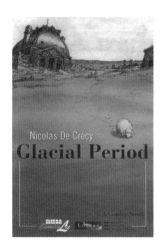

Plot: Thousands of years in the future, the planet is covered in a thick layer of ice. A group of explorers, accompanied by their genetically engineered dogs, uncover the long forgotten Louvre museum, and without any knowledge of the history that the art depicts, come to some appallingly daft conclusions about their ancestors. Meanwhile, a dog separated from the party discovers that the art itself, now rediscovered, is determined not to be lost again.

Review: This is an absurd, but enjoyable tale, and the first of a series of four beautifully executed books about—and produced in collaboration with—the famous Paris museum. De Crécy's delicate watercolor art is lovely, and he captures the myriad works that the museum contains extremely well, expertly blending reproductions of the originals into his work.

FURTHER READING: *Léon La Came; Salvatore*
SEE ALSO: *Streak Of Chalk; Dead Memory; Robot Dreams*

Writer: Warren Ellis
Artist: Various

Publisher: Wildstorm, 2004
ISBN: 1401202748

GLOBAL FREQUENCY: PLANET ABLAZE

Plot: What do you do when terrorists threaten to release the Ebola virus in central London, or a religious cult are about to blow the top off a building, or the world's first bionic man turns out to be psychotic? You call the Global Frequency, 1001 people around the world with extremely specialized skills, deployed by the mysterious Miranda Zero. This volume contains all of the above, plus alien viruses, Russian telekinetics, and more.

Review: A Warren Ellis script guarantees three things: good ideas, a ton of extreme violence, and a wicked sense of humor. Here, each story is illustrated by a different artist, including Steve Dillon and Glenn Fabry, and are of a universally high standard. Enormously good fun.

FURTHER READING: *Red; Strange Killings; Orbiter*
SEE ALSO: *Transmetropolitan; The Authority*

★
★   **Writer:** James Robinson   **Publisher:** Dark Horse, 2003
★   **Artist:** Phil Elliott   **ISBN:** 0878162976

15+ ILLEGAL ALIEN

Plot: Set in 1963, *Illegal Alien* is the story of a gaseous extra-terrestrial being who is forced to take over the body of murdered mobster Guido Palmano to escape the American military after a UFO crash. The alien goes to live with Guido's cousin and his family in London, and while he is pursued by mobsters and secret-service agents from both Britain and America, he slowly transforms the lives of every family member in a tale that encompasses everything from Beatlemania to clashes between Mods and Rockers.

Review: This is the second of artist Phil Elliott's collaborations with comics and screenplay writer James Robinson, the first being the arguably superior *Bluebeard* for Slave Labor Graphics. While Robinson went on to enjoy mainstream success, Elliott, with his simple yet expressive style, remains one of Britain's unsung national treasures.

FURTHER READING: *Bluebeard; Contraband*
SEE ALSO: *Starman: Sins of the Father; London's Dark*

★
★   **ISBN:** 1905437234   **Artist:** Carlos Ezquerra
★   **Writer:** John Wagner   **Publisher:** Rebellion, 2007

12+ JUDGE DREDD: ORIGINS

Plot: Dredd creators John Wagner and Carlos Ezquerra finally reveal the origins of Mega City One and the Judges, when Dredd discovers that Judge Fargo, the legendary Judge from whom he was cloned, might still be alive. He and a cadre of Judges travel across the radioactive Cursed Earth to discover the truth, with Dredd relating the events that led up to the great war, and making a few unexpected discoveries himself.

Review: *Judge Dredd* has a fine tradition of epic storylines. *The Cursed Earth* first appeared some 30 years ago, and this is a good addition to that saga. Wagner tells a cracking adventure story, and Carlos Ezquerra's dramatic art is spot-on as ever. It's not exactly groundbreaking, but if you're a Dredd fan, you'll love it.

FURTHER READING: *Judge Dredd: The Complete America; Chopper: Song Of The Surfer*
SEE ALSO: *Adventures In The Rifle Brigade; A History of Violence; Judge Dredd: The Complete Case Files 01*

Writer: Jack Kirby
Artist: Jack Kirby

Publisher: DC, 2005
ISBN: 1401204147

Ⓐ KAMANDI ARCHIVES

Plot: On a Planet of the Apes-style future Earth—after the "great disaster"—some animals have become sentient, others have mutated into monsters, and man has devolved to an ape-like state. One boy alone carries the torch of humanity. Brought up in a bunker (Command-D), Kamandi sets off to explore the world with the help of Ben Boxer and a doggie scientist called Dr. Canus, encountering bizarre dangers at every turn.

Review: At DC Comics in the 1970s, Jack Kirby was allowed to let his imagination run riot. *Kamandi* is one of four interconnecting series he created for them, and despite its simple structure, it proved to be the most popular title thanks to Kirby's clean artwork, fertile imagination, and ability to give a sense of pathos to Kamandi's quest for the remnants of humanity.

FURTHER READING: *The Eternals; Mister Miracle; Devil Dinosaur*
SEE ALSO: *Nexus Archives; Jack Kirby's New Gods; Essential Fantastic Four Volume 3*

Writer: Philippe Druillet
Artist: Philippe Druillet

Publisher: Heavy Metal Magazine, 2001
ISBN: 1882931653

8+ CHAOS: LONE SLOANE

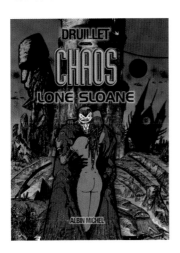

Plot: In the far future, Philippe Druillet's psychedelic antihero returns after apparently dying and being entombed in a golden casket for ten years among the stars. Revived by a mysterious woman, à la *Sleeping Beauty*, he avenges himself, causing chaos wherever he goes.

Review: After a 25-year hiatus Druillet returns with another installment of his interdimensional freebooter's adventures. One doesn't read Druillet for his bombastic and hard-to-follow far-future plots, but for his distinctive, baroque artwork with its ornately framed panels and unusual layouts. Although not quite as detailed as his original *Lone Sloane* stories, Chaos's artwork still retains an architectural majesty and atmosphere of depraved beauty.

FURTHER READING: *Six Voyages de Lone Sloane; Delirius; Nosferatu*
SEE ALSO: *Hard Boiled; The Magic Flute; Heart of Empire*

★ **Writer:** Warren Ellis **Publisher:** Titan Books, 2005
★ **Artist:** Chris Weston **ISBN:** 1840239247
★

MINISTRY OF SPACE

Plot: In 1945, British forces capture the German V2 rocket technology in Peenemunde, which leads to Britain winning the space race. By 2001, British space stations orbit the Earth, and British astronauts have claimed the Moon and Mars for Queen and Empire. When the Americans threaten to reveal the secret of Britain's success, the architect of the British space programme, Sir John Dashwood, is called to a hearing on the Churchill space station.

Review: Originally published as a three-issue series between 2001 and 2004, this story is a modern take on the *Dan Dare* style of Royal Air Force-in-space stories. The history of the British space mission is told in flashback while the main story suggests there is a dark secret to its financing, culminating in the truth being revealed.

Weston's spaceship designs successfully echo those of the *Dan Dare* spacecraft from *Eagle* comic 50 years earlier, while Ellis weaves a plausible alternative history of the space race in the post-war decades.

In addition to reprinting the original comic covers, the book has a sketchbook section showing Weston's early design concepts, photo references, and wireframe versions of some of the CGI models used in the final artwork.

FURTHER READING: *Ocean; Orbiter; The Filth*
SEE ALSO: *Scarlet Traces; Classic Dan Dare; League of Extraordinary Gentlemen*

Writer: Dean Motter and Paul Rivoche
Artist: Various

Publisher: I Books, 2004
ISBN: 0743493346

MISTER X: THE DEFINITIVE COLLECTION VOLUMES 1 AND 2

Plot: Mister X is an enigmatic figure who has returned after suffering a nervous breakdown to haunt the city he designed. Radiant City was supposed to be built in a way that would alter its inhabitants' mental states for the better. But the developers cut corners, and the result is a nightmare landscape in which people feel dehumanized and unsettled. Now it's full of gangsters, such as Arnie Zamora and his girlfriend Patrice, while ordinary people like Mercedes, the waitress who tries to befriend Mister X, don't understand why they feel so bad. How can Mister X put things right? Is he even the man we think he is?

Review: Drawing heavily on Modernist architectural theory, and looking at the construction of 20th century cities such as Brasilia, *Mister X* is far more entertaining than it sounds.

The character himself begins as one of those empty forms into which you can project all manner of things—even when his origin is revealed, you're left thinking, "This is *an* origin, it isn't necessarily *the* origin." The plot twists and turns, and after a shock revelation you're left questioning everything you previously thought was true. Volume one is drawn in a shading-free, black-and-white style with few right angles and shadows in all the wrong places, the art by The Hernandez Brothers perfectly reflects the superficially pretty yet deeply disturbing theme of the story.

FURTHER READING: *The Sacred and The Profane; Terminal City; The Prisoner*
SEE ALSO: *Locas; Heartbreak Soup; Signal to Noise*

★
★
★
★

Writers: Mark Wheatley and Marc Hempel
Artists: Marc Hempel and Mark Wheatley

Publisher: IDW Publishing, 2005
ISBN: 1932382917

15+ # MARS

Plot: A small party of colonists—including Morgana Trace, a paraplegic who can walk in zero gravity with the help of a computer—spend 10,000 years in stasis traveling to Mars with the intention of terraforming it for human colonization. But when they awake, all contact with Earth is gone and they find not a bare landscape, but a lush and surreal environment, with strange creatures (not to mention Norman Rockwell and Gauguin) popping up all over the place.

Review: *Mars* combines the adventure and sense of wonder of early science fiction with the 1960s interest in the inner landscape and the kind of philosophical pondering found in the films of Tarkovsky. The writing is experimental, with nonlinear plots, and the art wonderfully loose-lined without losing its sense of polish.

FURTHER READING: *Tug and Buster; Breathtaker*
SEE ALSO: *Gregory; A Distant Soil*

★
★
★
★

Writer: Hayao Miyazaki
Artist: Hayao Miyazaki

Publisher: VIZ Media LLC, 2004
ISBN: 1591164087

A # NAUSICAÄ OF THE VALLEY OF THE WIND: VOLUME 1

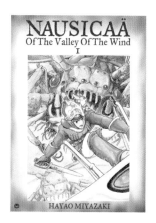

Plot: This volume introduces Nausicaä to a war between the Torumekian and Dorok empires. She meets the Torumekian Princess, Kushana, who is commanding forces that have been sent to confront the Doroks, but they are no match for the miasma that has been spreading from the forests. As Nausicaä begins to help those ruined by the warfare or the miasma, she finds herself in the role of The Blue Clad One, a predicted Messiah figure.

Review: Hayao Miyazaki is better known for his animation, but his ventures onto the printed page are just as striking. His compassionate scripting (with strong environmental and antiwar themes), deftness of characterization, and control of the emotional highs and lows are all first rate.

FURTHER READING: *Nausicaä Of The Valley Of The Wind: Volumes 2–7*
SEE ALSO: *The Legend Of Mother Sarah*

Writer: Pat Mills
Artists: Kevin O'Neill, Jesus Redondo and Bryan Talbot

Publisher: Rebellion, 2006
ISBN: 1905437110

THE COMPLETE NEMESIS THE WARLOCK VOLUME 1

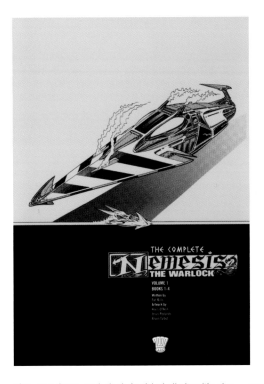

Plot: On a future earth that's fearful of all alien life, the human population lives in underground cities connected by travel tubes, while the alien rebel Nemesis and the forces of Credo wage war against the Termight Empire, led by the ghostly Torquemada. grand master of the human religious police who, although killed very early on, remains a spectral presence throughout the stories. The human Terminators led by Torquemada have taken their hatred of nonhuman life out into the galaxy in genocidal crusades, and now the aliens are fighting back.

Review: With an introduction by writer Pat Mills and an afterword by the original artist, Kevin O'Neill, this title covers the first four *Warlock* stories, originally published in *2000 AD* between 1980 and 1985.

This is a futuristic, supernatural story in which the humans are villains and the most bizarre aliens are heroes, and where even the hero's vehicle, called the Blitzspear, is a living entity. Nemesis is a cloven-hoofed, horned alien wizard, while his adversary, Thomas De Torquemada, is the

In addition to the four main "Books," this excellent compilation includes the *Comic Rock* stories that introduced the characters, two one-off stories from *Specials* and *Annuals*, fourteen *Nemesis* covers, and seven full-page pinups from the weekly.

FURTHER READING: *The Complete Nemesis The Warlock Volume 2; Robusters*
SEE ALSO: *Judge Dredd: The Complete Case Files 01*

★ **Writers:** Gainax and Hidekai Anno **Publisher:** Viz Media LLC, 2004
★ **Artist:** Yoshiyuki Sadamoto **ISBN:** 1591164001
★

NEON GENESIS EVANGELION

Plot: Shinji Ikari's father, head of N.E.R.V., an organization created by the U.N., has ignored him for years, but suddenly wants to see his bemused and angry 14-year-old son. Ikari Senior has developed E.V.A.s, semi-sentient robots that require psychic pilots, the Earth's only hope against Angels—alien robotic monsters. Within moments of their reunion, Ikari finds himself inside the brain of a robot, fighting for his life.

Review: Essentially the postmodern version of the classic Japanese "giant robot" story, Neon Genesis Evangelion moves extremely fast, reflects cultural trends, and is full of teenage angst—an emo comic before emo was invented. Yoshiyuki Sadamoto's artwork is dramatic and drags you through the story at a breathless pace.

FURTHER READING: *Sailor Moon; Der Mond: The Art of Neon Genesis Evangelion*
SEE ALSO: *Astro Boy*

Writer: Mike Baron
Artist: Steve Rude

Publisher: Dark Horse, 2005
ISBN: 1593073984

NEXUS ARCHIVES VOLUME 1

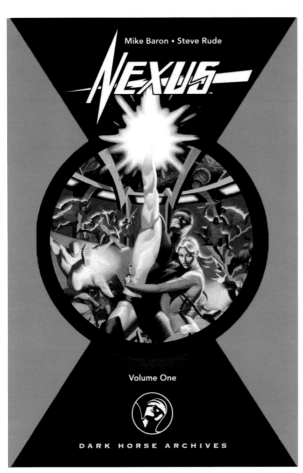

Plot: An alien called The Merk has given Horatio Hellpop almost limitless superpowers to defend his small homeworld, Ylum, but in return Horatio must police the universe as Nexus, killing mass murderers. If he refuses he's tormented by images of the suffering his target's victims have endured. Can Nexus come to terms with his role, especially when he discovers that his own father murdered millions?

Review: Mike Baron's future may have dated, but many of his ideas are still exciting. He makes Nexus a very human superhero, and surrounds him with an engaging cast of characters. Artist Steve Rude draws in a soothing, stripped-down style reflecting his interest in Alex Toth's animation designs (particularly *Space Ghost*), with bursts of Kirby-esque grandiosity to liven things up.

FURTHER READING: *Badger; The Alex Toth Reader*
SEE ALSO: *Madman: The Oddity Odyssey; Kingdom Come; Zorro*

★
★
★
★

Writer: Stan Lee, Roy Thomas, Jim Steranko
Artist: Jack Kirby, John Buscema, Jim Steranko,
Bill Everett, Joe Sinnott, Frank Giacoia

Publisher: Marvel Comics, 2000
ISBN: 0785107479

A # NICK FURY, AGENT OF S.H.I.E.L.D.

Plot: Nick Fury and S.H.I.E.L.D. fight to stop the evil Hydra organization from using the Overkill Horn to destroy the world's nuclear stockpile and take over the post-nuclear world. Fury later teams up with Captain America to fight the Yellow Claw, and a possible alien invasion.

Review: Collecting for the first time the *Nick Fury* strips from *Strange Tales* #150–168—the earliest works of Jim Steranko—this book captures not only the feel of 1960s Marvel comics, but also '60s pop culture in general. Thanks to Steranko's successful merger of Jack Kirby's layouts with his own style and influences such as Andy Warhol and Salvador Dalí, every page is unique, and stands as a genuine highlight of the Silver Age of Comics.

FURTHER READING: *Nick Fury: Who Is Scorpio?; Nick Fury and Wolverine: The Scorpio Connection; Nick Fury: Peacemaker*
SEE ALSO: *Marvel Visionaries;*

★
★
★
★
★

Writer: Robbie Morrison
Artists: Simon Fraser and Various

Publisher: Rebellion, 2004
ISBN: 1904265200

15+ # NIKOLAI DANTE:
THE ROMANOV DYNASTY

Plot: Imperial Russia, 2666, ruled by Tsar Vladimir the Conqueror. Rogue, thief, and lover, Nikolai Dante is an adventurer who robs from the rich—and gives to himself! Caught between the Tsar and the rival house of Romanov, can Dante survive as he gambles his way to prominence, or is he really "too cool to kill?"

Review: Serialized in *2000 AD* since the late 1990s, *Nikolai Dante* formed part of comics' second Golden Age. Unlike most action heroes with a soundbite and a huge gun, Dante is a charming character with a swashbuckling personality that's Han Solo by way of Errol Flynn. Cheeky, grand in scale, and highly recommended.

FURTHER READING: *Nikolai Dante Volumes 2–5*
SEE ALSO: *Lily McKenzie and the Mines Of Charybdis*

Writer: Dave Gibbons
Artist: Dave Gibbons

Publisher: Titan Books, 2006
ISBN: 1401203558

THE ORIGINALS

Plot: In an alternate postwar England, two friends, Lel and Bok, are desperate to join the sartorially elegant Originals gang and battle against the rival uncouth biker gang known as the Dirt. Acceptance takes both of them into the unknown, but yearned-for world of teenage approval.

Review: *The Originals* is reminiscent of Colin MacInnes' 1959 novel Absolute Beginners, chronicling the rise of the British teenager, and the 1979 movie *Quadrophenia*, based on *The Who's* album of the same name, and clashes between rival gangs of Mods and Rockers in 1960s Britain.

Gibbons doesn't miss a beat (pun intended), with the music, fashions, and social background of the characters. The Originals ride hover-Vespas, and are constantly in conflict with the Dirt, who are equipped with similar but more macho hover bikes. Gibbons captures the mood with his familiar street names and by crowning Lel with Roger Daltrey's 1960s hairstyle. The drugs, clubs, fashion, and evocative Mod-style posters are here, too.

As a homage it works well and Gibbons's black-and-white art suits the setting. The characters, however, can be stilted at times and the plot a little underwhelming and predictable. Gibbons's docudrama on post-pubescent angst skims over the surface of mob mentality without truly capturing the mindset of the characters and the amphetamine rush of their formative years.

FURTHER READING: *The Rann-Thanagar War; Give Me Liberty; Rogue Trooper*
SEE ALSO: *Watchmen; Dr Who*

★
★
★
★

Writer: Osamu Tezuka
Artist: Osamu Tezuka

Publisher: VIZ Media LLC, 2004
ISBN: 1591163005

12

PHOENIX VOLUME 4: KARMA

Plot: Set during the Nara period in 8th century Japan, this volume concerns the one-eyed, one-armed bandit, Gao, and the sculptor, Akanemaru. After Gao has disabled Akanemaru's arm, their paths diverge, but their fates are now inextricably linked until they face each other again as artistic rivals. Akanemaru is under orders to create a statue of Buddha, while Gao sculpts tortured faces. This is the story of how Gao and Akanemaru are driven in different ways by the Phoenix and its promise of immortality.

Review: Each volume of Tezuka's 12-part *Phoenix* saga can be read separately, and this—with the earliest setting, though actually the fifth in the chronology—is considered one of the very best, and therefore one of the best comics ever.

FURTHER READING: *Phoenix Volumes 1–3 and 5–11*
SEE ALSO: *Adolf; Ode to Kirihito; Nausicaä of the Valley of the Wind; Lost Girls*

★
★
★

Writer: Daniel Torres
Artist: Daniel Torres

Publisher: Dark Horse, 1998
ISBN: 1569712867

A

ROCCO VARGAS:
THE WHISPER MYSTERY

Plot: Rocco Vargas used to be a famous space captain, but retired to run a hotel and write science-fiction stories—until an old friend persuaded him to return to work, on Triton. In *The Whisper Mystery* he's dragged into a western-style showdown where the fate of the galaxy's illegal drug supply will be decided, and encounters his nemesis, a mysterious drug baron with a robotic arm known only as The Whisperer.

Review: Harking back to the crazy characters of classic crime comics, Spanish artist Daniel Torres populates his strips with weird-looking villains and grotesque professors. The art is highly stylized, with the panels carefully designed and full of lovely comedic detail, although it can be difficult to warm to the central characters because of the simple way they're drawn.

FURTHER READING: *Opium; Milady 3000: Magnus*
SEE ALSO: *Orient Gateway; American Flagg*

Writer: Frank Espinosa
Artist: Frank Espinosa

Publisher: Image, 2006
ISBN: 1582405859

ROCKETO: JOURNEY TO THE HIDDEN SEA VOLUME 1

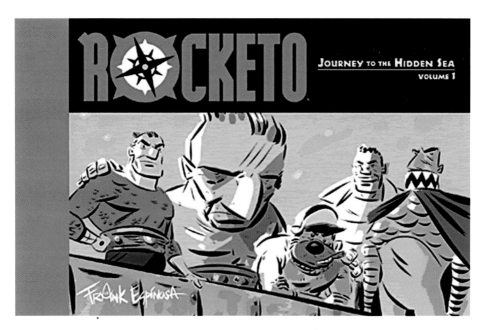

Plot: 2,000 years in the future, a mythical catastrophe has shattered the planet's magnetic field and only the genetically altered Mappers are able to navigate the ravaged terrain.

The square-jawed and well-muscled explorer Rocketo Garrison is one such individual, and accompanied by a motley crew of adventurers and warriors he sets out on a hazardous journey across uncharted territory in search of immense wealth.

Review: Frank Espinosa's futuristic action opus is set to run to four volumes, spanning two landscape-format trade paperbacks apiece. His story is set in a rich and vibrant far-future world that looks back to the two-fisted pulp science fiction of *Flash Gordon*, and features such well-worn genre clichés as flying vehicles, tentacled monsters, and giant robots. However, Espinosa puts a fresh spin on the theme with instantly appealing characters, an involving plot, and an overarching nautical theme that evokes classic maritime adventures.

Over the millennia, unfettered genetic modification has given rise a myriad established human/beast hybrid races, and this topical theme lends the story an intriguing additional facet, as well as explaining the multitude of bizarre beings that Rocketo and his comrades encounter. Espinosa's years of experience in animation show clearly in his sparse brushwork and considered design, and while the haphazard swathes of color can sometimes make an image difficult to decipher, his fluid style is genuinely unlike anything else in mainstream American comics.

FURTHER READING: *Samu; Rocketo: Journey To The Hidden Sea Volume 2*
SEE ALSO: *Kamandi Archives volume 1*

★
★
★
★

Writer: Frank Miller
Artist: Frank Miller

Publisher: DC Comics, 1987
ISBN: 0930289218

15+ RONIN

Plot: A 13th-century ronin avenges the death of his master by fighting a demon named Agat. With the aid of a mystical sword he defeats him—but not before the demon has cast a spell to imprison both their souls in the sword. Fast-forward 800 years to a dystopian New York where poverty is rife and the Aquarius corporation keeps a firm grip on power. Aquarius specializes in biotechnology, and with the aid of a telekinetic named Billy Challas, has perfected a new science which melds flesh and circuitry. When the spirits of the ronin and the demon are released from the sword, the demon spirit takes over the boss of Aquarius and the spirit of the ronin enters the body of Billy. The two slowly master their new world, building momentum toward a final battle. But the ronin must also avoid termination by Casey McKenna, the head of Aquarius Security.

Review: Originally a six-part miniseries in 1983, Frank Miller writes and draws this book, with Lyn Varley on colors. It's a bizarre manga-style tale that joins demons and feudal Japan with the 21st century world of corporate greed and out-of-control science, but it remains a compelling read. The speechless fight scenes are beautifully drawn, and Varley's color palette suggests a new Eden of biotechnology that could either flourish or rot. The McKenna character looks like an early prototype for Miller's *Martha Washington*.

FURTHER READING: *Samurai Executioner*
SEE ALSO: *Akira; Lone Wolf And Cub; Hard Boiled*

Writer: Ian Edginton
Artist: D'Israeli

Publisher: Dark Horse, 2003
ISBN: 1569719403

SCARLET TRACES

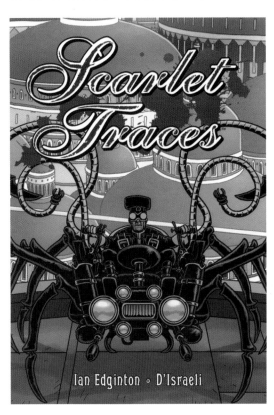

Plot: In the wake of the Martian invasion from H.G. Wells's *War Of The Worlds*, the British Empire now covers over two-thirds of the globe thanks to reverse-engineered Martian technology. It is now ten years since the invasion, and the dead bodies of young women are starting to appear, drained of blood, on the banks of the River Thames. The mystery is investigated by Captain Autumn and his manservant, former Sergeant Major Currie, when rumors begin to circulate that the deaths are being caused by a vampire. What they find is something far worse, and very real.

Review: After an extremely troubled gestation period, *Scarlet Traces* finally saw the light of day as a truly breathtaking work of fiction. Originally planned as a partially animated project for the now defunct *Cool Beans World*

website, only a handful of pages ever saw online publication. After Edginton and D'Israeli reacquired the rights to their work, *Scarlet Traces* finally saw print in *Judge Dredd Megazine* before being issued as a graphic novel by Dark Horse. From Ian Edginton's superb plotting and dialog to D'Israeli's beautifully realized steampunk rendition of Victorian Britain, *Scarlet Traces* is a real feast for the eyes and the mind. The vibrant colors, incredible design work, and obvious affection for the source material confirm this as a labor of love.

FURTHER READING: *War Of The Worlds (Dark Horse Adaptation); Scarlet Traces: The Great Game*
SEE ALSO: *The League of Extraordinary Gentlemen Volume 1; Planetary: All Over The World*

★
★
★

Writer: Alan Moore
Artist: Jim Baikie

Publisher: Titan, 2005
ISBN: 1904265308

A **SKIZZ**

Plot: Interpreter Zhcchz of the Tau-Ceti Imperium crashlands his spaceship on one of the restricted Hellworlds, where he takes refuge in an uninhabited building. On that Friday in August 1983, 15-year-old Roxy O'Rourke is in her parents' house alone when she discovers the alien in the garden shed. When the authorities finally capture "Skizz," "Rahk-See" and her friends decide to rescue him and reveal him to the world for his own safety.

Review: An early Alan Moore story from *2000 AD*, *Skizz* is a British take on *ET: The Extra-Terrestrial* set against a backdrop of unemployment in early 1980s Birmingham. While the characters and story are interesting, it has little of the depth of Moore's later work. Nevertheless, with Jim Baikie's expressive artwork, it remains an entertaining read.

FURTHER READING: *Skizz II: Alien Cultures;*
The Extraordinary Works Of Alan Moore
SEE ALSO: *The Complete D.R. And Quinch;*
The Complete Ballad of Halo Jones; A L I E E N

★
★
★
★

Writer: Teri Sue Wood
Artist: Teri Sue Wood

Publisher: Sirius Entertainment, 1998
ISBN: 1579890105

12+ **WANDERING STAR: VOLUME 1**

Plot: Casandra Andrews is the daughter of the President of Earth. She attends the Galactic Academy, where she is widely disliked simply because she is human. When the Bono Kiro attack, Casandra escapes the Academy on the spaceship, Wandering Star. Helped only by her two friends, Ellie, a Trillion, and the psychic, Madison, she must now somehow rally the Trillians to help drive back the invasion, while keeping one step ahead of her pursuers.

Review: Wood is concerned more with her characters' motivation than action— there's a lot of dialog, exposition, and discussion of feelings—but this is an appealing exploration of the lives and temperaments of the main characters and the world around them.

FURTHER READING: *Wandering Star: Volumes 2–3*
SEE ALSO: *A Distant Soil*

Writer: Andrew Stephenson
Artist: Trevor Goring

Publisher: Image Comics, 2006
ISBN: 1582406685

WATERLOO SUNSET

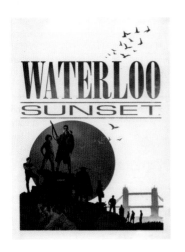

Plot: A future London, devastated by war, finds itself in the grip of a mysterious Cartel. This organization sends a woman to save London's bedraggled population from extinction—but a local alien vermin hunter is more interested in trading her to the local powers. However, both find themselves at the center of a conspiracy that requires their immediate termination. Whilst making their escape, they discover the true nature of London and its rapidly devolving society.

Review: It's easy to be confused by the language Stephenson's characters speak, a hotchpotch of Chaucer's Middle English, contemporary English idioms, and Orwell's Newspeak. Stephenson's ambition to portray the future not just visually but linguistically is a success, and Goring's black-and-white art enhances the desolation. Ultimately rewarding for those who value depth over eye candy.

FURTHER READING: *Pantera*
SEE ALSO: *Ring of Roses*

Writer: Grant Morrison
Artist: Frank Quitely

Publisher: Vertigo, 2005
ISBN: 9781401204952

WE3

Plot: *We3* is about a squad of three prototype "animal weapons" coming to terms with what they are as they flee captivity. Encased in robotic armor, they have been given the ability to speak, and although limited, this at least makes them able to communicate with each other. Hunted by the US Air Force, war breaks out between the two sides, with the three animals dispatching all soldiers sent against them with apparent ease.

Review: A heart-wrenching tale in which the three killing machines are the injured party. Frank Quitely's exquisite, almost cinematic, art brings a sheen to the violence, while the storytelling builds gradually to a climax. You'll yearn for the animals to become normal pets again, but feel strangely reassured by the fact that they could become cold-blooded killing machines at the drop of a hat.

FURTHER READING: *Animal Man Volume 2: Origin Of The Species*
SEE ALSO: *Batman: Arkham Asylum; All Star Superman; Animal Man Volume 1; The Invisibles Volume 1*

★ **Writer:** Various
★ **Artist:** Various
★

Publisher: Gemstone
ISBN: 1888472588

THE EC ARCHIVES: WEIRD SCIENCE VOLUME 1

Plot: Created during the Cold War, *Weird Science's* early stories, mostly written by Bill Gains and Al Feldstein, display a sweaty paranoia about all things foreign. Time and again the human characters turn out to be aliens or monsters in disguise, and when the humans do manage to make a useful scientific breakthrough, they either use it for petty means, are exterminated, or go mad before they can share the good news with the rest of humanity. The few stories that don't involve mad scientists usually revolve around UFOs and Roswell-style conspiracies.

Review: As science fiction, much of *Weird Science* is a nostalgia trip, very similar to the sci-fi movies of the period in tone and approach—although later issues of the comic did start to include more radical concepts. The original black-

and-white reprints had more of a period feel to them, but the computer recoloring in this volume cannot really dim the quality of the artwork from Wally Wood, a frequent flyer whose feverish attention to detail and gorgeous anatomy makes him the standout artist on the book. Harvey Kurtzman (who often wrote his own, generally more imaginative and light-hearted scripts) appears from time to time, as well as the reliable Joe Orlando and Jack Kamen, who could create a sense of creeping paranoia like no other.

FURTHER READING: *The EC Archives: Weird Science Volume 2; The Complete Weird Fantasy*
SEE ALSO: *Swamp Thing: Dark Genesis; EC Archives: Tales From The Crypt*

Writer: Brian K. Vaughan
Artist: Pia Guerra

Publisher: Vertigo, 2003
ISBN: 1840237082

Y: THE LAST MAN

Plot: Yorrick Brown was your average American literature graduate/escapologist/assistant monkey trainer, down to his last packet of Ramen noodles after buying an engagement ring for his long-distance girlfriend, when the plague struck: a plague that wiped out every single mammal on the planet in possession of a Y chromosome—except Yorrick, and his mischievous capuchin, Ampersand. The series follows Yorrick and Ampersand on their quest to solve the mystery of the plague, find a way to repopulate the planet, and perhaps try to stay alive by avoiding ninjas, amazons, and military forces if at all possible.

Review: Vaughan's characters throughout the series—including the secondary, and even tertiary players—are wonderfully well rounded. The histories, motives, and personal flaws are present and plausible, and at no point are you left feeling that a character's reaction to a situation or change in personality is unrealistic. This creates the kind of empathy that is essential for a series of this nature to endure. Pia Guerra's consistently phenomenal artwork is a genuine pleasure to behold—the attention to detail, costume design, and landscapes are all quite beautiful and there is great subtlety in the work as well as strength and drama.

FURTHER READING: *Ultimate X Men; Runaways Volume 1; Dr. Strange: The Oath*
SEE ALSO: *Ex Machina; Pride of Baghdad*

CHAPTER 9
SUPERHEROES

BIFF! BANG! POW!

Although the medium of comics is a universal one, it's fair to say that the superhero genre is predominantly American. Born in the 1930s, it achieved popularity during the war years with a roster of names that are familiar to this day. DC (then known as National) launched *Superman*, *Batman*, and *Wonder Woman*; publishing rival Timely (who would later become Marvel) came up with *Captain America*; Quality Comics added offbeat humor to the genre with the flexible *Plastic Man*; and Fawcett introduced a Superman clone called *Captain Marvel* (later to be repackaged as *Shazam* by DC to prevent infringement of Marvel's retrospective copyright on the word).

This Golden Age of superhero comics introduced many of the genre conventions that remain with us today— gaudy costumes, secret identities, larger than life villains, and impossible action scenes. By the 1950s, however, tastes had changed and readers turned instead to a glut of sensational crime and horror titles, sending the men in tights into temporary exile.

A revival of sorts began in 1956 with the introduction by DC of *The Flash* in *Showcase #4*. This was soon followed by other books, which introduced the concept of a super team—the *Justice League of America*—featuring all of DC's most popular characters. But despite DC's newfound enthusiasm for the genre, the true success story of the 1960s was to come from an unexpected quarter. Timely Comics had changed its name to Atlas and then to Marvel, but it was a second-rate company publishing monster comics and westerns. Taking a gamble, and noting the success DC were having with their costumed titles, Stan Lee and Jack Kirby decided to move Marvel back into the superhero market. The results were staggering. In just a few short years these men, with the help of a few other key talents, such as Steve Ditko, launched a new wave of comic book characters: the *Fantastic Four*, *Spider-Man*, the

Hulk, *Iron Man*, *Thor*, the *X-Men* and a revival of the *Captain America* character that had brought the company good sales during the war years.

Marvel's success may not have come overnight, but it was an unstoppable juggernaut once it got off the starting blocks. Kirby's art demonstrated a dynamic flair that was lacking in DC's more traditional titles, but it was Stan Lee's revolutionary approach of imagining the superheroes as real people with down-to-earth problems that really fired the public's imagination. These were heroes as ordinary human beings that teenagers could identify with.

While DC began to flounder (despite the success of the *Batman* TV series), Marvel stamped its mark on the 1960s, clever enough to move with the times, and responding to the hippy end of the decade with more cosmic and philosophical characters such as the Silver Surfer.

By the early 1970s, superheroes were once again a staple part of popular culture. In keeping with the progressive spirit of the first half of the decade, comics grew more serious, with deeply relevant storylines exploring subjects such as drugs, pollution, and racism. Dennis O'Neil's *Green Lantern/Green Arrow* was a brave and noteworthy attempt to inject contemporary issues into the superhero medium. In many ways the book was way ahead of its time—not until the new wave approach of the 1980s would such storytelling take center-stage again. Meanwhile, Jack Kirby defected from Marvel to DC, and set about creating the most ambitious storytelling concept of his career: the interlinked series of titles that formed his *Fourth World* concept of warring New Gods.

By the early 1980s, creativity had dipped. The major companies seemed content to coast on the successes of earlier decades. With a few notable exceptions, the writing and art had become routine, lacking the spark of ideas that had lit up the 1960s. But a new wave of writers and artists would soon change that. Key titles such as Frank Miller's *Daredevil* and *Elektra Assassin*; Alan Moore's *Watchmen*; Grant Morrison's *Doom Patrol*; and Peter Milligan's *Shade the Changing Man* redefined the concept of costumed superheroes. Characters that once inhabited a cartoon universe now seemed rooted in the real world. A darker tone took hold of the mainstream titles, rejecting the "suitable for children" traditions and the conventions of morality imposed by the Comic Code. Superheroes were no longer clean cut, incorruptible icons of goodness, but violent right-wing vigilantes, or mentally unstable individuals.

Shock and awe began to take hold of superhero titles as the '80s gave way to the '90s. Characters would die and then miraculously come back to life, or be found to have been clones, or shape-changing aliens, or related to some other character altogether. Existing continuity would be rewritten and revised on an almost monthly basis. Major story arcs, such as DC's *Crisis on Infinite Earths* or Marvel's *Civil War*, would cross over multiple titles and multiple issues in a ploy to sell as many comics as possible. Popular characters would be given additional titles and guest appearances to maximize exposure. Favorite big-name characters from earlier decades continued to dominate the stories, with few exceptions.

Famous writers from outside the medium, such as J. Michael Straczynski (creator of *Babylon 5*) and Joss Whedon (the genius behind *Buffy* and *Firefly*) would turn their hands to superhero stories, taking over runs of everything from *Spider-Man* to *X-Men*. Coinciding with the rise in popularity of superheroes in the cinema, the genre now seems to have achieved something that was denied it in previous decades: mainstream acceptance.

★
★
★
★

Writer: Alan Moore **Publisher:** DC Comics, 2006
Artist: Various **ISBN:** 1401200877

ACROSS THE UNIVERSE: THE DC UNIVERSE STORIES OF ALAN MOORE

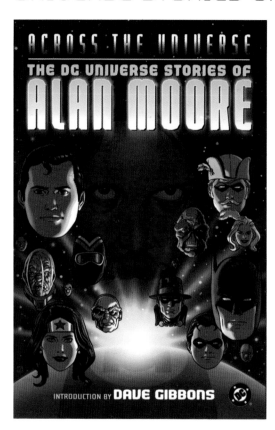

Plot: This book collects all of writer Alan Moore's superhero work for DC Comics, and while all were written in the 1980s, many continue to inform today's comics, and some have become classics. *Batman: The Killing Joke* contains perhaps the most sadistic Joker tale of them all, with the Clown Prince of Crime torturing both Commissioner Gordon and his daughter Barbara (aka Batgirl) to the brink of death, in scenes graphically rendered by the precise penmanship of artist Brian Bolland.

In the two-part Superman tale *Whatever Happened to the Man of Tomorrow*, Moore and definitive super-artist Curt

Swan bid a nostalgic farewell to the so-called "Silver-Age Superman" tales—those told from the 1950s to 1980s, just before John Byrne re-created the character from the ground up in *The Man of Steel*. The book's other Superman tale, *For the Man Who has Everything*, features birthday-boy Superman deluded into believing that he never left Krypton, an idyllic fantasy that goes horribly awry thanks to the machinations of the evil alien, Mongo. Also featuring Batman, Robin, and Wonder Woman, this psychological tale contains artwork by Dave Gibbons, who would go on to be Moore's artistic partner on the groundbreaking *Watchmen*. A dozen other comics complete this substantial collection.

Review: The three stories mentioned above, if available separately, would each rate an individual entry in this book, so important are they to the DC Comics canon. Gathered together, they represent an embarrassment of riches. While the other stories aren't quite as earth-shattering, they all showcase Moore's attention to detail in whatever genre he attempts. Some standouts from the shorter tales include the heavenly "possible origin" tale of DC's mysterious Phantom Stranger, and the surprising *Mojo Doesn't Socialize*, the tale of a Green Lantern far unlike—and more immense than—any other. Moore even gives a logical spin to the unlikely team-up between Batman and Moore's own version of Swamp Thing. Few other writers have created such a (relatively) small body of work for one company, yet made such a lasting impression upon it—making this book a must-have for any fan of DC superheroes.

FURTHER READING: *Doom Patrol:*
Crawling From The Wreckage; Watchmen
SEE ALSO: *Swamp Thing Volume 1;*
Promethea; Animal Man Volume One;

★
★
★
★
★

Writer: Frank Miller
Artists: Frank Miller, Klaus Janson, and Lynn Varley

Publisher: DC Comics, 2002
ISBN: 0930289234

12+

BATMAN: THE DARK KNIGHT RETURNS

Plot: In a possible future inspired by Reagan's America and 1980s culture, Batman reappears after 10 years of self-imposed retirement, in order to once again return law and order to the streets of Gotham City. But the villains—including the Mutants, Two-Face, and The Joker—are more dangerous than ever before, particularly as Batman's agility and endurance are hampered by his advancing years. Commissioner Gordon is just days away from retirement—and his successor, Ellen Yindel, along with most of the media, is convinced that Batman is one of the fundamental causes of the city's problems. On her promotion to commissioner she issues an immediate warrant for his arrest, putting Batman up against the law, something he's not been used to since his partnership with Gordon. Finally, Batman must face his ultimate nemesis—a government-neutered Superman, now the equivalent of a Man In Black, is sent after Bruce for a fight to the finish.

Review: Along with *Watchmen*, this reworking of the *Batman* mythos was responsible for the initial false start of graphic novels back in the late 1980s/early 1990s. Fantastically told and beautifully drawn, this was the backbone of the renaissance in re-imagining traditional superheroes in a much darker, grimmer light. This is a trend that continued for almost ten years, almost to the point of self-parody.

The pace is fast, and in between the action are the reports from various television stations, with so-called experts giving their conflicting opinions about how Batman affects society—one psychologist finds him particularly offensive, citing Batman as the reason why criminals such as Two-Face and the Joker appeared in Gotham in the first place. This is highlighted further by the Joker's catatonic condition that began when Batman retired. As soon as the reports start hitting the news of his return, the clown prince of crime is once again all smiles.

The book was originally issued as four "prestige-format" books. It was an instant hit and has remained in print ever since. Miller had cut his teeth on Marvel Comics' Daredevil, another grim, urban crime fighter, so his transfer to Batman was a logical move—and one that paid off handsomely.

FURTHER READING: *The Dark Knight Strikes Again; Batman: The Long Halloween; Batman: Dark Victory*
SEE ALSO: *Batman: Year One; Elektra: Assassin; Daredevil; Sin City*

★
★
★
★
★

Writer: Jeph Loeb
Artists: Jim Lee and Scott Williams
Publisher: DC Comics, 2003

ISBN (Volume One): 1401200605
ISBN (Volume Two): 1401200923

BATMAN: HUSH VOLUMES 1 AND 2

Plot: Someone is out to get Batman. Not just to kill him, but to destroy his life on every possible level. In a tale that twists and turns across every page, Bruce Wayne's alter ego is forced to call on all his skills as a detective in this tightly scripted whodunit thriller featuring a veritable who's who of the DC world. Joined by Robin, Nightwing, Huntress, Superman, and even Catwoman, the Caped Crusader faces an equally impressive roll call of villains that includes The Joker, The Riddler, The Scarecrow, Poison Ivy, and Ra's al Ghul, to name but a few. But this isn't a clichéd story of good against evil. Friends become foes and enemies become allies, leaving the hero unsure who to trust—even after the explosive climax.

Review: Collecting *Batman* comics #608–619, 2003's two-part *Hush* gained immediate notoriety as it marked Jim Lee's much-anticipated return to the drawing board. A key

artist in the mid-1990s (and considered the face of the X-Men for a time), Lee's days on the printed page appeared to be over when he swapped his pencils for publishing and became Editorial Director at Image Comics. However, in 1998 Lee left Image Comics, sold his Wildstorm imprint to DC Comics, and returned to his first love: drawing. The result was *Hush*.

Teaming up with writer Jeph Loeb, and with Scott Williams inking, Lee's return helps shape a sensual masterpiece that looks both forward and back into what—and more importantly, who—Batman really is, and what he could become. From the death of his parents, to his manipulation at the hands of an unseen foe, *Hush* presents the reader with the physical and psychological destruction of a tortured, heroic soul as he is forced to assess every relationship in his life—including those at the very heart of his existence.

At times brutal in its depiction of bloody violence, Alex Sinclair, who is arguably the unsung hero of the work, beautifully colors Lee's pencils and Williams's inks. His deliberate color palette changes to reflect the tone of the story, and drives the reader through the pages every bit as effectively as the images themselves and Loeb's well-paced script. The result is a truly collaborative page-turner that simply cannot be put down—from the first brooding page of Volume 1 to the final bittersweet frame of Volume 2.

FURTHER READING: *Batman: The Long Halloween;*
Batman: Dark Victory
SEE ALSO: *Batman: The Dark Knight Returns;*
Batman: Year One; Across The Universe

★
★
★
★
★

Writer: Stan Lee
Artist: Jack Kirby

Publisher: Marvel, 2007
ISBN: 0785126252

(A)

ESSENTIAL FANTASTIC FOUR VOLUME 3

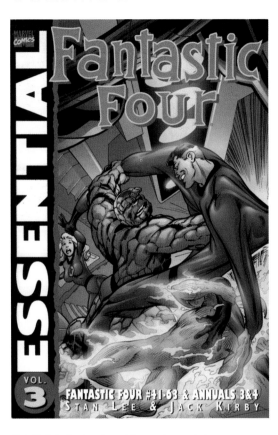

Plot: Their bodies transformed by cosmic rays during an ill-fated spaceflight, Reed Richards (Mr. Fantastic), Susan Storm (The Invisible Girl), Ben Grimm (The Thing), and young Johnny Storm (The Human Torch) vow to use their powers for the good of humanity as the Fantastic Four. This volume showcases two years of stories, including tales that established and defined the title, as well as the whole Marvel Comics mythos, for decades to come.

Without question, the three-issue *Galactus Trilogy* has become a superhero milestone. It introduces the threat of an amoral intergalactic being, Galactus, who ingests the energy of planets to survive, as well as his herald, the Silver Surfer, whose dedication to his master wanes as he learns about humanity. The tale's climactic battle between master and herald finds our four heroes mostly relegated to the sidelines, an almost unthinkable—yet dramatically appropriate—end to a superhero yarn.

Further adventures with new creations like the Inhumans and The Black Panther (comic-books' first mainstream black superhero), as well as the landmark battle between the Surfer and the dreaded Doctor Doom, mean the action never stops—not even at Reed and Sue's wedding!

Review: Stan Lee and Jack Kirby set the standard for superheroes with this period of the *Fantastic Four*. One of the most prolific and important cartoonists since the 1940s, Kirby reaches a new high with these tales, his artwork growing ever bolder, and his character and plot ideas exploding off the page, with Lee's stories and dialog perfectly complementing the artwork. Among the grand battles, however, we find *This Man, This Monster*, the most contemplative superhero story ever published at that time, a morality tale that's sometimes described as the title's single best issue. Indeed these are some of the finest superhero comics ever created, bar none. The foursome have

of course been translated to the big screen in several animated series (including one that replaced The Human Torch with a robot), the low-budget Roger Corman venture (so bad it's worth seeing once), and most recently the *Fantastic Four* and *Rise of the Silver Surfer* movies.

FURTHER READING: *Essential Fantastic Four Volumes 1, 2, 4-6*
SEE ALSO: *Essential Spider-Man Volume 2; Marvels*

★
★
★
★
★

Writer: Kurt Busiek
Artist: Alex Ross

Publisher: Marvel Comics, 2003
ISBN: 0785100490

12+

MARVELS

Plot: An innovative retelling of four key moments in the history of Marvel Comics, all seen through the lens of newspaper photographer Phil Sheldon. First, the Human Torch battles the Sub-Mariner during World War II. Then, as the Fantastic Four's Mr. Fantastic and the Invisible Girl prepare for their wedding, Sheldon finds himself drawn into the shadowy, tension-filled world of the emerging mutant population, in the form of a young, frightened girl. Next is the coming of Galactus, the world-devourer, after which the world seems to fear the heroes more and more. Finally, Sheldon finds himself caught up in the world of Gwen Stacy, Peter (Spider-Man) Parker's girlfriend, herself doomed to die at the hands of the Green Goblin.

Review: Busiek and Ross's nostalgic paean to Marvel's glory days was just what readers wanted in 1993. With its everyman protagonist, the book presented an innovative "you are there" approach; readers could imagine themselves as part of these classic tales, marveling at the wonders all around them. However, the book's main draw was the photorealistic painted artwork of Alex Ross, which managed to present the mundane alongside the magnificent. Ross has gone on to illustrate and create several other popular works, and his painterly style has influenced countless lesser-known works. But the unique impact of Marvels—its story and its storytelling—can't be denied. It was the deserving recipient of three Eisner awards.

FURTHER READING: *Earth X; Universe X; Justice; The Kingdom; Uncle Sam; Astro City: The Homecoming*
SEE ALSO: *Kingdom Come; Identity Crisis; Astro City: Life In The Big City;*

★
★
★
★
★

Writer: Warren Ellis
Artist: John Cassaday

Publisher: Wildstorm, 1999
ISBN: 1563896486

PLANETARY VOLUME 1: ALL OVER THE WORLD AND OTHER STORIES

THIS IS HOLY.

Plot: Meet the "archaeologists of the impossible," who explore Earth's secret history: Jakita Wagner, super-strong and super-intense; The Drummer, who talks to machines via vibration; and Elija Snow, master of cold, and over a century old. As Planetary, they uncover the sites of past events that seem suspiciously familiar, like a Japanese island filled with the skeletons of atomically mutated monsters, or a group of four astronauts who return to Earth with fantastic powers and a knack for technological innovation. The group's investigations are meant to benefit mankind, making genuine discoveries from the hidden or deliberately buried. However, certain factions oppose their efforts, and of course there's Planetary's own mysterious history to consider—and what of their insidious leader, the Fourth Man?

Review: *Planetary* delights in telling its stories, twisting genres to its own ends in a highly entertaining way. Each chapter loosely, and cleverly, explores a different science-fiction or fantasy convention—1950s horror movies, *Doc Savage*-type pulp novels, hard-edged science fiction, Hong Kong cop epics, and more. Cassaday's crisp, expressive images capture these styles perfectly, especially in the iconic and ever-malleable cover designs. Readers who prefer a bit of pulp with their fiction will lap this stuff up.

FURTHER READING: *X-Files; The Authority: Relentless*
SEE ALSO: *The League of Extraordinary Gentlemen;
Transmetropolitan*

★ **Writer:** Todd McFarlane   **Publisher:** Todd McFarlane Productions 2007
★ **Artist:** Todd McFarlane   **ISBN:** 1582405638
★
★

12+

SPAWN: COLLECTED EDITION VOLUME 1

Plot: Al Simmons is a highly decorated soldier recruited to a covert operations and assassination unit run by the US government. But when he starts questioning the true nature of his work, he is murdered by his own colleagues. Sent to Hell, Simmons is recruited by the devil Malebolgia to lead the Armies of Evil in the final battle against the Armies of Good—but Simmons only agrees to do this if he can be resurrected and returned to Earth to see his wife Wanda Blake again...

Simmons is tricked and returns to Earth as the superpowered and horrendously scarred warrior Spawn, instead of the man he once was. He also returns five years later, with amnesia, and his wife has since remarried. Dejected and alone, Spawn slowly pieces together the truth about who he is and how

he was betrayed, all the while defending the dispossessed of the downtown alley he chooses to call home. Also introduced are chalk-and-cheese detective duo Sam Burke and Twitch Williams; cyborg hitman Overtkill; the clown-like Violator; and Jason Wynn, the malevolent head of the US Security Group.

Review: This book collects issues 1–8 and 11–12 of *Spawn*, which sold a staggering 1.7 million comics when it debuted in 1992 via McFarlane's own studio. Since then, McFarlane has successfully expanded his creation into toys, a feature film, and a cartoon, as well as several spinoff books. With his current reputation as a savvy multimedia businessman, it is easy to forget that McFarlane is the same artist who

ESSENTIAL
GRAPHIC NOVELS

500

427

SUPERHEROES
Top 10 superhero graphic novels

made his name in the late 1980s on *Amazing Spider-Man* and as writer and artist on *Spider-Man* in 1990.

The art in *Spawn* possesses a real vibrancy and seamlessly switches between stunning battle sequences, semi-caricature in the scenes with Sam and Twitch, hallucinogenic fantasy sequences where Spawn returns to Hell, and urban squalor with the scenes in the alley. The coloring by Steve Oliff and Reuben Rude is excellent, too.

The moral universe of *Spawn* is based on Christian orthodoxy, but McFarlane's writing takes what it needs from this source material, creates a world of devils and angels, and pretty much ignores the rest.

Overall, McFarlane's writing is pretty slick and the banter between Sam and Twitch and the sarcastic ramblings of the Violator are very funny. It's a good read, and even if it does play the sentimentality card a little too often with Spawn lamenting his lost love and life, it is gothic fantasy meets adult vaudeville and a strong start to a fine series.

FURTHER READING: *Spawn: Collected Edition Volume 2; Spawn: Collected Edition Volume 3; Spider-Man: Birth of Venom; Spider-Man: Torment*
SEE ALSO: *Preacher Volume 1: Gone To Texas; Sandman Volume 1: Preludes And Nocturnes; Lucifer: Devil In The Gateway*

★
★
★
★
★

Writer: Stan Lee
Artists: Steve Ditko and John Romita

Publisher: Marvel Comics, 2005
ISBN: 0785118632

A # ESSENTIAL SPIDER-MAN, VOLUME 2

Plot: In this second 500 page volume of the *Essential Spider-Man* series, we see our hero meet his arch foe, the Green Goblin. After a number of confrontations he finally makes the startling discovery of the Goblin's true identity. Also included are Spidey's encounters with two other masked, mystery menaces; the first in a neverending series of J. Jonah Jameson's "*Spider-Slayers*;" a race against time for the life of Aunt May; and an epic adventure with Doctor Strange. Peter Parker's life is just as complicated. He loses Betty Brant, his first crush, to another man; he graduates from high school; and finally meets the girl his Aunt May has been trying to set him up with: Mary Jane Watson.

Review: Luckily for readers, this volume collects the end of artist Steve Ditko's defining run on the title, as well as the first handful of tales by John Romita, whose sleeker artwork brought a new sense of dynamism and romance to Spidey's—and Peter's— adventures. The book collects some of Ditko's finest artwork, produced just before he suddenly quit the book—and Marvel Comics. He not only illustrated but also plotted his latter issues, including the seminal oddcouple adventure with Spider-Man and fellow Ditko co-creation, Doctor Strange. Ditko also executed what many readers recall as the book's most visually stunning sequence, as Peter must draw on every last ounce of his strength to

BUT THEN, THE AMAZING TEEN-AGER GLIMPSES THE LIFE-SAVING SERUM-- SO NEAR, AND YET SO FAR-- SO HOPELESSLY FAR AWAY!

IT'S LYING THERE-- JUST BEYOND REACH-- AS THOUGH MOCKING ME-- TAUNTING ME--

*IT'S THE ONE THING-- THE **ONLY** THING-- THAT MAY SAVE AUNT MAY! AND I CAN'T BRING IT TO HER--!*

escape from being buried alive. When Romita came on board, Lee was immediately free to reveal the Green Goblin's true identity (apparently a bone of contention between Lee and Ditko). Having worked on romance comics for many years, Romita couldn't help but make the book's cast of characters more attractive, a distinct change from Ditko's more quirky depictions. Peter also became more extrovert. This aside, he still had enough problems in his life to stop it from running smoothly. For instance his Aunt May continued to have health problems, his romantic prospects improved, but were thwarted by his double life, and money problems continued to plague him.

With the quality of both the art and writing in these tales it's no wonder that they've influenced every writer and artist who has worked on the character ever since.

FURTHER READING: *Essential Spider-Man Volumes 1, 3-8; Essential Peter Parker, Spectacular Spider-Man Volumes 1-3*
SEE ALSO: *The Essential Doctor Strange Volume 1; Ultimate Spider-Man: Power And Responsibility*

★
★
★
★

Writer: Mark Millar
Artist: Bryan Hitch

Publisher: Marvel, 2004
ISBN: 0785109609

15+ THE ULTIMATES VOLUME 1

Plot: A glitzy reboot of Marvel's classic team of superheroes, making them relevant and interesting for a new, modern audience. Fan favorites Mark Millar and Bryan Hitch put the spectacular back into men in tight costumes hitting each other and breaking things.

Review: Do you know about *The Avengers*, Marvel Comics' great superhero team franchise? If you don't, this book is for you. If you do, well, this book will have some insider jokes you'll appreciate. But don't worry, it's not just some tired reheat—it's an attempt to do something much bigger.

The Ultimates is like a big-screen remake of *The Avengers*, boiling the strip down to its basic components and then weaving them into a massive visual spectacle. The characters might have a history and a back-story from other books, but all you really need to know is right in front of you.

The art is widescreen, detailed, and intricate, lovingly drawn by Bryan Hitch. Mark Millar's dialogue, too, is filmic—completely quotable, but like Tarantino, it falls a little short of naturalism. But what place does naturalism have in a Hollywood blockbuster? What place does naturalism have in

a story about a super soldier from World War II leading a government-sponsored team of superheroes against a gamma-irradiated monster in the middle of Manhattan?

This is all about the spectacle, and what a grand spectacle it is. Leaving aside the collateral damage to the New York City skyline, Hitch's heavily referenced character sketches are hugely evocative of the cinema—Nick Fury, traditionally depicted as a grizzled old cigar-chomping white guy (as portrayed by David Hasselhoff in the appalling movie Nick Fury: Agent of S.H.I.E.L.D.) is replaced by a character whose

look is based on Samuel L. Jackson. George W. Bush makes a guest star appearance, as does Freddie Prinze Junior and a host of others. This is a rollicking good popcorn-chomping romp of a comic that might not have much depth, but is utterly enthralling while you're reading it.

FURTHER READING: *Ultimates Volume 2; Ultimate Power; Ultimate Iron-Man*
SEE ALSO: *Civil War; Ultimate Spider-Man: Power And Responsibility; Marvels; Kingdom Come*

★ **Writer:** Alan Moore   **Publisher:** DC Comics, 1990
★ **Artist:** Dave Gibbons   **ISBN:** 0930289234
★
★
★

WATCHMEN

Plot: It's 1985. Richard Nixon is still president, America won the Vietnam War, the world is on the brink of nuclear war, and superheroes really exist. When one of the oldest and toughest of the costumed vigilantes, The Comedian, is murdered, rogue antihero Rorschach investigates. What he discovers is a vast conspiracy that's bigger than anyone can comprehend, with events stretching back to when the team first met one another.

Review: This is the daddy of all superhero graphic novels. Originally conceived as a 12-part reworking of old *Charlton Comics* heroes, the whole project grew to epic proportions. The book is so fêted because it was the first to treat superheroes "seriously," considering the implications of their actions upon their world. Moore and Gibbons's fanatical attention to detail—from creating Gunga Diner, the alternative fast-food joint, to the use of zeppelins as the primary means of air travel—pays off completely, creating an entirely believable, multilayered world. Despite the rather weak dénouement, the book still holds up as an exceptional case of what can be achieved in the comics medium.

FURTHER READING: *Watchmen Absolute Edition*
SEE ALSO: *Alan Moore's DC Universe; The League of Extraordinary Gentlemen; Promethea; V For Vendetta; Across The Universe*

★
★ **Writer:** Gardner Fox **Publisher:** DC Comics, 1997
★ **Artist:** Various **ISBN:** 1563890194
★

(A) # ALL STAR COMICS ARCHIVES, VOLUME 1

Plot: In the first story, our heroes recount their solo adventures to their teammates, but realize that their adventures were connected and are asked by the chief of the FBI to form a team. This sets the format for the series: first, a threat against the group is introduced; separate chapters follow in which the individual heroes deal with aspects of that threat; and a final chapter sees the whole team resolve it together. To begin with, the members of the team are the Atom, the Flash, Sandman, Spectre, Hawkman, r r. Fate, Green Lantern, and Hourman. The second story has them fighting foreign saboteurs while others include the mysterious Mr X trying to undermine the heroes, and Johnny Thunder becoming a replacement for the Flash.

Review: This volume reprints four issues (numbers 3 to 6) of *All Star Comics* from the early 1940s. The series had started as an anthology for some of the All-American superheroes, but the third issue presented something new—a team-up of those heroes as the Justice Society of America. These stories were written by Fox, accompanied by a variety of artists. Fun, if somewhat crude by today's standards, these are historically important superhero tales.

FURTHER READING: *All Star Comics Archives, Volumes 2–11; JSA All Star Archives; JSA All Stars*
SEE ALSO: *Identity Crisis; The Avengers: Kree Skrull Wars; JLA: A New Beginning*

Writer: Grant Morrison
Artist: Frank Quitely

Publisher: DC Comics, 2007
ISBN: 1401209149

ALL STAR SUPERMAN VOLUME 1

Plot: All of those goofy 1950s–1970s *Superman* stories didn't really need to be completely removed from existence by John Byrne in the 1980s, so this volume comprises DC's out-of-continuity fun stories. Morrison and Quitely show Superman being poisoned by solar radiation, telling Lois Lane his secret, introducing her to the Fortress of Solitude, Lois gaining Superman's powers, and a time-traveling Superman from the future.

Rating: Good goofy fun and lovely art from a couple of the UK's finest. If you fondly remember Elliot S. Maggin, this comic is for you. Collects the first six issues of the comic book.

FURTHER READING: *Superman: Man For All Seasons*
SEE ALSO: *Animal Man; Doom Patrol: Crawling From The Wreckage*

Writer: Grant Morrison
Artist: Chas Truog

Publisher: Vertigo, 2001
ISBN: 1563890054

ANIMAL MAN

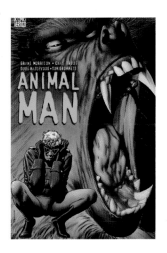

Plot: Small-time superhero Buddy Baker has the ability to mimic the natural powers of animals. After years living in the shadow of bigger and better heroes, he returns to his costumed alter ego, but instead of simply facing off against grandstanding villains, his adventures bring him face to face with the issues of vivisection, family relationships, vegetarianism, and a real-life Wile E. Coyote.

Review: Grant Morrison successfully pushed the boundaries of what was acceptable as a superhero title when he began his surreal interpretation of Animal Man. During a period in American comics (post-*Watchmen* and *Dark Knight Returns*) when writers were expected to produce dark, ultra-realistic, anti-heroes, Morrison wasn't afraid to explore more experimental storytelling techniques, and even embrace the absurd for the sake of originality.

FURTHER READING: *Animal Man: Deus Ex Machina*
SEE ALSO: *Doom Patrol: Crawling from the Wreckage*

★
★
★
★

Writer: Joss Whedon
Artist: John Cassaday

Publisher: Marvel, 2004
ISBN: 0785115315

ASTONISHING X-MEN VOLUME 1: GIFTED

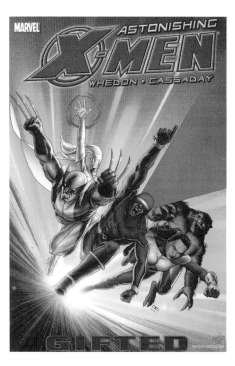

Plot: *Astonishing X-Men* starts with Shadowcat arriving at the Xavier Institute at the request of Cyclops, who tells her that he wants to reform the team to show the world that mutants aren't the malignant presence they've been portrayed as. A new team forms, consisting of Cyclops, Emma Frost, Wolverine, Shadowcat, Beast, and Shadowcat's pet dragon, Lockheed. Elsewhere, the superpowered alien, Ord, instigates a hostage situation and the X-Men storm into action. Meanwhile, at a press conference, Dr. Kavita Rao announces she has found a "cure" for the mutant strain. Beast visits Dr. Rao to find out more about this discovery, but while there he begins to suspect all is not as it should be with the firm funding the work.

Review: This novel collects the opening six issues of the *Astonishing X-Men* comic, which was launched in 2004. *Buffy* creator Joss Whedon takes the writing helm and his

clear and precise storylines make it a far less confusing read than most of Grant Morrison's convoluted *New X-Men* title. His dialog and characterization is particularly good—for example, Beast's moral dilemma when he fears he is devolving and may actually need a "cure" for his mutant genetics, is clever stuff. Cassaday's art is impressive and his intense character work helps invest the heroes with a real humanity. His detailed spreads and action sequences are also very strong.

FURTHER READING: *Astonishing X-Men: Dangerous; Astonishing X-Men: Torn*
SEE ALSO: *Buffy the Vampire Slayer: The Long Way Home; Planetary Volume 1: All Over the World and Other Stories*

Writer: Kurt Busiek
Artist: Brente E. Anderson

Publisher: Wildstorm, 1999
ISBN: 156389551X

ASTRO CITY: LIFE IN THE BIG CITY

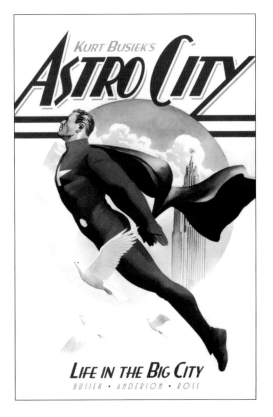

Plot: *Astro City* offers a whole new world of superheroes. Each chapter in this collection is a standalone story, highlighting different aspects or characters in the *Astro City* universe. A smalltime hood learns a hero's secret identity and tries to figure out how to profit from the knowledge. A beat reporter gets some advice from his editor on his first day on the job. A young woman tries to balance the demands of her family with her own hopes and desires.

Review: Superhero stories depicting costumed heroes protecting a city, patrolling the skies, and upholding justice have been part of comic-book storytelling from the early days of *Superman*. It is very rare that a new work comes along that provides a simple way to tell stories based on a whole new set of heroes.

Among these new heroes is Samaritan, a godlike caped hero with a tragic past; Winged Victory, a superwoman with a feminist twist; the Hanged Man, a mysterious figure who maintains a silent, protective vigil; and Jack-in-the-Box, a demonic-looking clown who deploys high-tech tricks.

But what makes this book so compelling are the "normal" people, the people who live their daily lives among these super beings. *Astro City* screams realism, providing a plausible social and cultural framework in which the stories can be told.

FURTHER READING: *Astro City: A Visitor's Guide; Astro City: Life In The Big City; Astro City: Confession*
SEE ALSO: *Marvels; Top Ten; Kingdom Come*

★
★
★
★

Writer: Warren Ellis
Artist: Bryan Hitch

Publisher: Wildstorm, 2000
ISBN: 1563896613

15+ THE AUTHORITY: RELENTLESS

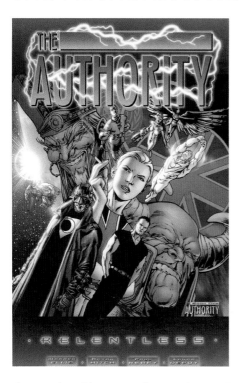

Plot: Formed out of the remnants of Stormwatch, a United Nations-sponsored superhero squad that was shut down after the deaths of most of its members, The Authority consists of Jenny Sparks, spirit of the 20th century, and alive since the beginning of it; Jack Hawksmoor, who can talk to the cities, and control them; Swift, a deadly and incredibly smart lady with a 20-foot wingspan; The Doctor, who can change the fabric of existence; The Engineer, who can do just about anything; and Apollo and The Midnighter, who are drawn from the same archetypes as Superman and Batman, respectively, but are much deadlier.

The Authority is probably the most powerful team in the world, existing to deal with global threats with extreme prejudice, and answerable to no one but themselves. In this volume, they have to stop an international terrorist crimelord, who's using superpowered clones to destroy cities, and then an invasion by a parallel universe.

Review: *The Authority* was the first big hit for both of its creators, and arguably changed the face of superhero comics. Ellis's characters are brilliant, but flawed, so nothing ever quite goes the way you expect. His dialog crackles with wit and sarcasm, while Hitch's art is spectacular as he effortlessly draws global invasions on a massive scale, and makes it look real. This is a very smart and knowing book, and near-essential reading for all superhero fans.

FURTHER READING: *The Authority: Under New Management; The Authority: Earth Inferno; The Authority: Revolution*
SEE ALSO: *The Ultimates; Transmetropolitan: Back On The Street; Planetary: All Over The World*

Writer: Roy Thomas
Artist: Neal Adams

Publisher: Marvel, 2000
ISBN: 0785107452

A THE AVENGERS: THE KREE-SKRULL WAR

Plot: The Avengers, "Earth's Mightiest Heroes"—including Marvel regulars Thor, Captain America, and Iron Man—find themselves, and the planet, caught in the middle of a star-spanning war between two alien races: the war-like Kree and the shape-changing Skrull. Although the Avengers are joined in battle by other heroes, such as the Inhumans and Captain Mar-Vell (himself a Kree), Earth's salvation might just depend upon ordinary teenager Rick Jones.

Review: This nine-issue story set the standard for every superhero space saga to follow, with Thomas and Adams determined to make the most complicated and engaging superhero epic of their the time (it was first published in the early 1970s). Fans revere it particularly for the artwork of Neal Adams, who drew the bulk of the story. Adams's most astounding scenes are of Ant-Man performing emergency surgery inside the mind of the android Avenger known as the Vision.

FURTHER READING: *Avengers: Assemble!*
SEE ALSO: *The Ultimates; X-Men: Dark Phoenix Saga*

★
★
★
★

Writer: Grant Morrison
Artist: Dave McKean

Publisher: DC Comics, 2005
ISBN: 1401204252

15+ BATMAN: ARKHAM ASYLUM

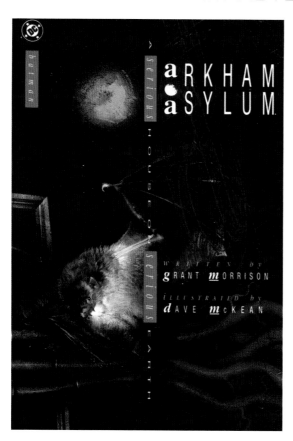

Plot: On April Fool's Day, the inmates of Arkham Asylum revolt and take over the institution. Of course, only Batman can stop them. As our hero wages a battle of wits and will against The Joker and other arch-villains, his own psyche becomes tainted by the asylum and he begins to doubt his own sanity.

Review: This psychological thriller brings depth and complexity to both Batman and his rogues' gallery, tearing them down to their archetypal roots and placing them against a backdrop of an *Alice Through the Looking Glass*-style asylum. Also included in the storyline is the history of the asylum and its founder Amadeus Arkham, who begins by wanting to help the mentally ill, but ends up questioning his own state of mind, particularly after the tragic death of his mother and the onset of his daughter's strange behavior. McKean's phantasmagorical illustrations, full of shadow and subjective imagery, complement and intensify Morrison's labyrinthine narrative. Moody, atmospheric, and enigmatic, *Arkham Asylum* demands to be read again and again.

FURTHER READING: *Batman: The Last Arkham*
SEE ALSO: *Signal to Noise; Violent Cases; Animal Man; Doom Patrol: Crawling from the Wreckage*

Writer: Frank Miller   **Publisher:** DC Comics, 2007
Artist: David Mazzucchelli   **ISBN:** 1401207529

BATMAN: YEAR ONE

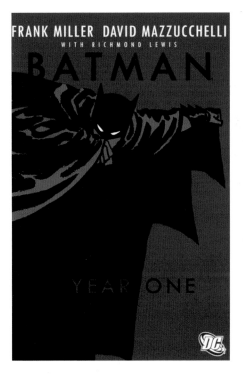

Plot: A retelling of Batman's origins, *Year One* focuses on police and government corruption, with as much attention given to the new police captain—and later Commissioner, Jim Gordon—as to Batman himself. Bruce Wayne's first, fumbling efforts to fight crime are recounted, as are his decision to don the batsuit and the uncertain beginnings of his partnership with Gordon (whose viewpoint humanizes the action). The book makes the Gotham City Police Department into a credible milieu (later explored in other comics), while also providing outrageous thrills, among them a new, seamier origin for Catwoman, and an encounter with the GCPD that ends with Batman summoning thousands of bats. *Year One* marks a return to the idea of Batman as a human vigilante on a par with Zorro, and furthers Miller's anti-authoritarian vision of the character.

Review: First published in 1987, *Year One* follows Miller's *The Dark Knight Returns*, but is different in tone and style,

and actually more cohesive and satisfying. While still recognizably Miller's, the story has been scaled down to capitalize on Mazzucchelli's elegant, understated visuals, which recall European variations on the Milton Caniff/Alex Toth school of graphic minimalism. This is a human Batman, with carefully choreographed action, a believable urban setting, beautifully muted colors (by Richmond Lewis), and a taut script—one of the best-ever interpretations of the character. The more down-to-earth elements of the film *Batman Begins* are derived from this book.

FURTHER READING: *Batman: The Long Halloween; Gotham Central Volume 1*
SEE ALSO: *The Dark Knight Returns; Daredevil By Frank Miller Omnibus Companion*

★ **Writer:** Gail Simone
★ **Artist:** Ed Benes

Publisher: DC Comics, 2004
ISBN: 1840238364

A # BIRDS OF PREY, VOLUME 1: OF LIKE MINDS

Plot: The unlikely crime-fighting duo of all-action girl, Black Canary, and former Batgirl, but now wheelchair-bound computer hacker, Oracle, operate together as Birds of Prey. But when the Canary is captured by mentally ill villain Savant, Oracle is offered her partner's life in exchange for some very bankable information: Batman's secret identity. Oracle responds by recruiting a third and rather more volatile member to the team.

Review: Relatively straightforward "old school" superhero material, enhanced by some occasionally witty and sharp dialog between the main characters. Gail Simone writes her female characters with a touch more sympathy than previous male writers, and in this story arc she touches upon various ethical issues associated with the consequences of crime fighting.

FURTHER READING: *She Hulk Volume 1: Single Green Female*
SEE ALSO: *Across The Universe: The DC Stories Of Alan Moore*

★
★ **Writer:** Rick Veitch
★ **Artist:** Rick Veitch

Publisher: King Hell Press, 2003
ISBN: 0962486442

18+ # BRATPACK

Plot: The city of Slumburg has more than its fair share of problems. The criminal element plays a part, but the city's superhero protectors themselves are morally corrupt. More interested in their merchandising residuals than public welfare, The Mink, Moon Mistress, King Rad, and Judge Jury save their worst tactics for their kid sidekicks, known popularly as the Bratpack. After the current crop of sidekicks is killed, the pastor at St. Bingo's church is forced to recruit replacements. Chippy, Luna, Wild Boy, and Kid Violence soon discover their new lives are more disturbing than they had anticipated.

Review: *Bratpack* is an extreme example of "tough love." Throwing any pretense of subtlety aside, Veitch employs thinly veiled substitutes for sidekick-sporting heroes such as Batman, Wonder Woman, and Green Arrow. Definitely not for the squeamish.

FURTHER READING: *The Maximortal; Batman: A Death In The Family;*
SEE ALSO: *Abraxas And The Earthman*

Writer: Stan Lee
Artist: Jack Kirby

Publisher: Marvel, 2003
ISBN: 078511176X

A MARVEL MASTERWORKS: CAPTAIN AMERICA VOLUME 1

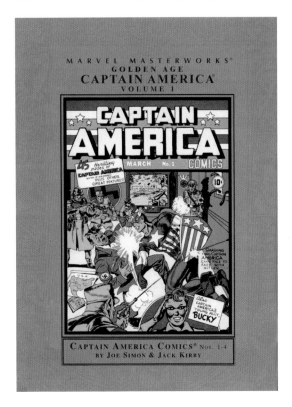

Plot: A collection of the earliest *Captain America* stories published by Marvel in the early 1960s after the character was rescued from comic-book limbo. Individual stories retell the character's origins, including flashbacks to his exploits in World War II, and reintroduce old 1940s comics characters such as the Red Skull, plus many new villains that are now familiar household names for superhero fans. Originally a super soldier, designed by scientists to combat Hitler and the Nazis, Captain America went on to act as Marvel's voice on the state of the nation.

as we know it today. The early 1960s were a fertile breeding ground of ideas for the legendary partnership of Stan Lee and Jack Kirby. Every comic published during that time seemed to bristle with new ideas. Although the stories may seem stylized and simple by today's standards, the sheer quantity of new characters and concepts that remain in common usage to this day proves beyond doubt the lasting power and influence of this unsurpassed creative team.

Review: Reprinting issues 59 to 81 of *Tales of Suspense*, this volume introduces many of the concepts and characters that in just a few short years would define the Marvel universe

FURTHER READING: *The Death of Captain America*
SEE ALSO: *Essential Fantastic Four Volume 3*

★ **Writer:** Mark Millar **Publisher:** Marvel, 2007
★ **Artist:** Steve McNiven **ISBN:** 078512179X
★

12+

CIVIL WAR

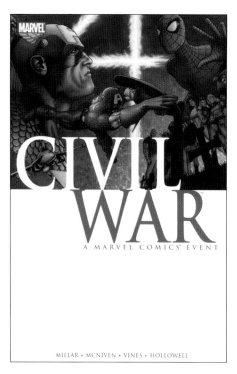

Plot: When the New Warriors, a group of young and inexperienced superheroes, are involved in a horrible explosion in Stamford, CT, killing hundreds of children, public and political anger leads to the Superhero Registration Act, or SRA. All superpowered individuals must register with the US Government and reveal their secret identities or be considered enemies of the state. Iron Man coordinates the heroes who register, while Captain America leads the resistance for those who feel that the SRA not only impinges upon their civil liberties, but also weakens the concept of liberty itself. Spider-Man initially sides with Iron Man, but after revealing his identity to the world and seeing the consequences the act brings to his family, and learning of the other-dimensional prison developed to house captured non-registered heroes, he joins the rebels. Distrust divides friendships, hero battles hero, and the country begins to suffer even more. The Registration side apparently wins, but the story is far from over.

Review: *Civil War* was a bold concept, a company-wide story that fundamentally altered characters and concepts, with long-term consequences. While far from perfect, it did unify the Marvel Universe more closely even than the classic 1960s stories in which characters regularly guest-starred in each other's books. Unlike DC's more plot-driven events, *Civil War* focused more closely on the characters themselves, drawing drama from personal interaction rather than menaces threatening the universe. For readers with an emotional investment in these characters, *Civil War* provokes reactions that few other superhero stories ever have.

FURTHER READING: *Civil War: Road to Civil War; Civil War: Front Line Parts 1 and 2*
SEE ALSO: *Bratpack; The Ultimates*

Writer: Marv Wolfman
Artist: George Pérez

Publisher: DC Comics, 2001
ISBN: 1563897504

Ⓐ CRISIS ON INFINITE EARTHS

Plot: The DC Universe is in peril—or, rather, the DC universes. From Earth-1 (home of "our" Superman and Wonder Woman) to Earth-3 (where Lex Luthor is a hero, and "our" heroes are villains), a crisis across space and time threatens to wipe out everything. The shadowy Monitor recruits heroes and villains from different worlds to stem the tide of oblivion. Along the way, some heroes disappear as if they'd never existed, while others, such as The Flash and Supergirl, die tragically.

Review: After decades of stories with increasingly complicated continuity, including the variety of Earths, DC editorial decided to "clean house." *Crisis* was the result: a year-long blockbuster that affected every title the company published. Buoyed by George Pérez's obsessively detailed artwork, the series streamlined DC's characters and history—until the patches began to show. Still, it marks a momentous event for the company.

FURTHER READING: *Infinite Crisis; 52*
SEE ALSO: *Crisis on Multiple Earths*

MARV WOLFMAN & GEORGE PÉREZ

Writer: Gardner Fox
Artist: Mike Sekowski

Publisher: DC Comics, 2002
ISBN: 1563898950

Ⓐ CRISIS ON MULTIPLE EARTHS VOLUME 1

Plot: Stemming from the groundbreaking *Flash of Two Worlds* story, the tales in this book helped expand the so-called DC Universe into a multiverse: a conglomeration of similar and not-so-similar Earths and other planets.

Review: Older readers at the time reveled in the nostalgia of seeing older heroes revived, even if it was only once a year, while younger readers gained quick comics-history lessons along with exciting, crisis-filled stories. Three decades of such stories inevitably created challenges for newer readers, as well as creators, so DC's universe was streamlined by *Crisis on Infinite Earths* in 1986. But you can't keep a good concept down, and the multiverse (or versions of it) has been brought back, most recently after the events of *Infinite Crisis* (2005). Everything new is old again.

FURTHER READING: *Crisis on Multiple Earths Volumes 2-3*
SEE ALSO: *Crisis on Infinite Earths*

★
★
★
★
★

12+

Writer: Frank Miller
Artist: Bill Sienkiewicz, John Romita Jr.,
David Mazzucchelli

Publisher: Marvel, 2007
ISBN: 0785126767

DAREDEVIL BY FRANK MILLER OMNIBUS COMPANION

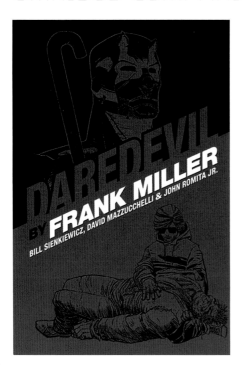

Plot: This omnibus edition gathers together three *Daredevil* stories penned by Frank Miller, all of which feature encounters with the hero's arch-nemesis, Kingpin. In *Love and War*, a graphic novel from 1986, Kingpin kidnaps and blackmails an eminent psychiatrist in an effort to save his ailing wife from a crippling mental illness. *Daredevil: The Man Without Fear* gathers together a five-issue miniseries from 1993 and provides a definitive account of the title character's origins. 1985's *Born Again* features a plotline in which the Kingpin learns of Daredevil's secret identity and uses the information to devastating effect.

Review: *Love and War*, despite sumptuous painted artwork by Bill Sienkiewicz, is ultimately a rather forgettable entry in the Daredevil canon. Much better is the *Daredevil: The Man Without Fear* miniseries, illustrated by John Romita, Jr., in which we learn how Daredevil first acquired his powers

and developed his abilities, and witness first meetings with classic characters from the series such as Foggy Nelson, Elektra, and the Kingpin. Best of all, though, is *Born Again*. Written around the same time as *The Dark Knight Returns* and *Batman: Year One*, when Miller was undeniably at the peak of his powers, *Born Again* is a lesser known, but equally accomplished work. David Mazzucchelli's artwork is the perfect realization of a grim and gritty storyline which charts the fall of Daredevil at the hands of the ruthless Kingpin, and the hero's ensuing struggle for salvation.

FURTHER READING: *Elektra Lives Again; Daredevil Visionaries—Frank Miller Volume 2; Daredevil Visionaries—Frank Miller Volume 3*
SEE ALSO: *The Dark Knight Returns; Batman: Year One; Sin City: The Hard Goodbye*

Writer: Grant Morrison
Artist: Richard Case

Publisher: Vertigo, 2000
ISBN: 1563890348

DOOM PATROL, BOOK 1: CRAWLING FROM THE WRECKAGE

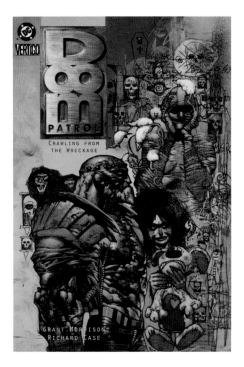

Plot: Groundbreaking surrealist adventures bursting out of an otherwise mundane and moribund superhero comic. After a massive series of traumas in a now mostly forgotten crossover story, a team of superheroes attempts to pick themselves up and recover. Normally this would be done quickly, almost as a pause between fight scenes, but in this volume no one really recovers.

Review: As the title says, this is a team that is crawling from the wreckage. This is the key to comics auteur Grant Morrison's vision of the Doom Patrol—these heroes aren't perfect supermen or Amazon women, but brittle, broken people—in the case of Rebus, quite literally fractured.

For Morrison, this, along with *Animal Man*, is where it all started—where he began to experiment with the comics form in earnest, bringing a much-needed infusion of new ideas into the superhero genre. Monsters from the children's classic *Struwwelpeter* help pose existential questions of being and nothingness. The art by Richard Case is equally distinctive, and helps reinforce the idea that from this volume forward, Doom Patrol would never again be just another bunch of superheroes.

Doom Patrol brought a great, renewed richness to American comics, and for that reason alone it is well worth reading.

FURTHER READING: *X-Men: E is for Extinction; Doom Patrol: The Painting That Ate Paris*
SEE ALSO: *Animal Man Volume 1*

★ **Writer:** Frank Miller **Publisher:** Panini (UK), 2005
★ **Artist:** Bill Sienkiewicz **ISBN:** 1904159893
★

15+ ELEKTRA: ASSASSIN

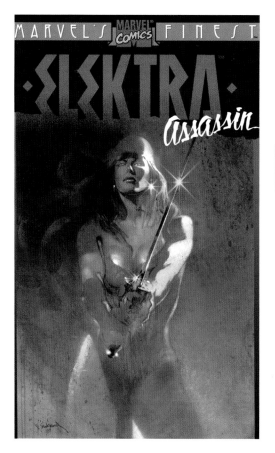

Plot: In this gonzo sequel/prequel to Miller's *Daredevil*, antiheroine Elektra escapes from a madhouse and sets out to stop the Beast—a sort of Antichrist who, in the form of politician Ken Wind, plans to trigger a nuclear war. She is aided by Garrett, a thuggish spy who at first tries to capture her, but then gets blown to bits, reborn as a cyborg, and controlled by Elektra's psychic powers. Satirical ultraviolence dominates, as Elektra and Garrett battle spies, ninjas, and an even nastier cyborg, leading to a mordantly funny end.

Review: *Elektra: Assassin* reprints an eight-issue miniseries from 1986-87 that trumps the satire of Miller's *Dark Knight*

Returns and nudges revisionist superheroes toward self-parody. It's a gleeful, viciously funny, paranoiac work, far from Miller's *Daredevil* in tone. Sienkiewicz's art, a riot of painting, drawing, and collage, blends Ralph Steadman-esque caricature and brazen expressionism. A career high for both creators, but certainly not an easy read.

FURTHER READING: *Elektra Lives Again*
SEE ALSO: *Stray Toasters; Daredevil*

Writer: Stan Lee
Artist: Steve Ditko

Publisher: Marvel, 2006
ISBN: 0785123164

THE ESSENTIAL DOCTOR STRANGE, VOLUME 1

Plot: The saga of Doctor Stephen Strange, Master of the Mystic Arts, from his not-so-humble beginnings as a spoiled surgeon to becoming Earth's best defense against mystical, other-dimensional menaces. While some stories occasionally wander into superhero territory, on the whole these sagas entail desperate magical confrontations with bizarre entities.

Review: This massive collection of the character's first four and a half years showcases, above all, the incomparable artistry of Steve Ditko, who conceived the title and depicted it in a style never before seen on the comics page—or anywhere else. His otherworldly scenes screamed "psychedelia" before the term even existed, and the good Doctor became a touchstone for the 1960s counterculture movement.

FURTHER READING: *Essential Doctor Strange Vol 2*
SEE ALSO: *Essential Doctor Strange*

Writer: Brian K. Vaughan
Artist: Tony Harris

Publisher: Wildstorm, 2005
ISBN: 1401206123

EX MACHINA, VOLUME 1: THE FIRST HUNDRED DAYS

Plot: The tale of a political superhero in a post-9/11 world, who takes on the ultimate challenge—serving as Mayor of New York City!

Review: The first thing that strikes you about *Ex Machina*, the latest addition to the trend of putting superheroes in more realistic situations, is that Brian K. Vaughan has obviously done his research. Fun facts about New York mayors proliferate. Tony Harris's photorealistic artwork reinforces the heightened reality. Unfortunately, the facts and the visuals often fail to gel with the rest of the narrative. It was always going to be difficult to create an interesting, engaging, and successful comic about politics, especially in the currently polarized political climate of the United States, but while it is not always successful, *Ex Machina* is at least an interesting attempt.

FURTHER READING: *Ex Machina: Volume 2: Tag*
SEE ALSO: *Y: The Last Man; Starman: Sins Of The Father*

★ **Writers:** Stan Lee and Marv Wolfman
★ **Artists:** Jack Kirby, Marie Sevrin, John Buscema,
★ Gene Colan, Moebius, and John Byrne

Publisher: Panini (UK), 2007
ISBN: 190523967X

A DEFINITIVE SILVER SURFER

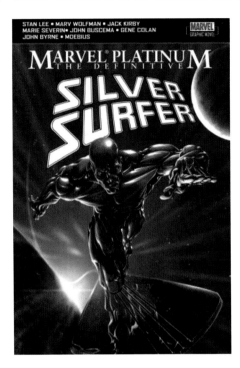

Plot: A collection of several key stories in the history of the Silver Surfer, beginning with arguably the best superhero story of the 1960s: the three-part *Coming of Galactus* by Stan Lee and Jack Kirby that introduced the Silver Surfer to Marvel comics and served as inspiration for the second *Fantastic Four* movie. Later tales surf through the 1970s and 1980s, offering highlights such as his origin story, an encounter with Bram Stoker's *Dracula*, and a prosaic and allegorical graphic novel with religious overtones drawn by French artist, Moebius. A less essential story covers his first encounter with the Hulk.

Review: The Silver Surfer has always stood out, even among Marvel's other angst-ridden heroes, as the quintessential "stranger in a strange land." In the best of these stories, particularly the unrepresentative collaboration between Stan Lee and Jean Giraud, aka Moebius, the character is used as a spiritual metaphor to examine various social and moral issues. Although it's conventional now, at the time it was a rare and bold example of such progressive writing in American superhero comics. In many respects, the early stories were a vehicle for Marvel writers to espouse various libertarian and ethical beliefs.

Parable does stand out, not just as a story by two of the world's biggest names in comics, but also in style. What Lee has done is give us a concept for Galactus as a God, but at 52 pages he doesn't allow the ideas to develop.

The individual stories can appear disjointed at times, because they cover a broad period of Marvel history and cross over multiple styles—from classic Kirby superhero art, to Gene Colan horror, to the unmistakably European style of Moebius.

FURTHER READING: *Essential Silver Surfer Volume 1*
SEE ALSO: *Essential Fantastic Four Volume 3*

Writer: John Byrne
Artist: John Byrne

Publisher: Marvel, 2001
ISBN: 0785107797

FANTASTIC FOUR VISIONARIES: JOHN BYRNE VOLUME 1

Plot: Wracked with guilt, Doctor Reed Richards attempts to cure The Thing of his condition, but unintentionally makes his appearance worse. The Fantastic Four also face old enemy Diablo again, and the combined force of Doctor Doom and the Puppet Master.

Review: Rivalled only by Stan Lee and Jack Kirby's original groundbreaking series, and later by Walt Simonson's brief stay with the title, John Byrne's epic run as both writer and artist begins here. This volume hints at the many changes that would be brought to Marvel's first family, including losing a member and finding a new home. As relevant and enjoyable today as when they were first published in the 1980s.

FURTHER READING: *Fantastic Four Omnibus Volume 1; Fantastic Four Omnibus Volume 2; Fantastic Four Visionaries: Walt Simonson*
SEE ALSO: *X-Men: The Dark Phoenix Saga*

Writer: Joe Casey
Artist: Tom Scioli

Publisher: Image Comics, 2006
ISBN: 1582407126

GØDLAND VOLUME 1: HELLO, COSMIC!

Plot: The only survivor of an ill-fated voyage to Mars, Commander Adam Archer receives powers of accelerated evolution from the Cosmic Fetus Collective. Along with his sisters Neela, Stella, and Angie (an anti-establishment, would-be punk), Archer encounters outlandish menaces that test even his own cosmic powers.

Review: *Gødland* updates the classic Marvel superhero formula for a new century in a way that's both nostalgic and fresh. Casey and Scioli wear their love of the classic *Fantastic Four* comics on their sleeve, creating a book that nearly explodes with far-out concepts, over-the-top villains, and excitement by the planet-load. Scioli's artwork (aided by Bill Crabtree's cosmic colors) positively krackles (sic) with Kirby-inspired machinery and designs of all types. And how can you not love a book with villains named Basil Chronus, or Friedrich Nickelhead, or Discordia, daughter of The Tormentor?

FURTHER READING: *Gødland: Another Sunny Delight; Code Flesh*
SEE ALSO: *Essential Fantastic Four Volume 3*

★
★
★

Writer: Dennis O'Neil
Artist: Neal Adams

Publisher: DC Comics, 2001
ISBN: 1401202241

(A)

GREEN LANTERN/GREEN ARROW COLLECTION VOLUME 1

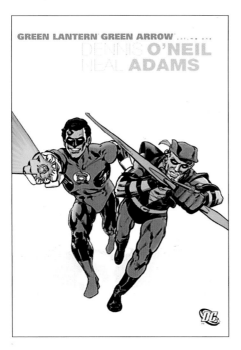

Plot: In 1970, Green Lantern and Green Arrow begin a journey across the seedy underbelly of America. Green Lantern (Hal Jordan) is portrayed as a stodgy conservative who needs hipster Green Arrow (former millionaire Oliver Queen) to explain to him, when confronting an altercation on the street, that the "fat cat landlord who owns this dump" was being roughed up by a "punk" because the landlord was evicting "a lot of old folks." In the iconic image that opens the series, an elderly black man says to Green Lantern, "I been readin' about you... How you work for the Blue Skins... and how on a planet someplace you helped out the Orange Skins... and you done considerable for the Purple Skins! Only there's skins you never bothered with--! ...The Black Skins! I want to know... How come?" Shocked and shamed by this realization, the two heroes venture forth to find the real America, encountering drug abuse, corporate greed, racism (including racism against Native Americans), and environmental destruction.

Review: This was a new type of superhero comic book for the time, actively engaging with social issues. O'Neil's writing can seem more than a touch overwrought today, but it still holds up, as does Neal Adams's influential artwork. Indeed, Adams's realistic style helped to ground these stories in a world recognizable as our own, not just some superhero fantasy land. While certainly of its time, the book addresses tensions and problems that resist easy answers today. Buy it and foster your sense of social justice.

FURTHER READING: *Green Lantern/Green Arrow Collection Volume 2*
SEE ALSO: *Green Arrow: Quiver*

Writer: Kevin Smith
Artist: Phil Hester

Publisher: DC Comics, 2003
ISBN: 1563899655

GREEN ARROW: QUIVER

Plot: Presumed dead for several years, Green Arrow (Oliver Queen) mysteriously returns to his hometown of Star City to find an almost unrecognizable world. It will take his fellow superheroes—including Aquaman, Batman, The Demon, The Spectre, his one-time love Black Canary, and his son (the new Green Arrow)—to help solve the mystery of his resurrection. Along the way there is a madman to defeat with a taste for the occult.

Review: Superstar filmmaker and comics fan Kevin Smith (Clerks, Mallrats) worked magic with this third-tier character, making the new *Green Arrow* series a bestseller. Deeply indebted to decades of DC history, the story may at first seem confusing, but by the end everything makes coherent sense—even the surprise appearance of some incredibly obscure characters. On its release, fans complained of needing a huge knowledge of the character in order to fully enjoy the book. What's more likely is that this sometimes-overlooked character now has a story that will make you seek out the back issues.

FURTHER READING: *Green Arrow: The Sounds of Violence; Green Arrow: Year 1*
SEE ALSO: *Green Lantern/Green Arrow Collection Volume 1*

★
★
★
★

Writer: Fletcher Hanks
Artist: Fletcher Hanks

Publisher: Fantagraphics, 2007
ISBN: 1560978392

ISBN: 1560978392

A

I SHALL DESTROY ALL THE CIVILIZED PLANETS!

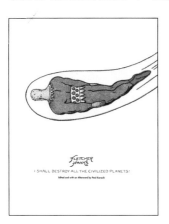

FLETCHER HANKS
I SHALL DESTROY ALL THE CIVILIZED PLANETS!
Edited and with an Afterword by Paul Karasik

Plot: Read about the crimebusting missions of Stardust the Super Wizard, "whose knowledge of interplanetary science has made him the most remarkable man who ever lived!" Find out why Big Red McLane, King of the North Woods and "loyal lumberjack for the Great Bend Lumber Company," isn't a household name, either!

Review: Originally published from 1939–1941, these stories overflow with strange concepts and even stranger anatomies. Hanks' inimitable style led Art Spiegelman and Françoise Mouly to label him "an obscure, heretofore unrecognized genius." There's no better introduction to the wild and wacky nature of many early superhero comics than this book.

FURTHER READING: *Art Out Of Time*
SEE ALSO: *Flaming Carrot: Flaming Carrot's Greatest Hits*

★
★
★
★

Writer: Brad Meltzer
Artists: Rags Morales and Michael Bair

Publisher: DC Comics, 2006
ISBN: 1560978392

ISBN: 1560978392

15+ # IDENTITY CRISIS

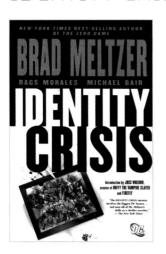

NEW YORK TIMES BEST-SELLING AUTHOR OF THE ZERO GAME
BRAD MELTZER
RAGS MORALES   MICHAEL BAIR
IDENTITY CRISIS
Introduction by JOSS WHEDON, creator of BUFFY THE VAMPIRE SLAYER and FIREFLY
"The IDENTITY CRISIS mystery involves the biggest DC heroes... and uses all of Mr. Meltzer's skills as a thriller novelist." — The New York Times
DC

Plot: In a *Justice League* story, Elongated Man's wife Sue Dibny is murdered. His superhero colleagues resolve to help find the murderer, but longstanding divisions in the superhero community stand in the way. It is revealed that Doctor Light raped Dibny years earlier, and had his memory wiped by Zatanna. He appears to be the obvious suspect, but when his memory returns, he proves innocent of the murder. Who is the real perpetrator?

Review: Brad Meltzer is a professional thriller writer, and comic-book fan, so this story takes a "realistic" view of superheroes. It's very readable and rolls along nicely, but some of the retroactive continuity—and adult themes such as the rape—don't mesh well. Fans of traditional DC superheroes should avoid this, but those who like a dash of modernity in their comics should give it a try.

FURTHER READING: *Justice League of America: The Tornado's Path*
SEE ALSO: *Kingdom Come; Watchmen; Ultimates*

Writer: Bruce Jones
Artist: John Romita Jr.

Publisher: Panini, 2002
ISBN: 1904159036

INCREDIBLE HULK: RETURN OF THE MONSTER

Plot: A recent rampage by the Hulk results in the televised death of a small boy. Now, hounded and hated even more than usual, Bruce Banner is on the run from the authorities and a vigilante public baying for his blood. With his fugitive status, he can count on only one ally—the mysterious Mr Blue—who he communicates with via a laptop.

Review: Bruce Jones returned to the classic theme of the early Stan Lee/ Jack Kirby tales in his reboot of the *Hulk* series: namely, the story of a fugitive Doctor Jekyll, living in fear of the shadow of his violent Mr Hyde self. This story concentrates on the human side of the character, with brief but savage appearances of his green-skinned alter ego, and is all the better for it.

FURTHER READING: *Incredible Hulk: Transformations*
SEE ALSO: *The Ultimates*

Writer: Robert Kirkman
Artists: Cory Walker and Ryan Ottley

Publisher: Image Comics, 2005
ISBN: 158240500X

INVINCIBLE: THE ULTIMATE COLLECTION VOLUME 1

Plot: Mark Grayson is a typical American high-school kid, but he's also the son of Omniman, the Earth's most powerful superhero, and his own inherited abilities have just been activated.

Review: Robert Kirkman's entertaining superhero soap opera uses the protagonist's inexperience to explore the many quandaries of the first-time hero, including which name and costume to adopt, and the pros and cons of belonging to a superteam. Cory Walker and Ryan Ottley's clean, stylized artwork helps to maintain a generally light tone, but Kirkman throws in more than the odd shock revelation and is not averse to showing the gory after-effects of a superpowered smackdown. This oversized hardback collects the first 13 issues and includes 80 pages of extras.

FURTHER READING: *Brit: Old Soldier; Battle Pope*
SEE ALSO: *The Walking Dead*

★
★ **Writer:** David Michelinie **Publisher:** Marvel Comics, 2008
★ **Artists:** Bob Layton, John Romita Jr., **ISBN:** 0785130950
★ Carmine Infantino

IRON MAN: DEMON IN A BOTTLE

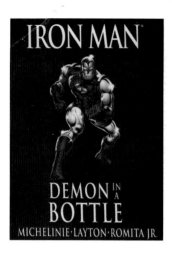

Plot: Tony "Iron Man" Stark has it all: the gleaming armor, high-tech weapons, and beautiful women. And then the downward spiral begins. He starts drinking after discovering that the spy agency S.H.I.E.L.D. is trying to buy up his company for weapons production. Villain and business rival, Justin Hammer, sends dozens of supervillains after him, and finally his remote-controlled armor kills an innocent man.

Review: Other stories in these creators' run were more fun, but what you get here is the frisson from the timeless story of a man who has it all and then throws it away due to the demon rum. Even a multimillionaire, good-looking superhero can be one step away from skid row.

FURTHER READING: *Essential Iron Man Volume 1; Iron Man: In Extremis; Iron-Man: Hypervelocity*
SEE ALSO: *Civil War; The Ultimates*

★
★ **Writer:** Jack Kirby **Publisher:** DC Comics, 1997
★ **Artist:** Jack Kirby **ISBN:** 1563893851

Ⓐ JACK KIRBY'S NEW GODS

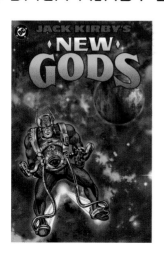

Plot: The old gods have died, to be replaced by the warring inhabitants of two worlds. Apokolips' ruler Darkseid employs his minions in his mad quest for the Anti-Life equation; New Genesis' High-father and his people, led by his foster son Orion, have pledged to stop him. The whole universe is at stake, but the battle comes to a head on Earth.

Review: When comics legend Jack Kirby quit Marvel Comics to work for DC in 1971, no one knew what to expect. What Kirby did was decades ahead of its time: he tried to create an entirely new mythology in the form of a massive epic, spread over four different titles. *New Gods* was the cornerstone of what came to be known as *The Fourth World*. His experiment was canceled mid-story, but the ideas he generated would soon become central to the DC Universe.

FURTHER READING: *Jack Kirby's Fourth World Omnibus Volumes 1–4; Jack Kirby's Fourth World: Featuring Mister Miracle*
SEE ALSO: *Essential Fantastic Four Volume 3*

Writer: Paul Grist
Artist: Paul Grist

Publisher: Image Comics, 2004
ISBN: 158240335X

JACK STAFF, VOLUME 1: EVERYTHING USED TO BE BLACK AND WHITE

Plot: Jack Staff, a British super-patriot from the World War II era, returns to present-day Castletown, looking no older than he did on his last appearance some 20 years before. This time he has to stop the Castletown Slasher, whose true identity, it transpires, is tied up with Jack's own history. Also involved is Jack's old nemesis The Spider, a group of trenchcoated investigators known simply as Q, and a raft of other fetchingly weird characters, among them the intrepid Becky Burdock, Vampire Reporter.

Review: Grist gives the superhero a delightful, self-mocking spin, mimicking British anthology comics. The story affectionately dusts off characters from Britain's venerable IPC Comics, and the whole thing is a fervent Valentine to comics past, brought to life by Grist's elegant black-and-white artwork.

FURTHER READING: *Jack Staff, Volume 2: Soldiers*
SEE ALSO: *Kane: Greetings from New Eden*

Writer: Keith Giffen and J.M. DeMatteis
Artist: Kevin Maguire

Publisher: DC Comics, 1991
ISBN: 0930289404

JUSTICE LEAGUE: A NEW BEGINNING

Plot: A new Justice League has formed, one without Superman or Wonder Woman, but featuring Batman, Dr. Fate, Martian Manhunter, Captain Marvel, and several lesser-known heroes, including the hotheaded Guy Gardner. They immediately have to deal with other-dimensional heroes, the Russian Rocket Red Brigade, the evil Gray Man, and a rogue satellite that's threatening nuclear armageddon. On top of all this, who is the mysterious Maxwell Lord, the industrialist who's bankrolling the new League?

Review: This book was pretty radical for 1987, bringing humor to the Justice League for the first time, and concentrating on the personalities in the League as much as the big events. It worked perfectly: Giffen and DeMatteis pitch the tone just right between drama and humor, and Maguire knocks it out of the park, artwise. Highly regarded, and justifiably so.

FURTHER READING: *Justice League International: Secret Gospel of Maxwell Lord;*
SEE ALSO: *Moonshadow; Identity Crisis*

★
★
★
★
★

Writer: Mark Waid
Artist: Alex Ross

Publisher: DC Comics, 1997
ISBN: 1563893304

KINGDOM COME

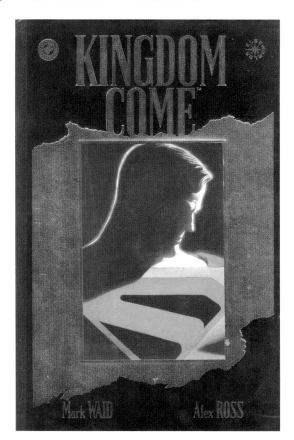

Plot: In a not-too-distant future, a morally corrupt new breed of superheroes, inspired by the hyper-violent (and now AWOL) Magog, has replaced the "old guard" of heroes. Superman, Wonder Woman, Green Lantern, and even Batman have gone underground. Spurred on by Wonder Woman, the self-exiled Superman is compelled to lead a resistance against the new generation, capturing and containing those who won't return to the straight and narrow. When Magog returns, who will prevail?

Review: Unlike Busiek and Ross's nostalgic Marvel epics, *Kingdom Come* looks to a possible future for its DC heroes. However, it's a future influenced by the then-common "grim and gritty" nature of superhero comics, and clearly Waid and Ross's sympathies lie with the old guard. That said, they create a tantalizing array of new characters with typically outlandish, yet photo-realistic, appearances. Half the fun for readers is trying to figure out just who these new heroes descend from or were inspired by. Even the old heroes get radical redesigns, perfect (of course) for a new line of action figures. As a possible destiny for the DC heroes, it continues to be fodder for debate among fans.

FURTHER READING: *Absolute Kingdom Come;*
Justice Volumes 1-3
SEE ALSO: *Marvels; Identity Crisis*

Writer: Michael Allred
Artist: Michael Allred

Publisher: Oni Press, 2002
ISBN: 1929998287

MADMAN: THE ODDITY ODYSSEY

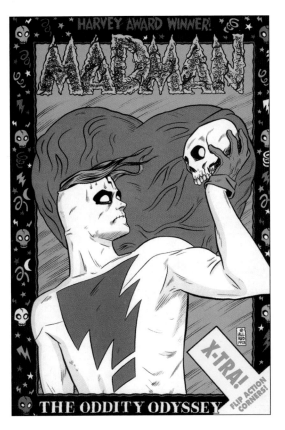

Plot: A mystery even to himself, Madman must race to find the elusive Dr. Flem so he can revive the frozen corpse of his mentor, Dr. Boiffard—the one man who may hold the key to his true identity. In the process, he must also locate and destroy Dr. Boiffard's journals to stop them from falling into the hands of the evil Mr. Monstadt. With only his trusty yoyo to protect himself, our hero battles injustice wherever he finds it, all the while pining for his love, Joe.

Review: Originally conceived as *The Spook*, and then briefly *The Goon*, *The Oddity Odyssey* reprints the first *Madman* series published by Tundra Press in 1992. Since then, *Madman* has been published by several companies, and it is interesting to see just how far the character of Frank Einstein has come

in the intervening years. Mike Allred's artwork, although very different from his more recent, cleaner work, is still distinctive, with the gray tone shading giving a noir feel to this debut. This sits in stark contrast to Laura Allred's bright colors that accentuate his later work on both *Madman* and *X-Force/X-Statix*. The storytelling occasionally gives *Madman* a dreamlike, surreal quality, just as the title suggests. Quirky and fun, *Madman* mixes genres, with zombies and clones sitting comfortably alongside humor and romance.

FURTHER READING: *Madman Gargantua; The Superman/Madman Hullabaloo!; X-Force: Famous; Mutant & Mortal; X-Statix Volume 1: Good Omens*
SEE ALSO: *Flaming Carrot Volume 3*

★
★ **Writer:** Matt Wagner   **Publisher:** Image Comics, 2004
★ **Artist:** Matt Wagner   **ISBN:** 158240609X

MAGE: THE HERO DEFINED VOLUME 2

Plot: Unwilling hero Kevin Matchstick takes on the role of the Pendragon and is forced to come to terms with the fact that he's reliving the Arthurian legend. Joined by a selection of heroic avatars (Hercules is a good ol' boy, The Monkey King a sour-faced Chinese waiter), old friends such as Mirth the wizard begin to worry that the power is going to his head.

Review: *Mage* is definitely a comic for card-carrying fantasy fans, and if it weren't for its willingness to recognize the ridiculous elements of the genre, it would be far too twee. However nerdy it gets, its sense of humor redeems it. Wagner's bold art, helped by Sam Keith's unfussy but elegant inks, is ultra-slick, with heavy backgrounds and clean action sequences. It may not be the cleverest comic around but it's delightful fantasy entertainment.

FURTHER READING: *Grendel*
SEE ALSO: *Elfquest Archives; Bone*

★
★ **Writer:** Archie Goodwin   **Publisher:** DC Comics, 1999
★ **Artist:** Walter Simonson   **ISBN:** 1563893746
★
★

MANHUNTER: THE SPECIAL EDITION

Plot: Brought back from the dead by the mysterious Council, Paul Kirk searches the world for clones of himself. Kirk makes it his mission to eradicate all his clones, and to bring down the Council once and for all.

Review: Collecting the multiple-award-winning short run of backup strips from *Detective Comics* in 1973 and 1974, Goodwin and Simonson's collaboration on *Manhunter* still holds up today. With the popularity of TV shows such as *24* it's easy to see why: *Manhunter* contains many of the plot twists, shadowy organizations, and stolen identities that still strike a chord with audiences today. This edition contains a new epilogue based on a plot by Goodwin and completed as a silent strip by Simonson after Goodwin's untimely death in 1998.

FURTHER READING: *Manhunter: Street Justice; Manhunter: Trial By Fire; Alien: The Illustrated Story*
SEE ALSO: *Thor Visionaries: Walter Simonson Volume 1; Nick Fury and Wolverine: The Scorpio Connection*

Writer: Pat Mills
Artist: Kevin O'Neill

Publisher: Titan Books, 2003
ISBN: 1840234520

MARSHAL LAW: FEAR AND LOATHING

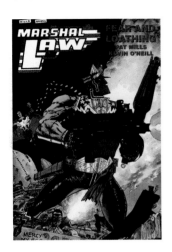

Plot: *Marshal Law* is set in a dark and broken future America, reeling from the aftermath of a vicious war with South America, a war it tried to win by employing superpowered soldiers. These soldiers have now returned home, and many have become superheroes. War veteran Marshal Law doesn't like superheroes very much, making him the ideal man to police them in the new city of San Futuro, built on the ashes of San Francisco.

Review: This is a wonderful piece of satire, outrageously violent, but very, very funny, poking fun at every superhero convention while remaining a gripping mystery. Mills is a master at this sort of story, having provided many of *2000 AD's* most enduring series, and contributes some very memorable lines. O'Neill's art is stunning, exaggerated to wonderful effect, with a superb rogues' gallery of characters. Certainly not for the squeamish, but recommended to anyone who likes their heroes with bite.

FURTHER READING: *Marshal Law: Blood, Sweat, and Fears; Marshal Law: Fear Asylum; Marshal Law: Day Of The Dead*
SEE ALSO: *The League Of Extraordinary Gentlemen*

Writer: Neil Gaiman
Artist: Andy Kubert; Richard Isanove

Publisher: Marvel, 2006
ISBN: 0785123113

MARVEL 1602

Plot: A strange anomaly has caused versions of the 1960s Marvel superheroes to exist in an Elizabethan past. The Queen's court physician, Doctor Stephen Strange, and her chief spy, Sir Nicholas Fury, confront dangers both political and cosmic. As the first child born in the Colonies, Virginia travels to England with her native American bodyguard Rojhaz and storms arise to threaten both humans and the enigmatic Witchbreed.

Review: *1602* was Gaiman's first project for Marvel Comics, bringing with it major expectations. The work received popular acclaim from the mainstream media, its epic scope and funhouse-mirrored view of the Marvel Universe enhanced by Kubert and Isanove's artwork.

FURTHER READING: *Marvel 1602: Fantastick Four*
SEE ALSO: *The League of Extraordinary Gentlemen*

★
★
★

Writer: Jack Cole
Artist: Jack Cole

Publisher: DC Comics, 1999
ISBN: 1563894688

A

THE PLASTIC MAN ARCHIVES, VOLUME 1

Plot: Plastic Man was once a crook called Patrick "Eel" O'Brian. During a robbery at the Crawford Chemical Works, Eel was shot and doused with an unidentified acid. He escaped, but passed out, only to awake in a monastery. He discovered that the acid had given him the ability to stretch and mold himself into any shape. Deciding to use his new abilities for good, he puts on a red-and-yellow costume and captures villains as Plastic Man.

Review: This volume reprints the first 20 issues of *Plastic Man* from *Police Comics*. These are unpredictable, surreal adventures full of humor and slapstick, despite the high body counts.

FURTHER READING: *The Plastic Man Archives, Volumes 2-8; The Classic Pin-Up Art of Jack Cole*
SEE ALSO: *Justice League: A New Beginning; Flaming Carrot*

★
★
★
★

Writer: Kyle Baker
Artist: Kyle Baker

Publisher: DC Comics, 2005
ISBN: 1401203434

A

PLASTIC MAN: ON THE LAM

Plot: Plastic Man flexes his way through a series of escapades which see him investigating his own dubious past life and ending up on the run from the law.

Review: It's rare, for some very good reasons, to find a graphic novel with a cover that actually smells of its lead character, as the plasticized ones on this book do. The emphasis on humor is fitting for Baker's interpretation of *Plastic Man*. It keeps to the spirit of Jack Cole's 1941 incarnation, with anarchic comedy that hits all its targets with the kind of cartoon intelligence only usually found in the best episodes of *The Simpsons* or Tex Avery's 1930s animation. Umbrage at Baker's cartoony art is pointless, because realism is not the key to the lampooning and satire that Baker captures here. And that's not stretching the point, either!

FURTHER READING: *Plastic Man: Rubber Bandits*
SEE ALSO: *Why I Hate Saturn; The Cowboy Wally Show*

Writer: Peter Milligan
Artist: Chris Bachalo

Publisher: Vertigo, 2003
ISBN: 140120046X

SHADE, THE CHANGING MAN: THE AMERICAN SCREAM

Plot: Shade, an otherworldly mind agent, comes to Earth to stop a psychic contagion known as "The Madness." However, he has to abandon his physical body and possess the body of a human—a serial killer who is about to be executed. Stranger still, Shade falls in with Kathy, the daughter of the killer's last victims.

Review: An unpredictable, disquieting revamp of Steve Ditko's *Shade* (1977–1978), laced with black humor, ultraviolence, and surprising tenderness. In these first six issues, Milligan's targets are obvious, but his complex, damaged characters are haunting. Bachalo's early work is rough but ambitious, using color holds and baroque layouts to match Milligan's hallucinatory scripting.

FURTHER READING: *Skreemer; X-Force, Volume 1: New Beginning*
SEE ALSO: *Human Target; Death The Hight Cost Of Living*

Writer: Bill Parker
Artist: C.C. Beck

Publisher: DC Comics, 1992
ISBN: 1563890534

SHAZAM! ARCHIVES, VOLUME 1

Plot: Billy Batson is a homeless 12-year-old boy who ekes out a living on the streets as a newsboy. One evening, a mysterious stranger leads him through a secret subway tunnel to the home of the wizard, Shazam. When Billy speaks the name of the wizard, magical lightning turns him into Captain Marvel, with the powers of six mythical heroes: the wisdom of Solomon; the strength of Hercules; the stamina of Atlas; the power of Zeus; the courage of Achilles; and the speed of Mercury.

Review: This volume contains stories from Fawcett's *Whiz Comics* 2–15, drawn in Beck's clean, clear art style. Captain Marvel was an instant success, earning him his own series and a "family" to rival Superman's.

FURTHER READING: *Shazam! Archives, Volumes 2–4; Shazam! Family Archives, Volume 1*
SEE ALSO: *Wonder Woman Archives*

★ **Writer:** Tom DeFalco **Publisher:** Marvel Comics, 2004
★ **Artist:** Pat Olliffe with Ron Frenz **ISBN:** 0785114416
★

A # SPIDER-GIRL VOLUME 1: LEGACY

Plot: High-school basketball star May "Mayday" Parker becomes a superhero after she develops spider-powers like her father, the retired Spider-Man. Besides battling new versions of the Green Goblin and Venom, she meets a new breed of villains—and heroes. But in her regular life she has bigger problems, like teenage relationships from Hell. And her parents, who are dead set against their little girl risking her life on a regular basis.

Review: Due to the fanaticism of its fans, *Spider-Girl* has survived several cancellation attempts. And it's not hard to see why the title inspires such devotion: along with its successor, *Amazing Spider-Girl*, this book puts the fun back into superhero comics. It reads like an updated take on the early Stan Lee/Steve Ditko *Spider-Man* comics. *Spider-Girl* balances action, melodrama, and humor nicely, never delving too deeply into the darker elements that have come to burden many contemporary superhero books.

FURTHER READING: *Amazing Spider-Girl Volume 1*
SEE ALSO: *Essential Spider-Man volume 2*

Writer: J.M. DeMatteis
Artist: Mike Zeck

Publisher: Marvel Comics, 2007
ISBN: 078512330X

SPIDER-MAN: KRAVEN'S LAST HUNT

Plot: Returning from his honeymoon with Mary Jane, Spider-Man is attacked by his old nemesis, Kraven the Hunter. But this time it's different: Kraven is dying, but he won't let himself pass away until he has not only defeated his greatest foe, but also become him. He shoots Spider-Man and buries him alive, then dons Spider-Man's costume and prowls the city. When Spider-Man recovers, he must face not only Kraven, but also Vermin, a crazed half-man, half-monster.

Review: This is some of the best writing to come from DeMatteis, who has crafted a tale that revolves around honor, obsession, and identity. The six chapters were always intended as a single, standalone tale. As a result, the tale has the coherence of a true graphic novel, while marking a definite finale to Kraven's personal saga.

FURTHER READING: *Spider-Man: The Black Costume Saga; Spider-Man; Torment*
SEE ALSO: *Spider-Girl Volume 1; Ultimate Spider-Man: Power And Responsibility*

★
★
★
★

Writer: James Robinson
Artist: Tony Harris

Publisher: DC Comics, 1996
ISBN: 1563892480

STARMAN: SINS OF THE FATHER

Plot: Opal City is the home of Ted Knight, the Starman, the World War II-era superhero who was a member of the Justice Society. Now he's retired, Knight's eldest son David has been training to take over the role. After years of preparation, he dons the costume, takes his first step into the air, and is immediately shot dead by an unknown sniper.

This starts a series of attacks on the Knight family, which forces youngest son Jack to assume the Starman role. A tattooed pop-culture addict, Jack's never been interested in the family legacy, but is now forced to face the children of his father's greatest enemy, with the help of his father and the mysterious Shade, an apparently reformed adversary of from Dad's past. As he learns to become a hero, he will learn more about himself, the legacy of the Starman name, and his estranged brother.

Review: Robinson and Harris both made their names on this book, and their obvious passion for the characters shines through on every page. Jack Knight is a brilliant creation, a flawed but extremely stylish hero who grows into the role thrust upon him in a totally believable way. Robinson's script crackles with imagination, and Tony Harris's stark, noir-ish artwork is equally apt in both action scenes and quieter moments. One of the finest mainstream superhero books ever published.

FURTHER READING: *Starman: Night & Day; Starman: Times Past; Starman: A Wicked Inclination*
SEE ALSO: *Ex Machina; Astro City; Crisis On Multiple Earths; Crisis on Infinite Earths*

Writer: Dan Jurgens, Jerry Ordway, Louise Simonson, and Roger Stern

Artist: Jon Bogdanove, Tom Grummett, Jackson Guice, and Jerry Ordway

Publisher: DC Comics, 1993
ISBN: 1563890976

SUPERMAN: THE DEATH OF SUPERMAN

Plot: Doomsday, a mysterious and incredibly powerful creature, tears a destructive path across America, heading straight for Metropolis. Along the way, it defeats the Justice League of America with one hand tied behind its back (literally!). In this battle to the death, Superman does all he can to stop Doomsday; but the more they fight, the stronger the creature becomes. Will Superman survive? The book's title is a bit of a giveaway.

Review: A media sensation when it first was serialized across four *Superman* titles (and one issue of *Justice League of America*), *The Death of Superman* was an attempt by DC Comics to show that the "big blue Boy Scout" was indeed their most important character. And it succeeded, at least

financially, with the books selling record numbers. By using Doomsday, an unknown menace, the story caused confusion and suspense for everyone, readers as well as characters. As the danger increased, the pages used fewer panels—by the last chapter, every page was a full panel, and you can feel the punches and see every detail of the destruction. Even though that final issue came complete with a black funeral armband, fans knew their hero would return—eventually.

FURTHER READING: *World without a Superman;*
The Return of Superman
SEE ALSO: *Superman: Man Of Steel;*
Kingdom Come; Identity Crisis

★
★
★
★

Writer: John Byrne
Artist: John Byrne and Dick Giordano

Publisher: DC Comics, 1991
ISBN: 0930289285

A

SUPERMAN: THE MAN OF STEEL

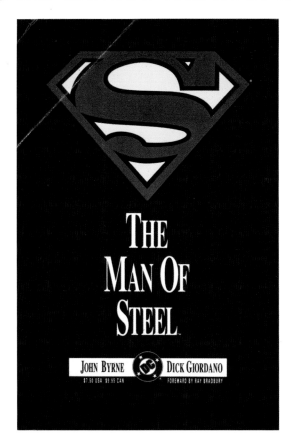

Plot: After 50 years of stories, Superman's history gets rebuilt from the ground up. Rocketed to Earth as a gestating fetus, baby Kal-El is found by the kindly couple Jonathan and Martha Kent, who raise him as their son, Clark. The boy gradually develops powers far beyond those of mortal men, and chooses to perform his deeds of derring-do as Superman. He falls for reporter Lois Lane, joins the staff of The Daily Planet, falls foul of business mogul Lex Luthor, encounters a suspicious Batman, and learns of his Kryptonian heritage.

Review: John Byrne, already a superstar for his art on Marvel's X-Men, was hired by DC Comics to breathe new life into their most iconic character. Taking some of his cues from Superman: The Movie Byrne recast Krypton as a cold and scientific society, and the Superman he drew bore more than a passing resemblance to Christopher Reeve. Byrne stripped away every bit of Superman's convoluted history and crowded cast of characters, presenting a new "Superman for the Eighties." This new start allowed writers and artists to move in unexpected directions, and to reimagine old concepts in new ways (Lex Luthor with hair!).

FURTHER READING: *Superman: Man For All Seasons;*
Superman / Batman: Enemies Among Us
SEE ALSO: *The Death of Superman*

Writer: Alan Moore
Artist: Joe Bennett and Rick Veitch

Publisher: Checker, 2002
ISBN: 0971024952

SUPREME: THE STORY OF THE YEAR

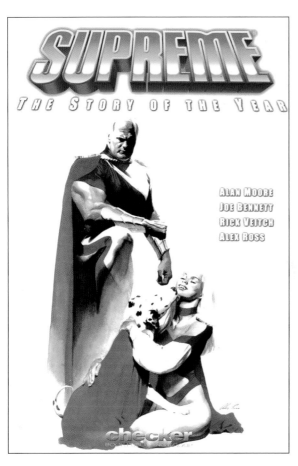

Plot: Omniman cartoonist Ethan Crane is also Supreme, an ultra-powerful superhero. When he discovers that he is only one of many incarnations of the hero, he is transported back to an Earth and a past he doesn't entirely remember. Together with an ever-growing cast of heroes, Supreme must confront the legacy of his most fearsome enemy, Darius Dax.

Review: Alan Moore transformed a violent and undistinguished Superman knockoff into a loving homage in this most "meta-" of superhero narratives. A superhero book about superheroes, Moore constructs an elaborate history for Supreme, conveyed brilliantly through faux flashbacks drawn by the talented Rick Veitch. This collection earned Moore an Eisner Award in 1997 for Best Writer.

FURTHER READING: *Supreme: The Return*
SEE ALSO: *Watchmen; Top Ten; The League of Extraordinary Gentlemen*

★
★
★
★

Writer: Walter Simonson
Artist: Walter Simonson

Publisher: Graphitti Designs, 2001
ISBN: 0785107584

A

THOR VISIONARIES:
WALTER SIMONSON VOLUME 1

Plot: When lame Dr. Donald Blake strikes his cane upon the ground, the cane becomes the mighty hammer Mjolnir, and Blake's true self is revealed: Thor, the Norse god of thunder! Seemingly invulnerable, Thor finally meets his match while fighting with an alien being, the improbably named Beta-Ray Bill, and loses control of Mjolnir, reverting him to his human self. Incredibly, Bill discovers that he too, can wield the hammer, and gains the power of thunder.

Reviews: When Walt Simonson took over *Thor* as writer and artist in 1983, the title soared to heights not seen since the book's Stan Lee/Jack Kirby epics almost two decades earlier. He applied his knowledge of Norse mythology generously throughout the book, augmenting Kirby's already fantastical design of Asgard and other godly realms with more authentic detail, and enriching his storylines with deep parallels to the earlier stories.

FURTHER READING: *Thor Visionaries: Walter Simonson Volumes 2-4*
SEE ALSO: *Ultimates; Avengers: Kree-Skrull War*

★
★
★

Writer: Kurt Busiek with Peter David
Artist: Mark Bagley and various

Publisher: Marvel, 2001
ISBN: 0785108173

THUNDERBOLTS:
JUSTICE LIKE LIGHTNING

Plot: After most of the major heroes in the Marvel Universe vanish into an alternate universe, a new team, the Thunderbolts, appear to fill the gap left by the Avengers. Led by the heroic Citizen V, they swiftly stop a rampaging Hulk, but in a strange twist, they're revealed as the Masters of Evil, scheming to take over the world. Having tasted the glory of heroism, however, not all of them are willing to return to their villainous ways.

Review: The twist works very well, and Busiek gives these second-rate supervillains some real personality, in a very old-school way. Bagley is also very good at what he does—non-flashy superheroics, told well. There's nothing too groundbreaking here, but it's solid, superior, mainstream superhero work.

FURTHER READING: *New Thunderbolts: One Step Forward;*
SEE ALSO: *Astro City: Life In The Big City; Civil War*

Writer: Alan Moore
Artist: Gene Ha

Publisher: Wildstorm, 2001
ISBN: 1563896680

TOP TEN BOOK 1

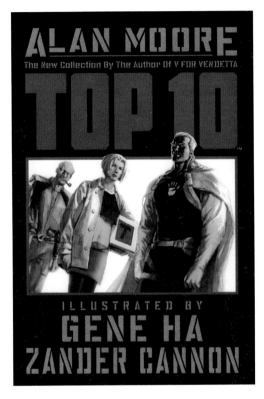

Plot: Rookie cop Robin Slinger is about to start her first day on the job. She's just joined the ranks of the Neopolis Police Department, in a city where everyone, from beggar to banker, has superpowers. She's inherited a box of weapon-infused toys from her ex-hero father, and joins the ranks of Precinct Ten, the only all-superpowered precinct in the city. Her fellow officers include devil worshippers, trolls, psychics, and a dog in a robotic body, and are led by an iconic ex-hero. Slinger and her new colleagues face drugs, prostitution, murder, domestic assault, and every other inner-city problem, but these are made infinitely worse when their suspects include aliens, robots, and gods. Even the mice have formed superteams...

Review: What could so easily have been a clichéd mess becomes one of the finest superhero books on the market in these skilled hands. Alan Moore is a master of making the incredible seem absolutely plausible, and the characterization and dialog is as authentic as any HBO TV show. He conveys the darkness of police life, with a wonderful thread of pitch-black humor running through it, and every potential cliché is teased into something new. Gene Ha's astonishingly detailed artwork is absolutely teeming with tiny little in-jokes and visual gags. *Top Ten* is aptly named—a more intelligent and imaginative crime book would be hard to find.

FURTHER READING: *Top Ten Book 2; Top Ten: The Forty-Niners; Top Ten: Beyond the Farthest Precinct*
SEE ALSO: *Promethea; The League Of Extraordinary Gentlemen; Watchmen*

★
★ **Writer:** Brian Bendis
★ **Artist:** Mark Bagley

Publisher: Marvel Comics, 2002
ISBN: 190415901X

Publisher: Marvel Comics, 2002
ISBN: 190415901X

A ULTIMATE SPIDER-MAN VOLUME 1: POWER AND RESPONSIBILITY

Plot: A new Spider-Man for a new millennium. From the spider's bite to his Uncle Ben's death, high-school kid Peter Parker tries to deal with a life of disappointment and tragedy. At least he has his best friend, Mary Jane, to help him along the way. A multi-issue re-telling of the first, 11-page *Spider-Man* story from 1962.

Review: Understanding that 40 years' worth of stories were making comic books difficult for new readers to follow, Marvel began an experimental line of books to re-introduce their characters to a new, younger readership in 2000. *Ultimate Spider-Man* was the first of the bunch, and it was a runaway success. Bendis, known for writing small-press crime comics, dug into his fanboy past and assembled familiar Spider-elements into fresh, new plots, while Bagley—initially reluctant to return to drawing *Spider-Man*— rose to the challenge, providing energy and storytelling chops. Their run as writer and artist eventually surpassed Lee and Kirby's run on the *Fantastic Four*, a testament to their popularity among readers both new and old.

FURTHER READING: *Spider-Man: Birth of Venom; Spider-Man: The Black Costume Saga*
SEE ALSO: *The Ultimates; Essential Spider-Man Vol 2*

Writer: Chris Claremont
Artist: Frank Miller

Publisher: Marvel Comics, 2001
ISBN: 087135277X

WOLVERINE

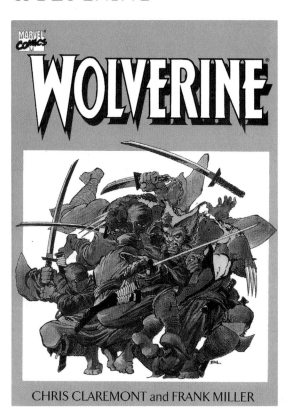

CHRIS CLAREMONT and FRANK MILLER

Plot: Wolverine, a former secret agent who's become a member of the X-Men, journeys to Japan when the love of his life, Mariko—who's also the head of one of the country's most powerful clans—cuts off all communication with him. When he arrives, Wolverine is stunned to learn that Mariko has undergone a forced marriage to settle a debt owed by her recently returned father, who's taken over as head of the family and has designs on running the Japanese underworld. Wolverine fights off all manner of death-dealing ninjas, as well as a duplicitous would-be lover and assassin named Yukio, before he can take on Mariko's father, regaining his honor—and Mariko.

Review: Originally a four-part miniseries for Marvel in 1982, the story was first devised when Claremont and Miller were traveling back from the San Diego Comic Convention. The idea was to take the violent, killing-machine character of Wolverine and give him some humanity, exploring what really makes him tick. Claremont's script is tight and hardly a word is wasted as complex issues such as loyalty, honor, and the Samurai code of Bushido are cleverly examined, while Miller's artwork flits between the brooding men-in-tights superheroics of his gritty run on *Daredevil* and the noir style he later employed in the *Sin City* series.

FURTHER READING: *Wolverine: Origin; Weapon X*
SEE ALSO: *X-Men: Dark Phoenix Saga; Daredevil: The Omnibus Companion*

★
★
★
★

Writer: William Moulton Marston
Artist: H.G. Peter

Publisher: DC Comics, 1998
ISBN: 1563894025

A

WONDER WOMAN ARCHIVES: VOLUME 1

Plot: Diana Prince is the Amazon in America, championing the fight against the invading German forces during World War II. She won her right to fight alongside mortals during a competition with her peers, and was bestowed with Amazon concentration. With her truth-inducing lasso and her bullet-deflecting bracelets, she becomes the ambassador to the "world of man."

Review: This collection starts the saga of Wonder Woman in her original World War II setting. Diana Prince was probably the first major female character to appear in comics—created by Dr. William Marston, a respected psychologist in his day, she was a reaction against the ubiquitous male stereotype, and *Wonder Woman* soon became a permanent fixture as a female role model for children.

FURTHER READING: *Wonder Woman Archives: Volume 2;*
Batman / Superman / Wonder Woman: Trinity
SEE ALSO: *Wonder Woman: Gods And Mortals*

★
★
★

Writer: George Perez, Greg Potter, Len Wein
Artist: George Perez

Publisher: DC Comics, 2004
ISBN: 1401201970

A

WONDER WOMAN VOLUME 1: GODS AND MORTALS

Plot: This volume re-establishes the origin of Diana (Wonder Woman) as the daughter of Amazon queen, Hippolyta, who is gifted with powers from her patron goddesses. Her first adventure, calls for her to prevent the war god, Ares, and his sons, Deimos and Phobos, from triggering a nuclear holocaust. Speaking only ancient Greek, Diana must also learn English with the help of new characters Julia Kapatelis, and her daughter Vanessa.

Review: This volume collects the first seven issues of the relaunch of the *Wonder Woman* title after DC's *Crisis on Infinite Earths*. This version of the character is linked far more closely to the Greek myths, creating a rich history from which to draw inspiration—all drawn with flair by Perez.

FURTHER READING: *Wonder Woman Volumes 2–4;*
Wonder Woman: Greatest Stories Ever Told
SEE ALSO: *Wonder Woman Archives;*
All Star Comics Archives Volume 1

Writer: Chris Claremont
Artist: John Byrne, Terry Austin
Publisher: Marvel Comics, 2006
ISBN: 0785122133

X-MEN: THE DARK PHOENIX SAGA

Plot: During a routine mission to establish contact with two newly discovered mutants, the X-Men learn of the existence of the Hellfire Club, a mysterious group bent on world domination. The team of heroes infiltrate the Hellfire Club, who turn out to be superhuman mutants themselves. A battle ensues, which the X-Men ultimately win, but, in the aftermath of the battle, the team's strongest member, Phoenix, loses control of her powers and is transformed into the malevolent, all-powerful Dark Phoenix. As her powers increase and events threaten to spiral out of control, external forces become involved in a mission to stop Dark Phoenix, while the X-Men are torn between their desire to save a teammate and their duty to safeguard mankind.

Review: Almost 30 years after its original publication, *The Dark Phoenix Saga* has aged remarkably well. The script and artwork are undeniably strong—Claremont and Byrne were at the height of their powers here—but what's really striking is the strength of characterization in the book. The creative team developed a cast that readers, over time, came to know and care for. On top of this solid foundation they laid a gripping storyline that saw the beleaguered X-Men constantly under attack and stretched to their limits.

FURTHER READING: *X-Men: Days of Future Past; X-Men: Phoenix Rising; Essential X-Men Volume 1*
SEE ALSO: *Astonishing X-Men: Gifted; Buffy The Vampire Slayer: The Long Way Home*

CHAPTER 10

WAR

WAR: WHAT IS IT GOOD FOR?

The war story has remained consistently popular throughout the history of comics. Used as propaganda, both pro- and anti-war, as well as providing the setting for less overtly political tales of combat and adventure, war comics have run the gamut of fact and fiction with stories designed to inspire and excite, inform and entertain.

You don't have to look any further for proof of war comics' perennial popularity than Britain's *Commando*, which publishes a staggering eight issues per month. Launched in 1961, *Commando* has achieved something that Hitler and the Axis powers never managed: making World War II last for 46 years (and counting...).

Not that World War II has the monopoly on settings for war comics. Film director and comics auteur Frank Miller's epic *300*, recently adapted into a film of the same name, travels back in time to 480 BC and the battle of Thermopylae—an encounter that pitted only 300 Spartans against the might of the Persian army under King Xerxes the Great. A tale he had loved since childhood, Miller's retelling is a work of passion, rendered in highly stylized art and told in large, lavish panels. It's spectacular and, with its focus on muscular, semi-naked men with their rigorous codes of masculinity, more than a little camp. Miller's *300* is undoubtedly a beautiful work of art, but it feels remote from the real brutality of war.

The reverse is true of *Charley's War*, by Pat Mills and Joe Colquhoun, a tale of doomed and idealistic youth among the trenches of the World War I. An unusual book, *Charley's War* used the documented experience of soldiers in the field as its inspiration in an effort to convey some of the real horrors of the trenches.

Keiji Nakazawa's *Barefoot Gen* draws heavily on the author's experiences of his life in Hiroshima, both before the atomic bomb and after. It is a fictional narrative, but has the veracious and authentic feel of non-fiction. The focus is not on the art of war, but on the violence it wreaks on civilian populations; the melted faces, brutalized bodies, and mysterious illnesses that follow conflict.

A companion piece of sorts is Raymond Briggs's *When the Wind Blows*. Most famous as a children's illustrator, here Briggs imagines what a nuclear strike on early 1980s Britain might have produced. Starring Jim and Hilda Bloggs, a warm, loving, elderly couple based on Briggs's own parents, we are forced to watch as they survive the initial nuclear strike, but slowly fall apart before our eyes—victims of a weapon, and a conflict, they cannot comprehend.

Joe Kubert, one of comics' elder statesmen, has a long history in the field of war comics; he, along with writer Robert Kanigher, was one of the defining creators behind DC's iconic soldier *Sgt. Rock*, a character who felt little affinity with the war, but was fiercely loyal to his fellow troops. In his later years, Kubert bridged the gap between fiction and non-fiction with two more standout works. *Fax from Sarajevo* was a collaboration born out of the experiences of his friend, the European comics agent Ervin Rustemagi, who was trapped during the Siege of Sarajevo and only able to communicate with the outside world via his fax machine. An even more intimate work is Kubert's own *Yossel*. Born in Poland in 1926, Kubert and his family emigrated to the USA shortly after his birth, escaping the devastation and genocide that was to ravage Poland. *Yossel* is the cartoonist's haunting speculation about the life he so narrowly escaped.

When it comes to war reporting in comics, the cartoonist who has made the subject his own is Joe Sacco. Coming from a background in journalism,

Sacco's breakthrough success was his documentary on life in Palestine, simply entitled *Palestine*. Sacco went on to document his experiences in the wake of the conflicts in the former Yugoslavia: *Safe Area Goražde* chronicles how the UN-designated "safe areas" were often anything but, while *The Fixer* offers a portrait of Nevin, a man who serves as a translator, guide, and facilitator for journalists looking to find their inside story.

The ongoing "war on terror" has prompted a new wave of war comics, bringing different approaches and breathing fresh life into the genre. First, there was *The 9/11 Report*. Initially published as a standard 568-page report into the events and circumstances leading up to the terrorist attack of September 11, the document was rendered in a more accessible, efficient, and effective 144-page graphic novel form by Sid Jacobson and Ernie Colon.

Later, in the wake of the subsequent US-led invasion of Iraq, came another unusual and attention-grabbing graphic novel, Brian K. Vaughan and Niko Henrichon's *Pride of Baghdad*. Based on a true story, the stars of the piece aren't soldiers or civilians, or even humans at all, but the animals of Baghdad Zoo—particularly its lions, led by the alpha male, Zill. What follows among the animals is a discussion of freedom and an allegorical allusion to the choices that remained open to the population of Baghdad in the days following the removal of Saddam Hussein.

New works continue to emerge, including *Iraq: Operation Corporate Takeover*, Sean Michael Wilson and Lee O'Connor's examination of how Western companies have profited from the Iraq war, and *Shooting War*, Anthony Lappé and Dan Goldman's plausible vision of a war on terror that is still going strong in 2011. While conflicts are still raging across the globe, war comics will thrive.

TOP 10 WAR GRAPHIC NOVELS

★
★ **Writer:** Sid Jacobson   **Publisher:** Hill and Wang, 2006
★ **Artist:** Ernie Colón   **ISBN:** 0670916730
★

15+

THE 9/11 REPORT:
A GRAPHIC ADAPTATION

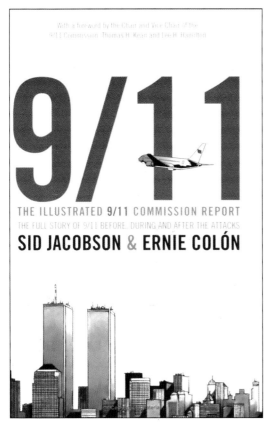

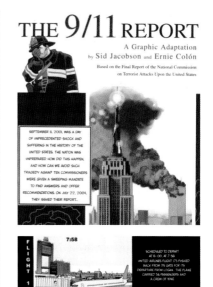

Plot: This graphic novel begins with a foreword from Thomas H. Kean and Lee H. Hamilton, the Chair and the Vice Chair of the 9/11 Commission. The graphic novel itself is divided into 13 chapters and begins with a chapter entitled *We Have Some Planes....*

This is a timeline charting the events from 8.00am on the morning of September 11, 2001, and it follows the fate of the four hijacked planes, the impact of two of them on the Twin Towers, one on the Pentagon, and one that never made its intended target of either the Capitol Building or the White House in Washington DC. The following five chapters examine the events that took place before this dramatic day—the foundation and emergence of the new threat of Al Qaeda, coupled with the evolution of US counter-terrorism. Chapters 7–10 chronicle the escalation of the 9/11 plot—including the training of the hijackers—before moving onto the attacks themselves and the US government's response to these attacks. Chapters 11–13 discuss the 9/11 Commission's recommendations on how future US governments could prevent a similar attack, and how they could be better prepared to tackle such a situation.

Review: The official *US Government 9/11 Report* comes in at 568 pages, and comprehensive as this may seem, its critics still claim it contained many omissions as well as being more than a little "flexible" with the truth. The graphic-novel version condenses the report into 130 pages, so a similar charge could also be leveled at this book—especially when the introduction by Kean and Hamilton tries to present it as the true story of "one of the most important and tragic events" in American history. But if you accept this report as one possible version of the truth, it's a gripping read. Writer Sid Jacobson does a sterling job of organizing his research and bringing order to the narrative, while artist Ernie Colón brings all the characters and events to life with a quiet dignity that imaginatively utilizes the different settings and employs clever graphic devices to maintain visual interest.

FURTHER READING: *Battlestar Galactica: Saga Of A Star World; Bruce Coville's Shapeshifters*
SEE ALSO: *Cancer Vixen; Last Day In Vietnam; When The Wind Blows*

★
★
★
★

Writer: Frank Miller
Artist: Frank Miller, Lynn Varley

Publisher: Dark Horse, 1999
ISBN: 1569714029

15+ # 300

Plot: *300* is an account of the battle of Thermopylae, in which the Spartan King, Leonidas, assembles a small army to protect Greece from the massed ranks of the invading Persian forces. When the Persian leader, Xerxes, offers the Greeks self-governance in return for ultimate submission, he is dismissed outright and war is declared.

Despite the ruling of the corrupt priests of Sparta, Leonidas sets off to war, taking with him a mere 300 warriors. Their numbers are soon swelled by the addition of soldiers from other regions, but even their combined army of around 7,000 men is nothing compared to the estimated 200,000 of the mighty Persians. Leonidas reasons that the battle can be won only if the Greeks have a superior tactical position and proceeds to advance north to Thermopylae (literally the

"Hot Gates"), a narrow mountain path that will channel the forces of the opposing army, reducing the effectiveness of their attack. However, the Spartans' plan is undone when they are betrayed by one of their own, Ephialtes, who tells the Persians of a secret mountain path that runs behind Leonidas' army. When the Greeks learn of their weakened position, many of them retreat, leaving only the 300 Spartan warriors of the title to fight a final, bloody battle in defence of their country.

Review: Readers seeking an historically accurate version of events should look elsewhere. Nor should they expect much in terms of characterization in a work that is essentially the comic-book equivalent of an action movie (fittingly, *300* was adapted for film in 2007). With the focus solely on the events

ESSENTIAL
GRAPHIC NOVELS

500

483

WAR

Top 10 war graphic novels

surrounding the battle there is little room for character development, and ultimately, it's impossible to feel any real sympathy for any of the protagonists.

However, viewed as an exercise in visual entertainment, *300* is a resounding success. Miller's artwork continues to impress, and in a welcome departure from the chiaroscuro style he so effectively employed in *Sin City*, the book features full-color artwork throughout. Yes, the deep shadows of the *Sin City* books are there in abundance, but here they are augmented by Lynn Varley's excellent color work. Varley, who brought so much to Miller's *The Dark Knight Returns*, creates a wonderfully evocative atmosphere, her subdued palette of yellows, ochres, and browns conjuring up the dusty heat of battle. Similarly, a change in format has improved the work immeasurably, and

this omnibus edition benefits from a landscape format, allowing the double-page spreads of the original comics to sit on a single page as Miller had originally intended.

Epic in scope and high on action, *300* will appeal to all those who require nothing more demanding than a glorious blood-soaked battle sustained over the course of 88 pages.

FURTHER READING: *Sin City: A Dame To Kill For*
SEE ALSO: *Age of Bronze; Dark Knight Returns*

★
★
★
★
★

Writer: Keiji Nakazawa
Artist: Keiji Nakazawa

Publisher: Last Gasp, 2004
ISBN: 0867196025

BAREFOOT GEN VOLUME 1: A CARTOON STORY OF HIROSHIMA

Plot: Drawing on his own experiences as a seven-year-old in Hiroshima when the atomic bomb was dropped, Keiji Nakazawa sets out, gently and persuasively, without preaching, to use the comic book as a medium to make sure such an atrocity never happens again. Following on from the success of his initial short strip about Hiroshima called *I Saw It*, *Barefoot Gen* is a huge body of work. Volume 1 is chiefly concerned with introducing us to Gen; his formidable mother, who struggles to cope with the privations of life during wartime; and the rest of his family and neighbors. Plenty of time is spent getting to know their quirks and personalities, giving the reader a huge emotional investment in their fate.

Review: Nakazawa's drawing brings out the simplicity and the straightforwardness of many of the people we meet. The story demonizes no one. Instead, it concentrates on showing us everyday life in the city during the war, exploring the Japanese mindset, and giving us a peek at domestic life and the concerns of a small child. He continues to show these small and touching details after the bomb has dropped, after he's shocked us with the death and destruction, and demonstrated the heartlessness of some citizens toward their sick and dying brethren. *Barefoot Gen* is unflinching, but ultimately more powerful for its moments of humor and its very ordinary take on one of the most momentous events of the 20th century.

It's strange to think of a Hiroshima survivor's story being joyful, but by filtering it through the awareness of a seven-year-old, who doesn't always understand what he is witnessing, that's exactly what it is. Nakazawa uses the child's optimism (or blind faith) for any given situation, enabling him to focus on the small, personal victories won by survivors in the immediate aftermath of the bomb—even if some of these temporary triumphs seem very hollow, considering how radiation-sick the walking wounded are soon to become.

Barefoot Gen mourns the dead, but also celebrates them in simple prose and softly drawn, often rounded, figures. Too much detail would almost be overkill: Nakazawa's drawing style is effective but quite cartoony, and it spares us the graphic details because, quite frankly, they aren't necessary to get the point across.

FURTHER READING: *I Saw It: The Atomic Bombing Of Hiroshima, A Survivor's True Story*
SEE ALSO: *Palestine; Persepolis; Safe Area Goražde; When The Wind Blows*

★
★
★
★
★

Writer: Pat Mills **Publisher:** Titan Books, 2005
Artist: Joe Colquhoun **ISBN:** 1840236272

CHARLEY'S WAR:
2 JUNE–1 AUGUST 1916

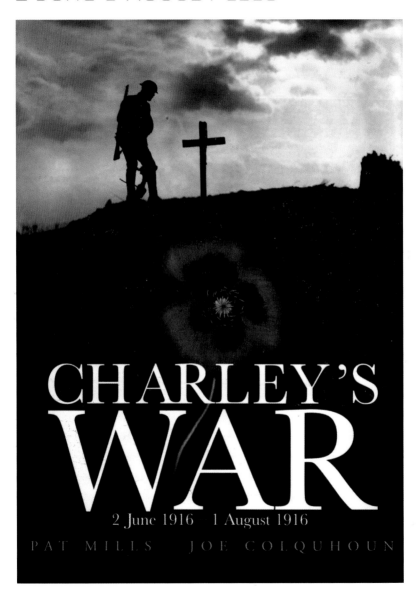

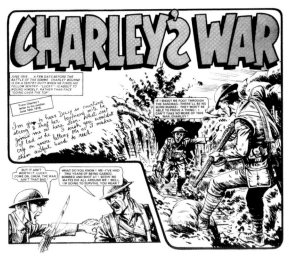

Plot: It is 1916, and 16-year-old Charley Bourne volunteers for the British Army. Despite being two years too young, he is accepted and after minimal training is sent to France. He discovers that life in the frontline trenches is very different than the way it is portrayed to the public—plagued by rats, flooding, and lack of food. Initial small-scale attacks against the German positions are only the precursor to the all-out attack on July 1—the devastating Battle of the Somme.

Review: *Charley's War* began in the weekly comic *Battle Action* in 1979, and this book reprints the first 29 weeks of the strip. Pat Mills's deeply researched stories and Joe Colquhoun's detailed artwork proved so well matched and so popular that the final two years of World War I ran for five years in the comic. Charley would continue to fight beyond the end of the Great War into the Russian War, eventually returning to France with the British Expeditionary Force at the beginning of World War II.

The early stories collected here show the horror of war through the eyes of the young and inexperienced Charley, his upbeat letters home contrasting with the grim reality of his daily existence. These bittersweet tales of trench warfare pull no punches in describing the dreadful living conditions, the futility of what the characters are ordered to do, and the

loss of life—all of which take their physical and mental toll on Charley and his friends. NCOs such as Charley's Sergeant, Old Bill, look after their men, but good officers die by leading from the front, while the bad officers, such as the sniveling Lieutenant Snell, survive by avoiding the fight. The combat, when it happens, is short, sharp, vicious, and often hand to hand, and the stories constantly remind you that whatever is happening to the characters, death is always a heartbeat away, and shows how the troops coped, or often didn't cope, with this grim reality.

In addition to the original stories, this book includes short articles on the background to the conflict, putting the stories into their historical perspective, and a commentary on each story by the original writer, Pat Mills. From the poignant photographic cover with its single red poppy, to the photographs of British soldiers from the Somme at the back, this is a magnificent publication and a benchmark of quality for graphic-novel reissues of weekly comic strips.

FURTHER READING: *Charley's War: 1 August–17 October 1916; Charley's War: Blue's Story; Life In Picture: Autobiographical Stories*
SEE ALSO: *War Stories; Adventures In The Rifle Brigade*

★
★
★
★
★

Writer: Joe Sacco
Artist: Joe Sacco

Publisher: Drawn & Quarterly, 2003
ISBN: 0224073826

15+

THE FIXER: A STORY FROM SARAJEVO

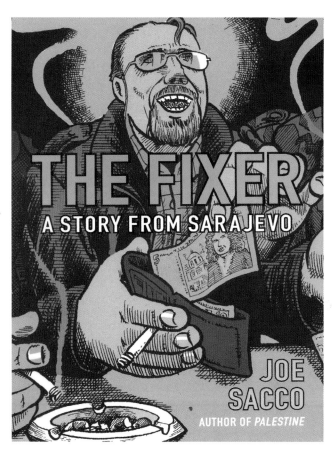

Plot: This is a portrait of a fixer—the journalist's best, and most important, friend—in the dying days of the Balkan wars of the early to mid-1990s. Joe Sacco has made a career in the field of documentary comics set in conflict zones. He first made his name on *Palestine* before moving on to the conflict in the Balkans, documenting life in one of the UN-declared "Safe Areas" in *Safe Area Goražde*. But the Balkan conflict was larger than one book...

Review: Like all wars, the conflict in the Balkans sucked in a great·many people, each with a story to tell. What we discover here is the vital role that the fixer plays for the

journalist as the gateway to those stories. He has the local knowledge, knows the human tragedy of his neighbors, and will persuade them to expose their pain. He also knows how to procure things in a war zone—from whisky and women, to tape recorders and other tools of the journalist's trade. A fixer is, first and foremost, a businessman, making a living from what he knows, making sure that he gives away only what deems justified by the payment he receives.

The fixer in this tale is a man called Nevin, a man who might have lived a very different life without the war. Like Sacco himself, we hear the story of Sarajevo through Nevin. The

ESSENTIAL
GRAPHIC NOVELS

500

489

WAR

Top 10 war graphic novels

details of Nevin's colorful life and his numerous brushes with hard men and criminals, both before and during the war, bring the Balkan conflict to life more than any mundane news report ever could.

In this book, it becomes obvious that Sacco has grown as both an artist and a documentary maker. This is not a collection of hasty impressions, as *Palestine* often seems to be, but detailed memories condensed, distilled, refined, and retold as an engaging narrative. The images stay with you: the dense crosshatching for the gloom of the Holiday Inn lobby and the bars of Sarajevo; the double-page view of the

route to the Sarajevo Holiday Inn, next to a burned-out tower block—an image recalled later when we see the same building at the start of the war. The Sarajevo Nevin depicts is a solid, real place, filled with people and stories. All these stories are available from the fixer—for a price.

FURTHER READING: *But I Like It; War's End*
SEE ALSO: *Palestine; Safe Area Gorazde; Persepolis*

★
★
★
★
★

Writer: Will Eisner   **Publisher:** Dark Horse, 2000
Artist: Will Eisner   **ISBN:** 1569715009

LAST DAY IN VIETNAM

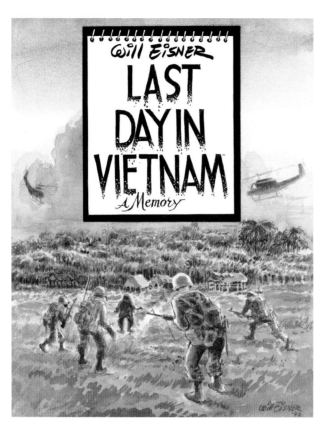

Plot: Eisner was stationed in Seoul, South Korea, in 1954 and Saigon in 1967—both times as a civilian contractor, supplying military guidance manuals in the form of comic books. *Last Day in Vietnam* contains six stories covering the conflicts and the short time Eisner spent in boot camp.

Review: The opening story involves a deskbound major, addressing the reader directly, as Eisner's guide. The themes of military overconfidence, the illusion of control, and the reality of fear quickly surface. Everything seems light and jolly but Eisner's incisive script suggests the truth behind the officer's words. In *The Periphery*, a Vietnamese guide gives a revealing account of how the Western world's media glorifies the war, knowing that boys' own adventure stories,

complete with depictions of technological superiority, will sell newspapers to eager readers back home while ignoring the personal tragedies of the conflict.

The Casualty wordlessly depicts how a US Marine never seems to learn from mistakes, falling for the same seductive and near-fatal booby trap every time, while *A Dull Day In Korea* chillingly shows a bored soldier deciding to liven up his day by shooting civilians. The antidote to this comes in the form of *Hard Duty*—short, touching, but poignant. A *Purple Heart For George* rounds off the collection, with soldiers trying to save an unfit soldier from transferring himself to the front line, only to fail and see him killed in action, then honored with a meaningless medal.

ESSENTIAL
GRAPHIC NOVELS

500

491

WAR

Top 10 war graphic novels

A lesser author may have resorted either to jingoism or didactic posturing, depending on their political persuasion. Eisner, however, intelligently allows his stories and characters to speak for themselves. He dispenses with the rigid, formulaic layout usually associated with comic books, allowing each borderless panel to flow into the next, which brings a sense of realism to his narrative.

FURTHER READING: *A Life Force; Comics & Sequential Art; Graphic Storytelling; Life In Pictures: Autobiographical Tales*
SEE ALSO: *Two-Fisted Tales; A Contract With God; The Best Of The Spirit*

★
★ **Writer:** Joe Sacco
★ **Artist:** Joe Sacco
★

Publisher: Fantagraphics, 2007
ISBN: 0224069829

18+ # PALESTINE

Plot: *Palestine* is a journal of Sacco's visit to Israel and the occupied territories of Palestine, told chronologically from the day of his arrival to the moment of his departure. He combines eyewitness reportage with illustrated footage of his interviews, giving a voice to the residents who endure the boredom, privation, and day-to-day minutiae of oppression in an occupied country. When presenting his interviews, Sacco usually lets his subject take over the narrative and the panels show the story from their perspective. As the story unfolds Sacco becomes less and less detached from the situation he is documenting and is drawn into the lives of the people he interviews, taking part in demonstrations, attending funerals, and encountering Israeli soldiers. Later he even shares food and lodgings with the Palestinians and takes great risks by breaking the curfew in the Gaza Strip.

Review: In December 1991 cartoonist Joe Sacco journeyed to the Gaza Strip and the West Bank to conduct over 100 interviews with Israeli and Palestinian residents, and to record his experiences. In doing so he almost single-handedly invented a new genre—comic-book journalism.

Sacco had already developed an interest in the Middle East and his previous comic series, *Yahoo*, had dealt with the first Gulf War. The results of the two months he spent in occupied

Palestine and Israel were published between 1993 and 2001 in a series of comics, which have since been collected into several editions. In 1996, the Columbus Foundation gave the first collection an American Book Award.

Palestine also explores the historical background of the conflict, taking a non-partisan approach to the sensitive subject matter. Sacco presents himself quite consciously as the gauche Westerner traveling to a country he doesn't know to confront a situation that is wholly unfamiliar to him and his mostly American readership. It is to his credit that he portrays what he finds without flinching or reverting to political or sentimental cliché.

To make sense of the apparently inexplicable situation, Sacco references Joseph Conrad's *Under Western Eyes*, Coppola's *Apocalypse Now*, and Edward Said's theories of Orientalism, to draw parallels between the occupation of the West Bank and the colonialism of former times. While Sacco is sensitive to the plight of the Palestinians, he is aware that *Palestine* gives a rather one-sided view of the conflict and he admits that it would take another whole book to present the situation from the Israeli perspective.

FURTHER READING: *But I Like It; War's End*
SEE ALSO: *Notes On A Defeatist; Safe Area Goražde; The Fixer; Persepolis*

★
★
★
★
★

Writer: Brian K. Vaughan **Publisher:** Vertigo, 2008
Artist: Niko Henrichon **ISBN:** 1401203140

15+ # PRIDE OF BAGHDAD

Plot: When US forces first occupied Iraq, a story emerged of a pride of lions escaping from Baghdad Zoo. This is a fictional version of that true story. Initially the lions are left pretty much for dead as their keepers give them one last meal and vacate the premises. American F-18s swoop overhead, bombing the zoo and the surrounding area. When the dust settles, the lions find themselves free. Brian K. Vaughan weaves an emotional tale as the lions are torn between the home they know and an unknown land.

Review: *Pride of Baghdad* won the IGN Best Original Graphic Novel award in 2006. Zill, the lead male; Safa, the matriarch; Ali, the young cub; and Noor, the fourth member of the pride, embark on their adventure into war-torn Baghdad after wrestling with their different views of freedom. Having understood the meaning of being in a zoo, Noor does not think that liberty can come so easily. Vaughan invests the lions with believably leonine "personalities," capturing all the cunning you would expect from the king

of beasts and keeping the pride together against all the odds. He avoids the trap of anthropomorphizing the creatures, and instead of magically bestowing human speech upon them, portrays their communication as growls and roars that are somehow intelligible to humans.

Niko Henrichon gives the book a stunning visual aspect, evoking the innocence of the lions' new lives, the grittiness of the war that surrounds them, the desolate land, and the heat of the sun. He keeps the animal forms intact while conveying emotion in the lions' faces, and story and art blend beautifully.

FURTHER READING: *The Runaways; The Escapist*
SEE ALSO: *Ex Machina; Y The Last Man*

★
★
★
★
★

Writer: Raymond Briggs **Publisher:** Penguin, 1988
Artist: Raymond Briggs **ISBN:** 0140094199

WHEN THE WIND BLOWS

Plot: In the English countryside, a retired couple learns of the possibility of nuclear war, but are sure that their government has prepared for such a crisis and will swiftly make things right if the situation arises. Even so, they prepare their house as best as they can by trying to follow the contradictory leaflets issued by the government. When the worst finally arrives, Hilda and James manage to survive, and attempt to return to their normal lives, but slowly succumb to radiation sickness—all the while maintaining their faith in the authorities that have deserted them.

Review: *When the Wind Blows* remains one of the most important works of fiction to be written about the threat of nuclear Armageddon. Briggs's graphic storytelling is masterful. The daily lives of Hilda and James are presented in colorful and densely packed pages as they obliviously

ESSENTIAL
GRAPHIC NOVELS

500

497

WAR

Top 10 war graphic novels

continue their everyday lives. But those images are contrasted with the approaching nuclear attack, rendered in murky and threatening two-page spreads. After a four-page bomb blast, life—of a sort—continues. But the promised government help never arrives, and the couple's radiation poisoning develops graphically, the pages becoming as pale as their diseased skin. While the tale's tragedy is tempered to a degree by the couple's deep and sustaining love, that love only makes their sacrifice that much more hollow. It's a powerful and affecting tale, and one for all ages.

FURTHER READING: *The Snowman; Fungus The Bogeyman; Ug: Boy Genius Of The Stoneage*
SEE ALSO: *Ethel and Ernest: A True Story*

★
★
★
★
★

Writer: Joe Kubert   **Publisher:** Ibooks, 2005
Artist: Joe Kubert   **ISBN:** 074347516X

15+ YOSSEL

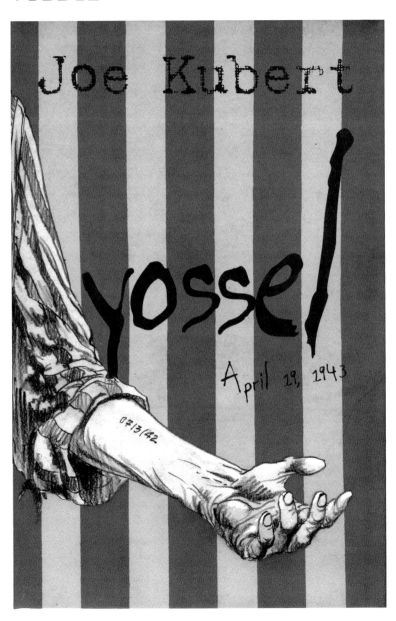

ESSENTIAL
GRAPHIC NOVELS

500

499

WAR

Top 10 war graphic novels

Plot: This book begins and ends on the day Yossel will probably die, in the last hours of the Warsaw uprising. In flashback we learn how his family lost everything and ended up in the Warsaw ghetto. We also see how the incredible talent the teenage Yossel has for drawing not only entertains so many of the ghetto's residents, it also brings him to the attention of the Nazi guards. Yossel is granted certain privileges by the guards because of his talent—much like Kubert himself in the years following the Depression, who at the same age, using his skills as an illustrator, was afforded the privilege of earning more than his father. These privileges can't save Yossel's parents and his sister from being deported to the death camps though, and it doesn't spare him the horrors that befell all Jews living in Poland under the Nazis. Like so many other brave young men and women in the ghetto, Yossel rises in open defiance against the Nazis and takes up arms, a struggle made all the more heroic by the certainty of defeat.

Review: Drawn in raw, hurried pencils that look as though they have been sketched on the run, Kubert wanted to convey the sense that the whole graphic novel had been written inside Yossel's mind as an escape from what he is witnessing. *Yossel* is a very personal "what if?" story, an alternate history whose events do not alter the course of recorded history, but lend it the poignancy of personal loss. Kubert's parents moved to the US from Poland in 1926. *Yossel* tells the story of what might have happened to Kubert and his family if they had stayed and become caught up in, the Nazi occupation of their country.

Kubert grounds *Yossel* in the historical truth of the ordeals and heroism of the denizens of the Warsaw ghetto, with an introduction that states "There's no question in my mind that what you are about to read could have happened."

FURTHER READING: *Fax From Sarajevo; Enemy Ace Archives Volume 1; Sgt. Rock: The Prophecy*
SEE ALSO: *Maus; Sgt. Rock Archives Volume 1; Tor*

★
★ **Writer:** Osamu Tezuka   **Publisher:** VIZ Media LLC, 1996
★ **Artist:** Osamu Tezuka   **ISBN:** 1569310580
★
★

15+ # ADOLF VOLUME 1

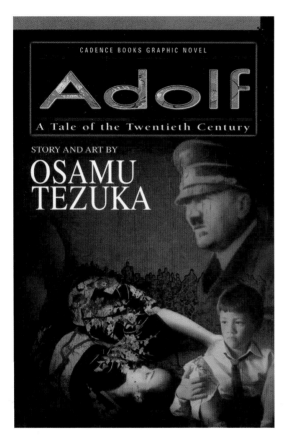

Plot: Primarily set during the period 1936–1945 (but with a conclusion set in 1970s Palestine), this is the story of three people called Adolf—one historical, Adolf Hitler, and two fictional, Adolf Kamil and Adolf Kaufmann. Kamil is a Jew living in Kobe, Japan, and Kaufmann is his best friend, half-Japanese and half-German. The plot concerns a document sent to Japan by the murdered brother of reporter Sohei Toge, who, in Berlin to cover the Olympics, is set on the trail of the document when he discovers that all traces of his brother's stay in Germany have been erased. Kaufmann's father is set the task of retrieving the document, which purports to prove that Hitler has Jewish blood. While Kaufmann becomes a member of the Hitler Youth and tries to reconcile that with his friendship with Jews, Kamil meets Toge, who is trying to publicize the document.

Review: This is a violent tale, part spy story and part history lesson. In keeping with its heartbreaking scenario, Tezuka uses a relatively realistic style, with few of the traditional manga exaggerations, as well as keeping his characterizations all convincingly portrayed—even Adolf Hitler. There are few truly great graphic novels, but this is one of them.

FURTHER READING: *Ode to Kirihito; Phoenix*
SEE ALSO: *V for Vendetta*

Writer: Garth Ennis
Artist: Carlos Ezquerra

Publisher: Vertigo, 2005
ISBN: 1401203531

ADVENTURES IN THE RIFLE BRIGADE

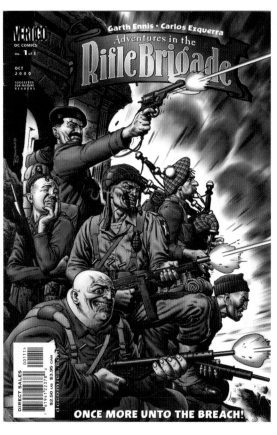

Plot: Back in the bad old days of World War II, when the dastardly Hun was threatening Blighty's golden shores, only one team could help bring back the stiff British upper lip—The Rifle Brigade! Led by the dashing Captain Darcy, the squad consists of the psychotic Yorkshireman Sergeant Crumb; working-class oik Corporal Geezer; explosives expert The Yank; suspiciously effeminate Second-Lieutenant "Doubtful" Milk; and The Piper, whose incessant bagpiping has caused men to try to rip their own heads off. These plucky heroes are sent on the most important, deadly, and top-secret missions—including the hunt for the Führer's infamous missing testicle—possibly with the hope that they don't come back!

Review: This book doesn't take itself too seriously, with Garth Ennis gloriously sending up the UK war comics of the 1960s and 1970s, adding a dash of foul language, a lot of smutty innuendo, and some nasty violence. Carlos Ezquerra's artwork is absolutely perfect—not surprising, because he drew several of those 1970s war comics. That said, this is very much Ennis on autopilot, and is fairly one-dimensional when compared with the depth of *Preacher* or *Hellblazer*.

FURTHER READING: *Battler Britton; Dicks; Hitman; Enemy Ace: War In Heaven*
SEE ALSO: *Preacher; Judge Dredd: Origins; War Stories; Hellblazer: Dangerous Habits*

★
★
★
★
★

Writer: Eric Shanower **Publisher:** Image Comics, 2001
Artist: Eric Shanower **ISBN:** 1582402000

AGE OF BRONZE VOLUME 1: A THOUSAND SHIPS

Plot: Enraged when servants of the King seize his family's bull as a prize for the festival games, the young goatherd, Paris, vows to go to Troy and win back the animal in the competition. Not only does he succeed in doing so, but it comes to light that he is the missing son of King Priam.

Abandoned as a baby after a prophecy warned he would bring doom to Troy, Paris is found and raised by one of the King's servants as his own. Welcomed back into the family, and eager to prove himself, Paris volunteers to rescue the King's sister, Hesione, from the Spartans. Instead, he takes it upon himself to return with Helen of Sparta, the most beautiful woman in the world, which starts the chain of events leading to the Trojan War.

Review: The first of a projected seven-volume saga, *A Thousand Ships* is a real labor of love from Eric Shanower.

Meticulously researched and immaculately drawn, Shanower's script strikes the right balance between providing the background to characters and events, and including enough action to make sure you don't lose interest. It's a real treat for fans of mythology and ancient history, and the deserving winner of two Eisner Awards.

FURTHER READING: *Age of Bronze Volume 2: Sacrifice; Age of Bronze Volume 3: Betrayal*
SEE ALSO: *White Death; Berlin: City of Stones; 300*

Writer: Mark S. Smylie
Artist: Mark S. Smylie

Publisher: Archaia Studio Press, 2007
ISBN: 193238622

ARTESIA: BOOK OF DOOM

Plot: Artesia is a Captain and concubine of Branimir, King of the Highland citadel of Dara Dess in Daradja. She is also the daughter of a witch, priestess of dread goddesses, and has power over spirits. Jealous of her military victories, Branimir conspires with emissaries from the Middle Kingdom to kill Artesia. After taking her bloody revenge on Branimir for his betrayal, Artesia learns that the Middle Kingdom has been invaded by the forces of the Empire of Thessid-Gola. Exhausted by their own campaigns, the other Citadel Kings of Daradja appoint Artesia their representative and she rides against the invaders.

Review: This epic fantasy is richly detailed and Smylie has fully mapped out the cultures, history, politics, and mythology of Artesia's world. His watercolor artwork is sympathetic to the story, while the writing is somber and intelligent, as concerned with the technicalities of war as with the characters, court intrigues, and battles that propel the story forward.

FURTHER READING: *Artesia Volume 2: Afield; Artesia Volume 3: Afire; Artesia: Adventures in the Known World (role-playing game)*
SEE ALSO: *Cerebus; Lost Girls*

Writer: B. Clay Moore
Artist: Jeremy Haun

Publisher: Image
ISBN: 1582405654

BATTLE HYMN: FAREWELL TO THE FIRST GOLDEN AGE

Plot: Set during World War II, a group of young heroes possessing special abilities, named the Watch Guard, are conscripted to the war effort. They could help tip the balance of the war, however their combined egos, along with the insidious government agenda, soon drive the group apart.

Review: Collecting the bestselling five-part series from Image, this explores the "what-if?" premise of heroes fighting on the front line of the Second World War (a nod to the Marvel and DC characters that were depicted doing the same back in the 1940s). The group can barely decide who's in charge, or who's the strongest, and unlike characters from the original stories from the '40s, this group going to war is very much a PR exercise, rather than having them perform heroic feats to win the day.

FURTHER READING: *The Golden Age*
SEE ALSO: *The Ultimates; Marvel Masterworks: Captain America*

★ **Writer:** Warren Ellis
★ **Artist:** Raulo Caceres
★

Publisher: Avatar, 2007
ISBN: 1592910408

18+ CRÉCY

Plot: Crécy, France, August 26, 1346: England's greatest battle. Outnumbered and driven to ground, the invading English army is forced to stand and fight the French. The ensuing conflict, recounted by William of Stoneham, will change modern warfare forever.

Review: Do not be deceived. Despite its brevity (clocking in at just 42 pages of story including a map), *Crécy* is a dense read. Built around a six-panel grid, Ellis's story packs in a lot of narrative. Treading similar ground to Frank Miller's *300*, it's a tale of a small, well-trained army overcoming a much greater foe. This time, though, the smaller army is the antagonist. There's a tongue-in-cheek tone to the story, but the battle is still brutally portrayed. The first-person narrative brings the period alive, as much through the coarse language and xenophobia as the description of warfare as a part of life. From the weekly longbow practice (part of English law

at time), to the constant threat of invasion by the French, it is clear that the English soldiers see war as a necessity for survival. Underhand tactics, such as the soldiers smearing their swords with excrement, are presented as matter of fact. Caceres's intricately detailed artwork complements Ellis's script superbly.

FURTHER READING: *Fell: Feral City; Orbiter; Ocean; Hellblazer: Haunted*
SEE ALSO: *Transmetropolitan: Back On The Street; Global Frequency: Planet Ablaze*

Writer: Brian Wood
Artist: Riccardo Burchielli

Publisher: Vertigo, 2006
ISBN: 1401210627

5+ # DMZ VOLUME 1: ON THE GROUND

Plot: A near-future America is plunged into civil war as secessionist states take up arms against the Federal government. The city of New York becomes a demilitarized zone and plunges into anarchy as the remaining civilians are left to fend for themselves. Into this urban anarchy comes a young news photographer, Matty Roth, who is determined to document the true story of the forgotten victims of the war.

Review: An excellent example of how intelligent science fiction can spotlight contemporary world issues. This is war, like those fought in Bosnia and Baghdad, in which every rooftop can hold a sniper and the armed forces can't tell the difference between friendlies and hostiles. Detailed art highlights every bombed-out building and burnt-out car, while Brian Wood's script concentrates on characterization rather than combat theatrics.

FURTHER READING: *DMZ: Body Of A Journalist; DMZ: Public Works*
SEE ALSO: *Palestine; 2020 Visions; The Losers: Ante Up*

Writer: Takao Saito
Artist: Takao Saito

Publisher: Viz Media LLC, 2006
ISBN: 1421502518

5+ # GOLGO 13 VOLUME 1: SUPERGUN

Plot: Golgo is an assassin who follows his own bleak code. He's more like Richard Stark's Parker than James Bond, although he's often compared to the latter. The first Golgo adventure dates from 1968, but this collection combines two stories from different periods. The *Gun at Am Shara* sees Golgo hired by the US government to prevent Saddam Hussein completing a supergun; the second story features a detective who gets his revenge on the gangster who killed his fiancé in a hit-and-run accident, by creating the impression he's hired Golgo 13.

Review: Like many long-running series, *Golgo 13* isn't particularly sophisticated, but the art is slick, simple, and stylish, and the steely inhumanity of the central character draws you into the story.

FURTHER READING: *Kage Gari; Modesty Blaise; Samurai Executioner*
SEE ALSO: *Lone Wolf and Cub; Crying Freeman; Lady Snowblood*

★
★
★
★
★

Writer: Art Spiegelman
Artist: Art Spiegelman

Publisher: Viking, 2004
ISBN: 0375423079

15+

IN THE SHADOW OF NO TOWERS

Plot: "I still believe the world is ending, but I concede that it seems to be ending more slowly than I once thought... so I figured I'd make a book." So writes Art Spiegelman in his introduction to this oversized board book, which collects his ten-page meditation on politics, hysteria, fear-mongering, and the end of the world—topics weighing heavily on his mind in the wake of 9/11. The size of a newspaper when open, the book also includes vintage comics pages from stalwarts like *The Yellow Kid* and *Foxy Grandpa*.

Review: Spiegelman put his heart into these pages, his always interesting layouts exploding with confusion and paranoia. Here, comic strips become a metaphor for life's impermanence as well as its resilience. A book of its time, it's an unfiltered glimpse into the artist's psyche.

FURTHER READING: *Open Me... I'm A Dog*
SEE ALSO: *Maus; Big Fat Little Lit*

Writer: Frank Miller
Artist: Dave Gibbons

Publisher: Dark Horse, 2008
ISBN: *NOT YET PUBLISHED*

THE LIFE AND TIMES OF MARTHA WASHINGTON IN THE 21ST CENTURY

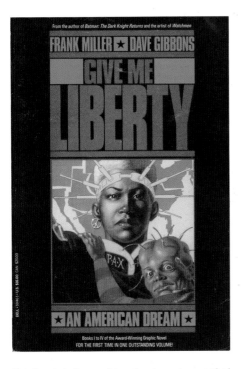

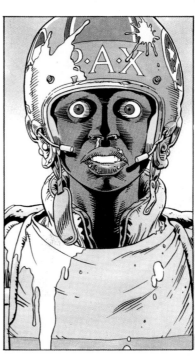

507

500

ESSENTIAL
GRAPHIC NOVELS

WAR
Best of the rest

Plot: In a dystopian near-future America, an impoverished but resourceful young African-American woman escapes from her ghetto prison, enlists with a peacekeeping force, and embarks on a series of high-concept, combat-oriented adventures. Although hampered by the machinations of her outlandish enemies—including gay neo-Nazis, heavily armed burger chains, and a dangerously obsessive-compulsive Surgeon General—her integrity and determination see her rise to become a respected and influential figure.

Review: Martha Washington has appeared in several miniseries and oneshots produced irregularly between 1990 and 2007, and one of the short stories featured here had only previously appeared in a limited-edition comic included with the Martha Washington action figure. The initial four-issue miniseries, *Give Me Liberty*, is a darkly entertaining romp that charts the fluctuating fortunes of a future America alongside those of its long-suffering protagonist. Frank Miller's rich, decade-spanning history is first and foremost an action adventure, however, and Washington is always right in the thick of it. Dave Gibbons is adept at depicting the smaller, human-interest aspects of the story, as well as the grandiose action set pieces that Miller's outrageous vision often demands. As with his groundbreaking DC series *The Dark Knight Returns*, Miller often employs the media as a storytelling tool, using TV news reports, magazine covers, and articles to enrich the story's background detail, as well as for their satirical mileage.

FURTHER READING: *Elektra Omnibus*
SEE ALSO: *Hard Boiled; The Originals; Ronin*

★
★
★
★

Writer: Gipi
Artist: Gipi

Publisher: First Second, 2007
ISBN: 1596432616

15+ NOTES FOR A WAR STORY

Plot: War breaks out in an unnamed Balkan country. Caught in this conflict are three homeless teenage friends who have drifted into a hand-to-mouth existence. It seems as if endless days of petty crime, black market deals, and dodging snipers will follow for all of them. But when they encounter organized crime and the lure of a thuggish, homegrown militia, they exchange their status as victims for something darker and more self-destructive.

Review: There is an assumed innocence in Gipi's gray, watercolored pencils that belies the corruption the youthful protagonists undergo during the conflict portrayed here. The techno-porn and "shock and awe" that characterized news coverage of the war is absent from Gipi's depiction, as is the visual paraphernalia of modern warfare. This bolsters the realism of the noncombatants' daily struggle with the casual and almost imperceptible disintegration of their community and the way of life they believed would always be a constant. Gipi's style is very matter-of-fact, with no complicated page layouts or busy panel progressions to disrupt the narrative. Ultimately, the book's strength lies in divorcing the perceived glamor of war from the palpable and enduring effects it has on individuals.

FURTHER READING: *Garage Band*
SEE ALSO: *Maus; Last Day In Vietnam; Palestine*

Writer: Joe Sacco
Artist: Joe Sacco

Publisher: Fantagraphics, 2002
ISBN: 1560974702

SAFE AREA GORAŽDE: THE WAR IN EASTERN BOSNIA 1992–1995

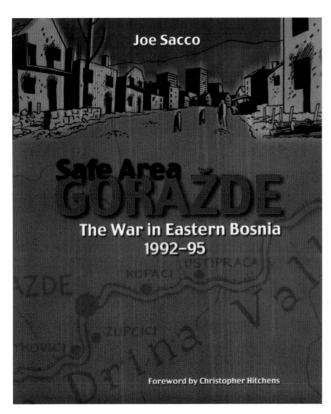

ESSENTIAL
GRAPHIC NOVELS

500

509

WAR
Best of the rest

Plot: *Safe Area Goražde* records Joe Sacco's four visits to a designated "safe area" in the Bosnian warzone during late 1995 and early 1996. By recording the everyday lives, fears, and hopes of the people he stayed with and talked to amid the increasing chaos of the town, he provides an affecting account of how war really effects civilians.

Review: Eschewing the kind of graphic photographs that familiarize us with daily atrocities and foster a dehumanizing distance between the viewer and the subject, Sacco's cartoons invite the viewer to empathize with the characters in a very direct and personal way. His artwork isn't complex; it's there to do a job, and it conveys emotion and danger brilliantly without using overdramatic gimmicks. Sacco knows when something doesn't need to be shown, and this makes his approach to the narrative all the more affecting, along with his own sense of guilt each time he leaves the area, knowing that his new friends don't have the option to step back. Sacco mixes interviews with his own "adventures" alongside them—fixing a hydroelectric generator, or simply finding food for dinner—as well as including some explanatory sections that put the circumstances into context. The combination of the three makes this a riveting read.

FURTHER READING: *War Junkie*
SEE ALSO: *Palestine; Persepolis*

★
★
★
★

Writer: Stan Lee
Artist: Jack Kirby, Dick Ayers

Publisher: Marvel, 2006
ISBN: 0785120394

A

MARVEL MASTERWORKS: SGT. FURY AND HIS HOWLING COMMANDOS, VOLUME 1

Plot: The Howling Commandos is the nickname of the First Attack Squad, stationed on a base in England and destined for missions into Europe during World War II. Fury is a cigar-chomping sergeant leading a group of soldiers who personify a number of cultural stereotypes—including "Dum Dum" Dugan, Gabe Jones, and "Izzy" Cohen. Together they team up with Captain America and fight villains such as Baron Strucker and Dr. Zemo.

Review: Lee's scripts are full of action, but leavened with a great deal of humor. The Commandos are some of the most larger-than-life soldiers ever to go to war, though death seeks them out soon enough. Kirby's artwork is always exciting, but Ayers made the series his own from the eighth issue.

FURTHER READING: *Marvel Visionaries: Jack Kirby Volume 1*
SEE ALSO: *Marvel Masterworks: Captain America*

★
★
★
★

Writer: Bob Kanigher, Bob Haney
Artist: Various

Publisher: DC Comics, 2002
ISBN: 1563898411

A

THE SGT. ROCK ARCHIVES, VOLUME 1

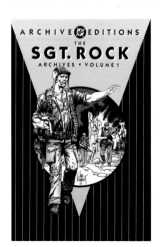

Plot: Platoon sergeant Frank Rock is the leader of Easy Company, whose number includes Bulldozer, Ice Cream Soldier, Jackie Johnson, Little Sure Shot, and Wildman. They serve on various World War II battlefields in North Africa, Italy, and Northern Europe during the course of the series. Although Rock has his superiors, he is usually the one who keeps his men alive against all odds, often by performing outrageously brave or seemingly impossible feats, just to get the job done.

Review: These stories are reprinted primarily from *Our Army at War* #81–96, but an earlier, prototype appearance is also included. Early episodes were drawn by Ross Andru, Russ Heath, Jerry Grandinetti, and Mort Drucker, but writer Bob Kanigher introduced Easy Company in #83 and would soon team up with Joe Kubert to become the strip's definitive creative team.

FURTHER READING: *The Sgt. Rock Archives, Volumes 2–3; The 'Nam*
SEE ALSO: *Charley's War; Sgt Fury And His Howling Commandos*

Writer: Ted Rall
Artist: Ted Rall

Publisher: NBM, 2003
ISBN: 1561633593

TO AFGHANISTAN AND BACK: A GRAPHIC TRAVELOGUE

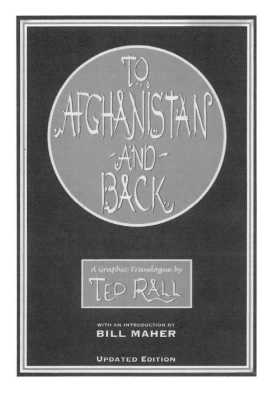

Plot: Ted Rall's firsthand reports of life in the Afghan war zone during the American-led invasion of 2001. Billed as a graphic travelogue, this is actually a dispatch from the first onslaught in the "war on terror." Moreover, only half of *To Afghanistan and Back* is comprised of comic strips; the other half contains the illustrated articles that Rall wrote for "The Village Voice," who was the sponsor that commissioned his trip to Afghanistan.

Review: Arguably, the labor-intensive medium of comics is not particularly well suited to the fast-moving world of current affairs, but that didn't stop Ted Rall, whose first impulse when an invasion of Afghanistan was mooted was to go there immediately. This is the record of what he experienced. When he arrives, it soon becomes apparent that the war doesn't have a front line; it is happening everywhere. Violence and death are a constant threat—in marketplace negotiations over faulty benzene heaters; in the knock at the door in the middle of the night. Rall's rough, angular style may not suit all tastes, but the strength of this book is in capturing the brief impressions, the flavor of adrenalin-soaked terror, and the brief flashes of exhilaration that make up the life of a correspondent in a war zone.

FURTHER READING: *Combat Zone: True Tales of GIs in Iraq*
SEE ALSO: *The Fixer*

★
★
★
★

Writer: Harvey Kurtzman and Various   **Publisher:** Gemstone Publishing, 2007
Artist: Various   **ISBN:** 1888472561

THE EC ARCHIVES: TWO-FISTED TALES VOLUME 1

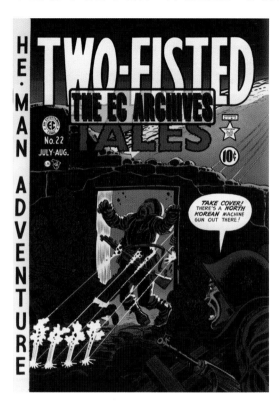

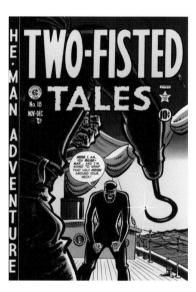

Plot: Originally conceived as an adventure series, *Two-Fisted Tales* got off to a rocky start, but when Harvey Kurtzman took over with the fourth issue, the title was transformed. *Two-Fisted Tales* broke away from flag-waving stereotypes and presented thoughtful, realistic tales, often questioning the ethics of war, usually told from the viewpoint of ordinary, often naïve, soldiers. It debuted during the Korean war, and while many of the most notable stories are set during that conflict, it also featured scripts set in the Civil War and World Wars I and II, and later touched on other conflicts. In addition to his other duties, Kurtzman illustrated a story in most issues himself, and did a superb job. His regular roster of artists—Jack Davies, John Severin, Will Elder, and Wally Wood—all produced memorable strips.

Review: Without a doubt, it is *MAD* creator Harvey Kurtzman's close control over the material in each issue that raises the majority of *Two-Fisted Tales* to "must-have" status. Forget about the war theme: these stories, despite their wartime settings, are fundamentally about humanity. Kurtzman employed many different narrative approaches to make sure the stories never repeated themselves, and was responsible for masterpiece after masterpiece.

FURTHER READING: *Two-Fisted Tales Volume 2*
SEE ALSO: *Sgt. Fury and his Howling Commandos; Charley's War*

Writer: Garth Ennis
Artist: David Lloyd, Cam Kennedy,
Carlos Ezquerra, and Gary Erskine

Publisher: Vertigo, 2006
ISBN: 1401210392

WAR STORIES VOLUME 2

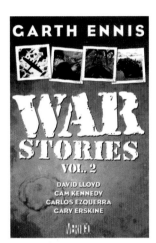

Plot: Four individual stories in one book. During the Spanish Civil War, four foreign combatants huddle together overnight in a shell hole, telling each other how they came to be there. In a World War II setting, a British bomber pilot takes his dedication for his job to the extreme; a British fighter pilot is launched from a merchant vessel to protect his convoy from torpedo bombers; and a Special Forces desert patrol embarks on a suicide mission.

Review: The contrasting styles of four different artists illustrate Garth Ennis's gritty tales of war. Lloyd's shadowy style is perfect for the night-time bombing raids; Ezquerra's gritty style emphasizes the grime of the shell hole; Erskine's clear style lifts the chaos of the airborne dogfights; and Cam Kennedy's sense of motion complements the hit-and-run tactics of the Special Forces. The wordy discussions of the participants make thoughtful tales out of what could otherwise have been familiar war stories.

FURTHER READING: *War Stories Volume 1; Battler Britton*
SEE ALSO: *Charley's War*

Writer: Rob Morrison
Artist: Charlie Adlard

Publisher: AiT/Planetlar, 2005
ISBN: 0970936060

WHITE DEATH

Plot: In the last months of 1916 on the Trentino mountain range, a private in the Italian army returns to his childhood home to find only a place of death and despair. Like the trenches of the Somme, the war on the Italian/Austro-Hungarian border is nothing more than the gain of a few hundred yards, followed by a retreat of a few hundred more. But here, there is an even more terrifying weapon, one that harnesses the power of nature itself. The White Death: thundering avalanches deliberately caused by cannon fire.

Review: Stunningly illustrated by Charlie Adlard using charcoal and chalk on gray paper, Rob Morrison's script is a real punch to the gut. Inspired by the cruel, shocking statistic that an estimated 60,000–100,000 troops were killed on the Italian front during World War I by deliberately triggered avalanches, *White Death* is a difficult but necessary read. Told through the eyes of Pietro Aquasanta, loyalties come to mean nothing, his friends die one by one, and everything is a means to an end for an uncaring officer class.

FURTHER READING: *Charley's War Volume 2*
SEE ALSO: *Charley's War; Nikolai Dante; The Walking Dead*

REFERENCE

INDEX AND CONTRIBUTORS

INDEX BY AGE

INDEX BY WRITER

INDEX BY ARTIST

INDEX BY TITLE

PUBLISHER INFORMATION

Aardvark-Vanheim
Cerebus Church And State © Dave Sim
Cerebus High Society © Dave Sim

Abrams Image
Mom's Cancer © Brian Fies

Abstract Studio
Strangers In Paradise © Terry Moore

Active Images
Skidmarks © Ilya
Spiral Cage © Al Davison
Strange Embrace © David Hine
Temptation © Glenn Dakin

AiT/Planet LAR
Astronauts In Trouble © Larry Young & Matt Smith
Couscous Express © Brian Wood & Brett Weldele
True Story Swear To God © Tom Beland
White Death © Rob Morrison & Charlie Adlard

Alternative Comics
Magic Whistle 9 © Sam Henderson

America's Best Comics
Promethea © America's Best Comics, L.L.C.
The League Of Extraordinary Gentlemen
© Alan Moore & Kevin O'Neill
Top Ten © America's Best Comics, L.L.C.

Amerotica
Omaha The Cat Dancer © Kate Worley
& Reed Waller

Andrews and McMeel
The Complete Calvin & Hobbes © Bill Watterson

Archaia Studio Press
Artesia Vol 1 © Mark S. Smylie
Mouse Guard Vol. 1: Fall 1152 © David Petersen

Archie Comics
Archie Americana Series: Best Of The Fifties
© Archie Comics

Avatar Press
Crécy (Warren Ellis) © Warren Ellis
Small Killing © Alan Moore & Oscar Zarate

Ballantine
American Splendor: The Life And Times Of Harvey Pekar
© Harvey Pekar

Black Dog & Leventhal Publishers
King Lear: Graphic Shakespeare © Ian Pollock
& Black Dog & Leventhal Publishers

Blast Books
Hell Baby © Hino Hideshi

Bloomsbury
Signal To Noise © Neil Gaiman & Dave Mckean

Checker Publishing Group
Clive Barker's Hellraiser: Collected Best, Vol. 1
© Clive Barker & The Checker Publishing Group
Little Nemo In Slumberland © The Estate Of
Windsor McCay
Supreme: The Story Of The Year © Alan Moore,
Joe Bennett, Rob Liefeld & The Checker
Publishing Group

Cinebooks
Lucky Luke © Cinebooks, Morris & The Estate
Of Rene Goscinny
Blake And Mortimer: The Yellow "M" © Cinebooks
& The Estate Of Edgar P. Jacobs
Thorgal—Child Of The Stars © Cinebooks

CMX
Gon © Masashi Tanaka And CMX

Dark Angel Productions
Blackjack: Blood And Honor © Alex Simmons

Dark Horse
300 © Frank Miller
Akira © Katsuhiro Otomo & Dark Horse Comics
Alice In Sunderland © Bryan Talbot
Aliens © Twentieth Century Fox & Film Corporation
Appleseed © Masamune Shirow & Dark Horse Comics
Astro Boy © Osamu Tezuka
B.P.R.D © Mike Mignola
Billi 99 © Sarah Byam, Tim Sale & Dark Horse Comics
Blade Of The Immortal © Hiroaki Samura
& Dark Horse Comics
Buffy The Vampire Slayer © Twentieth Century Fox
& Film Corporation
Cal Mcdonald © Steve Niles & Ben Templesmith
Conan Cover Art © Barry Windsor-Smith
& Dark Horse Comics
Concrete © Paul Chadwick
Crying Freeman © Kazuo Koike, Ryoichi Ikegami
& Dark Horse Comics
Dead Memory © Marc Antoine Mathieu
& Dark Horse Comics
Fafhrd And The Gray Mouser © The Estate
Of Fritz Leiber
Flaming Carrot © Bob Burden
Flood! © Eric Drooker & Dark Horse Comics
Ghost In The Shell © Masamune Shirow
& Dark Horse Comics
Goon © Eric Powell & Dark Horse Comics
Grendel © Matt Wagner
Groo © Sergio Aragones.
Gunsmith Cats © Kenichi Sonoda & Dark Horse Comics
Hard Boiled © Frank Miller & Geoff Darrow
Heart Of Empire © Bryan Talbot & Dark Horse Comics
Hellboy © Mike Mignola
Illegal Alien © James Robinson & Phil Elliott.
Lady Snowblood © Kazuo Kamimura, Kazuo Koike
& Dark Horse Comics
Last Day In Vietnam © Will Eisner Studios, Inc.
Little Annie Fannie © Playboy Enterprises Ltd.
Lonewolf And Cub © Frank Miller & Dark Horse Comics
Minotaur's Tale © Al Davison
Museum Of Terror © Junji Ito & Dark Horse Comics
Nexus © Mike Baron, Steve Rude & Dark Horse Comics
Oh My Goddess © Kosuke Fujishima
& Dark Horse Comics
Oldboy © Garon Tsuchiya, Mnegishi Nobuaki
& Dark Horse Comics
Pop Gun War © Farel Dalrymple
Rocco Vargas © Daniel Torres & Dark Horse Comics
Scarlet Traces © Ian Edington & Matt Brooker
Sin City © Frank Miller
Sock Monkey © Tony Millionaire
Star Wars © Lucasfilm Ltd.
Tale Of One Bad Rat © Bryan Talbot & Dark Horse Comics
The Towers Of Bois-Maury © Hermann & Dark Horse Comics
Too Much Coffee Man © Shannon Wheeler
& Dark Horse Comics
Zombie World © Mike Mignola, Pat Mckeown
& Dark Horse Comics

DC Comics
Across The Universe © DC Comics
All Star Comic Archives © DC Comics
All Star Superman © DC Comics
Batman: Arkham Asylum © DC Comics
Batman: Hush © DC Comics
Batman: The Dark Knight Returns © DC Comics
Batman: Year One © DC Comics
Birds Of Prey © DC Comics
Brooklyn Dreams © DC Comics
Crisis On Infinite Earths © DC Comics
Crisis On Multiple Earths © DC Comics
Elfquest Archives © Warp Graphics, Inc.
Green Arrow © DC Comics
Green Lantern/Green Arrow © DC Comics
Identity Crisis © DC Comics
Jack Kirby's New Gods © DC Comics
Justice League © DC Comics
Komandi Archives © DC Comics
Kingdom Come © DC Comics
Astro City: Life In The Big City © Juke Boy Productions
Light Brigade © DC Comics
Manhunter © DC Comics
Plastic Man: Archives Vol 1 © DC Comics
Plastic Man: On The Lam © DC Comics
Road To Perdition Script © Max Allan Collins.
Art © Richard Piers Rayner.
Ronin © Frank Miller Inc.
Sgt Rock © DC Comics
Shazam! © DC Comics
Starman © DC Comics
Stuck Rubber Baby © DC Comics.
Superman: Death Of Superman © DC Comics
Superman: Man Of Steel © DC Comics
The Spirit © Will Eisner Studios, Inc.
Tor © Joe Kubert
Watchmen © Alan Moore, Dave Gibbons & DC Comics
Wonder Woman: Archives Vol 1 © DC Comics
Wonder Woman: Gods And Mortals © DC Comics

DH Publishing
Hino Horror © Hino Hideshi & DH Publishing

Dennis Kitchen Publishing
Drawning Comics Is Easy © Dennis Kitchen Publishing

Dork Storm Press
Dork Tower © John Kovalic

Doubleday
Fagin The Jew © Will Eisner Studios, Inc.

Drawn & Quarterly
Berlin © Jason Lutes.
Chicken With Plums © Marjane Satrapi
Clyde Fans © G. (Seth) Gallant
Curses © Kevin Huizenga
Extended Dream Of Mr D © Max
Get A Life © Phillipe Dupuy
Golem's Mighty Swing © James Sturm
Hicksville © Dylan Horrocks
It's A Good Life If You Don't Weaken
© G. (Seth) Gallant
Jar Of Fools © Jason Lutes
Louis Riel © Chester Brown
Love That Bunch © Aline Kominsky Crumb
Moomin © Tove Jansson
Paul Has A Summer Job © Michel Rabagliati
Pyongyang © Guy Delisle
Shenzhen © Guy Delisle
Summer Blonde © Adrian Tomine
The Fixer © Joe Sacco

© The Estate Of Dori Seda
Justin Green's Binky Brown Sampler © Justin Green
My Troubles With Women © Robert Crumb
Pure Trance © Junko Mizuno

Little, Brown Young Readers
Tintin In Tibet © The Estate Of Herge

M Q Publications
Need More Love: A Graphic Memoir
© Aline Kominsky Crumb

MAD
Peepshow © Joe Matt

Main Street Books
Cartoon History Of The Universe 1 Vol. 1-7 © Larry Gonick

Marvel Comics
Alias © Marvel Characters, Inc.
Astonishing X-Men © Marvel Characters, Inc.
Avengers © Marvel Characters, Inc.
Captain America © Marvel Characters, Inc.
Civil War © Marvel Characters, Inc.
Criminal © Sean Philips & Ed Brubaker
Daredevil © Marvel Characters, Inc.
Doctor Strange © Marvel Characters, Inc.
Essential Fantastic Four: © Marvel Characters, Inc.
Essential Spider-Man © Marvel Characters, Inc.
Fantastic Four: Visionaries © Marvel Characters, Inc.
Incredible Hulk © Marvel Characters, Inc.
Iron Man © Marvel Characters, Inc.
Marvel 1602 © Marvel Characters, Inc.
Marvel Zombies © Marvel Characters, Inc.
Marvels © Marvel Characters, Inc.
Nick Fury, Agent Of S.H.I.E.L.D. © Marvel Characters, Inc.
Sgt. Fury And His Howling Commandos
© Marvel Characters, Inc.
Spider-Girl © Marvel Characters, Inc.
Spider-Man: Kraven's Last Hunt © Marvel Characters, Inc.
The Mighty Thor © Marvel Characters, Inc.
Thunderbolts © Marvel Characters, Inc.
Tomb Of Dracula © Marvel Characters, Inc.
Ultimate Spider-Man: Power And Responsibility
© Marvel Characters, Inc.
Ultimates © Marvel Characters, Inc.
Wolverine © Marvel Characters, Inc.
X-Men © Marvel Characters, Inc.

Metaphrog, Pap/Com
Louis © Metaphrog

NBM
After The Rain © Andre Julliard
Click © Milo Manara
Dr. Jekyll & Mr. Hyde © Lorenzo Mattotti & NBM
Dungeon: Duck Heart © Joann Sfar & Lewis Trondheim
Fairy Tales Of Oscar Wilde © P. Craig Russell
Glacial Period © Nicholas De Crecy
In Search Of Shirley © Cosey
Indian Summer © Milo Manara
Kafka: Give It Up & Other Short Stories
© Peter Kuper & NBM
L'il Santa © Louis Trondheim
Lone Sloane: Chaos © Philippe Druillet
Magic Flute © P. Craig Russell
Mister O © Louis Trondheim
Orient Gateway © Vittorio Giardino
Remembrance Of Things Past, Part Two:
Within A Budding Grove © Stephane Heuet & NBM
Streak of Chalk © Miguelanxo Prado
Tangents © Miguelanxo Prado

The Birthday Riots © Nabiel Kanan.
To Afghanistan And Back © Ted Rall
Treasury Of Victorian Murder: The Borden Tragedy
© Rick Geary
Yellow Jar © Patrick Antangen

Olympian
The Nocturnals © Dan Brereton

Oni Press
Alison Dare © J Torres And J Bone
Blue Monday © Chynna Clugston-Major
Courtney Crumrin © Ted Naifeh
Madman © Michael Allred
Queen & Country © Greg Rucka & Steve Rolston
Scott Pilgrim © Scott Pilgrim & Bryan Lee O' Malley
Wet Moon © Ross Campbell
Whiteout © Greg Rucka, Steve Lieber & Frank Miller

Orchard Books
Amazing Mr Pleebus © Nick Abadzis

Orion
Asterix And The Great Crossing
© Albert Uderzo & Orion Books

Palliard Press
Leonard & Larry: Domesticity Isn't Pretty © Tim Barela

Panini (UK) Ltd
Elektra: Assassin © Marvel Characters, Inc.
The Definitive Silver Surfer © Marvel Characters, Inc.
Doctor Who: Iron Legion © Pat Mills, Dave Gibbons
& Panini

Pantheon
Black Hole © Charles Burns
Boulevard Of Broken Dreams © Kim Deitch
Epileptic © David B.
Ethel & Ernest: A True Story © Raymond Briggs
Gemma Bovery © Posy Simmonds
Good-Bye, Chunky Rice © Craig Thompson
Ice Haven © Daniel Clowes
Jew Of New York © Ben Katchor
Julius Knipl, Real Estate Photographer © Ben Katchor
La Perdida © Jessica Abel
Perseopolis © Marjane Satrapi
The Big Book Of Hell © Matt Groening

Penguin Books Ltd
Maus © Art Spiegelman
When The Wind Blows © Raymond Briggs

Penguin Global
Corridor © Sarnath Banerjee

Perigree Trade
Amphigorey © Perigee Trade

Picador
City Of Glass: The Graphic Novel © Paul Auster,
David Mazzucchelli & Picador

Puffin
Big Fat Little Lit © Art Spiegelman

Pulp Theatre Entertainment
Brodie's Law: Project Jameson © Alan Grant & David Bircham

Rebellion
A. B. C. Warriors © Rebellion A/S
Complete Ballad Of Halo Jones © Rebellion A/S

D.R. And Quinch © Rebellion A/S
Fiends Of The Eastern Front © Rebellion A/S
Judge Dredd: Complete Case Files © Rebellion A/S
Judge Dredd: Origins © Rebellion A/S
Nemesis The Warlock © Rebellion A/S
Nikolai Dante © Rebellion A/S
Skizz © Rebellion A/S
Slaine: The Book Of Invasions © Rebellion A/S

Sasquatch Books
Making Comics © Scott McCloud
The Greatest Of Marlys © Lynda Barry

Scholastic Books
Bone © Jeff Smith

Sirius Entertainment
Scary Godmother © Jill Thompson
Wandering Star © Teri Sue Wood

Slave Labor Graphics
Johnny The Homicidal Maniac
© Jhonen Vasquez
Lenore © Roman Dirge
Milk And Cheese © Evan Dorkin
Skeleton Key © Andi Watsonn
Slow News Day © Andi Watson
Sugar Buzz © Ian Carney & Woodrow Phoenix

Sort of Books
Book Of Leviathan © Peter Blegvad

Sparkplug Comics
Bookhunter © Jason Shiga

Speakeasy Comics
2020 Visions © Jamie Delano

Spitfire Comics
Hookjaw © Pat Mills, Ramon Sola & Spitfire Comics

St. Martin's Griffin
Salon © Nick Bertozzi & St Martin's Griffin

Stone Bridge Press
Four Immigrants Manga © Stone Bridge Press

Studio Foglio
Girl Genius © Phil Foglio & Kaja Foglio

Telltale Press
Sam And Max © Steve Purcell

Three Rivers Press
Birth Of A Nation © Aaron Mcgruder
& Three Rivers Press

Titan Entertainment Group Ltd.
Casino Royale © Titan Entertainment Group Ltd.
Charley's War © Pat Mills, Joe Colquhoun & Titan
Entertainment Group Ltd.
Classic Dan Dare © Titan Entertainment Group Ltd.
London's Dark © James Robinson, Paul Johnson
& Titan Entertainment Group Ltd.
Marshal Law © Pat Mills, Kevin O'Neill & Titan
Entertainment Group Ltd.
Modesty Blaize © Titan Entertainment Group Ltd.
Nemi © Lise Myhre & Titan Entertainment Group Ltd.
Steel Claw © Titan Entertainment Group Ltd.
Tank Girl © Jamie Hewlett, Alan Martin & Titan
Entertainment Group Ltd.
Violent Cases © Neil Gaiman & Dave McKean

TokyoPop

Battle Royale © Koushun Takami, Yukito Kishiro & Tokyopop
Lupin III © Kazuhiko Kato
Blankets © Craig Thompson

Top Shelf Productions

Box Office Poison © Alex Robinson
Hey Mister © Pete Sickman-Garner
Hutch Owen © Hutch Owen
Lost Girls © Alan Moore & Melinda Gebbie
Monkey Vs Robot © James Kochalka
Owly © Andy Runton
Same Difference © Derek Kirk Kim
Three Fingers © Rich Koslowski
Tricked © Alex Robinson

Toptron Ltd.

Blue © Kiriko Nananan
The Times Of Botchan © Natsuo Sekikawa
& Jiro Taniguchi
Yukiko's Spinach © Frederic Biolet

Tor Books

Book Of Ballads © Charles Vess

Tundra Books

Kidnapped (Graphic Modern Text Edition)
© Tundra Books

Typocrat

Six Hundred Seventy Six Apparitions Of Killoffer
© Killoffer & Typocrat Press

Vertical

Buddha © Osamu Tezuka & Vertical, Inc.
Ode To Kirihito © Osamu Tezuka & Vertical, Inc.

Vertigo

100 Bullets © Brian Azzarello, Eduardo Risso & DC Comics
A History Of Violence © DC Comics
Adventures In The Rifle Brigade © DC Comics
Animal Man © DC Comics
Blood: A Tale © DC Comics
Can't Get No © DC Comics
Death © DC Comics
Demo © Brian Wood & Becky Cloonan
DMZ © Brian Wood & Riccardo Burchielli
Doom Patrol © DC Comics
Fables: 1001 Nights Of Snowfall © Bill Willingham
& DC Comics
Fables: Legends In Exile © Bill Willingham & DC Comics
Gregory © DC Comics
Hellblazer: All His Engines © DC Comics
Hellblazer: Dangerous Habits © DC Comics
Human Target © DC Comics
It's A Bird... © DC Comics
Lucifer © DC Comics
Moonshadow © DC Comics
Mr. Punch © Neil Gaiman & Dave McKean
Preacher © Garth Ennis & Steve Dillon.
Pride Of Baghdad © Brian K. Vaughan & Niko Henrichon
Sandman Vol 1: Preludes And Nocturnes © DC Comics
Sandman Vol 3: Dream Country © DC Comics
Sandman Mystery Theatre © DC Comics
Scene Of The Crime © DC Comics
Shade The Changing Man © DC Comics
Silverfish © David Lapham
Swamp Thing: Dark Genesis © DC Comics
Swamp Thing: Saga Of The Swamp Thing © DC Comics
The Books Of Magic © DC Comics
The Books Of Magic: Bindings © DC Comics
The Cowboy Wally Show © Kyle Baker

The Fountain © DC Comics
The Invisibles © DC Comics
The Losers © DC Comics
The Originals © Dave Gibbons
Transmetropolitan © Warren Ellis & Darick Robertson
V For Vendetta © Alan Moore, David Lloyd & DC Comics
War Stories © DC Comics.
We3 © Grant Morrison & Frank Quitely
Why I Hate Saturn © Kyle Baker
Y The Last Man © Brian K Vaughan & DC Comics

Viking

In The Shadow Of No Towers © Art Spiegelman & Viking

VIZ Media

Adolf © Tezuka Productions
Death Note © Tsugumi Ohba, Takeshi Obata/Shueisha, Inc.
Fullmetal Alchemist © Hiromu Arakawa/Square Enix
Fushigi Yugi © Yuu Watase/Shogakukan, Inc.
Golgo 13: Supergun © Tezuka Productions
Gunnm © By Yukito Kishiro/Shueisha, Inc.
Inuyasha © Rumiko Takahashi/Shogakukan, Inc.
Maison Ikoku © Rumiko Takahashi/Shogakukan, Inc.
Naoki Urasawa's Monster © Naoki Urasawa.
Naruto © By Masashi Kishimoto/Shueisha, Inc.
Nausicaä Of The Valley Of The Wind © Nibariki Co., Ltd.
Neon Genesis Evangelion © Tezuka Productions
One Piece © By Eiichiro Oda/Shueisha, Inc.
Phoenix Vol 4: Karma © Tezuka Productions
Ranma ½ © Rumiko Takahashi/Shogakukan, Inc.
Sanctuary © Sho Fumimura Ryoichi Ikegami Shogakukan
Video Girl Ai © Tezuka Productions

W. W. Norton

Contract With God Trilogy © Will Eisner Studios, Inc.
Kings In Disguise © James Vance, Dan Burr & W. W. Norton
The Plot © Will Eisner Studios, Inc.

Watson-Guptill

Mad, Spy Vs Spy © E.C. Publications, Inc.

Wildstorm

Authority © Warren Ellis, Brian Hitch
& Wildstorm Productions
Ex Machina © Brian K. Vaughan, Tony Harris
& Wildstorm Productions
Global Frequency © Warren Ellis & DC Comics
Greyshirt: Indigo Sunset © Rick Veitch
& Wildstorm Productions
Planetary © Warren Ellis, John Cassaday
& Wildstorm Productions
Steampunk © Joe Kelly, Chris Bachalo
& Wildstorm Productions

CONTRIBUTORS

Introduction Authors
Rob Cave, Fiona Jerome, Gene Kannenberg, Jr., and Rob Nott.

Review Authors
Nick Aldwinckle, Jaspre Bark, Jeremy Briggs, Paul Brooks, Steve Causer, Rob Cave, Michael Chester, Nigel Fletcher, Andy-Lee Fry, Chris Gatcum, Chris Glew, Ed Hipkiss, Steve Hooker, Fiona Jerome, Gene Kannenberg, Jr., Lisa Pike, Spike Ravenscroft, Chris Rice, Tim Seelig, Alex Sheers, and Asa Wheatley.

Picture Research
Jaspre Bark, Jeremy Briggs, Paul Brooks, Steve Causer, Nigel Fletcher, Fiona Jerome, Gene Kannenberg, Jr., Joel Meadows, Tim Pilcher, Chris Rice, Tim Seelig, and Alex Sheers.

Special Thanks
Carol Pinkus at Marvel. Eric Reynolds at Fantagraphics for all the images he supplied to us. Matt Smith at 2000 AD.

Paige Braddock, Sarah Baju, Dan Brereton, Aline Kominsky Crumb, Al Davison, Evan Dorkin, Elsa Esparbé, Daryn Guarino, Ian Gibson, Kathleen Glosan, Julie Graves, Emily Harbison, Ilya, Denis Kitchen, Joe Kubert, Clint Langley, Terry & Robyn Moore, Bill Marks, Chris Martin-Smith, John & Sandra @ Metaphrog, Dean Motter, Terry Nantier, Daley Osiyemi, Jim Ottaviani, Andy Runton, Jeff Smith, Mark Smylie, Richard Starkings Chris Staros, Jason Shiga, Fred Van Lente, Rick Veitch, Teri Wood, Julie Weir, Matt Wagner, and Larry Young.